ENGLISH VOCABULARY IN USE

Vocabulary reference and practice

with answers

Fourth Edition

Pre-intermediate & Intermediate

Stuart Redman

CAMBRIDGE
UNIVERSITY PRESS

Shaftesbury Road, Cambridge CB2 8EA, United Kingdom

One Liberty Plaza, 20th Floor, New York, NY 10006, USA

477 Williamstown Road, Port Melbourne, VIC 3207, Australia

314–321, 3rd Floor, Plot 3, Splendor Forum, Jasola District Centre, New Delhi – 110025, India

103 Penang Road, #05–06/07, Visioncrest Commercial, Singapore 238467

Cambridge University Press & Assessment is a department of the University of Cambridge.

We share the University's mission to contribute to society through the pursuit of education, learning and research at the highest international levels of excellence.

www.cambridge.org
Information on this title: www.cambridge.org/elt

First published 1997
Fourth edition

40 39 38 37 36 35 34 33 32 31 30 29 28 27 26 25 24 23 22

Printed in Dubai by Oriental Press

A catalogue record for this publication is available from the British Library

ISBN 978-1-316-62831-7 Edition with answers and eBook
ISBN 978-1-316-63171-3 Edition with answers

Cambridge University Press & Assessment has no responsibility for the persistence or accuracy of URLs for external or third-party internet websites referred to in this publication and does not guarantee that any content on such websites is, or will remain, accurate or appropriate. Information regarding prices, travel timetables, and other factual information given in this work is correct at the time of first printing but Cambridge University Press & Assessment does not guarantee the accuracy of such information thereafter.

Contents

Thanks   5

Introduction   6

Learning

1 Learning vocabulary   8

2 Keeping a vocabulary notebook   10

3 Using a dictionary   12

4 English language words   14

The world around us

5 Country, nationality and language   16

6 The physical world   18

7 Weather   20

8 Animals and insects   22

People

9 The body and movement   24

10 Describing appearance   26

11 Describing character   28

12 Feelings   30

13 Family and friends   32

14 Growing up   34

15 Romance, marriage and divorce   36

Daily life

16 Daily routines   38

17 The place where you live   40

18 Around the home   42

19 Money   44

20 Health   46

21 Clothes   48

22 Fashion and buying clothes   50

23 Shopping   52

24 Food   54

25 Cooking   56

26 City life   58

27 Life in the country   60

28 Transport   62

29 On the road   64

30 Notices and warnings   66

Education and study

31 Classroom language   68

32 School education   70

33 Studying English and taking exams   72

34 University education   74

Work and business

35 Jobs   76

36 Talking about your work   78

37 Making a career   80

38 Working in an office   82

39 Running a company   84

40 Business and finance   86

Leisure and entertainment

41 Sport and leisure   88

42 Competitive sport   90

43 Books and films   92

44 Music   94

45 Special events   96

Tourism

46 Travel bookings   98

47 Air travel   100

48 Hotels and restaurants   102

49 Cafés   104

50 Sightseeing holidays   106

51 Holidays by the sea   108

Communication and technology

52 Newspapers and television   110

53 Phoning and texting   112

54 Computers   114

55 Email and the Internet   116

Social issues

56 Crime 118
57 Politics 120
58 Climate change 122
59 War and violence 124

Concepts

60 Time 126
61 Numbers 128
62 Distance, dimensions and size 130
63 Objects, materials, shapes and colour 132
64 Containers and quantities 134

Functional language

65 Apologies, excuses and thanks 136
66 Requests, permission and suggestions 138
67 Opinions, agreeing and disagreeing 140
68 Likes, dislikes, attitudes and preferences 142
69 Greetings, farewells and special expressions 144

Word formation

70 Prefixes: changing meaning 146
71 Suffixes: forming nouns 148
72 Suffixes: forming adjectives 150
73 Compound nouns 152

Phrase building

74 Word partners 154
75 Fixed phrases 156
76 Fixed phrases in conversation 158
77 Verb or adjective + preposition 160
78 Prepositional phrases 162
79 Phrasal verbs 1: form and meaning 164
80 Phrasal verbs 2: grammar and style 166

Key verbs

81 *Make*, *do* and *take*: uses and phrases 168
82 Key verbs: *give*, *keep* and *miss* 170
83 *Get*: uses, phrases and phrasal verbs 172
84 *Go*: meanings and expressions 174
85 The senses 176

Words and grammar

86 Uncountable nouns 178
87 Verb constructions 1 180
88 Verb constructions 2 182
89 Adjectives 184
90 Prepositions: place and movement 186
91 Adverbs 188

Connecting and linking

92 Time and sequence 190
93 Addition and contrast 192
94 Reason, purpose, result, condition 194

Style and register

95 Formal and informal English 196
96 Completing forms and CVs 198
97 Writing an essay 200
98 Formal letters and emails 202
99 Informal emails and messages 204
100 Abbreviations 206

Answer key 208

Phonemic symbols 245

Index 246

Acknowledgements 262

Thanks

Sabina Ostrowska wrote two new units for the Fourth Edition: Unit 46, *Travel Bookings* and Unit 49, *Cafés*. The publishers would like to thank Sabina for her contribution to this edition.

Introduction

To the student

This book will help you learn more than 2,000 words and phrases, and you can use it without a teacher. There are 100 units in the book. You can study them in any order, but the first four units have information about vocabulary that will help you with your learning.

Here is what the pages look like:

The left-hand page presents the new vocabulary.

New vocabulary is in **bold**.

The right-hand page practises the new vocabulary.

There is an example in each exercise to help you.

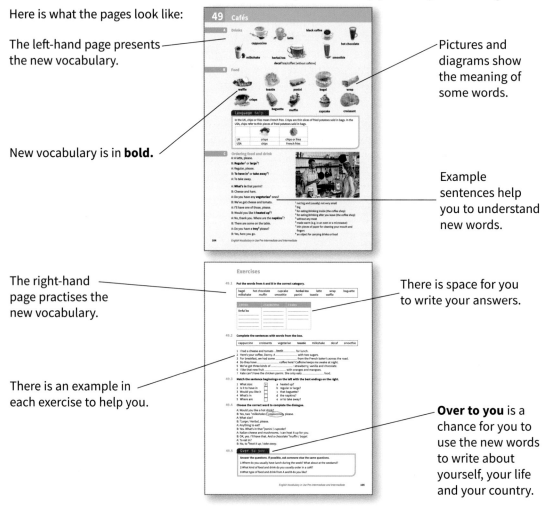

Pictures and diagrams show the meaning of some words.

Example sentences help you to understand new words.

There is space for you to write your answers.

Over to you is a chance for you to use the new words to write about yourself, your life and your country.

After you do the exercises, you can check your answers in the **Answer key** at the back of the book. You will also find possible answers for most of the **Over to you** exercises.

The **Index** at the back of the book has all the new words and phrases from the units, with a phonemic transcription to help you with pronunciation.

It is a good idea to have a dictionary when you use the book. Sometimes you may want a bilingual dictionary, so you can find a translation; sometimes the book asks you to use an English dictionary for an exercise. You also need a notebook when you are studying. The study units 1–4 in this book will give you ideas and information to help you to use your notebook and become a better learner. I hope you enjoy using this book.

To the teacher

This book can be used in class or for self-study. It is intended for learners at the upper A2 level and B1 level on the Council of Europe scale, and teaches more than 2,000 words and phrases. The vocabulary is organised around common everyday topics, but also contains units on different aspects of language such as phrasal verbs, uncountable nouns and link words and phrases. These units provide key information about lexis, but also help to ensure that learners are exposed to the most important vocabulary for their level. The first four units are dedicated to aspects of vocabulary learning such as record keeping and dictionary use. The book has been written so that units can be studied in any order, but I recommend you look at these four study units first, as they provide learners with important advice about vocabulary learning in general.

Throughout the book, vocabulary items have been chosen for their usefulness in a wide range of everyday situations, and this task has been made easier by having access to the English Profile (EP). Forming part of a large research programme sponsored by the Council of Europe, the EP helps teachers and students identify the words or phrases that a learner can be expected to know at each level of the Common European Framework. The words and phrases have mainly been selected using the Cambridge Learner Corpus, examination wordlists and classroom materials, and in this book the main focus is on words and phrases at the upper end of the A2 level and across the B1 level.

Much of the new vocabulary (on average about 25 items per unit) is presented through different types of text, and then explained immediately after the item appears, or in a separate glossary below the text; some words are presented in tables or lists, and contextualised in sentence examples; some of the new vocabulary is presented in pictures and diagrams.

The new vocabulary is then practised on the right-hand pages through a wide range of exercise types. These pages generally progress from easier to more difficult exercises, with items often tested receptively first, e.g. through a matching or grouping exercise, before moving on to more challenging productive exercises such as gap-fill texts or sentence transformations. In many units, the final exercise is called **Over to you**. This indicates a personalised exercise, in which learners have an opportunity to use some of the new vocabulary to talk about themselves, their lives and their country, and sometimes to express their own personal opinions. These make ideal classroom speaking activities for pairs or groups, but many of the exercises on the right-hand page can be adapted for speaking practice. For example, where there are short question and answer dialogues, students can first read the dialogues out loud, then one student can ask the questions, and their partner has to respond appropriately using target vocabulary from the unit, but without referring to the book.

There is a comprehensive Answer key at the back of the book, as well as an Index of all the vocabulary taught with a phonemic pronunciation guide and a unit reference to where each item appears.

Find more resources for teachers at www.cambridge.org/elt/inuse

We hope you enjoy using this new edition.

Study unit 1 — Learning vocabulary

A Using this book

It's a good idea to have a **routine** when you use this book. [something you do often and usually in the same way] For example:

- a **weekly** routine when you study a new unit for **at least** [not less than] 30–45 minutes;
- a **daily** routine when you **revise** that unit. [study it again] You may only need to revise for five or ten minutes each time.

1.1 Over to you

Write your answers.

1 How often can you spend at least half an hour or forty-five minutes on a unit?

....

2 How often can you revise? How much time can you spend when you revise? Where will you do it?

....

B Studying a new unit

When you are studying a unit for the first time, you need to be **active** when you are learning.

- With a new word or phrase, **say it aloud** [speak it so you can hear it], and repeat it to yourself **silently** [in your head, not speaking]. If you have the eBook that goes with the book, use it to check the pronunciation.
- Use a **highlighter pen** to mark words you think are important or difficult.
- Write down new words and phrases in your notebook. (See Unit 2 for more information.)
- Always try to write an example sentence for new words. You can choose an example from this book or a dictionary, but an example from your own life will often help you to remember a word, e.g. I _shared_ a flat with an Australian girl when I was in London last year.
- Do exercises in pencil, then you can **rub** them **out** (using a **rubber**) and do them again later. This is a good way to revise vocabulary.

1.2 Over to you

Write your answers.

1 Which of these things do you do now when you are learning vocabulary?

....

2 What will you do in the future? ....

....

C Revising a unit

When you are revising a unit one or two days later, it is also important to be as active as possible.

- Test yourself, e.g. look at a word and cover the meaning. Can you remember what the meaning is? If you can't, check the meaning, then come back to the word in five minutes' time and test yourself again.
- Look at what you wrote in your notebook when you first studied the unit. Is there any new information you want to add, e.g. something about the pronunciation, or a common word partner? (See Unit 2.)
- Diagrams may help you to organise some of the vocabulary differently, and help you to remember it.

Who took
my pen?

Let's take a
break now.

1.3

take

I took notes
during the lecture.

What size shoes
do you take?

Over to you

Write your answers.

1 Do you revise vocabulary that you study? If so, how often? ....
....

2 Will you try to revise more often in the future? If so, will you use some of the ideas above?

....

D   ## Expanding* your vocabulary

- When you learn a word, e.g. *dirty*, think of **synonyms** *(syn)* [words with a similar meaning] or **opposites** *(opp)* in your language. Look them up in a bilingual dictionary to find the English words, then look up the English words in an English dictionary to check the meaning. From this, you will find that the opposite of *dirty* is *clean*, and you may also find **filthy** [very dirty].

*making something bigger

1.4   **Using this method, find opposites for the words in bold.**

1 My room is very **clean**.   *opp* _dirty_..............................
2 It's a **permanent** job.   *opp* ....
3 He was **kind** to all of his animals.   *opp* ....
4 Babies have very soft, **smooth** skin.   *opp* ....
5 Where's the **entrance**?   *opp* ....
6 Was the bird **dead**?   *opp* ....
7 Did they **accept** the invitation?   *opp* ....

- Building word families (see Units 70–72) will also help to expand your vocabulary. From a noun, verb or adjective, you can often find related words in the dictionary with a similar meaning. So, you can often learn two or three words, and not just one, e.g. **argue** *v* = have an angry discussion; *n* = **argument**.

1.5   **Use a dictionary to find the related parts of speech for the words in bold.**

1 She gave me some **advice**.   *verb* _advise_........................
2 We mustn't **argue**.   *noun* ....
3 I will have to **revise** this unit.   *noun* ....
4 Is there a **choice**?   *verb* ....
5 I want to **expand** my vocabulary.   *noun* ....
6 The two boys are very **different**.   *noun* .... *verb* ....
7 They need to **communicate** more.   *noun* .... *adj* ....

- Try to read and listen to English as much as possible. The more you read and listen, the more you will learn. When you read, try to:
  - Highlight or underline interesting new words.
  - Highlight words if they are familiar but you can't remember the meaning.
- There is a lot of spoken English on the Internet which you can play again and again. Try to make a note of interesting words and look up the meaning.

1.6   **Over to you**

Now choose a unit that interests you. Study the left-hand page, then do the exercises in pencil. Wait for at least 24 hours, revise the unit, then answer these questions.

1 How many answers did you get right the first time? ....
2 How many answers did you get right the second time? ....

cup saucer mug

A What do you do?
This is what some students do.

RAFAEL I **write down** new English words and phrases in my notebook, and next to each one I write a Spanish **translation**. I usually write down if a word is a *noun, verb, adjective*, and so on.

KAZUO I sometimes write a word in phonemics because English pronunciation is very difficult for me. But my notebook is a **mess** [nothing is in a good order; *syn* **untidy**]. I like to **draw** pictures.

EUN I sometimes **make a note of** new words in my notebook, but I often **forget** [don't remember]. I usually write a translation, and sometimes I write example sentences as well.

ANDREY I've got a notebook. I don't use it much but when I do, I try and list words by **topic**, so I put all the animals together, and all the clothes words together, and so on. I find it's easier to remember the words this way.

DONATA I **note down** new words and phrases. Sometimes I **translate** them **into** Polish, and sometimes I write an **explanation** [a description of what something means] in English if it is not difficult. For example:
kitten — a very young cat

B Tips for your notebook
A **tip** is a piece of advice to help you. Here are some tips for your notebook.

- Put words from one **topic** in the same place, e.g. food in one place, clothes in another, etc. Don't **mix** them **up** [put them together with no order]. You can also have grammar topics, e.g. 'uncountable nouns', or a page for words that all have a connection, e.g. words and phrases that were all in a story you read in English. Some words and phrases will go in more than one topic.
- If you can't find a topic for a new word or phrase, e.g. *useful* or *in particular*, put them in a different place in your notebook, e.g. a page for each day or each week, or perhaps one page for every English lesson you have. Write the **date** clearly at the top, e.g. Monday 14th May.
- When you write down new vocabulary, write a translation if it is **necessary** [you need it; *opp* **unnecessary**], but also write the meaning in English if it is possible, or draw pictures.
- If possible, add synonyms, opposites, other parts of speech, etc. (See Unit 1.)
   awful *adj* = terrible (*syn* **dreadful**)
   enjoy *v* = like something and get pleasure from it   *n* = **enjoyment** *adj* = **enjoyable**
- Example sentences help you with the grammar of a word, or with word partners (collocations).
   I **enjoy** liv**ing** in a big city. (NOT I enjoy ~~to live~~ in a big city.) (See Units 87–8.)
   I **spent two weeks in** Rome. (NOT I ~~passed~~ two weeks in Rome. You *spend* time in a place.)
   (See Unit 74.)
- Remember, words often have more than one meaning that you need to know, e.g. a **tip** is also money that you give, for example, to a waiter for serving you in a restaurant.

Exercises

2.1 Organise the words into the topics below. One word can go in two different topics. Use a dictionary to help you.

~~diet~~	branch	lay the table	count *v*	dig *v*	ground	flour	add up
raw	leaf	minus	butcher	thousand	frozen	zero	butterfly

food	garden	numbers
diet		

2.2 Explain these words in English, or draw a picture, or if you think an explanation is too difficult and a drawing is not possible, write a translation instead.

1 raw *not cooked* ....
2 dig ....
3 butcher ....
4 leaf ....
5 flour ....
6 lay the table ....
7 add up ....
8 minus ....

2.3 What information could you include with these words? The answers are all on the opposite page.

1 forget   *opposite – remember* ....
2 awful ....
3 necessary ....
4 translate ....
5 tip ....
6 enjoy ....

2.4

Over to you

Answer the questions. If possible, compare your answers with someone else.

1 Look again at what the students said on the opposite page. What are the good things that they do? Underline them.

2 Do you do all of these things? ....

3 Is there anything you don't do now, but will do in the future? ....
....

4 At the moment, which person's notebook is most like your notebook? ....

5 What are the most useful tips on the opposite page for you? ....
....

A **What dictionaries do I need?**

A **bilingual** dictionary [using two languages] is easy for you to understand, and quick and easy to use. A dictionary in English will give you reading practice in English and many more examples of how words are used. If possible, use both. These are good dictionaries in English for your level, and most of them are available online:

Cambridge Learner's Dictionary   Oxford Wordpower Dictionary
Longman Active Study Dictionary   Macmillan Essential Dictionary

B **Information in dictionaries**

If you **look up a word** [find a word in a dictionary] using the *Cambridge Learner's Dictionary*, the information is shown like this:

pronunciation using **phonemic symbols** (see page 247)

a **definition** explains the meaning

bold *italics* show common word partners (see Unit 74)

● ● ● ⟨ ⟩   ↻ ⚲ ⌂

fun¹ /fʌn/ *noun* [u]

1 enjoyment or pleasure, or something that gives you enjoyment or pleasure

*She's **great fun** to be with.*
***Have fun!** (= enjoy yourself)*
*It's **no fun** having to work late every night.*

2 for fun/for the fun of it
for pleasure and not for any other reason

3 make fun of sb/sth
to make a joke about someone or something in an unkind way.

The other children at school used to make fun of his hair.

part of speech (= noun)

[U] tells you that *fun* is uncountable (see Unit 86)

fixed **phrases** using the word are shown in **bold** (see Units 75–6)

examples are in *italics*

3.1 **Correct the spelling mistakes. Use a dictionary to check your answers.**

1 allways ....*always*.....................   6 confortable ....
2 realy ....   7 accomodation ....
3 unfortunatly ....   8 beautifull ....
4 expecially ....   9 unbeleivable ....
5 cloths ....   10 neccesary ....

3.2 **In the word *island* /ˈaɪlənd/, the letter 's' is silent (not pronounced). Use your dictionary to find the silent letters in these words.**

1 knee   2 comb   3 castle   4 salmon   5 receipt

C **Defining words**

'Defining words' are words that dictionaries use when they **define** [explain] the words in the dictionary. Some of these are quite common.

emphasise [give something more attention and importance], e.g. My teacher has always emphasised the importance of writing down new words in a notebook.
relating to or **connected to/with** [having a relationship with someone or something], e.g. *musical* is connected with / related to *music*
amount [how much there is of something], e.g. £5 million is a large amount of money.
official [done by the government or someone in authority], e.g. A passport is an official document.
behave [do or say things in a particular way], e.g. People can behave strangely when they're nervous.

Exercises

3.3 Complete the dictionary definitions using words from the box.

| ~~connected with~~ emphasise relating to behave official amount |

1 **industrial** /ɪnˈdʌstriəl/ 1 adjective ...*connected with*...... industry
2 **sum** /sʌm/ noun [C] an .... of money
3 **pretend** /prɪˈtend/ verb [I,T] to .... as if something is true when it is not
4 **certificate** /səˈtɪfɪkət/ noun [C] an .... document that gives details to show something is true
5 **not at all** /nɒt ət ɔːl/ used instead of 'no' or 'not' to .... what you are saying: I'm not at all happy about it
6 **legal** /ˈliːɡəl/ adjective .... the law

D Using a dictionary

- When you use a dictionary to check the meaning of a word, put a **tick** (✓) next to it. Each time you return to a page with a tick, **see** [find out] if you remember the word.
- When you meet a new word or phrase in a text, first try to **guess the meaning** [try to think of the meaning when you don't know it]. Then, use a dictionary to see if your **guess** was correct.
- Don't just read the dictionary definition. Example phrases and sentences show you how a word or phrase is used, and they help you to understand the meaning more clearly.
- If you look up a word in a bilingual dictionary and get two or three different translations, check these words in an English dictionary to see which translation is the best one for the situation.
- Remember that many words have more than one meaning. The first meaning in the dictionary is not always the one you want. You may need to read through the different meanings.

3.4 Answer the questions, and use an English dictionary to check the answers.

1 What does *puppy* mean? *It's a very young dog.*
2 Is the correct spelling *organize* or *organise*? ....
3 What part of speech is *extremely*? ....
4 What kind of noun is *advice*? ....
5 What preposition follows the verb *rely*? ....
6 Look up *friend*, and then the words in **bold** that are often used with it. Can you complete these phrases? *She's an* .... *friend; he's my* .... *friend; you* .... *friends with people.*

3.5 Match the sentences on the right with the different meanings of *post* on the left.

post¹ /pəʊst/ *noun*

1 System [no plural] UK (US mail) the system for sending letters, parcels, etc
Your letter is **in the post**.
I'm sending the documents **by post**.

2 Letters [u] UK (US mail) letters, parcels, etc that you send or receive
Has the **post arrived/come yet?**

3 Job [c] *formal* a job
A part-time post.
A teaching post.

4 Pole [c] a long, vertical piece of wood or metal fixed into the ground at one end.
I found the dog tied to a **post**.

1 He's applied for a post overseas.
2 Did you send the cheque by post?
3 I tied the flag to a post.
4 We haven't had any post yet.

A Parts of speech

❝I have a brown leather chair by the window, and I often sit there in the morning to listen to music.❞

In the sentence above, *I* is a **pronoun**; *chair, window, morning* and *music* are all **nouns**; *have, sit* and *listen* are **verbs**; *brown* and *leather* are **adjectives**; *often* is an **adverb**; *by* and *to* are **prepositions**; *the* is a **definite article**; *a* is an **indefinite article**; *and* is a **conjunction** or **link word**.

Here are two more examples:

❝We saw an elephant at the zoo yesterday.❞
Elephant and *zoo* are nouns; *saw* is a verb; *at* is a preposition; *an* is an indefinite article; *the* is a definite article.

❝It was a cold night, so I walked quickly.❞
Was and *walked* are verbs; *cold* is an adjective; *night* is a noun; *quickly* is an adverb; *so* is a link word.

B Grammar

When you are learning vocabulary, you need to know certain things about different words; for example, if nouns are **countable**, e.g. *books, apples, chairs*; or **uncountable**, e.g. *information* (NOT ~~informations~~), *advice* (NOT ~~advices~~). (See Unit 86.)
With verbs, you need to know if they are **regular**, e.g. *work, live*, etc; or **irregular**, e.g. *go/went, take/took*. You will also need to learn the grammar of **phrasal verbs**, e.g. *take something off, wake up*. (See Units 79–80.)
You also need to learn certain groups of words as **phrases**, e.g. *at the moment, never mind, see you later*. (See Units 75–6.)

C Word building

In the word *uncomfortable*, *un-* is a **prefix**, and *-able* is a **suffix**. Other common prefixes include *in-* and *dis-*, e.g. *incorrect* and *dislike*. Common suffixes include *-ment* and *-ive*, e.g. *improvement* and *attractive*. (See Units 70–72.)

D Pronunciation

Dictionaries show the pronunciation of a word using **phonemic symbols**, e.g. *book* /bʊk/, *before* /bɪˈfɔː/, *cinema* /ˈsɪnəmə/.
Every word has one or more **syllables**, e.g. *book* has one syllable, *before* has two syllables, *cinema* has three syllables.
It is important to know which syllable to **stress**, e.g. on *before* it is the second syllable (beˈfore), on *cinema* it is the first syllable (ˈcinema). The vertical mark ˈ shows where the stressed syllable begins.

E Punctuation

Every sentence must begin with a **capital letter** and end with a **full stop**. Some sentences have a **comma**, which often shows a **pause** [when you stop reading or speaking for a short time] in a long sentence. Did you also know that a question must end with a **question mark**?

Exercises

4.1 Put the words into the correct columns.

~~noun~~   comma   phonemic symbol   adverb   stress
question mark   syllable   preposition   full stop   adjective

parts of speech	punctuation	pronunciation
noun		

4.2 There is one word missing in each line of the text. Where does the missing word go? What could it be? What part of speech is it?

Last year I went to for my holiday. I spent the first
week Seville staying with a couple of friends, and
then I a train to Barcelona, where I spent another
ten days. It is beautiful city and I had a marvellous
time. I stayed in a very hotel right in the centre, but
I didn't mind spending a lot money because it was a
wonderful and it was very convenient. My brother was
the person who recommended it; he goes Spain a lot
and he stays anywhere else. I may go back next year
if have enough time.

1 *Spain (noun)*
2 ....
3 ....
4 ....
5 ....
6 ....
7 ....
8 ....
9 ....
10 ....

4.3 Answer the questions.

1 What type of verb is **break**?   *an irregular verb*
2 What does a sentence begin with?   ....
3 What do you put at the end of every sentence?   ....
4 What's missing here.   ....
5 What shows you there is a pause in the middle of a long sentence?   ....
6 What type of noun is **butter**?   ....
7 What type of verbs are **pick somebody up** and **grow up**?   ....
8 What are **full stop** and **comma** examples of?   ....
9 How do dictionaries show the pronunciation of a word?   ....
10 Is the 'a' in **phrase** pronounced the same as **can**, **can't** or **late**?   ....

4.4 Mark the stress on each word. How many syllables are there?

'English 2   informal   opposite   syllable
decide   adjective   education   pronunciation

4.5 Look at these words and answer the questions.

cheap   dangerous   kind   lucky

1 What part of speech are these words?   *adjectives*
2 Can you change the first two words into adverbs? ....
3 Is the pronunciation of *kind* like *wind* (noun) or *find* (verb)?   ....
4 What prefix do you need to form the opposite of the last two words?   ....
5 What suffix makes a noun from *kind*?   ....

5 Country, nationality and language

A Who speaks what where?

country	nationality	language
Australia	Australian	English
Brazil	Brazilian	Portuguese
China	Chinese	Mandarin (and Cantonese)
Egypt	Egyptian	Arabic
France	French	French
Germany	German	German
Greece	Greek	Greek
Israel	Israeli	Hebrew
Italy	Italian	Italian
Japan	Japanese	Japanese
(South) Korea	Korean	Korean
Poland	Polish	Polish
Russia	Russian	Russian
Saudi Arabia	Saudi Arabian	Arabic
Spain	Spanish	Spanish
Switzerland	Swiss	Swiss-German, French, Italian
Thailand	Thai	Thai
Turkey	Turkish	Turkish
the UK (United Kingdom)*	British	English
the USA (United States of America)	American	English

*the UK (England, Scotland, Wales and Northern Ireland)

I **come from** Argentina, so I'm **Argentinian** and my **first language** is Spanish. The **capital** is Buenos Aires, which has a **population** of more than 10 million people.

Common mistakes

He's **E**nglish. (NOT He's ~~english.~~); We ate **French** food. (NOT We ate ~~France~~ food.)

I went to **the USA**. (NOT I went ~~to USA.~~) I also visited **the UK**. (NOT I also ~~visited UK.~~)

B Parts of the world

The **continents** in the world are **Europe**, **Africa**, **Asia**, North America, **South America**, Australia [Australia and New Zealand] and Antarctica.

We also use these terms for different parts of the world:
the Middle East (e.g. United Arab Emirates, Saudi Arabia), **the Far East** (e.g. Thailand, Japan), **the Caribbean** (e.g. Jamaica, Barbados), **Scandinavia** (Sweden, Norway, Denmark, Finland).

C The people

When we are talking about people from a particular country, we add 's' to nationalities ending in '-i' or '-(i)an', but we need the definite article (the) for most others.

Brazilians/Russians
Thais/Israelis } are …

The British / The French
The Swiss / The Japanese } are …

With both groups we can also use the word 'people', e.g. Brazilian people, British people, etc.

Exercises

5.1 **Answer the questions.**

1 What nationality are people from Poland? _Polish_ ....
2 What nationality are people from Thailand? ....
3 What language is spoken in Spain? ....
4 Where do people speak Hebrew? ....
5 Where do people speak Mandarin? ....
6 What language is spoken in Brazil? ....
7 What language is spoken in Egypt? ....
8 What nationality are people from Germany? ....
9 Write down three countries whose first language is English. ....
10 Write down three languages spoken in Switzerland. ....

5.2 **What parts of the world are these countries in? Write the continent, e.g. Europe, or the area, e.g. the Far East.**

1 Germany _Europe_ ....   4 Italy ....
2 Japan ....   5 Jamaica ....
3 Saudi Arabia ....   6 Argentina ....

5.3 **Underline the main stress in the words in the box, and practise saying them. Use the pronunciation in the index to help you.**

Brazilian	Japan	Egyptian	Arabic	Scandinavia
Chinese	Portuguese	Australia	Saudi Arabia	

5.4 **Write the answers.**

1 Bangkok is the capital of _Thailand_ .   4 Moscow is the capital of ....
2 Ankara is the capital of ....   5 Buenos Aires is the capital of ....
3 Seoul is the capital of ....   6 Athens is the capital of ....

5.5 **Complete the sentences with the name of the people from the country on the right.**

1 I've worked a lot with _the French_ .   FRANCE
2 I know lots of ....   GERMANY
3 We do a lot of business with ....   JAPAN
4 I used to know a lot of ....   ISRAEL
5 I have always found .... very friendly.   BRAZIL
6 People often say that .... are very reserved.   BRITAIN
7 .... are very organised.   SWITZERLAND
8 I met a lot of .... on my trip to Moscow.   RUSSIA

5.6 ## Over to you

Answer the questions for you, then ask a friend – if possible, someone from a different country – and write their answers.

1 What's your nationality? ....
2 What's the capital city and population of your country? ....
3 What's your first language? ....
4 What other languages do you speak? ....
5 Which countries have you visited? ....
6 Which countries would you like to visit? ....

A Facts

The Krubera-Voronja **Cave**

Beijing-Hangshou Grand **Canal**

The Angel **Falls**

DID YOU KNOW...?

Two thirds of the **surface**[1] of the **Earth**[2] is **covered in** water.

El Azizia in Libya is the hottest place **in the world**, where **temperatures** of **over**[3] 57 °C (57 **degrees** Celsius) have been recorded.

The coldest place **on earth** is probably Vostok in Antarctica, which reached a temperature of **minus** 89 °C.

The Krubera-Voronja **Cave** near the Black Sea coast in Georgia, is the deepest cave in the world. It is **over** 2000 metres deep.

The Beijing–Hangzhou Grand **Canal** is the longest canal in the world. It is 1,794 kilometres long.

The highest **waterfall** in the world is the Angel Falls in Venezuela. It is 979 metres high.

The Amazon Rainforest is the largest **rainforest** in the world, **covering** 40% of the South American continent.

The Pacific is the largest **ocean** in the world, and is nearly twice the size of the Atlantic Ocean.

[1] the top or outside part   [2] the planet we live on   [3] more than

Language help

Cover can mean that something is over something else, e.g. *The surface was* **covered in** *water; The ground was* **covered with** *snow.* Cover can also refer to the size of something, e.g. *The Amazon rainforest* **covers** *40% of South America*, or the distance you travel, e.g. *We* **covered** *ten miles in one day.*

B Geography

Switzerland **consists of** [is made or formed from] three main geographical **regions** [areas in a country or the world]: The Swiss Plateau, The Jura, and The Alps. Switzerland is a land of **contrasts** [big differences], with completely different **landscapes** [the appearance of an area of land]. The **climate** [weather conditions] can also change within a very short **distance**. For example, Ascona **in the south** has an almost Mediterranean climate, but the Dufour Peak in Valais has a very cold climate. The **distance** between the two is just 70 kilometres.

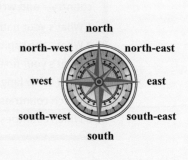

Exercises

6.1 **Look at the map of Switzerland and complete the sentences.**

1 Zurich is _in the north_ ....
2 The Jura mountains are ....
3 Geneva is ....
4 St Gallen is ....
5 Basel is ....
6 Lake Constance is ....
7 Locarno is ....

6.2 **Test your knowledge. Can you complete these sentences without looking at the opposite page?**

1 Two thirds of the .._surface_................... of the Earth is covered in water.
2 Vostok in Antarctica is the ....
3 El Azizia in Libya is the ....
4 The Krubera-Voronja .... is the deepest in the world.
5 The Beijing–Hangzhou Grand .... is the longest in the world.
6 At 979 metres the Angel Falls is the highest .... in the world.
7 The Amazon is the largest ....
8 The largest .... in the world is the Pacific.
9 The .... we live on is called the Earth.

6.3 **Complete the sentences.**

1 Mount Everest is the highest mountain in the .._world_...................... .
2 In the autumn, the ground is .... in leaves that have fallen off the trees.
3 You find this animal in the semi-desert .... of Australia.
4 Brazil is a country of .... : large empty areas inland, and cities near the coast.
5 The Amazon rainforest .... 40% of the South American continent.
6 Mountains and lakes are typical of the .... in Switzerland.
7 It was a freezing night. The .... was well below zero.
8 Switzerland .... of three main geographical regions.
9 It takes the moon just under 28 days to go round the ....
10 People say Cape Town in South Africa has a wonderful .... : sunny for much of the year, and never too hot or very cold.
11 The .... from London to Paris is 340 kilometres; that's less than the .... from London to Edinburgh.
12 When the temperature fell to .... 10 .... Celsius, all the schools in the town closed.

6.4 `Over to you`

Answer the questions about your country and your region.

1 What are the highest and lowest temperatures?

2 Do you like the climate?

3 Are there any regions which have a very different landscape from the rest of the country?

4 Do you have any long canals, or famous caves or waterfalls?

5 How would you describe the landscape in the region where you live?

6 What's the distance from the place where you live to the next big town?

7 Weather

A Weather conditions

Notice that it is very common to form adjectives by adding *-y*.

noun	adjective
fog	**foggy**
cloud	**cloudy**
the cold	cold
ice	**icy**

noun	adjective	verb
sun	**sunny**	the sun is **shining**
wind	windy	the wind is **blowing**
snow	**snowy**	it's **snowing**
rain	**wet**	it's raining

There are common word partners to describe weather conditions:

It was very cloudy this morning, but the **sun came out** after lunch. [appeared]
The accident happened in **thick fog** [bad fog].
We had some **heavy rain** at the weekend. [a lot of rain; *opp* **light rain**]
There was a **strong wind** when we were on the boat. [a lot of wind]
The **wind** has **blown** all the apples off the tree.
It rained in the morning, but the **sky** was **clear** by lunchtime. [no clouds]
It's been **extremely cold** today. [very; also **extremely hot/windy**]

B Rain and storms

For heavy rain we often use the verb **pour**, e.g. **pour with rain**. For short periods of light or heavy rain, we use the noun **shower**. A **storm** is heavy rain with strong winds.
It **poured with rain** this afternoon.
Look, it's really **pouring (with rain)** now.
We had a couple of **heavy/light showers** this morning.

A period of hot weather sometimes ends with a **thunderstorm**.
First it becomes very **humid** [the air feels very warm and wet],
then you hear **thunder** and see **lightning**, and it's followed by heavy rain.

C Temperature*

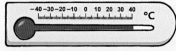

40 degrees Celsius

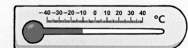

10 degrees below zero

| **boiling**
[very hot] | hot | warm | not very warm
(also **cool**) | cold
(also **chilly**) | **freezing**
[very cold] |

* how hot or cold it is

Language help

Cool can either mean slightly cold in a negative way, e.g. *We've had a cool summer*; or slightly cold in a pleasant way, e.g. *The water in the pool was lovely and cool*.

Mild is often used in a positive way to describe weather that is not as cold as usual, e.g. *It's been a mild winter*.

Exercises

7.1 **Match the words on the left with the words on the right.**

1 a sunny   [e]   a with rain
2 heavy   [ ]   b fog
3 a strong   [ ]   c sky
4 a clear   [ ]   d and lightning
5 pour   [ ]   e day
6 thick   [ ]   f rain
7 thunder   [ ]   g wind

7.2 **Write short sentences to describe the weather conditions in each picture.**

1 *It's foggy.* .... 3 .... 5 ....

2 .... 4 .... 6 ....

7.3 **True or false? If a sentence is false, change it to make it true.**

1 When it's foggy, you need sunglasses. *False. When it's foggy you can't see very well.* ....
2 It's nice to sit outside when it's freezing. ....
3 If you're boiling, you might enjoy a swim. ....
4 A shower is a type of wind. ....
5 If it's chilly, you may want to put on a coat. ....
6 If it's humid, the air will be very dry. ....
7 A mild winter means it is colder than usual. ....
8 If it rains, the road will be wet. ....

7.4 **Complete the sentences.**

1 We had really thick ..*fog*.......................... this morning.
2 I don't mind wet weather if it stays quite mild. I just hate the ....
3 We had a heavy .... this morning, but it only lasted a few minutes.
4 It was .... with rain when we left the house.
5 It was minus ten .... in New York yesterday. It is often below .... here in winter. It's .... cold!
6 It's getting very humid. We might have a .... later.
7 It was cloudy and grey this morning, but when the sun .... out it was quite hot.
8 What's the .... today? It feels much colder than yesterday.
9 It was hot sitting in the sun, but under the beach umbrella it was nice and ....

7.5

Over to you

Do you have these weather conditions in your country? When do you have them?

humid weather   storms and thunderstorms   strong winds
thick fog   temperatures below zero   showers

8 Animals and insects

A Pets and farm animals

In the UK, many people **keep pets** [animals that live with people]. The most common are dogs and cats, but people also keep birds, e.g. **parrots**, that are usually in a **cage**. Children sometimes keep **mice** (*sing* **mouse**) and **rabbits.** Some people keep more unusual animals as pets, e.g. **frogs**, **snakes** and **spiders**.

Farms in the UK may have sheep, pigs, cows, horses, **donkeys**, chickens, **goats** and a **bull**.

B Wild animals

The pictures show a number of **wild animals** [animals that normally live in natural conditions]. If you are lucky, you may see these animals **in the wild** [living free], but you will probably see them in a **zoo**. Some of these animals, for example tigers, are now quite **rare** [not often seen or found]. It is important that we **protect** [keep safe] these **endangered animals**.

C Insects

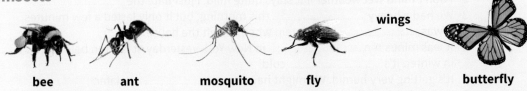

D Sea creatures

Many different **creatures** [living things, e.g. animals] live in the sea.

Exercises

8.1 **Put the words into the correct columns.**

| goat monkey goat fly bull bee elephant pig |
| mosquito tiger donkey camel ant leopard butterfly |

farm animals	wild animals	insects
goat		

8.2 **Look at the underlined letters in each pair of words. Is the pronunciation the same or different? Use the index to help you.**

1 wh<u>a</u>le w<u>a</u>ter *different*
2 c<u>a</u>t c<u>a</u>mel *same*
3 b<u>ea</u>r b<u>ee</u>
4 le<u>o</u>pard mosqui<u>to</u>
5 l<u>i</u>on t<u>i</u>ger

6 <u>g</u>oat <u>g</u>iraffe
7 sp<u>i</u>der w<u>i</u>ld
8 c<u>a</u>mel sn<u>a</u>ke
9 leopa<u>r</u>d sha<u>r</u>k
10 m<u>o</u>nkey fr<u>o</u>g

8.3 **Complete the sentences.**

1 Cats and dogs are the most common ..*pets*.......................... in the UK.
2 I've only seen .... animals in zoos or on TV.
3 I don't like keeping birds in a .... ; they need more space.
4 I hate ants and mosquitos. In fact, I hate all ....
5 It's hard to see tigers in the wild because they are now ....
6 Some animals are disappearing, so we must .... them.

8.4 **Start each sentence with a suitable creature from the opposite page.**

1 *Sharks*............................ can swim very long distances.
2 .... are very clever and are similar to humans.
3 .... can travel through the desert for long distances without water.
4 .... can be 25 metres in length.
5 .... can eat leaves from tall trees when they are standing on the ground.
6 .... sometimes change their skin several times a year.
7 .... can pick things up with their trunk.
8 .... are kept as pets, usually in cages, and some can even talk!

8.5 `Over to you`

Answer the questions. If possible, compare your answers with someone else.

1 Have you got any pets? What pets?

2 Have you ever seen animals in the wild? What did you see? Where?

3 How do you feel about birds in cages and wild animals in zoos?

4 Are you frightened of any creatures, e.g. mice?

9 The body and movement

A Parts of the body

The outer part of the body is covered in **skin**. Too much sun is bad for your skin.

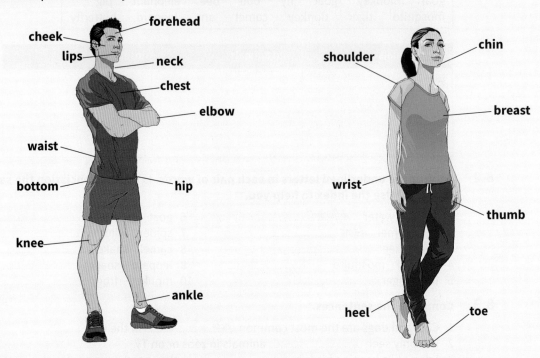

B Movements with your mouth, face and head

People **breathe** through their nose or mouth. You **breathe in** and **out** about 12–15 times a minute.

People **smile** when they're happy, and sometimes **smile at** people to be polite.

People **laugh at** things which are funny.

People sometimes **cry** if they're very unhappy, or receive bad news.

People in some countries **nod their head** [move it up and down] to mean 'yes', and **shake their head** [move it from side to side] for 'no'.

People often **yawn** when they're tired, and sometimes when they're bored.

C Common expressions

shake hands
with someone

fold your
arms

comb your
hair

wave to
somebody

blow your
nose

Exercises

9.1 Find ten more words for parts of the body, either across or down.

T	H	U	K	C	A	P
O	N	H	N	H	N	I
E	C	H	E	E	K	O
H	I	P	E	S	L	C
E	A	N	K	T	E	H
E	L	B	O	W	E	I
L	I	P	S	K	I	N

toe ....

....

....

....

....

....

9.2 Match the words on the left with the words on the right.

1 shake   `e`   a your hair
2 wave   ☐   b your nose
3 comb   ☐   c to somebody
4 fold   ☐   d your head
5 blow   ☐   e hands
6 nod   ☐   f your arms

9.3 Label the picture.

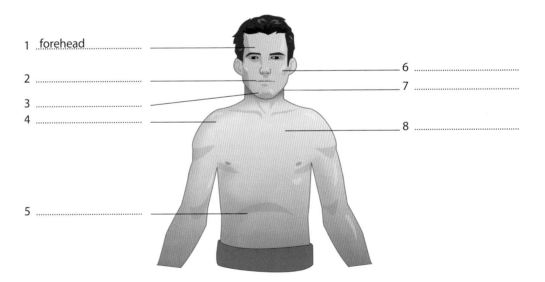

1 forehead ....

2 ....

3 ....

4 ....

5 ....

6 ....

7 ....

8 ....

9.4 What do these actions often mean? (There may be several possible answers.)

1 People often smile *when they're happy.* ....
2 They often breathe quickly after ....
3 They laugh ....
4 They may wave to somebody ....
5 They blow their nose ....
6 They shake their head ....
7 And nod their head ....
8 They cry ....
9 They yawn ....

10 Describing appearance

A Describing beauty

Your **appearance** is the way you look, and we sometimes use different words to talk about **beauty** in men and women.

WOMEN can be **attractive** or **good-looking** [nice to look at], and we often use **pretty** [attractive] to describe a girl. We use beautiful or **gorgeous** for women who are very attractive.

MEN can be attractive and good-looking, but also **handsome**. If men are very attractive, we can say they are gorgeous or very good-looking, but not usually beautiful.

Liam has become quite **handsome**.
Olivia was very **pretty** when she was younger.

Bella looks **gorgeous** in that dress.
They're a very **good-looking** couple.

> ### Language help
>
> The opposite of beautiful is **ugly**, but it is not very polite to describe someone as ugly; **ordinary** [not special or different] is more polite. It also isn't polite to say that someone is fat; **overweight** is more polite.

B Size

We can talk about a person's **height** [how tall or short they are] and their **weight** [how heavy they are], e.g. *I'm **roughly** [about; syn **approximately**] one metre eighty (tall), and I **weigh** just under eighty kilograms*. If someone is not tall or short, you can describe them as **medium height**. If a person is very similar to most other people in height and weight, you can say they are **average**.

A: How tall is Hannah?
B: **Medium height**, I'd say.

A: Is Marco quite big?
B: No, about **average**.

C Hair

| **blonde** (or **blond**) | **fair** | brown | **dark** | black |

straight   **wavy**   **curly**

> ### Common mistakes
>
> Remember that 'hair' is uncountable, e.g. She's got straight **hair**. (NOT She's got straight ~~hairs~~.)
> Also: She's got long black hair. (NOT She's got ~~a~~ long black hair.)

D Talking about someone's appearance

A: **What does** Sophia's boyfriend **look like**? [Can you describe his appearance?]
B: He's blond, and quite good-looking.
A: Is he tall?
B: Er, **tallish** [quite tall], but he's got **broad** shoulders [wide; opp **narrow**]. He looks very **athletic** [strong, healthy and often good at sports]. I think he does a lot of sport.
A: Is he quite **smart** [clean, tidy and stylish]?
B: Yeah, he **dresses** quite **well** [the clothes he wears are quite nice].

> ### Language help
>
> We can use the suffix **-ish** at the end of some adjectives to mean 'quite', e.g. She's got **longish** hair, and at the end of some numbers to mean 'more or less', e.g. He's **twentyish**.

Exercises

10.1 **Complete the sentences.**

1 She's got straight *hair* .

2 Isabella is very good-.................................. .

3 Beata's got blonde ....

4 Her brother's got very broad ....

5 That's a nice suit: Jack's very .... today.

6 I would say he was medium ....

7 Charlotte's hair is fair but her brother's is quite ....

10.2 **Find six more pairs of words in the box. Why are they pairs?**

~~attractive~~	height	average	~~good-looking~~	weight	narrow	roughly
tall	curly	approximately	medium	wavy	broad	weigh

Attractive and good-looking are similar in meaning. ....

....

....

....

....

....

....

10.3 **Complete the dialogues using words that are similar to the underlined words.**

1 A: She's <u>good-looking</u>.
   B: Yes, very *attractive* .

2 A: María José looked <u>beautiful</u> last night.
   B: Yes, absolutely ....

3 A: Her boyfriend's quite <u>good-looking</u>.
   B: Yes, he is rather ....

4 A: Andreas looks very <u>strong and healthy</u>.
   B: Yes, I think he's very ....

5 A: That girl is <u>attractive</u>, isn't she?
   B: Yes, she's very ....

6 A: Ethan's getting <u>fat</u>.
   B: Yes, he is a bit ....

7 A: Did you think he was a bit <u>ugly</u>?
   B: Yes, he was quite ....

8 A: Is she <u>about</u> 25?
   B: Yes, ...

9 A: He's just <u>above average height</u>.
   B: Yes, he is .... , isn't he?

10.4

Over to you

Answer the questions.

1 How tall are you? ....

2 What's your hair like? ....

3 Think about one of your best friends. What does he/she look like? ....

....

....

11 Describing character

A What are you like?

Describe your character[1]

Choose the number that describes you. For example, in the first line
1 = very positive, 3 = not very positive or negative, 5 = very negative.

	1	2	3	4	5	
I think I'm very **positive**[2].	●	○	○	○	○	I'm quite a **negative** person.
I'm usually **reliable**[3].	○	○	●	○	○	I'm quite **unreliable**.
I'm quite **confident**[4].	○	●	○	○	○	I'm quite **shy**[5].
I'm **hard-working**[6].	●	○	○	○	○	I'm quite **lazy**.
I have a good **sense of humour**[7].	○	○	○	●	○	I'm usually quite **serious**[8].
I'm usually quite **patient**[9].	○	○	●	○	○	I'm quite **impatient**.
	1	2	3	4	5	

[1] what you are like as a person
[2] believe that good things will happen
[3] can be trusted to do what people expect you to do
[4] feeling sure about yourself and your abilities
[5] not confident, especially about meeting or talking to new people
[6] putting a lot of effort into your work and spending a lot of time on it
[7] the ability to laugh and understand when something is funny
[8] a serious person is quiet and doesn't laugh very much
[9] able to stay calm and not get angry, especially when things take a lot of time

Common mistakes

A: What's he like? (NOT How
   is he like?)
B: He's very **nice**. (NOT He's
   like very nice.)

B Opposites

positive	negative
generous [happy to give more money or help than is usual]	**mean**
honest [an honest person tells the truth]	**dishonest**
clever, intelligent [able to learn and understand things quickly]	**stupid**
calm [relaxed and not worried or frightened]	**nervous, anxious**

Language help

We use **kind** to describe someone who wants to help people a lot, and **nice**, **friendly**
or **pleasant** for someone who is happy to talk to people. The opposites are **unkind**,
unfriendly and **unpleasant**.

C Describing a friend

"The first thing I would say about my best friend is that she's very **sensible**[1]. I've never
known Emilia to do anything **silly**[2], and I know I can always **trust**[3] her. She's also very
creative[4]; she makes things, and she's a very **talented**[5] artist. I **wish**[6] I had her **talent**."

[1] practical; doesn't do stupid things
[2] not sensible, a bit stupid
[3] be sure that she is honest
[4] good at thinking of new ideas
  and using her imagination

[5] has a natural ability
[6] I would like to have her
  talent but I haven't got it.

Exercises

11.1 Find five pairs of opposites and put them into the correct columns.

nice	mean	sensible	lazy	calm	generous
unpleasant	hard-working	silly	nervous		

positive	negative
nice	

11.2 Write the opposites using the correct prefix.

1 *un*..kind   3 ....pleasant   5 ....honest

2 ....friendly   4 ....patient   6 ....reliable

11.3 Describe the person in the sentences, in one word.

1 My brother is in the office from 8 am to 6 pm every day. *hard-working*
2 He has never bought me a drink in ten years. ....
3 She often promises to do things but sometimes she forgets. ....
4 My teacher explains things again and never gets angry. ....
5 Emma finds it difficult to meet people and talk to strangers. ....
6 Noah is practical and doesn't do anything stupid. ....
7 Our teacher is nice, but he's quiet and he doesn't laugh a lot. ....
8 Danya is very relaxed and doesn't seem to worry about things. ....
9 My boss is really good at using his imagination to think of new ideas. ....
10 Ava can play several musical instruments. ....

11.4 Complete the sentences.

1 My sister can't wait for anything; she's so ....*impatient*........ .
2 I get very .... before exams; I need to try and relax a bit more.
3 I .... I could paint as well as your brother; he's so creative.
4 Adeline hasn't done a thing since she's been here. Honestly, she's so ....
5 I always have a laugh with my cousin – he's got a great sense of ....
6 My younger sister is able to understand new ideas so quickly; she's very ....
7 If Sarah says she'll do it, then she'll do it. I .... her completely.
8 He'd like to be relaxed and confident, but it's just not part of his ....
9 He failed his exams, but he isn't .... He just didn't do any work.
10 Aurora helped me bake some cakes last week; she's very ....

11.5   **Over to you**

Complete the quiz on the opposite page for yourself. From all the words on the opposite page, which one would you most like to be, and which is the one you would hate to be? If possible, compare your answers with someone else.

12 Feelings

A How do you feel?

Language help

We use **emotion** and **feeling(s)** for something which someone feels strongly about, e.g. love, hate or anger. **Emotions** are part of our character, e.g. *Timo is a very **emotional** person*. [shows his feelings easily] **Feeling** is often plural, e.g. *She doesn't like talking about her **feelings***.

> I'm very **proud**[1] **of** my son's success, but I'm a bit **disappointed**[2] that the local paper hasn't shown more interest in the story.

> The politicians seem **confused**[3] about what to do, so I'm not **hopeful**[4] that things will improve.

[1] feeling good because you (or someone you know) has done something well
[2] unhappy because someone or something was not as good as you hoped.

[3] not able to think clearly or understand something
[4] feeling positive about a future situation

> We were **curious**[5] to see what all the noise was about, but I felt **anxious**[6] when I saw how angry the men were, and really **scared**[7] when they started coming towards us.

> I think Harry ended the relationship because his girlfriend was getting **jealous**[8], but now he's quite **upset**[9].

[5] wanting to know or learn about something
[6] worried
[7] afraid; *syn* **frightened**

[8] unhappy and angry because someone you love seems too interested in another person
[9] unhappy because something unpleasant has happened

Language help

adjective	noun	adjective	noun
proud	**pride**	disappointed	**disappointment**
jealous	**jealousy**	confused	**confusion**
curious	**curiosity**	anxious	**anxiety**

B The effect of the weather on our feelings

Why do people say they feel more **cheerful** [happy] when the sun shines, and **miserable** [unhappy] when it's raining? Why do some people suffer from SAD (seasonal affective disorder), which makes them feel **depressed** [unhappy, often for a long time, and without hope for the future] during long dark winters? Can the weather really affect our **mood** [the way we feel at a particular time], or is it just in our imaginations?

C The effect of colour on our emotions

COLOUR can have an **effect** on our mood, but how do specific colours relate to our emotions?

RED can make us feel **energetic**[1], but it can also indicate **anger**[2].

PINK though, is softer and more about maternal love and **caring for**[3] people.

GREEN is associated with nature and is good for people suffering from **stress**[4].

BLUE is relaxing and helps us to be **creative**[5], but too much dark blue can make us depressed.

[1] wanting to be busy and doing a lot of things
[2] being angry
[3] looking after someone, especially someone young or old

[4] feelings of worry caused by difficult situations such as problems at work
[5] good at thinking of new ideas or using our imagination

Exercises

12.1 **Cover the opposite page. Complete the tables.**

adjective	noun
angry	*anger*
jealous	
confused	
	pride

adjective	noun
disappointed	
	curiosity
anxious	
	emotion

12.2 **Find the best sentence ending on the right for each of the sentence beginnings on the left.**

1 He was very anxious when ☐ c
2 He was very jealous when ☐
3 He was very scared when ☐
4 He was very proud when ☐
5 He was very upset when ☐
6 He was very miserable when ☐

a he heard his aunt had died.
b his father appeared on TV with the Prime Minister.
c his 14-year-old daughter didn't get home until 2 am.
d he saw the man coming towards him with a knife.
e he was ill.
f his best friend went out with the girl he really liked.

12.3 **Match the words and faces.**

anxious ....*1*....   scared ....   cheerful ....   upset ....   confused ....   depressed ....

1   2    3   4   5   6

12.4 **Complete the sentences.**

1 My aunt had to ..*care*.......................... for her elderly mother for years.
2 I can't tell whether Mia is happy or not; she never shows her ....
3 I'm much more .... in the mornings. By the afternoon I feel tired.
4 Weather has a big .... on the way I feel.
5 He's been under a lot of .... recently because of the amount of work he has to do.
6 Oliver's cheerful one minute and miserable the next; his .... changes all the time.
7 It's been a depressing month, but I'm .... things will get better next month.
8 I don't like walking home in the dark. I get very ....

12.5
Over to you

Answer the questions. If possible, compare your answers with someone else.

1 Does colour or the weather have an effect on your emotions? How?

2 Do you ever suffer from stress? Why?

3 Does your mood change a lot from day to day? Why?

4 Do you feel more energetic at certain times of the day? Why?

13 Family and friends

A Relatives*

RELATIVES

My father died when I was nine, and so my mother was a **widow**[1] with four young children. She **remarried** five years later, so now I have a **stepfather**. As he is not my real father, I call him by his first name, which is Dieter. I've got an **elder**[2] brother called Thomas and two younger sisters, Anya and Claudia, who are **twins**[3]. We're a **close family**[4].

My mother is an **only child**[5], but I've got two uncles on my father's side. One is married with two children, and the other is married with three children, so **altogether** I have five **cousins**. I **get on well with**[6] Uncle Rolf, and he always tells me I'm his favourite **nephew**. Of his **nieces**, I think he likes Anya best.

Recently my brother Thomas **got married**. His wife's name is Sabine, so I now have a **sister-in-law**[7] as well.

* members of your family; *syn* **relations**
[1] a woman whose husband has died
[2] older
[3] two children born to one mother at the same time
[4] a family who like each other and stay together a lot
[5] without brothers or sisters
[6] have a good relationship with
[7] (also **mother/brother/son-in-law**, etc.)

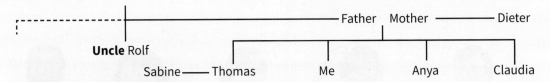

```
                                    Father   Mother ————— Dieter
        Uncle Rolf
     Sabine —— Thomas       Me          Anya          Claudia
```

Common mistakes

It's more common and more natural to say '**Thomas's** wife' (NOT ~~the wife of Thomas~~) or '**Anna's** younger sister' (NOT ~~the younger sister of Anna~~).

B Friends

FRIENDS

My **best friend** is Florian, an **old** school **friend**[1]. We **got to know each other**[2] when we were in the same class at school. We've been **mates**[3] **ever since**[4], and our **friendship** is very important to both of us. He spends a lot of time with my family, and his **current**[5] girlfriend is actually one of Thomas's **ex**-girlfriends. But we all get on really well.

Florian

Language help

We use the prefix **ex-** for a relationship we had in the past but do not have now, e.g. *The children stay with my **ex**-husband at the weekend; I saw an **ex**-girlfriend of mine yesterday.*

Exercises

13.1 **Look at the family tree, then complete the sentences below.**

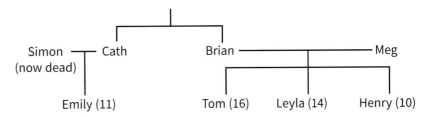

1 Simon died two years ago, so Cath is a _widow_ .
2 Leyla is Cath's ....
3 Tom is Cath's ....
4 Cath is Meg's ....
5 Simon was Brian's ....
6 Tom is Leyla's .... brother.
7 Emily is Leyla's ....
8 Emily is an .... child.

13.2 **Which words are being defined?**

1 Your _current_ .... boyfriend is the one that you have now.
2 .... means get married again.
3 .... are all the members of your family.
4 Your .... friend is the one you like more than any other.
5 An .... friend is someone you have known for a long time.
6 .... are two children born to one mother at the same time.
7 .... is an informal word for a friend.
8 .... is the noun when two people are friends.
9 Your .... is the man who is married to your mother but is not your father.

13.3 **Complete the text.**

❝I was still going out with James when I met my husband, Ben. We ¹ _got to know_ .... each other because we went to the same gym twice a week. We went out with each other for about 18 months, and we got ² .... three years ago, so ³ .... we've been a couple for almost five years. We've continued to go to the gym ever ⁴ .... we got married, and I still quite often see James when we're there. It's nice if you can still ⁵ .... with an ⁶ ....-boyfriend or -girlfriend.❞

13.4

Over to you

Answer the questions for you, then, if possible, ask a friend and write their answers.

1 Are you an only child? If not, do you have elder brothers or sisters? ....

2 Do you get on well with other members of your family? ....

3 Are you a close family? ....

4 Who was the last person in your family to get married? When? ....

5 Who's your best friend? ....

6 How long have you known him/her? ....

7 How did you get to know each other? ....

A Ages and stages in the UK

| 0 months | 12 months | 3 years | 12 years | 18 years | 40 years | 65 years | 80 years |

Age	Stage
0	**birth** [the moment a baby is born]
Up to 12 months	a baby
12 months – 3 years old	a **toddler**
3–12 years old	a child: this period is your **childhood**
13–18 approximately	a **teenager**: during this period you are **in your teens**
18+	an **adult**
40+ approximately	people are **middle-aged** [in the middle of their lives]
60 or 65	**retirement** [when people stop work; they are **retired**]
80+	old age (we usually describe people as **elderly**)

B Approximate ages

I'm **in my early twenties** [21–23].
My parents are **in their mid-fifties** [54–56].
My grandmother is **in her late seventies** [77–79].
My grandfather is **nearly/almost eighty** [he's probably 79].
My English teacher's **approximately/roughly** thirty.
[about 30 / more or less 30]

Common mistakes

We can say, **he's 30** or **he's 30 years old**. (NOT he ~~has~~ 30 or he's 30 ~~years~~)
Also: a **30-year-old man** (NOT a 30-~~years~~-old man)

C Past and present

PAST AND PRESENT

My grandmother's name was Mary. She's **dead**[1] now. She died about ten years ago when I was in my teens, but I remember her well. She was **brought up**[2] on a farm in Wales, and her parents were very **strict**: as a teenager, they didn't **allow**[3] her to listen to the radio or go to parties in the village. **In the end**[4], she decided to leave home and get a job in Cardiff. **At first**[5] it wasn't easy, but she **managed**[6] to find work, and she also met the man who became her husband: my grandfather. My mother was born four years later. She had a very different childhood. She grew up in the city, she **was allowed to** go to parties, and when she was in her teens, her parents **let**[7] her **stay out late**[8]. My mum is the same with me.

[1] not living; opp **alive**
[2] looked after until you are an adult
[3] give permission
[4] finally, after a lot of time or thought
[5] at the beginning
[6] was able (but it was difficult)
[7] allowed
[8] not go home until late

Language help

Let and **allow** have the same meaning. **Let** is slightly more informal, and **allow** is often used in the passive.
*My dad **let me drive** his car. I **was allowed to drive** my dad's car.*
***You're not allowed to** smoke in that room.* (NOT ~~It's not allowed to~~ smoke in that room.)

Exercises

14.1   **Complete the sentences.**

1   Isabella is only six months old – she's still *a baby* .
2   Louis was 22 a few months ago, so he's in his ....
3   Amelia is 35, so she's in her ....
4   Abigail will be 13 this year, so she'll soon be a ....
5   William is 53 and his wife is 47, so they're both ....
6   Joan is 80 this year, so she is quite ....
7   Michael was a bus driver for 40 years but he's now ....
8   Leon is 18 this year, so legally he becomes ....
9   The boys are 14 and 16, so they're both in their ....
10 Holly is just over a year old and she's starting to walk, so she's a .... now.

14.2   **Are the sentences true or false about Mary's life on the opposite page? If a sentence is false, change it to make it true.**

1   Mary was brought up in the city. *False. Mary was brought up on a farm.*
2   She grew up in Wales. ....
3   Her parents let her do what she wanted. ....
4   She wasn't allowed to listen to the radio. ....
5   Life was easy when she went to Cardiff. ....
6   She couldn't get a job in Cardiff. ....

14.3   **Rewrite the sentences without using the underlined words and phrases. Keep a similar meaning.**

1   My parents <u>are dead</u> now.   My parents *aren't alive now* .
2   It was hard but <u>finally</u> I did it.   It was hard but ....
3   She's <u>approximately</u> my age.   She's ....
4   They're <u>almost</u> thirty now.   They're ....
5   <u>I had to do what</u> my parents <u>wanted</u>.   My parents were ....
6   My parents <u>let me</u> stay up and watch TV.   I was ....
7   My mum <u>looked after me</u> in Scotland.   I was ....
8   I <u>was able</u> to pass my exams <u>but it wasn't easy</u>.   I ....
9   I <u>didn't go home until</u> late.   I ....
10 <u>I was allowed to</u> wear what I liked.   My parents ....
11 I was happy <u>as a child</u>.   I had a happy ....
12 My grandparents <u>don't work any more</u>.   My grandparents are ....

14.4   ▐ `Over to you` ▐

> **Answer the questions. If possible, ask a friend and write their answers.**
>
> **1** Where were you brought up? ....
>
> **2** What do you particularly remember about your childhood? ....
> ....
> ....
> ....
>
> **3** Were your parents strict? What weren't you allowed to do when you were a child? ....
> ....
> ....
> ....
>
> **4** How late were you allowed to stay out when you were a teenager? ....
> ....

15 Romance, marriage and divorce

A Romance

"I had my first **date**[1] when I was 16, and it was terrible. I took a girl to the cinema but she didn't like the film and looked bored all evening; it was a bad start. Then, when I was 17, I **went out with**[2] a girl for three months, but we **broke up**[3] when she met a boy who was two years older than me, and had a car. My first **serious relationship**[4] was when I went to university. I **got to know**[5] Melanie because we were on the same course. At first we were just friends, then we started going out with each other, and after a few months we realised we were **in love**. We **got engaged**[6] **a couple of**[7] years after we left university and then …"

[1] a planned romantic meeting
[2] had a romantic relationship with
[3] the relationship ended
[4] important romantic relationship
[5] became friends with
[6] formally agreed to marry
[7] two, perhaps three

B Marriage*

(bride)groom

bride

"… we **got married**[1] the following year. We didn't want a big **ceremony**[2], so we had the **wedding**[3] in the local church near Melanie's home with just family and a few friends. Afterwards we had the **reception**[4] in a small hotel nearby, and then went on our **honeymoon**[5] to Greece."

* the time when you are married
[1] became husband and wife
[2] an important public event
[3] the ceremony when people get married
[4] the wedding party
[5] a holiday just after getting married

Common mistakes

She **got to know** Darren at university. (NOT She ~~knew~~ Darren at university.)

Now they plan to **get married**. (NOT They plan to get ~~marry~~; or They plan to ~~married~~.)
She's getting married **to** Darren next year. (NOT She's getting married ~~with~~ Darren next year.)

C Children

"Just over three years later Melanie **got pregnant**, and our first child, Cal, was born just two days after our fourth wedding **anniversary**[1]. We had a big **celebration**[2]."

[1] a day that is exactly one or more years after an important event
[2] a time when you do something you enjoy because it is a special day

Language help

adjective	noun		verb	noun
engaged	**engagement**		**celebrate**	celebration
pregnant	**pregnancy**		**marry**	marriage

D Divorce*

"Things started to **go wrong**[1] when I got a job as manager of a sportswear company. I was working six days a week and I had to do a lot of travelling. It was difficult for Melanie as well. She was working during the week, then at weekends she was often **alone / on her own**[2] with two young children. I felt I couldn't **give up**[3] my job, and in the end Melanie decided to **leave**[4] me. The following year we **got divorced**[5]."

* when a marriage officially ends
[1] become a problem
[2] without other people
[3] stop doing
[4] stop living with me
[5] the marriage officially ended

Exercises

15.1 **Put the events in a logical order.**

I went out with Gabriel. ☐
We got married. ☐
I got pregnant three months later. ☐
We got engaged. ☐
I got to know Gabriel. ☐
Our son was born just after our first anniversary. ☐
We went on our honeymoon. ☐
I met Gabriel at a party. ☐ *1*
We had a big reception. ☐

15.2 **Which words are being defined?**

1 The big party you have after the wedding. *reception*
2 A romantic meeting you plan before it happens. ....
3 The period of time when you are married. ....
4 How you describe a woman who is going to have a baby. ....
5 The day that is exactly one year, or a number of years, after an important event. ....
6 The name given to the woman and man on their wedding day. .... and
....
7 Stop doing a job or activity. .... something up

15.3 **Complete the dialogues.**

1 A: When did they get *engaged* ....?
   B: Last week. They plan to get married in a .... of years.

2 A: Where did they meet?
   B: I think he got .... her at university.
   A: And now they're married?
   B: Yes, the .... was last week.

3 A: Is it going to be a big wedding?
   B: No, they're having a small .... in the village church.
   A: And what about the reception?
   B: They're having a reception but no .... They're going straight back to work.

4 A: So, it's all over.
   B: Yes. Lily .... him and moved out last month.
   A: Oh dear. Have they had problems for a long time?
   B: I think it all started to go .... when they moved to Woodbridge.
   A: And what about Oliver? Is he alone now?
   B: Yes, completely on .... He doesn't want any new relationships yet.
   A: But the marriage is definitely over?
   B: Yes, I'm afraid they're getting ....

15.4 **Over to you**

Answer the questions for you, then, if possible, ask a friend and write their answers.

1 Can you remember your first date? (When, and who with?)

2 Can you remember your first serious relationship? (Who was it with? Did you break up, or are you still with the same person?)

3 Whose was the last wedding you went to?

4 What was the last big celebration (other than a wedding) that you went to?

16 Daily routines

A Sleep

"During the week I usually **wake up**[1] about 7.30 am. If I don't, my mum **wakes me up**. I **get up**[2] a few minutes later. In the evenings I **go to bed** about 10.30 pm, and usually **go to sleep**[3] **straight away**[4]. If I **have a late night**[5] I try to **have a sleep**[6] in the afternoon when I get home from college."

[1] stop sleeping
[2] get out of bed
[3] start sleeping; *syn* **fall asleep**
[4] immediately
[5] go to bed very late; *opp* **have an early night**
[6] a short period of sleeping, e.g. half an hour

B Food

"I have coffee and **cereal** for breakfast, then **have a light lunch**[1], maybe a sandwich and an apple, and a **snack**[2] in the afternoon. We have our **main meal** in the evening. If Mum's late home from work, she **doesn't bother**[3] to cook; we just get a **takeaway**[4] instead. One of us has to **feed**[5] the cat as well."

cereal

[1] have a small meal
[2] a small amount of food you eat between meals
[3] doesn't do something because there is no reason or because it is too much work
[4] a meal you buy in a restaurant but eat at home
[5] give food

C Bathroom routines

"I usually **have a shower** when I get home from college because my sister, Rosie, and my brother, Marcus, spend so much time in the bathroom in the morning. I only have time to **have a wash** and **clean my teeth** (*syn* **brush my teeth**), before Rosie comes in to **put on** a bit of **make-up**. In the winter I sometimes **have a bath instead of**[1] a shower. I like to lie in the bath and listen to music."

Marcus **having a shave**

Rosie **putting on make-up**

[1] in place of (a shower)

D Housework*

"**Fortunately**[1] we've got a **cleaner**[2] who **does** a lot of the **housework**, and that includes **doing** my **washing**[3]. But I still have to **make** my **bed** and **do** some of my **ironing**, and I sometimes **do the shopping** with Mum."

ironing

* the work of keeping a home clean and tidy
[1] happening because of good luck; *syn* **luckily**
[2] a person who cleans
[3] washing my clothes

Language help

When we **do the shopping**, we buy food at the supermarket; when we **go shopping**, it is a leisure activity and we perhaps buy clothes, DVDs, books, etc.

E Spare time*

"On weekdays I usually **stay in**[1] and watch TV in the evening. At the weekend I **go out** quite a lot with my friends, either to the cinema or just to a café, and I **eat out**[2] once a week. Sometimes friends **come round**[3] and we **chat**[4] about clothes, music and college."

* time when you are not working
[1] stay at home
[2] eat in a restaurant; *opp* **eat in**
[3] visit me in my home
[4] have an informal conversation

Exercises

16.1 **Find seven more expressions with *have* + [noun] and *do* + [noun] from the opposite page.**

have *a shower* .... have .... have .... have ....
do .... do .... do .... do ....

16.2 **Match the words on the left with the words on the right.**

1 get up ⬚ *g*   a the dog
2 fall ⬚   b my teeth
3 make ⬚   c make-up
4 put on ⬚   d a week
5 go ⬚   e the bed
6 clean ⬚   f to sleep
7 feed ⬚   g early
8 once ⬚   h asleep

16.3 **One word is missing in each sentence. What is it and where does it go?**

1 Does it cost much to have a cleaner to ˅the housework? *do*
2 My mother usually me up around 7:30, then I get up about 7:45.
3 If I have a in the afternoon, I usually eat fruit instead of chocolate.
4 I always go on Friday and Saturday, often to the cinema or a club.
5 Sometimes friends round to the flat and we play computer games.
6 I eat at the weekend, usually in a local Italian or French restaurant.
7 I don't with a full meal at lunchtime; I usually just have a light lunch, like a salad.
8 I often have for breakfast – usually cornflakes or something like that.
9 I don't like doing housework; I have a husband who does most of it.
10 When I get emails, I try to reply to them straight.

16.4 **Complete the dialogue with a word or phrasal verb from the opposite page in each gap.**

A: Don't ¹ *bother* .... to cook dinner tonight.
B: Why not?
A: We could go out ² .... of eating here.
B: Yeah. Where?
A: Well, I'd like to try that new Korean restaurant.
B: That's miles away. No, I think I'd rather ³ .... and have an ⁴ .... night.
A: But it's Friday.
B: Yes, I know, but I'm tired. Why don't we ask Ryan and Charlotte to ⁵ ....?
   You don't have to cook, we can order a ⁶ .... And we can have a nice
   ⁷ .... round the dining table; much better than a noisy restaurant.

16.5

Over to you

Find three facts from the opposite page that are similar in your routine, and three that are different. Complete the table.

similar	different
1	....
2	....
3	....

17 The place where you live

A Location*

"We live **on the outskirts of town**[1], and it's a very nice **location**. We used to live in the centre, but we **moved**[2] to our present flat when we had children because there's more **space**[3] for them to play and it has nice **views**[4]."

* the place and position of something
[1] on the edge of town
[2] changed the place where we live

[3] an area that is empty or not used
[4] the things you can see from a place

B Our flat

"This is where we live. We **rent**[1] a flat **on the second floor**. There's a family in the flat **downstairs**[2], and a young French couple **upstairs**, on the top floor. It's a modern **block of flats**[3], and it's quite good, although the **lift**[4] is small, and there's no **air conditioning**[5]."

[1] pay money every week/month to use it because it isn't ours
[2] on a lower level of a building
[3] a building with a number of flats in it
[4] the machine that takes people up or down a floor
[5] a system that keeps the air cool

> ### Language help
>
> **Flat** is more common in British English; **apartment** is used in American English but is becoming more common in British English. Apartments are usually in large buildings; flats can be in a large building or part of a larger house.

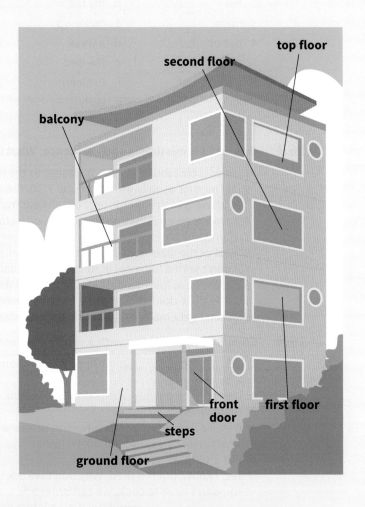

top floor
second floor
balcony
first floor
front door
steps
ground floor

C A house in the country

"My parents **own**[1] a **cottage**[2]. It's a **charming**[3] house and **has lots of character**[4], but like many old buildings, it's quite **dark** (*opp* **light**), quite difficult to **heat**[5], and it doesn't have **central heating**[6]."

[1] they bought it
[2] a small house, that is old and attractive, and usually found in the country
[3] pleasant and attractive
[4] it is interesting and unusual
[5] make warm or hot
[6] a system that heats a whole house

cottage

Exercises

17.1 **Are the sentences about the people on the opposite page true or false? If the sentence is false, change it to make it true.**

1 They live in a house. _False. They live in a flat._
2 They used to live on the outskirts of town. ....
3 They own their flat. ....
4 They've got nice views from their flat. ....
5 They live on the first floor. ....
6 There's a lift in the building. ....
7 A French couple live downstairs. ....
8 They own a cottage. ....
9 The cottage has lots of character. ....
10 The cottage is quite cold. ....

17.2 **Are these generally positive or negative features of a home?**

views _positive_   air conditioning ....   character ....
dark ....   charming ....   no central heating ....

17.3 **Label the pictures.**

1 _a block of flats_   2 ....   3 ....   4 ....   5 ....
    6 ....

17.4 **Complete the sentences.**

1 Our flat doesn't have air _conditioning_ .
2 I live .... the second floor, and my cousin lives ...., on the first floor.
3 My old flat was very small, but this one has much more ....
4 The flat's in a great .... : it's near the centre of town but opposite a park and very quiet.
5 We live on the .... of town, but it's only a twenty-minute walk to the centre.
6 The flat is on the third floor, but we can sit outside on the ....
7 It's a very big house, so it costs a lot of money to .... in the winter.
8 I'm on the second .... I usually use the stairs, but take the .... if I'm feeling lazy.
9 I live in Paris. I used to live in Marseilles, but I .... to Paris when I left university.
10 I love my apartment. It has big windows, so it's nice and .... inside.

17.5

Answer the questions about your home.

1 Do you live in a house or flat?

2 If you live in a flat, what floor is it on?

3 Do you own your home or rent it?

4 Are you in the centre, or on the outskirts of your town?

5 How long have you lived there?

6 Do you have these things:

   air conditioning?   central heating?
   a balcony?

A Different homes

"When we first got married, we lived in a one-bedroom flat with a small kitchen, a living room and a bathroom. When our first child was born, she had to **share** our bedroom. [use something at the same time as someone else] Now we live in a four-bedroom house. Our bedroom has an **en-suite bathroom** [a bathroom connected to the bedroom], our two teenage children have their **own** rooms [they do not have to share], we have a **spare room** for guests, and another bathroom. Downstairs, there's a living room, a dining room and a **study** [a room where people can work]. We've also got a lovely big kitchen with a fridge-freezer, a cooker with two ovens and a **dishwasher** [a machine for washing dishes]. Next to it, there's a small **utility room** where we keep the **washing machine**."

> ### Language help
> We usually talk about a **sink** in the kitchen, but a (**wash**)**basin** in the bathroom.

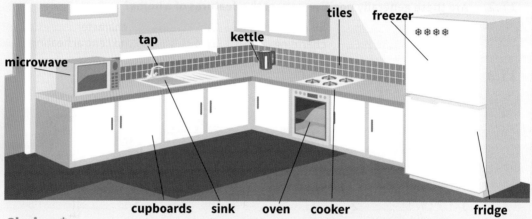

microwave · tap · kettle · tiles · freezer · cupboards · sink · oven · cooker · fridge

B Choices*

* when you decide between two or more possibilities

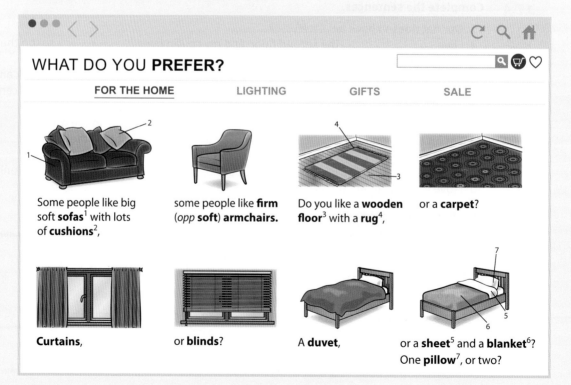

WHAT DO YOU PREFER?

FOR THE HOME   LIGHTING   GIFTS   SALE

Some people like big soft **sofas**[1] with lots of **cushions**[2],

some people like **firm** (*opp* **soft**) **armchairs**.

Do you like a **wooden floor**[3] with a **rug**[4],

or a **carpet**?

Curtains,

or **blinds**?

A **duvet**,

or a **sheet**[5] and a **blanket**[6]? One **pillow**[7], or two?

Exercises

18.1 **You are in the kitchen. Where would you put these things?**

1 milk? *in the fridge* ....
2 food that you want to heat very quickly? ....
3 meat that you are going to cook? ....
4 dirty clothes? ....
5 dirty saucepans? ....
6 clean cups and saucers ....
7 frozen food that you want to keep for several weeks? ....

18.2 **What are these things, and which room(s) do you usually find them in?**

1 girdef   *fridge, in the kitchen* ....
2 snik   ....
3 nacitusr   ....
4 shiconus   ....
5 ktelet   ....
6 bashniswa   ....
7 cparte   ....
8 lipowl   ....
9 shiwang chameni ....
10 kocero   ....
11 chmariar   ....
12 leits   ....

18.3 **Complete the sentences.**

1 I'm happy with curtains or .... *blinds* ....; I really don't mind.
2 We used to have a .... floor, but it was a bit noisy so we put down a carpet.
3 When I got my new bedroom, my mum gave me a .... of curtains or blinds.
4 My mum works at home, so she spends all day in the .... on the computer.
5 As a child I had to .... a room with my sister, but now I've got my .... bedroom.
6 We often have guests to stay, but fortunately we've got a .... room.
7 'Dad, there's no water coming out of the .... in the kitchen sink.'
8 Some people like a sheet and .... , but I prefer a ....
9 There's a family bathroom, but I've got my own .... shower room next to the bedroom.
10 Our kitchen is small but we have a .... room for the washing machine.

18.4 **Over to you**

Answer the questions. If possible, compare your answers with someone else.

1 What have you got on your kitchen floor? ....

2 What have you got on the bathroom floor? ....

3 What have you got on the floor in the living room? ....

4 Have you got curtains or blinds in your bedroom? ....

5 Have you got a duvet or sheets and blankets on your bed? ....

18.5 **Over to you**

Look at section B on the opposite page again. Which do you prefer, and why? Compare your answers with someone else if possible.

19 Money

A Notes and coins

In the UK the **currency** [type of money used] is **sterling** [pounds]; in America it is **the dollar**; in much of Europe it's **the euro**.

Notes
e.g. ten pounds, twenty euros,
a ten-pound note, **a twenty-euro note**

Coins (in the UK)
e.g. fifty pence (usually spoken as **fifty p**),
a pound, **a fifty-pence piece**, but **a one-pound coin**

B Managing your money

"I've had a **bank account** for a few years now, and I make sure my account is always **in credit**[1]. I go to the **cashpoint** once a week, so I always have some **cash**[2] with me, and I **check**[3] my account online once a week to see how much money I've got."

[1] having money in the account
[2] money in the form of notes and coins
[3] look at the details of it

cashpoint

C Money problems

"When I went to university, I had to get a **student loan**[1] to pay my **fees**[2]. That meant I had to be careful and make sure I didn't **waste money**[3], but by the time I finished my degree I **owed**[4] a lot. One good thing is that I don't have to pay it back until I get a job and I'm **earning**[5] a **reasonable amount**[6] of money. At the moment I'm **saving up**[7] for a new laptop; the one I have is very slow and keeps going wrong. I'd love to have a car as well, but I **can't afford**[8] it."

[1] money you borrow to pay for your studies
[2] money you pay to use something, or for a service, e.g. a lawyer's fee
[3] use it badly
[4] had to **pay back** a lot of money to the bank

[5] receiving money for the work I do
[6] quite a lot; $1 million is **a large amount**
[7] keeping money to buy something in the future
[8] don't have enough money to buy one

D Accommodation*

"This year I'm **renting** a flat with three friends of mine. We had to pay one month's **rent** as a **deposit**[1], but it's a nice place, quite **good value for money**[2], and the landlord isn't **charging**[3] us to use his garage."

* places where you live or stay
[1] money you pay for something you are going to use, which is then returned to you when you have finished using it
[2] good for the amount of money you pay
[3] asking someone to pay an amount of money

> ### Language help
>
> We use **rent** when we pay to use something for a long period of time, e.g. *rent a flat*.
> The noun *rent* is the amount you pay, e.g. *The **rent** is £400 per month*. We use **hire**
> when we pay to use something for a short period of time, e.g. *I **hired** a bike for the day*.
> Both verbs are used with cars, e.g. *We **rented/hired** a car when we were on holiday*.

Exercises

19.1 **Answer the questions as quickly as possible.**

1 Is sterling a currency? .... *Yes* ....
2 Is a five-pound note worth less than a fifty-pence piece? ....
3 If you rent something, do you own it? ....
4 If you waste money, do you use it well? ....
5 Can you get money from a cashpoint? ....
6 If you are in credit, do you have money in your account? ....
7 Do you pay back a bank loan? ....
8 Is the currency in the United States of America called the euro? ....
9 Do you normally get back a deposit? ....
10 If you 'can afford' something, do you have enough money for it? ....

19.2 **Which words are being defined?**

1 A flat, usually round piece of metal used as money. *coin* ....
2 Money you borrow from a bank. ....
3 Money you pay to someone for a professional service, e.g. a school. ....
4 Money in the form of notes or coins. ....
5 Money you pay to live in a building that you don't own. ....
6 A machine where you can get money. ....
7 The type of money used in a country. ....

19.3 **Rewrite the sentences without using the underlined words and phrases. Keep the same meaning.**

1 He's <u>getting</u> £300 a week in his job.   He's *earning £300 a week in his job.* ....
2 She <u>used</u> the money <u>badly</u>.   She ....
3 I <u>don't have enough money</u> to go.   I ....
4 We could <u>rent</u> a car.   We could ....
5 He <u>asked</u> us <u>to pay</u> £25.   He ....
6 I<u>'ve got to pay back</u> a lot of money.   I ....
7 I always <u>look at</u> my account carefully.   I always ....

19.4 **Complete the text.**

❝I'm nearly 20 now, and I've been [1] *saving up* .... for a car for the last two years. I've been putting money into my bank [2] .... , and I try to put in exactly the same [3] .... every month: £75 from money that I [4] .... doing a job two evenings a week, and £50 that my parents are lending me each month. That means I now [5] .... them £1200, but they said I don't have to [6] .... them .... until I've got a full-time job. At the moment I'm still living at home, so I don't have to pay for my [7] .... , although I will start paying my parents a bit of rent when I finish college and get a job.❞

19.5

```
Over to you
```

Answer the questions.

1 Have you got a bank account? If so, how long have you had it?

2 How often do you check your account?

3 How often do you use a cashpoint?

4 Have you ever had a bank loan? What did you have the loan for?

5 Are you saving up for anything at the moment?

6 Do you rent the place where you live? If so, did you have to pay a deposit?

A Common problems

What's the matter?	What you should do
A: I've got a **sore throat**[1] and a **temperature**.[2]	B: That sounds like **flu**. You should see a doctor.
A: I've **cut** my arm; it's **bleeding**.[3]	B: Put a **bandage**[4] round it.
A: I've got a terrible **cough**.[5]	B: Go to the chemist and get some cough **medicine** [something you take to treat an illness].
A: I've got a **headache**.	B: Take some **tablets**[6] for the pain. (also **pills**)
A: I **feel sick**.[7]	B: Go to the bathroom quickly!

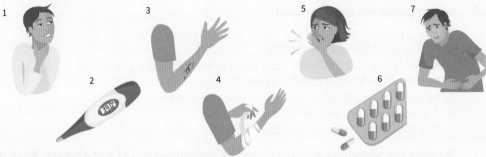

B Describing pain

We can use different words to describe **pain**. An **ache** describes pain that is not always strong, but often continues. It is used with certain parts of the body.
I've got a **headache**.   Aria's got **stomach ache**.
My dad **suffers from** [often has the pain of] **backache**.

For other parts of the body we often use **pain**.
I've got a **pain** in my shoulder/foot.

Ache can also be a verb to describe pain that continues for some time.
By the end of the day my feet were **aching**.

For stronger or more sudden pain, we usually use the verb **hurt**.
My throat **hurts** when I speak.
I hit my leg on the table and it really **hurts** / it's very **painful**.

C Serious illnesses

For **serious** [bad] illnesses, you will probably go into hospital. A person who stays in hospital is called a **patient**. Many patients need an **operation** [when special doctors, called **surgeons**, cut into the body for medical reasons; also called **surgery**].

Lung cancer can be caused by smoking.
Heart attacks can happen very suddenly.
Hepatitis is a **disease** affecting the **liver**.

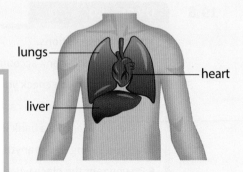

Language help

Disease is used to talk about more serious medical problems, often affecting certain parts of the body, e.g. heart disease. **Illness** is used to talk about serious and minor medical problems and those affecting the mind, e.g. mental illness. Disease is not used about a period of illness, e.g. He died after a long illness. (NOT He died after a ~~long disease~~.)

Exercises

20.1 **Look at the underlined letters in each pair of words. Is the pronunciation the same or different? Use the index to help you.**

1 <u>a</u>che   p<u>ai</u>n   *same*
2 c<u>o</u>ld   st<u>o</u>mach   *different*
3 c<u>ou</u>gh   thr<u>ou</u>gh ....
4 fl<u>u</u>   c<u>u</u>t ....

5 l<u>i</u>ver   d<u>i</u>sease ....
6 st<u>o</u>mach   <u>o</u>peration ....
7 <u>ch</u>emist   a<u>ch</u>e ....
8 p<u>a</u>tient   b<u>a</u>ndage ....

20.2 **Complete the sentences with *a* or nothing (–).**

1 She's got ....–.... hepatitis.
2 I've got ....*a*.... cough.
3 I'm getting .... sore throat.
4 Ben's got .... headache.
5 Luis's got .... temperature.

6 I've got .... backache.
7 Zarita's got .... flu.
8 My uncle had .... heart attack.
9 She's got .... cancer.
10 I've got .... pain in my foot.

20.3 **Complete the dialogues.**

1 A: Does your finger hurt?
   B: Yes, it's very *painful* ....
2 A: What's wrong with Dimitrios?
   B: He feels .... I think it's something he ate.
3 A: Did you hit your foot?
   B: Yes, and it really ....
4 A: My hand's bleeding quite badly.
   B: Well, put a .... round it.
5 A: Your finger's ....
   B: I know. I cut it using that knife.
6 A: Does Tanya still .... from bad headaches?
   B: Yes, she gets them all the time.
7 A: What's the matter?
   B: My back .... from sitting at that computer all day.
8 A: I understand Lena has had quite a .... illness.
   B: Yeah. She was in hospital for over a week.

20.4 **Find five more pairs of words. Why are they pairs?**

| ~~lung~~ heart surgeon tablets/pills attack liver |
| operation ~~cancer~~ hepatitis sore medicine throat |

lung and cancer – because you can get lung cancer. ....
....
....
....
....

20.5 **Over to you**

Answer the questions. If possible, compare your answers with someone else.

1 What do you usually do if you get a headache?

2 How often do you get a cough or a sore throat?

3 Have you ever been a patient in hospital? If so, what was it like?

4 Have you ever had surgery?

5 Are there some medicines you always keep in your home? What are they?

A Smart, stylish and casual

I think the woman looks **stylish** [wearing nice clothes and looking attractive; also **well-dressed**].
The man is **smartly dressed** [clean and tidy and suitable for formal situations].
The boy's clothes are more **casual** [comfortable and suitable for informal situations].

- earring
- top
- necklace
- bracelet
- ring
- skirt
- sleeve
- boots
- tights
- button
- suit
- tie
- collar
- scarf
- pocket
- cap
- T-shirt
- rucksack
- jumper/sweater
- zip
- jacket
- jeans
- trainers

B Verbs and phrases used with clothes

As soon as I get up, I have a shower and **get dressed** [put on my clothes]. I don't eat breakfast.

I have to **wear** a suit and tie to work, but I usually **take off** my tie before lunchtime. [remove it; *opp* **put something on**]

I prefer jackets with a zip; it's easier to **undo** a zip [open a zip, buttons, etc.] and it's also much quicker to **do it up**.

I think I look good **in black** because dark colours **suit** me. [I look good in dark colours; *opp* **bright** colours]

When I get home from work, I usually **change into** a pair of jeans.

Common mistakes

I like **clothes**. (NOT I like ~~cloth~~ or ~~cloths~~.)
I like your new **trousers**. (NOT I like your new ~~trouser~~.)

Exercises

21.1 **Put the words into the correct columns.**

> ~~boots~~ earrings button top ring jumper bracelet scarf
> necklace zip pocket cap sleeve tights collar

items of clothing	jewellery	parts of clothing
boots		

21.2 **Find five more things that are different in the pictures.**

1 *The first woman is wearing a ring; the second isn't.* ....
2 ....
 ....
3 ....
 ....
4 ....
 ....
5 ....
 ....
6 ....
 ....

21.3 **Complete the sentences.**

1 Why don't you take ......*off*.......................... your coat?
2 Madison looks really nice .... purple.
3 He was very smartly- .... this morning. He had his best suit on.
4 It took me ages to put .... these boots.
5 You should wear bright colours more often; they .... you.
6 Julia couldn't do .... the zip on her jacket.
7 I changed .... a pair of jeans as soon as I got home.
8 I took my tie off and .... the top button of my shirt.
9 My brother takes his books to school in a .... He says it's easier to carry them on his back.
10 I had a quick shower, got .... , then joined the others for breakfast.

21.4

Women, answer these questions.	Men, answer these questions.
1 What jewellery do you usually wear?	How often do you wear a suit?
2 Which colours suit you best?	How often do you wear a tie?
3 Do you prefer smart or casual clothes?	Do you usually do up the top button of your shirt?
4 Do you generally look quite stylish?	Do you often change into jeans after school or work?
5 Do you often wear a hat or a cap?	Do you often wear a hat or a cap?
6 Do you often wear T-shirts or trainers?	Do you often wear T-shirts or trainers?

A Fashion

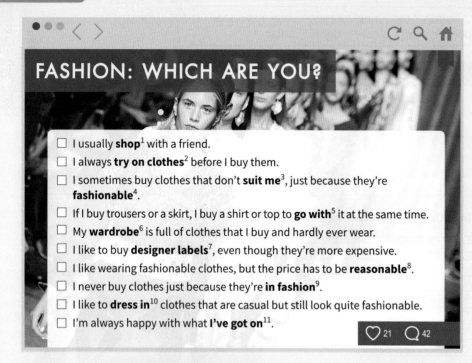

FASHION: WHICH ARE YOU?

- ☐ I usually **shop**[1] with a friend.
- ☐ I always **try on clothes**[2] before I buy them.
- ☐ I sometimes buy clothes that don't **suit me**[3], just because they're **fashionable**[4].
- ☐ If I buy trousers or a skirt, I buy a shirt or top to **go with**[5] it at the same time.
- ☐ My **wardrobe**[6] is full of clothes that I buy and hardly ever wear.
- ☐ I like to buy **designer labels**[7], even though they're more expensive.
- ☐ I like wearing fashionable clothes, but the price has to be **reasonable**[8].
- ☐ I never buy clothes just because they're **in fashion**[9].
- ☐ I like to **dress in**[10] clothes that are casual but still look quite fashionable.
- ☐ I'm always happy with what **I've got on**[11].

♡ 21   💬 42

[1] buy things in shops
[2] put clothes on in a shop to see what they are like
[3] look good on me
[4] popular at that particular time
[5] look good together
[6] a large cupboard for keeping clothes in
[7] clothes made by famous designers, e.g. Versace, Dolce & Gabbana
[8] not expensive
[9] fashionable
[10] wear a particular type, style or colour of clothes
[11] am wearing

Language help

If two things **match**, they are a similar colour or type. If two things **go with** each other, they look good together.
*Catherine's bag **matches** her coat. Catherine's bag **goes with** her coat.*
If something **suits** you, it looks good on you. If something **fits** you, it is the right size.

B In a clothes shop

A **shop assistant** [a person who works in a shop] is **serving** different customers [helping them to buy things].

 Shop assisstant Can I help you?

 Customer 1 No, **I'm being served**, thanks. [another shop assistant is already helping me]

 Shop assisstant Do you need any help?

 Customer 2 Yes, I've just tried on this jacket in a **size** 12, and it didn't really **fit** me; it's a bit **tight** [too small around the body; *opp* **loose**/big]. Have you got it in a bigger size?

 Shop assisstant We have got a size 14, but not in pink, I'm afraid.

 Customer 2 Oh, **that's a shame** [that is disappointing; *syn* **that's a pity**]. OK. **I'll leave it**, thanks. [I have decided not to buy it; *opp* **I'll take it/them**]

 Shop assisstant OK. I'm sorry about that. … Can I help you?

 Customer 3 Yes, **I'm looking for** a skirt and this looks nice. [I want to find a skirt] Can I try it on?

  Shop assisstant Yes, of course. The **changing rooms** are down there. [the place where you can try on clothes]

Exercises

22.1 **Are these pairs similar in meaning or different in meaning?**

1 *in fashion* and *fashionable* ....*similar*............
2 *wardrobe* and *changing room* ....
3 *I'll take it* and *I'll leave it* ....
4 *match something* and *go with something* ....
5 *tight* and *loose* ....
6 *fit someone* and *suit someone* ....
7 *that's a shame* and *that's a pity* ....

22.2 **Rewrite the sentences starting with the words given. Keep a similar meaning.**

1 I often shop with my mother. I often go ....*shopping with my mother*...................................... .
2 These watches are fashionable. These watches are in ....
3 Your top matches your skirt. Your top goes ....
4 I like what I'm wearing. I like what I've ....
5 Those trousers suit you. Those trousers look ....
6 Are they the right size? Do they .... ?
7 I'd like it to be quite loose. I don't want it to be too ....
8 She always wears black. She always .... in black.

22.3 **Which words are being defined?**

1 be the right size ....*fit*..................................
2 not cheap, but not expensive ....
3 a large cupboard for keeping clothes in ....
4 popular with people at a particular time ....
5 the place where you try on clothes in a shop ....
6 Armani and Calvin Klein are examples of this ....
7 a person who works in a shop ....
8 look after customers and help them to buy things ....

22.4 **Complete the dialogues.**

SHOP ASSISTANT: Can I help you?
    CUSTOMER 1: I'm [1] ....*looking for*.............. a top. This one's quite nice. I think I'll
                [2] .... it on.

SHOP ASSISTANT: Of course. The [3] .... room is just over there.

SHOP ASSISTANT: Do you need any help?
    CUSTOMER 2: No, I'm being [4] .... , thanks.

SHOP ASSISTANT: How was the top?
    CUSTOMER 1: I'm afraid it didn't [5] .... very well. It was a bit
                [6] .... under the arms.

SHOP ASSISTANT: Oh, that's a [7] .... Would you like a bigger size?
    CUSTOMER 1: No, I don't think so. In actual fact, it wasn't just the [8] ....
              I don't think it [9] .... me, actually. I think it's really for a younger
              person. I'll [10] .... it, thanks.

22.5

Over to you

Look at the text at the top of the opposite page again. Which statements are true for you?
If possible, compare your answers with someone else.

A | In a supermarket

sweets

basket

shelves

checkout

trolley

SHOPPING & MONEY ⟨ ⟩

How do supermarkets **make us**[1] spend more money?

They put **fresh**[2] bread, as it smells lovely, near the **entrance**[3] to make us feel hungry – and hungry shoppers spend more. They also rearrange things and put them in different places; this makes us spend more time in the store and that means spending more money. They put sweets and chocolate near the checkout, so it is easy to add bars of chocolate to our basket or trolley while we are waiting in the **queue**[4]. And they put the most expensive **items**[5] on the middle shelves where you are more **likely**[6] to see them. And be careful of **special offers**[7], e.g. three for the price of two. People often buy more than they need and **throw away** half of it.

[1] cause us to do or be something, e.g. *I don't like rain; it **makes me** depressed*.
[2] just made/cooked
[3] the place where you go into a building
[4] a line of people who are waiting for something
[5] an *item* is a single thing
[6] If you are likely to do something, you will probably do it.
[7] cheaper prices than normal

B | Shopping centres and street markets

Some people like modern **shopping centres**[1] because everything is **under one roof**[2] and it is **convenient**[3]. There's a **wide range**[4] of shops, and if there is anything wrong with something you buy, the shop will **replace**[5] it, or give you a **refund**[6].

Other people prefer going to **street markets** because they like the **atmosphere**[7] you get from the different **stalls**. Food and clothes are also usually cheaper in street markets. Sometimes you can try to agree a lower price for something you buy in a street market; we call this **haggling**. Of course, if you don't like what you buy in a street market, you can't normally take it back and get a refund.

stall

[1] large covered shopping areas
[2] in one place
[3] practical and easy to use
[4] different things of the same type
[5] exchange it for another one
[6] money that is paid back to you when you return something
[7] the feeling in a place or situation

Exercises

23.1 **True or false? If a sentence is false, change it to make it true.**

1 If you have a lot of things to buy, you need a basket.
False. If you have a lot of things to buy, you need a trolley.
....

2 Supermarkets arrange things to make us spend more money.
....

3 The checkout is where you pay for things.
....

4 Expensive items are on the top shelves.
....

5 If something is fresh, it has just been made.
....

6 There are often lovely smells near the entrance.
....

7 Sweets are often near the checkout.
....

8 It's always a good idea to buy things on special offer.
....

23.2 **Mark the main stress on these words. Use the index to help you.**

'atmosphere   convenient   checkout   entrance   a refund   replace   item

23.3 **Are these statements true of shopping centres, street markets, or both?**

1 They are usually quite modern.   *shopping centres* ....
2 Everything is under one roof.   ....
3 You buy things from stalls.   ....
4 You can haggle.   ....
5 You can normally get refunds.   ....
6 They can be very convenient.   ....

23.4 **Complete the sentences.**

1 I took the shoes back to the shop, but they wouldn't give me a ....*refund*.......................... .
2 It .... me angry when shops refuse to give you a refund or .... things.
3 I often buy bananas but forget to eat them, and then I have to .... them away.
4 When I got to the checkout, there was a long .... of people waiting.
5 There's a special .... on melons – buy one, get one free!
6 The vegetables are near the .... , where we came in.
7 I like that supermarket because they have a wide .... of meat and cheese.
8 In my local street market, there's just a really nice .... : it's very busy, but everyone is friendly and there's lots of colour.
9 I am more .... to buy something if it's a special offer, because it seems cheaper.

23.5

Over to you

Answer the questions. If possible, ask someone else the same questions.

1 How often do you shop in supermarkets? What do you think of them?

2 How often do you go to shopping centres? Do you like them?

3 How often do you go to street markets? Do you like them?

4 Do you haggle for things when you're shopping?

5 Have you ever asked for a refund?

24 Food

A Fruit

pineapple   **peach**   **strawberry**   **bunch of grapes**   **olives**

pear   **melon**   **lemon**   **coconut**

B Vegetables

beans   **peas**   **onion**   **garlic**   **carrot**   **mushrooms**

aubergine   **courgette**   **pepper**   **cabbage**   **broccoli**   **spinach**

C Salad

A **salad** is usually a mixture of uncooked ingredients. In Britain it mainly has **lettuce**, as well as **tomato**, **cucumber,** onion, and other things. We often put **salad dressing** (usually **oil** and **vinegar**, or perhaps oil and lemon) on salad.

lettuce   **tomato**   **cucumber**   **oil**   **vinegar**

D Meat, fish and seafood

Animal:	cow	**calf** [young cow]	**lamb** [young sheep]	pig	**chicken/hen**
Meat:	**beef**	veal	lamb	**pork**	chicken

A person who does not eat meat is a **vegetarian**.

salmon   **prawns**   **mussels**   **crab**

Exercises

24.1 Write down one vegetable and fruit beginning with these letters.

		vegetable	fruit
1	the letter *p*	.peas........................	....
2	the letter *g*	....	....
3	the letter *m*	....	....
4	the letter *s*	....	....
5	the letter *o*	....	....

24.2 Find a word from each box where the underlined letters are pronounced the same.

carr<u>o</u>t 1	<u>o</u>nion
lett<u>u</u>ce	pr<u>aw</u>n
<u>au</u>bergine	s<u>a</u>lmon

tomat<u>o</u>	mel<u>o</u>n 1
p<u>o</u>rk	ch<u>i</u>cken
l<u>a</u>mb	m<u>u</u>shroom

24.3 Which is the odd one out in each group, and why?

1	pork	veal	(salmon)	beef	*salmon is a fish, the others are meat* ....
2	lettuce	cabbage	tomato	cucumber	....
3	pork	lamb	beef	crab	....
4	peach	onion	pepper	courgette	....
5	crab	broccoli	mussels	prawn	....
6	carrots	chicken	beans	aubergine	....

24.4 Do you usually eat the skin (the outside) of these fruits? (Answer *Yes*, *Sometimes* or *No*.)

pineapple	*No*........................	peaches	....
melon	....	pears	....
grapes	....	lemon	....

24.5 Answer the questions.

1 What do we call the meat from a cow, lamb, calf, and a pig? .....*beef*............... , ... , ... , ...

2 What's the main ingredient in a green salad? ....

3 What are the two most common things we put in salad dressing? .... and ....

4 What do we usually call someone who doesn't eat meat? ....

5 What do we call a number of grapes that grow together? A .... of grapes.

24.6 `Over to you`

Using words from the opposite page, complete these sentences about yourself and your country. If possible, compare your answers with someone else.

1 .... is/are more common than ....

2 .... is/are more expensive than ....

3 A mixed salad usually has .... , ... , ... , ...

4 We don't often grow ....

5 We don't often eat ....

6 .... is/are my favourite ....

25 Cooking

barbecue

frying pan

saucepan

grill

oven

A Ways of cooking food

You **boil** potatoes or rice in a **saucepan**.
You can **fry** sausages in a **frying pan**.
You **grill** toast or meat under a **grill**.
You **roast** meat [using oil] in the **oven**.
You also **bake** cakes [without oil] in the oven.
You **barbecue** meat and fish on a **barbecue**.
Food which is not cooked is **raw**.

B Preparing and cooking food

Peel the potatoes [remove the skin] and boil them.
While they're boiling, **chop** an onion. [cut it into small pieces]
Fry the onion before **adding** some chopped tomatoes. [putting them together with the onions]
Then **stir** it all for a few minutes. [move it around in a saucepan using a spoon]

C What does it taste like?

Chefs [people who cook food in a restaurant as a job] always **taste** the food [put a small amount in their mouth to see what it is like] while they are cooking.
I don't like the **taste** of too much garlic.
I tried the soup and it **tasted** a bit strange.
Michel's food is very **tasty** [has a good taste].
Indian food is a bit too **spicy** for me [with a strong hot flavour].
You get ice cream in different **flavours** [the type of taste that food or drink has, e.g. vanilla, coffee, strawberry, etc.].
Lena said her pasta was **horrible** [terrible, unpleasant], but I thought it was **delicious** [fantastic, with a wonderful taste].

> ### Language help
>
> We use the word **sour** to describe the taste of lemons (*opp* **sweet**), but usually **bitter** to describe coffee that is strong and has a sharp unpleasant taste (*opp* **smooth**).
> Strong, dark chocolate can also be described as bitter, but this is not always negative.

D Are you a good cook?

❝I'm a bit nervous when I cook, so I always follow a **recipe** [the cooking instructions for a particular dish, e.g. lasagne], and make sure I have all the right **ingredients** [the different food you need to make a particular meal] before I start. However, I am quite good at making **pies**, especially apple **pie**.❞ (Pie is pronounced /paɪ/ like 'my'.)

apple pie

> ### Common mistakes
>
> A person who cooks well is a good **cook** (NOT a good ~~cooker~~). The **cooker** is the large piece of equipment you use for cooking. You could also say that you are **good/bad** at cooking (NOT good/bad ~~in~~ cooking), e.g. *I'm quite good at cooking fish.*
>
> Also we 'cook' a type of food, e.g. *I'm cooking some beef*, but we 'make' a dish, e.g. *I'm making dessert.* (NOT I'm ~~cooking~~ dessert.)

Exercises

25.1 **Write down five more ways of cooking food.**

boil............................. , ... , ... , ... , ... ,
....

25.2 **How do you pronounce the underlined letters? Use the index to help you.**

chef   Is it like <u>sh</u>oe or <u>ch</u>ief? _shoe_   oven   Is it like l<u>o</u>ve or l<u>o</u>nely?
raw   Is it like n<u>ow</u> or d<u>oor</u>?   pie   Is it like p<u>ea</u> or l<u>ie</u>?
sour   Is it like m<u>ore</u> or h<u>our</u>?   saucepan Is it like f<u>our</u> or fl<u>ower</u>?

25.3 **Cross out the wrong word in each sentence. Write the correct word at the end.**

1 The paella was very ~~tasteful~~. _tasty_.............................
2 My brother is a very good cooker.   ....
3 Don't forget to heat up the fry pan before you add the aubergine.   ....
4 This chocolate is very sour.   ....
5 I'm afraid my mother has never been very good in cooking.   ....
6 You can buy this ice cream in five different tastes.   ....

25.4 **Which words are being defined?**

1 The flavour that something has in your mouth when you eat it.   _taste_.............................
2 A person who cooks food as their job.   ....
3 Having a good taste.   ....
4 The large piece of equipment in the kitchen for cooking food.   ....
5 The word to describe the taste of lemons.   ....
6 Not cooked.   ....
7 Having a fantastic taste.   .... The opposite is ....

25.5 **Explain what the person did, using the correct word.**

1 I got the list of food and cooking instructions.   You got the ..._recipe_................. .
2 I bought all the food I needed for the dish.   You bought all the ....
3 First I removed the skin of the potatoes.   You .... the potatoes.
4 I cooked the potatoes in water.   You .... the potatoes.
5 Then I cut the onions into small pieces.   You .... the onions.
6 I cooked the onions in a frying pan.   You .... the onions.
7 I put the potatoes together with the onion.   You .... the potatoes
                                                            to the onion.
8 I put in some milk and moved it round in the pan.   You put in milk and .... it.
9 Then I put a little in my mouth to see what it was like. You .... it.

25.6
Over to you

Answer the questions. If possible, compare your answers with someone else.

1 Do you eat these things in your country?

  a) raw fish   **b)** roast beef   **c)** fried rice   **d)** baked potato   **e)** barbecued chicken

2 Do you like these things?

  a) bitter chocolate   **b)** spicy food   **c)** chocolate-flavoured ice cream   **d)** the taste of garlic

3 How often do you cook food on a barbecue?

4 Are you a good cook? If so, what are you good at?

A The rush hour*

66 For me, the rush hour is the worst time of day. Everywhere is busy, and everyone seems to be **in a hurry**[1]. I usually drive to work, but sometimes I **get stuck**[2] in **traffic jams**[3], and when I get to work I find there's **nowhere to park**[4] because the **car park**[5] is already full. But if I get the bus, it takes me longer, and that makes the journey very **stressful**[6]. When I get home in the evenings I often feel **exhausted**[7] – more from the travelling than from my work. 99

* the time when people travel to and from work
[1] want to go somewhere / do something quickly
[2] become unable to move or go anywhere
[3] long lines of cars that are not moving
[4] no place to leave the car
[5] place to leave a car
[6] causing a lot of worry
[7] very tired

Common mistakes

The situation was **stressful**, and I was very **stressed** (NOT I was ~~stressing~~, or it was ~~stressing~~).
I couldn't find a **car park**. OR I couldn't find a **parking space**. (NOT I couldn't find a ~~parking~~.)

B The nightlife*

66 One of the **advantages of**[1] living in the city is the **nightlife**. The **town centre** is always **lively**[2] in the evening, and there is a wide **variety of**[3] bars, clubs and restaurants to go to. If you are more interested in **culture** and **cultural activities,** you can go to the cinema, the theatre, concerts, art galleries, etc. 99

* places to visit in the evening for social reasons
[1] the positive things about a situation; *opp* **disadvantages**
[2] full of activity
[3] many different things

C Advantages and disadvantages

66 Cities always seem **crowded**[1], and they can be **dirty** (*opp* **clean**) and **dangerous** (*opp* **safe**) places to live. **Pollution**[2] is worse in big cities, and so is the **crime rate**[3]. I only walk home **at night**[4] if I'm with a friend. When I'm on my own, I get a taxi.

Life in cities is also more expensive. Flats cost a lot, and I think you get better **value for money**[5] in a smaller town or village.

On the positive side, **you get**[6] a real **mix**[7] of people and nationalities in a big city; that makes life more interesting. I also enjoy the fact that there's always something **going on**[8] in a big city, so life is never **dull**[9]. 99

[1] full of people; *opp* **quiet**
[2] dirty air and water
[3] the number of crimes that happen
[4] in the period when it is dark
[5] If something is **good value for money**, you are happy with what you receive for the amount of money you pay.

[6] you find / there exists
[7] different types
[8] happening
[9] boring; *opp* exciting

Exercises

26.1 **Match the words on the left with the words on the right.**

1 town   [d]   a for money
2 traffic [ ]   b hour
3 night [ ]   c rate
4 value [ ]   d centre
5 crime [ ]   e space
6 rush [ ]   f jam
7 car [ ]   g life
8 parking [ ]   h park

26.2 **Write the opposite.**

1 It's safe.   *It's dangerous.* ....   4 It was very exciting. ....
2 It was crowded. ....   5 There are advantages. ....
3 It's very clean. ....   6 There's a place to park. ....

26.3 **Complete the dialogues with one word in each gap.**

1 A: Is there plenty to do in the evening?
   B: Yes, the ...*nightlife*............... is great.
2 A: And are there lots of .... activities in the town?
   B: Yes. There's a cinema, theatre, concerts, and so on.
3 A: Is it good for shopping?
   B: Yes, there's a .... of shops.
4 A: Are you worried about walking home late in the evening?
   B: Yes, it can be dangerous at ....
5 A: Is the traffic bad?
   B: Yes, I often get .... in traffic jams.
6 A: Is your flat expensive?
   B: Well, it's not cheap but I think it's quite good .... for money.

26.4 **Rewrite the sentences without the underlined words. Keep the meaning the same.**

1 There were <u>different types</u> of people there.   There was a good ...*mix*............... of people there.
2 I was <u>very tired</u>.   I was ....
3 I was very <u>nervous and worried</u>.   I was very ....
4 The place is always <u>full of activity</u>.   The place is always very ....
5 The <u>air is dirty</u>.   There's a lot of ....
6 They want to do everything <u>very quickly</u>.   They want to do everything in a ....
7 There was nowhere to <u>leave the car</u>.   There was nowhere to ....
8 There isn't much <u>happening</u> here.   There isn't much .... here.
9 Poverty <u>doesn't exist</u> here.   You don't .... here.

26.5

Over to you

Answer the questions. If possible, compare your answers with someone else.

1 What's the rush hour like where you live?

2 What's the nightlife like in your town?

3 Is it good for cultural activities?

4 Is there much pollution?

5 Is the crime rate bad?

6 What are the advantages/disadvantages of where you live?

A Surrounded by nature

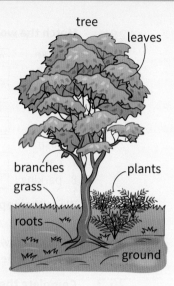

"I grew up in the **countryside** where I was **surrounded by**[1] nature. As children, we used to play on the **banks**[2] of the river and in the **woods**[3]. In the summer we **picked**[4] apples and blackberries; in the autumn we often picked mushrooms. The **seasons**[5] were all different, and I loved the **scenery**[6], the **open spaces**[7], and the **fresh air**[8]. I still do."

[1] nature was everywhere around me
[2] the side of the river
[3] groups of trees
[4] took them from the tree/plant

[5] spring, summer, autumn, winter
[6] the natural beauty you see around you
[7] empty areas of land
[8] naturally clean air

Common mistakes

I like being **in the countryside**. OR I like being **surrounded by nature**. (NOT I like being ~~in the nature~~.)

B Working in the country

"My uncle **owns**[1] a farm. He **keeps**[2] a few animals, but mostly he grows **crops** like barley, wheat and potatoes. **Farming** is a hard life: my uncle is usually **up**[3] at five in the morning, and sometimes his work isn't finished until **sunset**[4]."

[1] has (something that legally belongs to him)
[2] owns and looks after them

[3] not in bed
[4] when the sun goes down in the evening

C The disadvantages of country life

"**The worst thing about** living in a **village**[1] is that **there isn't much to do** in the evening, apart from going to the village pub. The nearest town is eight miles **away**[2], and **public transport**[3] is **hopeless**[4]. And, of course, **you don't get**[5] many shops in a village."

[1] a place smaller than a town
[2] a distance from a place
[3] buses and trains for people to use

[4] terrible
[5] there aren't / you don't find

Exercises

27.1 **These things all grow, but what are they? Put the letters in the right order.**

1 seret   *trees* ....
2 sargs   ....
3 velase   ....
4 odows   ....

5 tnpsal   ....
6 toros   ....
7 chesranb   ....
8 roscp   ....

27.2 **Complete the dialogues.**

1 A: It must be beautiful when the sun goes down over the valley.
   B: It is. The ...*sunsets*............... are lovely here.

2 A: Have you ever lived in a town?
   B: No, I've always lived in the ....

3 A: Is Dad .... yet?
   B: He must be. He's not in bed.

4 A: Is it your dad's farm?
   B: No, he doesn't .... it. He's just the farm manager.

5 A: Do you enjoy the summer?
   B: Yes, but spring is my favourite ....

6 A: Did it rain a lot last night?
   B: Yes. When I went outside this morning, the .... was very wet.

7 A: Do they .... many animals?
   B: Yes, they've got sheep, cows and goats.

27.3 **Look at the picture in section B again, then cover it and complete the text.**

We walked alongside the [1] ...*fence*..................... , opened the [2] .... , and said 'hello' to the man on the [3] .... We then followed the [4] .... across the [5] .... and down into the [6] .... We stopped and had a picnic by the river. After that, we walked up through the [7] .... and then finally back to the [8] .... , where we stopped and bought some eggs.

27.4 **Cover the left-hand page. Complete the advantages and disadvantages of living in the country.**

Some of the best things about living in the country are:
• the beautiful [1] *scenery*.....................
• the open [2] ....
• the fresh [3] ....
• being able to go out and [4] .... fruit
• the fact you are [5] .... by nature.

Some of the [6] .... things about living in the country are that:
• you don't [7] .... many shops
• [8] .... transport is [9] ....
• there isn't [10] .... to do in the evening, and the nearest town might be a long way [11] ....

Over to you

What do you think are the advantages and disadvantages of living in the countryside? Do you agree with the ideas above? Can you think of any other advantages and disadvantages? If possible, discuss your ideas with someone else.

28 Transport

A Vehicles

Vehicle is the general word for all types of road transport.

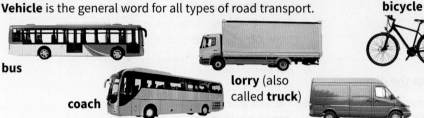

bicycle

bus

coach

lorry (also called **truck**)

van

motorbike

B Travelling around

bus/coach	train	plane	taxi	bicycle
bus/coach driver	train driver	**pilot**	taxi driver	**cyclist**
(£) **bus fare**	**train fare**	**airfare**	fare	
get / catch / go by	get / catch / go by	**fly**	get/take	**go by bike / cycle / ride a bike**
get on/off	get on/off	get on/off	**get in / out (of)**	get on/off
bus stop / bus station	**platform** / train station	airport	**taxi rank**	
journey	journey	**flight**		

I **go** to work **by bus**. It's only three **stops**.

We **got the train** to Cardiff, but the **journey** was terrible.
When the **bus fares** went up last month, my dad started **cycling** to work.
I **got out of** the taxi and almost walked away without paying the **fare**.
If there are more **flights**, **airfares** should be cheaper.
We were going to **get the train** to Paris, but in the end we decided to **fly**.

> **Common mistakes**
>
> It was a good **journey**.
> (NOT It was a good ~~travel~~.)

C Are you happy with public transport?*

Where I live buses are not very **convenient**[1]; the nearest bus stop is half a mile **away**[2]. And when I do get the bus, I often have to **wait in a queue**[3] for about twenty minutes, and then three come along at the same time!

People are always **complaining about**[4] the bus service, but where I live it's good. I've got a bus stop **round the corner**[5] and buses **run** every ten minutes for most of the day, and they're usually **reliable**[6].

I get the train to work. Trains are expensive – a **return**[7] to London is forty pounds – but I've got a **season ticket**[8], and that makes it cheaper. My only real **complaint** is that if I **miss**[9] my train, I have to wait half an hour for the next one.

* buses and trains for people to use
[1] near or easy to use
[2] the distance from a place
[3] stand in a line
[4] saying they are unhappy / not satisfied with
[5] very near
[6] you can trust them
[7] a ticket for a journey to a place and back
[8] a ticket you can use many times within a period of time without paying each time
[9] don't catch (a train or bus)

Exercises

28.1 **Choose the correct word(s) to complete the sentences.**

1 We were late, so we had to *get / catch* a taxi.
2 You mustn't *ride / drive* a motorbike without a helmet in the UK.
3 She told him to *get in / get on* the car and fasten his seat belt.
4 The *journey / travel* to the airport takes half an hour.
5 Trains to the airport *travel / run* every half hour.
6 The pilot didn't want to *drive / fly* the plane in such bad weather.
7 They left a bit late and *lost / missed* the bus.
8 I see that train *fares / tickets* are going up again.
9 You mustn't speak to the bus *pilot / driver* when he is driving.
10 We must get *off / out* the bus at the next *station / stop*.

28.2 **Test your knowledge. Can you label the vehicles without looking at the opposite page?**

1 *bus* .... 3 .... 5 ....

2 .... 4 .... 6 ....

28.3 **Complete the sentences.**

1 I wasn't happy with the service, so I made a ......*complaint*...... .
2 The flight was fine but we had a terrible .... from the airport to our hotel.
3 Where I live, the public transport is not very .... because the nearest bus stop is two kilometres .... , and there are no trains at all.
4 The train station is just round the .... from where I live.
5 Buses are not very .... Sometimes they come every five minutes, but other times you have to wait for forty minutes.
6 When I got to the bus stop there was a long .... of people.
7 Train fares are crazy: a .... to Glasgow costs more than two singles.
8 People are always .... about the buses, but I don't think they're that bad.
9 I use the trains every day for work, so I've got a .... ticket.
10 Your train is going to depart from .... six at 10:25.

28.4

Over to you

Answer the questions about transport in your country. If possible, compare your answers with someone else.

1 Are trains more reliable than buses?

2 Are return tickets usually twice the price of a single?

3 Is where you live convenient for public transport? Why? / Why not?

4 How often do you take a taxi? Why, and where do you go to?

5 How often do you ride a bike?

29 On the road

A Roads

traffic lights

(road) junction

a bend in the road
(this road **bends**
to the right)

pedestrian crossing

road signs

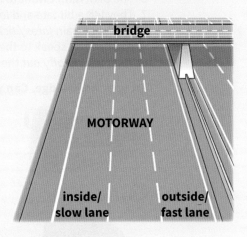

no overtaking
[you can't pass
another car]

speed limit

bridge

MOTORWAY

**inside/
slow lane**

**outside/
fast lane**

B Finding your way

"Yesterday, I **got lost**[1] **on my way to**[2] the airport. I decided to use side roads and go **via**[3] the village of Pensford, but I took the wrong **turning**[4] just before I got there, and I **ended up**[5] in a supermarket car park. Fortunately I was able to **ask** someone **the way**[6], and a very kind woman **directed**[7] me to the A38, where I could then follow **signs** for the airport."

[1] didn't know where I was
[2] while I was going to (the airport)
[3] go through somewhere to get to a destination
[4] corner where one road meets another
[5] found myself in a place I didn't expect to be in
[6] ask how to get to a place
[7] told me how to get to a place

C An accident

"I saw an **accident** this morning on the **main road**[1] into town. A **pedestrian**[2] – a young boy – stepped off the **pavement**[3] and into the road just as a car was **approaching**[4]. The driver **braked**[5], but the car **swerved**[6] and **crashed into** a **parked car**[7] on the opposite side of the road. Fortunately the driver wasn't **injured** but both cars were quite badly **damaged**."

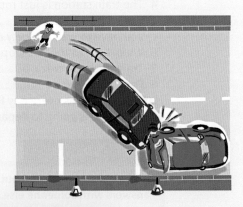

[1] important road
[2] a person walking
[3] the place where pedestrians walk
[4] coming closer
[5] put his foot on the **brake** to stop the car
[6] changed direction suddenly and
   without control
[7] a car next to the pavement, not moving

> ### Language help
>
> You **damage** a thing [harm or break it] but **injure** a person [hurt them]. The related nouns are **damage** and **injury**, e.g. *There was a lot of **damage to** the bike, but the cyclist only had minor **injuries**.*

Exercises

29.1 **Which words are being defined?**

1 part of a road that is separated from other parts by a line   *lane* ....
2 people who are walking   ....
3 the place where people usually walk   ....
4 the place where people can cross the road   ....
5 the place where two roads meet   ....
6 the thing you put your foot on to stop a car   ....
7 a message or symbol beside the road that gives information   ....

29.2 **Complete the information for these road signs.**

1 50 mph *speed* ....   3 ....   5 end of   7 a ....
   limit   ....   in the road

2 there is only one   4 no ....   6 low ....   8 ....
   ....

29.3 **Rewrite the sentences on the left starting with the words given. Keep a similar meaning.**

1 I asked him how to get to the bank.   I asked him the ...*way*........... to the bank.
2 I didn't know where I was in the town centre.   I got .... in the town centre.
3 You can ask someone to tell you how to get here.   You can ask someone to .... you.
4 I went through Ledbury to get to Malvern.   I went to Malvern .... Ledbury.
5 I was going to the station.   I was on my .... to the station.
6 We arrived unexpectedly by the river.   We .... up by the river.
7 I turned left instead of right.   I took the wrong ....

29.4 **Complete the text.**

I was on the [1] ...*main*................... road into town today and I saw an [2]................... .
I was [3]................... a roundabout when the guy behind tried to [4]...................
me and the driver in front of me. He was driving too fast – over the [5]...................
limit – and he lost control of the car. He had to [6]................... to avoid a car on the
other side of the road, and in the end he [7]................... into a tree. The car was badly
[8]................... , but to my surprise, the man got out of the car with no [9]................... at all.

29.5 ```
Over to you
```

Answer the questions about your own country. If possible, compare your answers with someone else.

**1** Do you have a speed limit on motorways? If so, what is it?

**2** How many lanes do motorways usually have?

**3** Do drivers usually stop for pedestrians at pedestrian crossings? If not, why not?

**4** Do many people park their cars on the pavements? Why? / Why not?
```

30 Notices and warnings

A Notices

on a machine that is not working, e.g. vending machine (above)

in the window of a hotel; the hotel is full

outside a theatre; all the tickets have been sold

outside a museum; you can go in free

B Do this!

wait in a line on the other side of this notice, e.g. in a bank or post office

stay on the right side, e.g. on the underground

do not walk on the grass

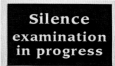

be quiet, an exam is happening now

C Don't do this!

you cannot leave your car here

you cannot go in here

you cannot go out here

on a hotel door; leave me to sleep

don't put a bag down and walk away

do not give food to the animals

D Warnings*

Take care you don't hit your head on a low door.

Be careful. There's a step.

be careful, this **parcel** will break easily

*something that tells you that something bad may happen

66 English Vocabulary in Use Pre-intermediate and Intermediate

Exercises

30.1 **Complete these notices and warnings. More than one answer may be possible.**

1 NO ...*PARKING*...................................
2 MIND THE ....
3 ADMISSION ....
4 OUT OF ....
5 NO ....
6 DO NOT ....

7 PLEASE QUEUE ....
8 MIND YOUR ....
9 PLEASE DO NOT ....
10 KEEP OFF ....
11 KEEP ....
12 SILENCE EXAMINATION ....

30.2 **Where could you see these notices or warnings?**

1 *On a door in a public building.*...

2 ....

3 ....

4 ....

5 ....

6 ....

7 ....

30.3 **What notice could you see in each of these places?**

1 on the underground   *Keep right* ....
2 in a waiting area in a busy airport ....
3 on the door of a hotel room at 9 am ....
4 in front of garage doors ....
5 above the window of a train ....
6 on a door going into a low room ....
7 outside a museum or art gallery ....
8 outside a room where students are doing an exam ....

30.4 **Write down five more notices from the opposite page that you could see in a school or college.**

Mind your head ....
....
....
....
....
....
....

30.5 **Over to you**

Look for other notices (in English or your first language). Can you understand the English notices? Can you translate the ones in your own language? Try to find four more notices in the next week.

31 Classroom language

A Equipment and uses

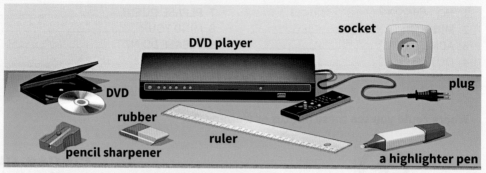

You use a rubber to **rub something out**, e.g. writing.
You use a ruler to **measure** something.

You use a pencil sharpener to **sharpen** pencils.
You use a highlighter pen to **highlight** a word.

B Classroom activities

Teachers or students do these things in the classroom.

look up a word in a dictionary [find the meaning of a word]
borrow someone's dictionary or rubber [use it and then return it]
plug in the DVD player [put the **plug** in the electric **socket**]
turn up the volume on the DVD player [increase the volume; make it louder; *opp* **turn (it) down**]
correct students' English [give the correct English if students make mistakes]

> ### Language help
>
> If **you lend someone something**, you give it to them for a period of time; if **you borrow something from someone**, you get it from them.
> Could **you lend me** your pen? means the same as Could **I borrow** your pen?

Teachers may ask students to do these things in the classroom.

I'd like you to work with a **partner** [someone else, i.e. another student].
Henrique, could you **swap places** with Lorena? [change seats / sit in each other's seats]
Kim, could you **share** your book with Petra? [use it together at the same time]
Repeat this sentence after me. [say it again]

C Questions about vocabulary

Q: **What does** *tiny* **mean**?
A: It means 'very small'.

Q: **How** do you **pronounce** *weight*?
A: It's pronounced /weɪt/, like *wait*.

Q: How do you **spell** *bicycle*?
A: B-I-C-Y-C-L-E.

Q: How do you **use** the word *wow*?
A: We use it to show that we think something is fantastic or surprising, e.g. *Wow*, look at that car.

Q: Could you **explain the difference between** *lend* and *give*?
A: If you lend something to someone, they have to give it back. If you give something to them, they can keep it.

> ### Language help
>
> | verb | noun | verb | noun |
> | --- | --- | --- | --- |
> | mean | **meaning** | spell | **spelling** |
> | pronounce | **pronunciation** | explain | **explanation** |
> | repeat | **repetition** | use | **use** |

Exercises

31.1 **Match the words on the left with the words on the right.**

1 explain $\boxed{g}$ a places
2 look up $\boxed{}$ b a mistake
3 sharpen $\boxed{}$ c a word
4 swap $\boxed{}$ d with a partner
5 plug in $\boxed{}$ e a dictionary
6 work $\boxed{}$ f the DVD player
7 borrow $\boxed{}$ g the meaning
8 correct $\boxed{}$ h a pencil

31.2 **Answer the questions.**

1 What do you put in a DVD player? *a DVD* ....
2 What do you use a dictionary for? ....
3 What do you put in a socket? ....
4 What do you use a rubber for? ....
5 Why do you share a book? ....
6 What do you use a highlighter pen for? ....
7 What do you use a pencil sharpener for? ....
8 What do you use a ruler for? ....

31.3 **Here are some answers about *swap*. Write the questions.**

1 A: *What does 'swap' mean?* ....
   B: It means to change something for something else.
2 A: ....
   B: Like shop or stop.
3 A: ....
   B: S-W-A-P.
4 A: ....
   B: You could say: *I can't see the board from here. Could you* **swap** *places with me?*

31.4 **Read the sentences on the left, then write a suitable request on the right.**

1 You want to look up a word.   Could I *borrow your dictionary?* ....
2 You can't hear the DVD player.   Could you ....
3 You need to borrow a dictionary.   Could you ....
4 You didn't hear what the teacher said.   Could you ....
5 You want to know the difference between   Could you ....
   lend and *borrow*.   ....
6 You need to use someone's ruler.   Could I ....
7 You want to sit in someone else's seat.   Could we ....

31.5 `Over to you`

Think about your last lesson (in English or any other subject). Did you do any of these things:

use a highlighter pen?   share a book with anyone?   use a rubber?
look up any words?   borrow anything?   lend someone a pencil?
swap places with anyone?   use a ruler?

32 School education

The school system

This is the **system** for **state education** in most parts of England and Wales. State schools are free and operated by the country. Parents pay to send their children to **private** schools.

age	education
3	Almost all children **attend** [go to; *fml*] **nursery school** for up to 15 hours a week.
5	Everyone starts **primary school**.
11	**Pupils** [students at school] go to **secondary school**.
16	Pupils **take/do** GCSE **exams**, in up to ten subjects. Then they can go to a college for **vocational** [job] **training**, e.g. hotel management or travel and tourism courses, or they can **stay at school** for two more years.
18	Pupils take 'A' level exams in three or four subjects, and then they can **leave school** and **get a job** or **go on to** university [continue their education at university], or go to a college for further education/training, e.g. teaching or business studies.

The school timetable

The school day is **divided into** about 5–7 lessons, and over the course of a week, most pupils **do/study** about ten **subjects**, including English, maths, history, science, etc. There's usually a one-hour lunch **break** [period of rest between work], and a break in the morning and afternoon as well.

> ### Language help
>
> In American English the subject is **math**, but in British English it is **maths**.

The school year is usually divided into three **terms** [periods of study], with each term being about 13 weeks, although some schools are now having shorter terms and more frequent holidays. At the end of the school year, pupils usually **take/do** exams before they **break up** [end classes for the term]. After the summer holidays, they **go back** [return] for the new school year.

School rules*

"**In the past** schools generally had more rules, and if you **broke the rules**[1], you were **punished**. At my school, for example, pupils sometimes had to **stay behind**[2] and write an essay. I used to **get into trouble**[3] for wearing **lipstick**.

I remember we had to **call** the **male** teachers 'sir' and **female** teachers 'miss', and we had to **wear** a horrible **uniform**[4]. Nowadays, the **atmosphere**[5] is more **relaxed**[6]: older pupils can often **dress**[7] the way they want – as long as they're reasonably **smart**[8] – and the teachers are not as **strict**[9]."

* instructions telling you what you must or must not do

[1] did something wrong
[2] stay in a place when others leave
[3] do something wrong and be punished
[4] special clothes
[5] the feeling in a place or situation

[6] comfortable and informal
[7] wear clothes
[8] well dressed and not too casual
[9] A strict teacher punishes pupils who do something wrong.

lipstick

Exercises

32.1 **Match the words on the left with the words on the right.**

1	go	[e]	a the rules
2	leave	[ ]	b a uniform
3	take	[ ]	c into trouble
4	wear	[ ]	d at school
5	study	[ ]	e to school
6	stay	[ ]	f school
7	get	[ ]	g an exam
8	break	[ ]	h a subject

32.2 **Complete the sentences about state schools in England.**

1 When they're three, children can go to *nursery* .... school.
2 At the age of five they go to .... school.
3 At the age of eleven they go to .... school.
4 When they're sixteen they .... exams, and afterwards they can go to a college for .... if they want.
5 Many pupils .... at school for another two years and do 'A' levels.
6 Nowadays, a lot of pupils .... to university after they leave school.

32.3 **Choose the correct word to complete the sentences. Sometimes both are correct.**

1 We *take / do* exams in the summer. *Both are correct.*
2 The school *timetable / schedule* is more or less the same every day.
3 The day is divided *into / out of* seven lessons.
4 The pupils *do / study* about ten subjects.
5 There is usually a *rest / break* three times a day.
6 Schools often *break out / break up* after they finish exams.
7 After pupils leave school, many of them *take / get* a job.
8 Pupils can *wear / dress* the way they want.

32.4 **Complete the sentences.**

1 There were three *terms* .... in the school year.
2 I had to .... a uniform.
3 I had to call the .... teachers 'sir' and .... teachers 'miss'.
4 I occasionally got into .... at school for doing things I shouldn't do.
5 The teachers at my school were strict, and they .... pupils who broke the rules.
6 My school had a really nice, relaxed ....

32.5

Over to you

Answer the questions about the education system in your country. If possible, compare your answers with someone else.

1 Do you have state schools and private schools?

2 Do all children have nursery education?

3 When do children go to primary school and secondary school?

4 Do all schools have the same terms?

5 When can children leave school?

6 Do pupils normally have to wear a uniform, or can they wear what they want?

7 Are teachers usually quite strict?

8 Is the atmosphere quite relaxed in most schools?

33 Studying English and taking exams

A How are they getting on?*

This is what Nastya, an English teacher, thinks about some of her students.

Nastya

66 Jade has a **wide vocabulary** [knows a lot of words] and speaks very **accurately** [without mistakes], but she needs to practise her speaking more in order to become more **fluent** [able to speak naturally without stopping]. 99

66 Angel is quite fluent, but his **accent** [the way he pronounces words] is not very good. In particular, he has problems with certain **consonants** [letters of the **alphabet** (a–z), which are not the **vowels** a, e, i, o, u]. 99

66 Jose has no problem **making himself understood** [saying things in a way people understand], but he needs to **increase** his vocabulary [make it bigger], because at the moment it's quite **basic** [elementary; *syn* **simple**]. 99

66 Olga is always **willing to** [happy and ready to] **experiment** with language [try something new to see what it is like]. For that reason she sometimes **gets things wrong** [makes mistakes], but she learns from her mistakes and she's making a lot of progress. 99

66 Andreas is a fantastic language learner. He **picks** things **up** [learns things without trying] very quickly, and he **has a good ear for language** [is good at hearing, repeating and understanding sounds and words]. 99

*What progress are they making?

Common mistakes

We use adjectives with nouns, and adverbs with verbs.
He's a **fluent** speaker. (NOT He's a ~~fluently~~ speaker.) She speaks **accurately**. (NOT She speaks ~~accurate~~.)
I need to speak English **well**. (NOT I need to speak English ~~good~~.)

B Examinations

Language help

You can **take** or **do** an exam (NOT ~~make~~ an exam). If you are successful and do well, you **pass**; if you are not successful and do badly, you **fail**. Before taking an exam, you **revise for** the exam. [study /prepare for the exam] Sometimes you can also **retake** an exam. [do it again]

66 My students are **taking** the Cambridge English: First **exam** in June, and for some of them it will be **hard work**[1]. I think Angel might fail, but he's **doing his best**[2], so with a bit of luck he might pass. I expect most of the others to pass. Andreas is a strong **candidate**[3], and I'm sure he'll get a good **grade** (*syn* **mark**). I think Jade and Olga will also **do well**.

At the moment I'm trying to **get through**[4] the coursebook so that we can do some **revision**[5]. I think the most important thing is to do some **exam preparation**[6]. Today I want the students to **do/write an essay**[7]. Most of them still find it difficult to write accurately, so I need to **work on** that with them. 99

[1] work that requires a lot of effort
[2] making as much effort as he can; *syn* **trying his best**
[3] someone who is taking an exam
[4] finish
[5] revise for the exam
[6] getting ready for the exam
[7] a short piece of writing about a particular subject

Exercises

33.1 **Choose the correct word to complete the sentences. Sometimes both are correct.**

1 We *made* /(*got*) something wrong in the first question.
2 I had to *do* / *write* an essay.
3 My sister picks *up* / *out* languages very quickly.
4 I will have to *revise for* / *revise* my exam next week.
5 The students always *do* / *make* their best.
6 Tomas wants to *do* / *take* the exam in June.
7 Karin *failed* / *lost* the exam, but she can retake it next year.

33.2 **Complete the sentences. The first letter has been given to help you.**

1 There are twenty-six letters in the a. *lphabet* ....
2 A+ is the highest g.............................. you can get.
3 There are over 100 c.............................. taking the exam.
4 We had to write an e.............................. for homework in not more than 200 words.
5 I need to w.............................. on my grammar; it's not very good.
6 I need to i.............................. my vocabulary; it's still very b.............................. .
7 A and E are v.............................. ; B, C and D are c.............................. .
8 Studying for my exam is h.............................. w.............................. , but it will be worth the effort.
9 Our teacher was always w.............................. to help us with our exam preparation.

33.3 **Rewrite the sentences on the left starting with the words given. Keep a similar meaning.**

1 Can you retake the exam?   Can you do *the exam again* .... ?
2 They will need to revise for the exam.   They will need to do some ....
3 I will work as hard as I can.   I will do ....
4 We need to prepare for the exam.   We need to do some ....
5 I make mistakes.   I get ....
6 I can listen and repeat things accurately. I have a good ....

33.4 **Complete the dialogues.**

1 A: Do you think Natasha will do well?
  B: Yes, I'm sure she'll *pass* .... the exam.
2 A: Is her pronunciation good?
  B: No, she has quite a strong ....
3 A: Can Elke speak naturally without stopping?
  B: Yes, she's quite ....
4 A: And does she make many mistakes?
  B: No, she's quite .... when she speaks.
5 A: Does Victor know a lot of English?
  B: No, but he can make himself ....
6 A: Will you finish the book?
  B: Yeah, we should get .... it.
7 A: Did Amy do .... in her exam?
  B: Yes, she got 80%.

33.5

Over to you

Answer the questions. If possible, ask someone else the same questions.

Do you think you …
… can make yourself understood?   … have a wide vocabulary?
… have a strong accent?   … have a good ear for language?
… are quite accurate?   … pick things up quickly?
… are quite fluent?   … often experiment with new language?

A Subjects

You can **do/study** these subjects at university but not always at school.

medicine (to become a doctor)	**law** (to become a lawyer)
engineering (to become an engineer)	**architecture** (to become an **architect**)
economics (to become an **economist**)	**psychology** (to become a **psychologist**)
business studies (to become a **businessman/ woman** and **go into business**)	

B Studying at university

Some students go to university because they enjoy studying, others just want a **qualification**[1]. First, however, you have to get good **grades** in your final school exams to **get a place** at many universities. You can then **study for / do a degree**[2]. If you complete the course **successfully**, you get your **degree**[3] and receive a **certificate**[4]. In the UK, most degree courses **last**[5] three years, although some take longer, e.g. medicine or law.

I've got a **degree in** economics.

Teachers at university are usually called **lecturers**, and most of the **teaching** is done through **lectures**[6]. The most senior lecturers have the title **Professor**. Students doing **arts** subjects, e.g. English or history, will spend time working in the **library** and writing **essays**[7]. Students doing **science** degrees, e.g. physics or chemistry, will probably spend a lot of their time working in a **laboratory** (*infml* **lab**).

library   **laboratory (lab)**

[1] something that you get when you are successful in an exam
[2] do a course at university
[3] (also the word for) a university qualification
[4] a document that shows you have completed a course successfully
[5] continue for
[6] the lecturer talks and the students listen
[7] short pieces of writing on a particular subject

Language help

noun	verb	adjective
qualification	**qualify**	**qualified**
success	**succeed (in sth / in doing sth)**	**(un) successful**

C Postgraduate degrees

When students are doing their first degree, they are called **undergraduates**. When they complete their degree, they are **graduates**. Some graduates **go on to do** [do something in the future] a Master's, e.g. in the UK an MA (Master of Arts) or MSc (Master of Science). These are called **postgraduate degrees**. The longest one is a PhD (Doctor of Philosophy) where students **do research** [make a detailed study of one particular subject] for at least three years.

Exercises

34.1 **Complete the sentences.**

1 To become a psychologist you need to study *psychology* .
2 To become an engineer you need to study ....
3 To become a doctor you need to study ....
4 To become an economist you need to study ....
5 To become a lawyer you need to study ....
6 To become an architect you need to study ....

34.2 **Put the sentences in the correct order.**

I did a degree course.   ☐
I passed with good grades.   ☐
I got a Master's.   ☐
I did a postgraduate course.   ☐
I did my final exams at school.   ☐ *1*
I became an undergraduate.   ☐
I got a place at university.   ☐
I got a degree in business studies.   ☐

34.3 **Are the sentences about English universities true or false? If a sentence is false, correct it.**

1 The teachers are all called professors.   *False. Most teachers are called lecturers.*
2 Anyone can go to university if they want to.   ....
3 Some students go to university just to get a qualification.   ....
4 Most university degree courses in the UK last two years.   ....
5 Students go to lectures at university.   ....
6 If you are unsuccessful, you get a degree.   ....
7 Students studying for their first degree are called graduates.   ....
....
8 Science students have to write a lot of essays.   ....
....
9 A PhD is a postgraduate degree.   ....
10 If you study arts subjects, you work in a laboratory.   ....
....

34.4 **Complete the text.**

Stephen got very good [1] *grades* in his final school exams, and he went to university and got a [2] .... in economics. He then [3] .... to do an MSc.
The course [4] .... a year, and at the end of it, he had an offer to go [5] .... business with a friend. After two years though, he decided to go back to university to do [6] .... for a PhD. He knows it will be three years' work without much money, but he loves studying, and never went to university just for a [7] .... that would get him a good job earning a lot of money.

34.5

Over to you

Answer the questions. If possible, compare your answers with someone else.

1 Do you need to pass exams before you can go to university in your country?

2 How long do most degree courses last?

3 In England the first degree is called a BA or BSc. What are they called in your country?

4 Do you have similar postgraduate degrees in your country?

5 Do you get a certificate when you finish your degree?

35 Jobs

A Working with your hands

builder
[**builds** or **repairs** homes]

carpenter
[makes things using **wood**]

plumber
[**installs** and **repairs** water pipes, etc.]

electrician
[**installs** and **repairs** electrical things, e.g. lights]

mechanic
[**repairs** cars when there is a problem]

Language help

When something is damaged or broken, we often use **repair** or **fix**.
*Dad **repaired/fixed** the window for me.*   *I need someone to **fix/repair** the computer.*

With small pieces of equipment we can also use **mend**; with clothes we often use mend.
*Could you **fix/repair/mend** my watch?*   *I've **mended** your trousers for you.*

B Professions*

job	what he/she does
architect	**designs** buildings
lawyer	**represents** people with legal problems
engineer	**plans** the building of roads, bridges, machines, etc.
accountant	controls the financial situation of people and companies
university lecturer	teaches in a university, e.g. gives **lectures**

* jobs that need a lot of training and/or education

C The medical profession

These people **treat** people or animals. [give medicine or medical help]

GPs [general practitioners: doctors who don't work in a hospital], **dentists** [people who look after your teeth] and **vets** [animal doctors] all work in a place called a **surgery**. In hospital there are **nurses** who look after people, and **surgeons** who **operate on** people. [open the body to remove or repair a part that is damaged]

D The armed forces and the emergency services

My son **joined** the army when he was 18. [became a member of]

gun

soldier
(in the **army**)

sailor
(in the **navy**)

pilot
(in the **air force**)

police officer
(in the **police force**)

fireman/ firefighter (in the **fire brigade**)

Exercises

35.1 Match the job on the left with something the person uses on the right.

1	lecturer	c	a	a gun
2	plumber		b	wood
3	accountant		c	books
4	builder		d	pipes
5	soldier		e	bricks
6	carpenter		f	numbers

35.2 Write down *one* job from the opposite page that would be difficult for the person in 2–6, and *three* jobs that would be difficult for the person in 7–9.

1 Someone who didn't go to university.   *dentist*
2 Someone who is always sick on a boat.   ....
3 Someone who is not interested in cars.   ....
4 Someone who is afraid of dogs.   ....
5 Someone who is afraid of heights and high places.   ....
6 Someone who is terrible at numbers and maths.   ....
7 Someone who isn't good at working with their hands.   ....
8 Someone who cannot see very well.   ....
9 Someone who will not work in the evening or at weekends.   ....

35.3 Test your knowledge. Can you write down what these people do without looking at the opposite page?

1 A university lecturer *teaches university students.* ....
2 A vet ....
3 An architect ....
4 An electrician ....
5 A lawyer ....
6 A surgeon ....
7 A mechanic ....
8 A dentist ....
9 An engineer ....

35.4 Complete the dialogues.

1 A: She's a police officer.
  B: *Really? When did she join the police force?* ....
2 A: He's a sailor.
  B: ....
3 A: He's a fighter pilot.
  B: ....
4 A: She's a soldier.
  B: ....
5 A: He's a firefighter.
  B: ....

35.5 `Over to you`

Write a list of friends, relatives or neighbours who have jobs. What does each person do?

36 Talking about your work

A What do you do?

People can ask what job you do in different ways; you can answer in different ways.

 A: **What do you do**?

 B: I **work in** sales / marketing / a bank, etc.

 A: **What do you do for a living?**

 B: **I'm a** doctor / hairdresser, etc.

 A: **What's your job?**

 B: **I work for** Union Bank / Fiat / Sony, etc.

B What does that involve?*

James and Emma are business **consultants** [people who help others in a particular area]. They **advise** people who want to **set up** [start] a business, especially in health and fitness. James **deals with** the marketing [does the work in marketing; *syn* **handle**], while Emma is **responsible for** [in control of; *syn* **in charge of**] **products** [things that people make/**produce**] such as towels, equipment, beauty products, etc.

Common mistakes

> I have a lot of work to do. (NOT I have a lot of ~~works~~ to do.)
> She **advises** me. (NOT She ~~advices~~ me.) BUT She gives me **advice**. (NOT She gives me ~~advise~~.)
> My job involves a lot of travel. OR My job involves travelling. (NOT My job involves ~~to travel~~.)

Amy is a manager in a veterinary surgery. She **runs** [organises or controls] the **day-to-day** [happening every day] business of the surgery and is in charge of a small team: three receptionists, an accounts manager and a secretary. Her work involves a lot of **admin** [short for administration] such as buying food, medicine and equipment; she also handles any **complaints** that customers make. [when customers **complain** / say that something is wrong or is not satisfactory]

* What do you have to do exactly?

C Pay

Most workers **are paid** [receive money] every month; this is called a **salary**. Your **income** is the total amount of money you receive in a year. This might be money from one job; it might be money from two jobs. We can express this in different ways:
My **income** is about £25,000. OR I **earn/make** about £25,000 **a year** [every year].
Some of that income you can keep, but some goes to the government; in the UK this is called **income tax**, e.g. *I lose 20% of my income in income tax.*

Language help

> A **salary** is money paid to professional people, e.g. doctors or teachers, and to office workers for the work they do, and is usually paid into a person's bank account every month. **Wages** are usually paid for each hour/day/week of work to people who do more physical jobs, e.g. building or cleaning.

D Conditions*

Most people work **fixed** hours [always the same], e.g. 9 am to 5.30 pm. We often call this a **nine-to-five** job. Other people have to **do/work overtime** [work extra hours]. Some people get paid for overtime; others don't. Some people have good working conditions, e.g. nice offices, paid holidays, extra time **off** [not at work] for a new mother and father when a baby is born, etc. There is also a **minimum wage** [an amount of money workers receive, and employers cannot pay less than this].

* the situation in which people work or live

Exercises

36.1 **Tick (✓) the words which are directly connected with *money*.**

pay ✓   earn   handle   wages
salary   income   consult   product

36.2 **Match the words on the left with the words on the right.**

1 set up	b	a	clients
2 in charge		b	a company
3 deal		c	overtime
4 earn		d	with complaints
5 do		e	of a small department
6 advise		f	money

36.3 **Rewrite the sentences on the left starting with the words given. Keep a similar meaning.**

1 What do you do?	What's *your job?*
2 I'm a marketing assistant.	I work
3 I'm employed by the government.	I work
4 I earn £34,000 a year from my two jobs.	My
5 What do you have to do exactly?	What does your job
6 I'm responsible for the reception area.	I'm in
7 What's your job?	What do you do for
8 I have to read government reports.	My job involves
9 I advise clients.	I give
10 I complained about the service.	I made

36.4 **Complete the texts. Put one word in each gap.**

Alexander Carpenter works [1] *in* sales, and he's a regional manager. He [2] the north-west region and he's [3] for a small team of five other sales people. His job [4] a lot of travelling within the region, and he's in contact with his team on a day-to-[5] basis. It's not a nine-to-[6] job: Alexander has to do a lot of [7] . Fortunately he can [8] a lot more money by doing this, and his working [9] are quite good. After income [10] he makes £60,000 [11] year. Recently his wife had a baby, but the company gave him extra time [12] to be with her after the birth.

Kelly Bradbury is a financial adviser for a bank. She specialises in mortgages, which means that she [13] people who want to buy a flat or a house. At the moment Kelly spends a lot of her time [14] with young people who are trying to buy a property for the first time, which is not easy. She works [15] hours – 9 am to 5 pm – and she doesn't have to [16] overtime.

36.5 **Over to you**

Answer the questions about working conditions in your country. If possible, compare your answers with someone else.

1 What are normal working hours for most office jobs in your country?

2 How much income tax do most people pay? (e.g. 10% or 20% of what they earn)

3 Do male and female workers normally get time off if they have a baby? If so, how much?

4 Is there a minimum wage? If so, do you know what it is?

37 Making a career

A Getting a job*

“When I left school, I **applied for**[1] jobs in different companies, and finally, after sending out lots of **CVs**[2] and having some **interviews**[3], a small company **employed** me[4]. I didn't earn a lot, but the company gave me some **training**[5], which was good.”

* finding a job
[1] wrote a letter of **application** for
[2] a document which describes your education and the jobs you have done
[3] a meeting where someone asks you questions to see if you are suitable for a job
[4] gave me a job
[5] help and advice to learn how to do a job or activity

Common mistakes

I had **some training**. (NOT I had a training.) You can also **go on / do** a **training course** [a period of organised help and advice, often in a different place] (NOT formation or stage).

B Promotion

“I worked hard and soon I was **promoted** [given a better job with more responsibility]. They also gave me a good **pay rise** [more money]. It was really good **experience** [knowledge you get from doing something such as a job], and when my boss left the company a few years later, they gave me an important **promotion** [a move to a higher job in the company].”

C Resignation*

“By my mid-twenties, I was getting a bit bored, and decided I wanted to work **abroad** [in another country]. So, I **quit my job** [told the company I was leaving; *syn* **resign**] and started looking for jobs in the UK. After a couple of months I got a job in London. At first I liked it, but …”

* when you say officially you are leaving a job

D Unemployment*

“After six months, I got fed up with the job – and I think I was enjoying myself too much to work very hard. Finally, the company **sacked** me [told me to leave the company; *syn* **gave me the sack**], and after that I was **unemployed** [without a job; *syn* **out of work**] for two months. Finally I got a **part-time** job [working only part of the day or week; *opp* **full-time** job] in the kitchen of a restaurant.”

* when people do not have a job

Common mistakes

Claudio didn't **have a job**. (NOT He didn't have a work.)

E Success and retirement*

Claudio

“I loved the restaurant. I learned how to cook, and two years later I became manager. Three years after that I opened my **own** restaurant. [belonging to me / it was my restaurant] It was very **successful** [it did well and made money], and twenty years later, I **owned** five restaurants, and I was the **owner** of two hotels. I believe anyone can **succeed** [be successful] if they work hard enough – and have a little bit of luck. Last year, aged sixty, I **retired** and went back to Italy.”

* the time when people stop work, often at 60 or 65

Exercises

37.1 **Match the answers on the right with the questions on the left.**

1 Why did they sack him? ☐ c
2 Why did they promote him? ☐
3 Why did he apply for the job? ☐
4 Why did he retire? ☐
5 Why did he quit his job? ☐
6 Why did he go on the course? ☐

a Because he was 65.
b Because he needed more training.
c Because he was late for work every day.
d Because he was out of work.
e Because he was the best person in the department.
f Because he didn't like his boss.

37.2 **Complete the table.**

verb	noun	adjective
employ	(un)employment	
promote		
retire		
resign		
	success	
own		

37.3 **Complete the sentences.**

1 Lucy is hoping to ..*get*.............................. a job in a travel agency when she leaves school.
2 I decided to work .... to see what life was like in another country.
3 I don't want a full-time job. I'd prefer to work ....
4 She .... her job when her boss refused to give her a pay ....
5 I didn't earn much money in the job, but it was still good .... because the company sent me on several training ....
6 After they sacked me, I was out of .... for six months.
7 It's not easy to .... in business; you need ability and luck.
8 I think you should definitely .... for that job.
9 Ivan was terrible as a tour guide; that's why they gave him the ....
10 I've worked for other people most of my life, but I'd really like to run my .... company.
11 I used to .... a company but it wasn't a .... ; I lost a lot of money.
12 If she's interested in that job, she'll have to write a letter of ....

37.4

Over to you

If you have a job, answer the questions. If possible, ask someone else the same questions.

1 Have you been promoted since you started working at your present company?

2 Do you normally get a good pay rise at the end of each year?

3 Have you been on many training courses since you started work?

4 Would you like to go on more training courses in the future?

5 Have you ever resigned from a job, or been given the sack?

A Office equipment

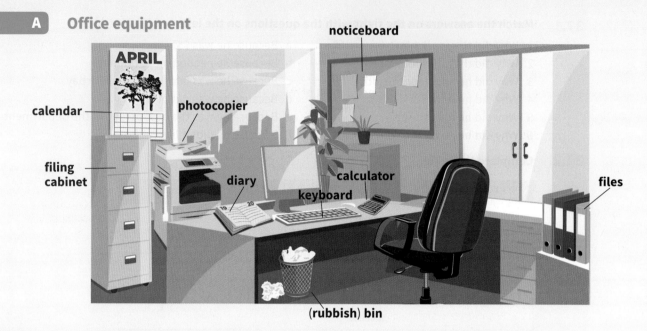

calendar — filing cabinet — photocopier — diary — keyboard — noticeboard — calculator — files — (rubbish) bin

B Office work

Josh works for a company which **produces**[1] furniture. He doesn't work in the factory where the furniture is produced, but in the offices across the road.

His job **involves**[2] quite a lot of **paperwork**[3]. He **types**[4] letters to different companies, sends out **invoices**[5] to customers and sends emails.

He also has to **arrange**[6] visits to other companies, **make appointments**[7] for his boss, and sometimes he **shows** visitors **round** the factory. Occasionally he has to **attend**[8] meetings with his boss, but one of Josh's most important tasks is to **organise**[9] the office party every year.

[1] makes
[2] includes doing
[3] work that uses paper, e.g. reports, forms
[4] writes using a keyboard
[5] documents showing how much the customer has to pay
[6] plan and prepare
[7] arrange a time when you meet someone
[8] go to; *fml*
[9] plan and arrange

Language help

verb	noun
arrange	**arrangement**
organise	**organisation**

verb	noun
attend	**attendance**
produce	**production**

C Office problems

Josh is having a bad day today. The photocopier has **broken down**[1], the computer **isn't working** and the printer has **run out of**[2] paper. On top of that, two of his **colleagues**[3] are **absent**[4], just when there is **loads of**[5] work to do.

[1] stopped working
[2] has no more
[3] people you work with
[4] not in the office; *syn* **off**
[5] lots of; *infml*

Exercises

38.1 **Finish the noun in each sentence.**

1 I've just got myself a new *key*...*board*................ .
2 I threw all that stuff in the *rubbish* ....
3 He put most of the stuff in the *filing* ....
4 It's a very boring job and I spend most of my time doing general *paper*.. .
5 I told him to put the details on the *notice*.. .

38.2 **Which words are being defined?**

1 The place where you throw away paper you don't want.   *bin*..
2 People you work with.   ....
3 Something you put on a wall which tells you the date.   ....
4 A book where you write down appointments and things you have to do.   ....
5 A piece of paper which shows a customer what they have bought and what they must pay.
   ....
6 An electronic device that helps you to add up numbers and do maths.   ....
7 An informal word meaning 'lots'.   ....

38.3 **Complete the dialogues.**

1 A: What does the company do?
  B: It .*produces*.................... electronic equipment.

2 A: I've .... to see the bank manager on Friday, but I think I'm going to be away.
  B: OK. Do you want me to make another .... for you?
  A: Yes, please. That would be great. Next Thursday or Friday, if possible.

3 A: Why can't we use the printer?
  B: It's .... of ink.

4 A: Do you have to .... meetings?
  B: Yes, sometimes, if my boss is away and he can't go.

5 A: We've got some visitors coming tomorrow.
  B: Right. Would you like me to .... them .... the factory?

6 A: What does your work .... ?
  B: Basically, I have to .... people's travel arrangements and hotel accommodation.

38.4 **Rewrite the sentences using the words in capitals. Keep a similar meaning.**

1 My boss isn't here today. OFF   My boss .*is off today*..
2 The photocopier is broken. WORK   The photocopier ....
3 We're very busy today. LOADS   We ....
4 I have to go to a meeting. ATTEND   I have to ....
5 We don't have any more paper. RUN OUT   We ....
6 Why isn't he here this morning? ABSENT   Why ....

38.5 `Over to you`

> **Have you got a job? If so, are these statements true for you? If you haven't got a job, answer for someone you know.**
>
> | | | |
> |---|---|---|
> | I do lots of paperwork. | I attend meetings. | I send loads of emails. |
> | I organise events. | I type letters. | I show people round. |
> | I use a photocopier. | I send invoices. | I repair things that break down. |

A A successful business

This is the story of a company that has **achieved a great deal** [a lot] in a short period of time.

Language help

If you **achieve** something, you have been successful in something that needed a lot of work and effort. The noun is **achievement**, e.g. *Writing a book has been my greatest **achievement**.*

LOCAL BUSINESS SPOTLIGHT

DENHAM FARM BAKERY

DENHAM Farm Bakery

DENHAM FARM BAKERY¹ is a family business, with three different **generations**² (father, son and granddaughter) of the family **currently**² working with a team of 90 **employees**. The company **was set up**³ in 1991 with the **aim**⁴ of producing **a variety**⁵ of bread of the highest **quality**⁶. The Denham family saw there was a **growing demand**⁷ for organic products in the 1990s, and they soon became **experts**⁸ **in** the field of organic bread-making.

The company is **run**⁹ from a factory in Ilminster, where the bread is baked **daily**¹⁰ and then **delivered**¹¹ to shops across the south-west of England. The **firm**¹² has **expanded**¹³ a great deal in the last 20 years, but it still remains a family business.

¹ place where bread and cakes are made or sold
² now, at the moment (NOT ~~actually~~)
³ started (used about a company or organisation)
⁴ a plan of what you hope to achieve
⁵ different types
⁶ how good or bad something is
⁷ when more people want to buy something

⁸ people with skill/knowledge in something
⁹ organised and controlled
¹⁰ every day
¹¹ taken (to shops)
¹² company or business
¹³ become bigger

B A view of a company

< > +   80% ▭

MORGAN & STENSON

Morgan & Stenson are a firm of **accountants**¹. They were **formerly**² Stenson & Son, but were **taken over**³ by JS Morgan five years ago. James Morgan **took up** the **position**⁴ of senior partner, and the company changed its name to Morgan & Stenson. The **headquarters**⁵ of the firm are in Newcastle, but they have five other **branches**⁶ in different parts of the north-east of England.

James Morgan is a **former** owner of a football club, with many **contacts**⁷ in the football world, so many of his **clients**⁸ are footballers.

Last year the company **attracted** a lot of **attention**⁹ when it became the first firm of accountants to advertise on local TV and radio. At the time, James Morgan said it was his **ambition**¹⁰ to change the **image**¹¹ that people have of accountants.

¹ people who control a person or company's money
² in the past but not now
³ JS Morgan got control of Stenson & Son
⁴ started in the job
⁵ the place where the main office is
⁶ offices that are part of the company

⁷ people you know
⁸ people who pay someone for a service
⁹ caused people to notice it
¹⁰ something someone wants to achieve
¹¹ the way that people think of them

Language help

We usually talk about an **ex**-wife/boyfriend, etc., but a **former** president/career/banker, etc. Shops and organisations have **customers**; lawyers, accountants, etc. have **clients**. We **take up** a job or activity, but we **set up** a company.

Exercises

39.1 **Tick (✓) the words which refer to people.**

headquarters   employee ✓   branches   expert   bakery
accountant   quality   client   contacts   variety

39.2 **Replace the underlined word(s) with a word or phrase that has a similar meaning.**

1 The food is delivered <u>every day</u>.   *daily* ....
2 There is a real <u>need</u> for food of this quality.   ....
3 Our <u>plan</u> is to open another branch.   ....
4 The <u>company</u> is doing well.   ....
5 We have 25 <u>workers</u>.   ....
6 I <u>started</u> the business ten years ago.   ....
7 Their <u>main offices</u> are in Sheffield.   ....
8 He's hoping for a <u>position</u> in the company.   ....
9 The firm is <u>getting bigger</u>.   ....
10 The company made <u>a lot</u> of money last year.   ....

39.3 **Choose the best word to complete the sentences.**

1 They're experts *in* / *on* farming.
2 When did you *set up* / *take up* tennis?
3 Her law firm has many famous *clients* / *customers*.
4 She's actually my *ex-* / *former* wife; we got divorced last year.
5 When did they *set up* / *take up* the company?
6 The shop assistant was serving a *client* / *customer*.
7 Marcel used to work here, but he's *currently* / *actually* working abroad.
8 Are they planning to *take up* / *take over* the company?
9 George Bush is *a former* / *an ex-* president of America.

39.4 **Rewrite the sentences using the words in capitals. Keep a similar meaning.**

1 He makes different cakes. VARIETY   He *makes a variety of cakes.* ....
2 They were very successful. ACHIEVE   They ....
3 I know a lot of people in banking. CONTACTS   I ....
....
4 They used to be called BMG. FORMERLY   They ....
5 I've always wanted to fly a plane. AMBITION   It's ....
....
6 She has a great knowledge of finance. EXPERT   She ....
7 People noticed the adverts. ATTRACT   The adverts ....

39.5 **Complete the text.**

Danielle Spinks set up her motorbike courier service (DCS) in 1979. If you wanted to send documents across London, Danielle promised to [1] *deliver* them in less than one hour. It was only a small [2] _____ , but DCS [3] _____ immediate success, so Danielle set up another [4] _____ of the company in Manchester, which was [5] _____ by her brother, Darren. The business soon [6] _____ rapidly, and it is now Danielle's [7] _____ to have a branch of her courier service in every major city in England.

A Rise and fall

These verbs describe **trends** [movements] in **sales** [how much you sell], prices, etc.

When sales or prices **rise / go up / increase**, they can do it in different ways:

They can rise **slightly** [a bit]. ➡

They can rise **gradually** [slowly over a long period]. ↗

They can rise **sharply** [quickly and by a large amount]. ↗

The opposite can also happen. Prices or sales can **fall / go down / decrease** slightly, gradually or sharply. If prices don't rise *or* fall, they **stay the same**. ➡

We use certain prepositions to say by how much something rises or falls.
The price has risen **by** 10 pence.   Sales fell **from** 8,000 units **to** 6,500 units.

Rise/increase and **fall/decrease** can also be used as nouns, with certain prepositions.
There's been a **gradual rise in** prices.   We've seen a **slight increase in profit**.
There's been a **sharp fall in sales**.   Profits were £5 million, which is a **decrease of** 10%.

Language help

> **Profit** is the money you receive from your business after you have paid all your costs (*opp* **loss**). *Last year the company **made a profit of** €2 million but this year they could **make a loss**.*

B Financial language

> With the **economy**[1] now improving, banks are reporting positive **signs**[2] that the number of **loans**[3] is increasing.

> With **inflation**[4] expected to rise, there are **growing fears**[5] that **interest rates**[6] could go up by as much as **2%**[7] next year.
>
> EUROPE

Figures[8] published yesterday show that **trade**[9] between the two countries has now risen for the fifth year **in a row**[10].

> ■ CURRENCY
>
> Although the **value**[11] **of** the pound fell slightly against the dollar yesterday, the news that sales rose in the last **quarter**[12] has **raised**[13] hopes that we may be coming out of **recession**[14].
>
> ➡ *Read full story*

[1] the system by which a country's trade, industry and money are organised
[2] something which shows something is happening
[3] money that you borrow
[4] the rate at which prices increase
[5] increasing worries
[6] (see language help below)
[7] this is spoken as *two per cent*

[8] an amount shown in numbers, e.g. 500
[9] buying and selling between countries
[10] one after another with no break
[11] the money that something can be sold for
[12] (in business) a period of three months
[13] increased; you can also **raise prices**
[14] a time when the economy is not successful

Language help

> **Interest** is what the bank **charges** you [asks you to pay] when you borrow money from them, and the **interest rate** is how much you must pay as a **percentage**, e.g. **5%, 8%**, etc. So, if you borrow £100 for a year and the interest rate is 15% a year, you'll have to **pay back** £115.

Exercises

40.1 **Choose the correct word to complete the sentences.**

1 We made a profit *of* / *for* six million euros.
2 Sales rose *to* / *by* 10% last year.
3 The value of the shares fell *from* / *for* 240 pence to 225 pence.
4 There was a fall *of* / *from* 5% in the value of the shares.
5 There has been a gradual rise *with* / *in* profits.
6 The company made a loss two years *on* / *in* a row.
7 What's the current value *of* / *in* the euro?

40.2 **Which words or phrases are being defined?**

1 The amount of money that something can be sold for.   *value*
2 Money you borrow from a bank for your business.   ....
3 What the bank charges you when you borrow money.   ....
4 The rate at which prices increase.   ....
5 The money that a company receives for its goods after paying all the costs.   ....
6 Buying and selling goods and services between countries.   ....
7 A movement in sales, prices, etc. over a period of time.   ....

40.3 **Complete the two short texts, then answer each of the two questions.**

1 If you get a bank .... of €500 for one year and the bank .... you 20% ...., how much will you have to .... to the bank at the end of the year? ....

2 If you take out a similar amount from another bank, and the interest .... is 15 ...., how much will you .... at the end of the year? ....

40.4 **Look at the graph and complete the text.**

The [1] *graph* .... shows sales [2]...................................... for the last three and a half years. Three years ago sales [3]...................................... slightly and reached 100,000 units by the end of the year. The company [4]...................................... a profit of almost £500,000 and decided to [5]...................................... the price from £8.95 to £10.25. It had an immediate effect: there was a [6]...................................... [7]...................................... in sales over the year. It was bad news, and the company made a [8]...................................... . And in the next year sales [9]...................................... the same. However, in the first two [10]...................................... of this year, they have [11]...................................... [12]...................................... for the first time in many years.

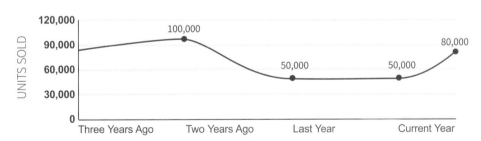

40.5 **Over to you**

Can you answer these questions about your own country?

1 What is the inflation rate at the moment?

2 If you borrow money from the bank, what is the approximate interest rate you will be charged?

3 Do you think the economy is doing well or badly?

4 When was the last time your country was in recession?

5 What is the value of your currency against the dollar?

41 Sport and leisure

A Sports

goalkeeper · net

skis

stick

swimming costume

sport	person	verb(s)	place
athletics	**athlete**	run, jump, throw, etc.	**track** (in a **stadium**)
motor racing	**racing driver**	drive/**race**	track
swimming	**swimmer**	swim/race	pool
boxing	**boxer**	**box**/fight	**boxing ring**
skiing	**skier**	**ski**	ski slopes
football	footballer	play	**pitch** (in a stadium)
ice hockey	ice hockey player	play	ice hockey **rink**
golf	golfer	play	golf **course**
basketball	basketball player	play	basketball **court**
sailing	**sailor**	**sail**	on the sea or a lake

Language help

We **play** sports such as football, ice hockey, tennis, golf and basketball.
*I **play** football in the winter.*   *I **play** basketball twice a week.*
We use **go** with other sports and activities, especially those ending in **-ing**.
*I **go** swimm**ing** in the lake during summer.*   *We often **go** rock climb**ing** in the mountains.*
We use **do** with **a lot of** / **a bit of** + -ing.
***I did a bit of sailing** in the holidays.*   *I don't **do a lot of running** these days.*

B Leisure activities*

tent

camping

rock climbing

jogging

yoga

going to the gym

We often **go camping** in the summer, and we usually **do a bit of rock climbing** as well.
My best friend **does a lot of yoga**. She **works out** in the gym two or three times a week as well.
My brother enjoys jogging, and it **keeps him fit** [helps his body to stay in good condition].
My mum does a bit of jogging as well – just **for fun** [because she enjoys it; *syn* **for pleasure**].
I'm afraid I don't **do** any **exercise** at all.

* activities in your free time

Exercises

41.1 **Put the words into the correct columns.**

> ~~swimming~~   golfer   court   track   jump   pitch   net
> motor racing   stick   basketball   athlete   box   skis   race
> goalkeeper   racing driver   sail   rink   skiing   swimming costume

sport	person	place	verb	equipment
swimming				

41.2 **Complete the sentences with the correct verb.**

1 We .*play*.................... football in the winter at my school.
2 Do you .... much exercise?
3 I .... basketball in the summer and winter.
4 We always .... in the winter, as long as there is enough snow.
5 I .... a bit of yoga when I was younger.
6 We used to .... camping in the mountains.
7 I .... a lot of swimming in the summer.
8 If you want to .... fit, you need to run three or four miles every other day.
9 I used to .... in the gym, but I'm getting a bit old for that now.

41.3 **What is the sport and who is the person?**

1 *skiing*.....................
  skier.....................
2 ....
  ....
3 ....
  ....
4 ....
  ....
5 ....
  ....

41.4 **Complete the last word in each sentence.**

1 Do you know the size of a boxing ....*ring*.................... ?
2 I used to play ice ....
3 We played golf in Scotland, where they have some fantastic golf ....
4 My dad plays golf. He's not a serious golfer; he just plays for ....
5 If the girls go swimming, they must remember to take their swimming ....
6 We watch a lot of motor ....
7 I love swimming, and it helps to keep me ....
8 My sister enjoys rock ....
9 You can't go camping unless you have a ....
10 Running is good exercise, so four or five times a week I go ....

41.5 **Over to you**

> **Answer these questions. If possible, compare your answers with someone else.**
>
> **1** What sport or leisure activities do you do? Why do you do it/them?
>
> **2** What sport do you watch, and where?

42 Competitive sport

A Winning and losing

In football, you can talk about the **score** [the number of goals a team has] like this:

Spain played Poland and they **won** the game.	= Poland **lost** the game.
Spain **won** 2–0 (spoken as *two nil*).	= Poland **lost** 2–0.
Spain **beat** Poland (2–0). (NOT Spain ~~won~~ Poland.)	= Poland **lost** (2–0) **to** Spain.
Spain **defeated** Poland (2–0).	= Poland **were defeated** (2–0) **by** Spain.
Spain and Italy **drew** 1–1 (spoken as *one all*) OR It was **a** 1–1 **draw between** Spain and Italy.	

Language help

The **score** at the end of a game is also the **result**.
The final score/result was 2–0.   The score at half-time was 1–0. (NOT The ~~result~~ at half-time was 1–0.)

B Competitions

A **competition** is an organised event in which people try to win something by being the best, the fastest, etc. **Individuals**, such as tennis players Serena Williams or Rafael Nadal, and **teams** such as Manchester United, **take part in** [join with others in] different types of competition. Tennis players and golfers enter **tournaments** such as the French Open; football and ice hockey teams play in **league** competitions, where they **play against** different teams. Many teams also play in **cup** competitions (similar to tournaments), e.g. the FA Cup or the World Cup, which ends with two teams playing against each other in a **final**. The **winners** (*opp* the **losers**) are the **champions**, e.g. Germany became World Cup champions in 2014, and Philipp Lahm received the cup as **captain** of the winning team.

C Reporting sports events

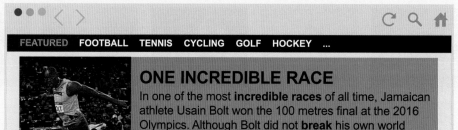

FEATURED   FOOTBALL   TENNIS   CYCLING   GOLF   HOCKEY   ...

ONE INCREDIBLE RACE

In one of the most **incredible races** of all time, Jamaican athlete Usain Bolt won the 100 metres final at the 2016 Olympics. Although Bolt did not **break** his own world **record**[1] of 9.69 seconds, he achieved a great **victory**[2] running an **outstanding** time of 9.81 seconds. Usain Bolt has now won three gold medals in three consecutive Olympic Games, also known as the 'triple triple'.

Another win for Kim Clijsters

Kim Clijsters won the women's US Open last night for the second time. She first won the **championship**[3] in 2005, but **gave up**[4] tennis in 2007 to have a baby. She returned in 2009, and is the first mother to win a grand slam for 29 years.

Canadian Grand Prix

There was a **superb** race for the Canadian Grand Prix. The **winner**[5], Lewis Hamilton, passed Sebastian Vettel and won by five seconds. But Nico Rosberg now **leads**[6] the drivers championship with 107 points.

[1] run faster than anyone in the world before
[2] the time when you win a game or a competition
[3] an important competition to decide who is the best
[4] stopped playing
[5] the person who wins
[6] is in front of others during a competition, e.g. At half-time, Milan are leading 1–0.

Language help

Superb, **incredible** and **outstanding** can describe something or someone that is very good and of a very high quality, e.g. *Pelé was a **superb** footballer.*

Exercises

42.1 **Complete the verb forms with the correct past tense and past participle.**

1 win / *won* / *have won*
2 lose / .... / ....
3 beat / .... / ....
4 draw / .... / ....
5 break / .... / ....
6 give up / .... / ....

42.2 **Choose the correct words to complete the sentences. Sometimes both are correct.**

1 It was a fantastic (victory) / defeat for the team.
2 Lionel Messi was *outstanding* / *incredible* for Barcelona.
3 At half-time in the game, the *score* / *result* is 1–0 to Arsenal.
4 The French Open is a famous tennis *cup* / *tournament*.
5 Croatia *beat* / *defeated* Germany 3–2.
6 We *won* / *beat* the other team 4–1.
7 The UEFA Cup is a great *competition* / *league*.

42.3 **Complete the sentences.**

1 It was a good game but unfortunately we ...... *lost* ...... 3–2.
2 The .... at half-time was 2–1, but the final .... was a draw.
3 Holland .... England 2–1, so they are in the semi-final.
4 Brazil .... 1–1 with Argentina last night.
5 Serena Williams has won the Wimbledon .... at least six times.
6 Carolina Kluft broke the heptathlon world .... again last night.
7 There are 20 teams in the .... , and each team plays the other teams twice.
8 Bradley Wiggins .... part in the *Tour de France* in 2009 and finished fourth.
9 I think Novak Djokovic is going to win. He's .... 5–2 in the final set.
10 Argentina are playing .... Brazil next week.

42.4 **Complete the crossword. What is the vertical word in grey?**

1 competition in which people run, drive, etc.
2 the opposite of *win*
3 a group of people who play together
4 a synonym for *outstanding*
5 stop doing a regular activity
6 the leader of a team
7 someone who wins something
8 when you win a competition
9 the last part of a competition
10 the opposite of *winner*
11 a type of sports competition

	1		
	R	A	C	E

42.5 **Over to you**

Answer the questions. If possible, compare your answers with someone else.

1 Have you ever taken part in a sports competition?

2 Have you ever won anything?

3 Have you ever been captain of a team?

4 Have you ever come first, second or third in a race?

5 Have you ever watched an individual or team in a final, at the game or on television?

43 Books and films

A Books

"I used to hate **literature**[1] at school, but now I read a lot. I started off with **fiction**[2]. I read hundreds of **novels**[3], mostly **thrillers**[4] and **science fiction**[5]. My favourite **author**[6] is John le Carré.

Recently, I've started reading quite a lot of **biographies**[7], and even some **poetry**[8]. Two of my favourite **poets** are Antonio Machado and Federico García Lorca. They both wrote **poems** in the early 20th **century**."

[1] serious and important writing
[2] stories about imaginary people and events
[3] fiction books
[4] exciting stories, often about crime
[5] stories about the future
[6] someone who writes books
[7] stories of a person's life, written by another person
[8] pieces of creative writing in short lines

B Films

How do you decide which films you are going to see?

If it's a **horror film** [a film that makes people frightened, e.g. *Dracula*], I usually go and see it. I love horror films.

If a film gets good **reviews** [opinions in a newspaper or magazine], then I often go and see it.

If there's a big **star** [a famous actor] in it, then I am more likely to see it. I don't normally go and see films if I don't recognise the names of the **actors** [the people who are in films].

I'm not interested in films that are serious or **complicated** [difficult to understand]; I only go to the cinema for **entertainment** [things you see or do to enjoy yourself].

I like **comedies** [films that are funny] and especially **romantic comedies** [comedies that have a love story]. I'll go and see anything that Ashton Kutcher is in!

I look to see **what's on** [what films are being shown at the cinema], and go to anything that I **fancy** see**ing** [want to see; *infml*].

For me, the **film director** [the person who tells the actors what to do, e.g. Spielberg] is the most important thing. I always go and see the **latest** film [the newest, most recent] by directors I really like such as Ben Affleck.

Language help

noun	person	verb
entertainment	**entertainer**	**entertain**
review	**reviewer**	**review**
acting	actor	**act**
directing	director	**direct**

Exercises

43.1 **Find twelve more words, across or down, connected with books and films.**

act ....

....

....

....

....

....

....

L	I	T	E	R	A	T	U	R	E
P	E	S	A	U	T	H	O	R	T
A	C	T	O	R	N	R	G	D	R
C	H	F	I	C	T	I	O	N	E
T	A	P	U	R	F	L	S	F	V
E	N	O	V	E	L	L	T	I	I
P	O	E	T	R	Y	E	A	L	E
C	O	M	E	D	Y	R	R	M	W

43.2 **Cross out one wrong word in each sentence. Write the correct word at the end.**

1 Many ~~poems~~ are around 300 pages. *novels* ....
2 Cinema grew in popularity in the first half of the 20th year. ....
3 I enjoy science fiction because I like stories about the past. ....
4 What's happening at the cinema? ....
5 We went to see the film because there was a good article in the newspaper. ....
6 I've been reading a new autobiography of Alfred Hitchcock by Donald Spoto. ....
7 Comedies should make people frightened. ....

43.3 **Complete the sentences with the correct form of the word on the right.**

1 William Wordsworth is a very famous ....*poet*............ .   POETRY
2 I thought the film was good ....   ENTERTAIN
3 Johnny Depp is one of my favourite ....   ACT
4 My daughter wrote a lovely .... for her school magazine.   POETRY
5 I thought the .... in the film was a bit unnatural.   ACT
6 I like him very much; he's a great ....   ENTERTAIN
7 I didn't agree with what the .... said.   REVIEW
8 Who's your favourite .... ?   DIRECT

43.4 **Complete the dialogue.**

A: What's ¹ ....*on*........................ at the cinema?
B: Er, there's the ² .... film by Pedro Almodóvar. It only came out yesterday.
A: Oh, the guy who ³ .... *Julieta*. He's a very good ⁴ .... , but I don't understand some of his films – they're a bit ⁵ .... for me. Anything else ⁶ .... ?
B: Well, a couple of romantic ⁷ .... , which may be fun. And they're showing *The Kite Runner* again.
A: Oh, what's that?
B: It's a film based on the ⁸ .... by Khaled Hosseini. It's a very good book. Do you ⁹ .... seeing that?
A: Yeah, why not.

43.5 **Over to you**

Answer the questions. If possible, compare your answers with someone else.

1 Do you read novels or poetry? If so, what do you like? Who are your favourite authors?

2 Do you go to the cinema? If so, how do you decide which films to go and see?

3 Do you often read film reviews?

4 What are your favourite films? Who are your favourite actors?

A Musical taste*

People's **taste in** music is different. I like **pop music**, my brother likes **folk music** [music written and played in a traditional style], and my dad prefers **classical music**.

My brother and I like going to concerts to see groups **perform** [play] **live** [in front of a large group of people, called an **audience**; pronounced to rhyme with *five*]. My dad just listens to music at home; he isn't interested in **live performances**. When I listen to music I am mostly interested in the **tune** [the musical notes], but my brother is more interested in the **lyrics** [the words of a song].

*the type of music that you like

B Musical instruments and musicians

piano (pianist)

guitar (guitarist)

keyboard (keyboard player)

cello (cellist)

saxophone (saxophonist)

trumpet (trumpeter)

drums (drummer)

bass guitar (bass guitarist)

violin (violinist)

flute (flautist)

C People in music

A **composer** is someone who writes music, usually classical music.
A **songwriter** is someone who writes songs, e.g. Paul McCartney, Adele, Ed Sheeran, Chris Martin.
A **conductor** is someone who stands in front of an **orchestra** [a large group of musicians who play different instruments] and **conducts** [leads] them.
An **opera singer** is someone who sings **opera** [a play in which the words are sung].
A **ballet dancer** is someone who dances in a **ballet**.
A **solo artist** is someone who sings or plays music but is not part of a group, e.g. Beyoncé, Jay-Z, etc.
Famous **groups/bands** are The Arctic Monkeys, U2, etc.

D Making an album

When groups **record** an **album** [put eight or ten songs into one collection] or a **single** [one song], they do it in a **recording studio**. Then, when the album **comes out** [is available for people to buy], it is usually **advertised** in the media [there are **adverts** on TV, online etc.]. Many people **download** their favourite **tracks** [individual songs from an album] or albums from the Internet.

Exercises

44.1 **Match the words on the left with the words on the right.**

1 classical   [c]   a studio
2 solo   [   ]   b singer
3 recording   [   ]   c music
4 musical   [   ]   d dancer
5 opera   [   ]   e artist
6 ballet   [   ]   f instrument

44.2 **Complete the sentences.**

1 There was a very big __audience__ for their last concert – nearly 10,000 people.
2 I think their new .... is a great song.
3 The new .... has songs written by other people. It .... out next week.
4 I've listened to a lot of their music but I've never seen them perform ....
5 Their new album was .... in a studio near my home.
6 The band has a new album out and it's being .... on TV.

44.3 **Find five more pairs of words. Why are they pairs?**

| flute   ballet   audience   album   dancing   orchestra   concert |
| conductor   flautist   composer   classical music   recording studio |

A flautist is a person who plays a flute.

....
....
....
....
....
....

44.4 **Can you complete this music quiz with words from the opposite page?**

1 Florence Welch is the main singer and __songwriter__ for her group Florence + the Machine.
2 The Berlin Philharmonic is an .... Herbert von Karajan was the .... from 1955 to 1989.
3 Placido Domingo and Luciano Pavarotti were both great ....
4 *Waterloo* was Abba's first Number 1 hit ....
5 *Sergeant Pepper* is the most famous .... by The Beatles.
6 Eric Clapton is a great rock ....
7 Yo Yo Ma is a great classical ....
8 Rachmaninoff is a famous ....
9 Puccini composed .... such as *La Bohème*.
10 Who was the very famous .... artist who sang *Thriller*? ....

44.5 **Over to you**

Answer the questions. If possible, ask someone else the same questions.

1 What music do you like? Is your taste in music different from your parents'?

2 Who's your favourite solo artist, group or composer?

3 What was the last single or album you bought or downloaded?

4 When was the last time you heard or saw a group or orchestra perform live?

5 Are you usually more interested in the tune or the lyrics of a song?

6 Do you play a musical instrument? What do you play?

A A fireworks display

The Sydney **fireworks**[1] **display**[2] is **held**[3] every year, and more than one million people **gather**[4] at Sydney **harbour**[5] on New Year's Eve to **celebrate**[6] the new year. All age groups are **involved**[7] in the event. At 9 pm there is 'Family fireworks' for families with younger children. After that a large number of boats **parade**[8] around the harbour. Finally, at midnight, there is a **spectacular**[9] fireworks display for almost fifteen minutes in which more than 4,000 kilograms of fireworks light up the night sky.

[1] (see picture)
[2] a show for people to watch
[3] organised
[4] come together
[5] area of water where ships are kept and are safe from the sea
[6] do something enjoyable on a special day
[7] included (in an event or activity)
[8] move around as part of a group, often to celebrate something (*parade* is also a noun)
[9] looking extremely good or exciting

B An arts festival

The Edinburgh **Festival**[1] is an **annual**[2] event, and is the largest arts festival in the world. It **consists of**[3] at least six different festivals which **take place**[4] in the city and **last**[5] for almost six weeks during August and early September. The most **popular**[6] festival is The Fringe, which has **up to**[7] 500 daily performances in dance, music, drama and comedy in 180 places across the city.

[1] a number of special events often continuing for several days
[2] happening once a year
[3] is made of
[4] happen

[5] continue
[6] liked by many people
[7] the maximum (is 500)

C The Chinese Spring Festival

The Spring Festival (or Chinese New Year) is the biggest **traditional** festival in China. It has been celebrated for about 4,000 years, and takes place every year at some point between 21 January and 20 February. On the day before the festival starts, people from **all over**[1] China return to their family homes and gather for a big meal. The next day, many people **dress up**[2], and children receive money from their parents in red envelopes to **bring them luck**. Another popular **custom** is to put two-line poems on the gates outside each home.

[1] everywhere (in China)
[2] wear special clothes

Language help

A **custom** is something that people usually do. A **tradition** is a very old custom that has continued for a long time. The adjectives are **traditional** and **customary**.
*It is **traditional** to give each other presents.*
*It is **customary** to take your shoes off before you enter a mosque.*
*We went to a **traditional** Greek wedding (NOT a ~~Greek traditional~~ wedding).*

Exercises

45.1 **Complete the definitions.**

1 A display is a show for people to ....*watch*.......... .
2 If you are involved in an activity, you are .... in it.
3 If you can have up to 25 people, 25 people is the ....
4 If an event is spectacular, it looks very good or ....
5 A harbour is a place where .... are kept.
6 If people parade round the streets, they .... round the streets in a group.

45.2 **Rewrite the sentences using the word in capitals. Keep a similar meaning.**

1 The festival happens in the summer. TAKE   *The festival takes place in the summer.*.........
2 The children wear special clothes. DRESS   ....
3 People come from everywhere in Japan. ALL ....
4 They hold the event every year. HELD   ....
5 Do you do anything special for
   your birthday? CELEBRATE   ....
6 The festival happens every year. ANNUAL   ....

45.3 **Complete the text.**

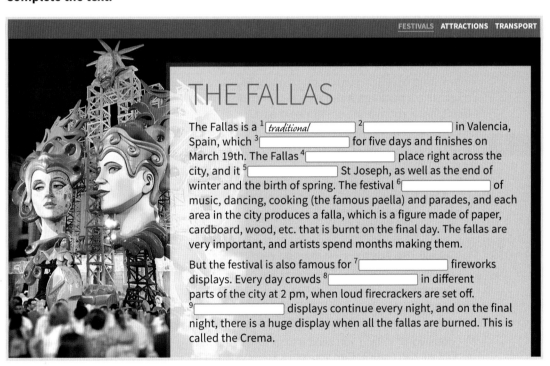

FESTIVALS ATTRACTIONS TRANSPORT

THE FALLAS

The Fallas is a ¹[*traditional*] ²[_____] in Valencia, Spain, which ³[_____] for five days and finishes on March 19th. The Fallas ⁴[_____] place right across the city, and it ⁵[_____] St Joseph, as well as the end of winter and the birth of spring. The festival ⁶[_____] of music, dancing, cooking (the famous paella) and parades, and each area in the city produces a falla, which is a figure made of paper, cardboard, wood, etc. that is burnt on the final day. The fallas are very important, and artists spend months making them.

But the festival is also famous for ⁷[_____] fireworks displays. Every day crowds ⁸[_____] in different parts of the city at 2 pm, when loud firecrackers are set off. ⁹[_____] displays continue every night, and on the final night, there is a huge display when all the fallas are burned. This is called the Crema.

45.4 **Over to you**

Think about a festival you know and answer the questions. If possible, ask someone else.

1 What kind of festival is it? Is it an arts festival or a traditional festival?

2 How often is it held?

3 When and where does it take place?

4 How long does it last?

5 What does it consist of?

6 Are there any special traditions or customs as part of the festival?

A   Types of holidays

adventure holiday

skiing holiday

family holiday

beach holiday

go on a cruise

city break

B   Online booking

Many people book their holiday **accommodation**[1] on the Internet. To **book online**[2], you need to search for your **destination**[3] and the dates when you plan to travel. You can look for hotels or **B&Bs**[4]. Often websites have low prices, especially in winter. It is helpful to read the online **reviews**[5] before you book the accommodation. A popular option for a **weekend break**[6] is to rent an apartment in an interesting city. But if you want to make life easy, you might like a **package holiday**, which includes the flight, hotel room and sometimes meals.

[1] a place where you stay
[2] to make a reservation using the Internet
[3] a place where you plan to travel
[4] bed and breakfast: a small hotel where breakfast is included in the price
[5] a description of a hotel, restaurant, etc, written by people who've been there
[6] a short holiday during a weekend

C   Renting a private apartment

> ● ● ● ✉ Reply   Forward
>
> To   Irene Sanders x   CC BCC
> From   Oliver Weiss x   11:02 AM (2 hours ago)
>
> Subject   Re: Apartment with mountain view
>
> Dear Irene,
>
> We have arrived at your apartment. We **picked up**[1] the keys from the neighbours without any problems. We like the apartment a lot, but we have a few questions. We can't find the **wi-fi password**[2]. Could you send it to us? Also, the **listing**[3] said that there was an **iron**[4] in the kitchen, but we can't see it. Can you let us know where it is? Finally, it's very cold and we can't find the instructions for the **central heating**[5]. Where do we **switch it on**[6]?
>
> Where's the **nearest** supermarket? And can you **recommend**[7] a **nearby**[8] restaurant for dinner? Somewhere cheap would be great!
>
> All the best,
> Oliver and Jo

[1] collect
[2] a secret group of letters and numbers, for connecting to wireless Internet
[3] written description of something to buy or rent
[4] a small machine that makes clothes smooth and flat
[5] a system that keeps a building warm
[6] make it start working
[7] say something is good
[8] not far

Exercises

46.1 **Match the holiday types on the left with their descriptions on the right.**

1 a cruise   [c]   a   a holiday where there are activities for children as well as adults
2 beach holiday   [ ]   b   a winter holiday in the mountains
3 skiing holiday   [ ]   c   a holiday where you sleep on a boat and travel from one place to another
4 adventure holiday   [ ]   d   a short holiday where you visit a city
5 family holiday   [ ]   e   a holiday where you stay near the sea
6 city break   [ ]   f   an unusual, exciting holiday, possibly with some danger, e.g. rock climbing or walking in the jungle

46.2 **Complete the dialogues with words from B.**

RUTH: Shall we book somewhere for our ¹ *weekend* .... break?

HARRY: What about this hotel? It has great ² .... online. Five stars!

RUTH: I'd prefer somewhere a bit smaller, with breakfast included.

HARRY: OK, here's a nice ³ .... in the countryside.

HANS: Have you found any ⁴ .... yet?

PAULA: Yes, I've booked a four-star hotel in the city centre.

HANS: Was it very expensive?

PAULA: No, it was part of a ⁵ ...., so the hotel was included in the price.

46.3 **Circle the words from B and C to complete each sentence.**

1 Many travellers prefer to (book) / *take* their holiday online, rather than on the phone.
2 Spain is a popular holiday *accommodation* / *destination* among British holiday-makers.
3 If you book a *package holiday* / *weekend break*, you don't have to book flights separately.
4 The apartment *listing* / *password* doesn't say if it has wi-fi or not. We'll have to email them.
5 The *central heating* / *iron* is broken and Sara's clothes are all creased.
6 The house has *listing* / *central heating*, so it is warm all through the winter months.

46.4 **Look at C opposite. Correct the mistakes.**

1 When you arrive, you can pick ~~out~~ the keys from the reception desk. ..*up*..................................
2 I recommence renting a car, as public transport is not very good. ....
3 The nearer train station is a five minute walk away. ....
4 The wi-fi passport is written on a piece of paper next to the computer. ....
5 I like staying in this area. There are quite a few nice cafés nearly. ....
6 To switch out the air conditioning, press this button. ....

46.5   `Over to you`

Answer these questions. If possible, compare your answers with someone else.

1 What type of holiday from A do you prefer?

2 Do you read hotel reviews before you book online?

3 Where do you like to stay when you travel: in a hotel, in a B&B or in a private apartment?

A   Departure*

When you arrive at an airport, the **departures board** will show you the **flight numbers** (e.g. BA735), departure times (e.g. 08.40), and **destinations**[1].

At **check-in / the check-in desk**, someone will check your ticket and **weigh**[2] your luggage. If it is more than, for example, 20 kilograms, you will have to **pay excess baggage**[3]. You can take your hand luggage with you on the **aircraft**[4]. You also get your **boarding card**[5] and then you can go through **passport control**, where someone **checks your passport**[6], and into the departure lounge, where you can buy things in the **duty-free** shop, e.g. cigarettes and perfume.

Shortly before **take-off**[7], you go to the place where you get on the plane, e.g. **Gate** 3 or **Gate** 5. When you **board the plane**[8], you can put your hand luggage in a small cupboard above your seat called an **overhead locker**. You then have to **fasten your seat belt**. If there are no **delays**[9], the plane moves slowly to the **runway**[10], then it takes off.

passenger

luggage

suitcase

hand luggage

trolley

AIRLINES

fastening a seatbelt

* when you leave a place, at the start of a journey
[1] where the flights are going to
[2] see how heavy something is
[3] pay extra for your luggage
[4] plane
[5] a piece of paper you must show to get on the plane
[6] looks at your passport carefully
[7] when the plane takes off / leaves the ground
[8] get on the plane
[9] when you have to wait longer than expected
[10] the large road that planes use for take-offs and **landings**

Common mistakes

My **flight** number is BA640. (NOT My ~~fly~~ number is BA640.) I slept the whole **flight**. (NOT I slept the whole ~~fly~~.)

B   Arrival*

When the plane **lands**[1], there is always an **announcement**[2] from a member of the **cabin crew**[3] telling passengers to wait until the plane completely stops before they stand up. Then you get off the plane and walk through the **terminal building**[4] to passport control. When you've got your luggage from **baggage reclaim**[5], you **go through customs**[6] and leave the airport.

* when someone or something arrives
[1] arrives on the ground
[2] spoken information to a group of people
[3] the people on the aircraft who look after the passengers
[4] the airport building
[5] the place where you collect your luggage
[6] go through the area where your luggage may be checked to make sure you don't have anything illegal.

Exercises

47.1 Complete the words or phrases using words from the box.

~~board~~	number	crew	card	control	luggage
reclaim	free	baggage	building	desk	locker

1 departures _board_
2 excess ....
3 check-in ....
4 hand ....
5 terminal ....
6 duty ....

7 flight ....
8 overhead ....
9 boarding ....
10 cabin ....
11 baggage ....
12 passport ....

47.2 Answer the questions.

1 What's the place where the airline staff check your ticket? _the check-in desk_
2 Who are the people that travel on a plane? ....
3 What do airline staff weigh at the check-in desk? ....
4 What's the piece of paper they give you at the check-in desk? ....
5 What do we call the place you're travelling to? ....
6 What do airport staff do at passport control? ....
7 What do we call the place where you get on the plane? ....
8 What do you call the bags that you can take on the plane with you? ....
9 What's the part of the airport where the plane takes off and lands? ....

47.3 Complete the email.

● ● ●   ✉   Reply   Forward

To   [Tom x]   CC BCC
From   [Ellie x] [▾]   11:52 AM (10 hours ago)

Hi Tom

I've just arrived in Rome but I'm still recovering from a really terrible ¹[_flight_]. When we were in the airport in Manchester there was an ²[   ] telling us that there would be a one-hour ³[   ] because of bad weather, but when we finally ⁴[   ] the plane, there was a further delay before we could ⁵[   ]. There was more bad weather over France, and we all had to ⁶[   ] our seat belts, which worried me a bit. In fact, I was almost sick, but the cabin ⁷[   ] were really nice.

It was still raining and very windy when we ⁸[   ] in Rome and I was really glad to get off the plane and get into the ⁹[   ] building. I really hope the return ¹⁰[   ] is a lot better.

See you soon.

Ellie

47.4 ▐ Over to you ▌

Answer the questions. If you don't fly very much, ask someone else.

1 What is the best part and the worst part of the flight?

2 When do you often have delays, and why?

3 What do you usually do on the aircraft during the flight?

4 What's the first thing you do on arrival?

5 Do you ever have anything to declare when you go through customs?

A   Hotel facilities and rooms

HOTEL LE ROUGE

The hotel is located near The Louvre, Notre Dame and top department stores right in the **heart**[1] of Paris. Hotel **facilities** include: **room service**[2], **Internet access**[3], **air conditioning**[4] and **parking**. Our choice of **single**[5], **double**[6] or **twin**[7] rooms are all equipped with **satellite TV**[8], air conditioning, direct-dial telephone, **mini-bar**[9], and personal **safe**[10]. Bathrooms come with a bath or shower and hair dryer.

[1] centre
[2] staff will bring food and drink to the room
[3] use of the Internet
[4] a system that keeps the air cool
[5] a room for one person

[6] a room for two people with one big bed
[7] a room for two people with two beds
[8] TV with many channels from different countries
[9] a small fridge
[10] a box to keep money and valuable items in

B   Staying in a hotel

Rooms are often **available**[1] during the week, but many hotels are **fully booked**[2] at weekends or during the holidays, so you may need to **book a room**[3] **in advance**[4]. When you arrive, you **check in at reception**[5]; at the end of your **stay**[6], you **check out**[7].

[1] you can find one
[2] all the rooms are taken
[3] arrange/plan to have a room; *syn* **reserve**
[4] before you go

[5] say you have arrived and get your room key
[6] the period of time you spend in a place
[7] pay your bill and leave the hotel

C   Going to a restaurant

It's often a good idea to **book a table / make a reservation** if you go to a restaurant at the weekend. Many restaurants offer **three-course** meals which **include** [have as part of the meal] a **starter** (e.g. soup), **main course** (e.g. meat or fish) and **dessert** (e.g. fruit with ice cream). Prices sometimes include 10% **service** as well [amount of money you pay for being served by the waiter]. If service isn't **included**, it's normal to leave a **tip** [extra money you give to the waiter/waitress].

D   Ordering a meal

WAITER: **Are you ready to order**? [Have you decided what to eat?]
CUSTOMER: Yes, I think so. I'd like to start with the spicy prawns, and then **I'll have** the fillet steak, with French fries and a **mixed salad** [lettuce with other vegetables].
WAITER: How would you like your steak? (**Rare, medium** or **well-done**?)
CUSTOMER: **Medium**, please. And I'd like some mineral water as well.
WAITER: **Still** or **sparkling**?
CUSTOMER: Er, sparkling.

> ### Common mistakes
>
> **I'll have** the steak. (NOT ~~I take~~ the steak.)

Exercises

48.1 **Put the words into the correct columns. Write titles for the other two groups.**

rare	starter	mini-bar	sparkling	main course
room service	medium	dessert	still	well-done	safe

steak			water
rare			

48.2 **Match the words on the left with the words on the right.**

1 service   *g*   a room
2 room   ☐   b access
3 double   ☐   c meal
4 three-course   ☐   d conditioning
5 main   ☐   e service
6 Internet   ☐   f TV
7 air   ☐   g included
8 satellite   ☐   h course

48.3 **Complete the sentences.**

1 Have you booked a ......*room*...... ?
2 Could you first check in at .... ?
3 Do you want a single or a .... ?
4 Does the price include .... ?
5 I .... the soup, and then the fish for my main course.
6 The hotel .... included Internet access, 24-hour reception and a restaurant.
7 Service wasn't included, so I left a 10% ....
8 The hotel is in the .... of the town, close to all the main attractions.
9 Would you like a .... salad with your main .... ?
10 At the end of your .... at a hotel, you normally have to .... out by midday.

48.4 **Rewrite the sentences on the left starting with the words given. Keep a similar meaning.**

1 I was able to use the Internet.   I had Internet ...*access*.......... .
2 Did you book a table?   Did you make a .... ?
3 The hotel was fully booked.   There were no rooms ....
4 You don't pay extra for service.   Service is ....
5 Did you book it before you went?   Did you book it in .... ?
6 Is there somewhere to leave the car?   Do you have .... ?
7 Have you decided what you want to eat?   Are you ready .... ?

48.5 `Over to you`

You are staying in a hotel in your own country. Are these facilities important to you? Why? / Why not?

mini-bar   24-hour room service   air conditioning   satellite TV
Internet access   parking   restaurant   a personal safe

49 Cafés

A Drinks

  **black coffee**

cappuccino latte hot chocolate

 **milkshake** herbal tea smoothie

decaf tea/coffee [without caffeine]

B Food

waffle   toastie   panini   bagel   wrap

crisps

baguette   muffin   cupcake   croissant

Language help

In the UK, *chips* or *fries* mean *French fries*. *Crisps* are thin slices of fried potatoes sold in bags. In the USA, *chips* refer to thin pieces of fried potatoes sold in bags.

UK	crisps	chips or fries
USA	chips	French fries

C Ordering food and drink

A: A latte, please.

B: **Regular**[1] or **large**[2]?

A: Regular, please.

B: **To have in**[3] or **take away**[4]?

A: To take away.

A: **What's in** that panini?

B: Cheese and ham.

A: Do you have any **vegetarian**[5] ones?

B: We've got cheese and tomato.

A: I'll have one of those, please.

B: Would you like it **heated up**[6]?

A: No, thank you. Where are the **napkins**[7]?

B: There are some on the table.

A: Do you have a **tray**[8] please?

B: Yes, here you go.

[1] not big and (usually) not very small
[2] big
[3] for eating/drinking inside (the coffee shop)
[4] for eating/drinking after you leave (the coffee shop)
[5] without any meat
[6] made warm (e.g. in an oven or a microwave)
[7] thin pieces of paper for cleaning your mouth and fingers
[8] an object for carrying drinks or food

Exercises

49.1 Put the words from A and B in the correct category.

| bagel | hot chocolate | cupcake | ~~herbal tea~~ | latte | wrap | baguette |
| milkshake | muffin | smoothie | panini | toastie | waffle | |

1 Drinks	2 Sandwiches	3 Cakes
herbal tea	....	....
....	....	....
....	....	....
....	....	
....	....	

49.2 Complete the sentences with words from the box.

| cappuccino | croissants | vegetarian | ~~toastie~~ | milkshake | decaf | smoothie |

1 I had a cheese and tomato ....*toastie*.............. for lunch.
2 Here's your coffee, Danny. A .... with two sugars.
3 For breakfast, we had some .... from the French baker's across the road.
4 Do they have .... coffee here? Caffeine keeps me awake at night.
5 We've got three kinds of .... : strawberry, vanilla and chocolate.
6 I like that new fruit .... with oranges and mangoes.
7 Kate can't have the chicken panini. She only eats .... food.

49.3 Match the sentence beginnings on the left with the best endings on the right.

1 What size: | b | a heated up?
2 Is it to have in | | b regular or large?
3 Would you like it | | c that baguette?
4 What's in | | d the napkins?
5 Where are | | e or to take away?

49.4 Choose the correct word to complete the dialogue.

A: Would you like a hot drink?
B: Yes, two [1]*milkshakes* / (*cappuccinos*), please.
A: What size?
B: [2]*Large / Herbal*, please.
A: Anything to eat?
B: Yes. What's in that [3]*panini / cupcake*?
A: Italian cheese and mushrooms. I can heat it up for you.
B: OK, yes. I'll have that. And a chocolate [4]*muffin / bagel*.
A: To eat in?
B: No, to [5]*heat it up / take away*.

49.5

Over to you

Answer the questions. If possible, ask someone else the same questions.

1 Where do you usually have lunch during the week? What about at the weekend?

2 What kind of food and drink do you usually order in a café?

3 What type of food and drink from A and B do you like?

Sightseeing holidays

A   Things to see

market   **castle**

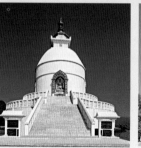

palace

fountain

mosque

cathedral   temple   statue

B   Tourist activities

activity	example
• **go sightseeing** [visit famous places; also **see the sights**]	We **went sightseeing** almost every day. I like to **see the sights** when I visit a place.
• **do** a bit of / a lot of **sightseeing**	I didn't **do** a lot of **sightseeing** in Warsaw.
• **have a look round** [visit a place casually, often on foot]	We **had a look round** the shops. I want to **have a look round** the museum.
• **explore** [go round a new place to see what is there]	We **explored** the flower market.
• **go out** [leave home / your hotel to go to a social event, e.g. restaurant or theatre]	On holiday we **went out** every night.
• **get lost** [lose one's way]	I **got lost** three times in London.
• **have** a great/nice/terrible **time**	They **had a lovely time** in Venice.
• buy **souvenirs** [something you buy or keep to remember a place or holiday]	We bought some dolls as **souvenirs**.

C   Describing places

The word **place** can describe a building, an area, a town, or country, e.g. Bruges is a lovely **place** [town] and we found a really nice **place** [hotel] to stay.

❝The **guidebooks** [books with information about places] say the Alhambra in Granada is **magnificent** [very good or very beautiful], but it's always **packed** [very crowded] with tourists in the summer.❞

❝São Paulo is a **lively** place [full of life and activity], and there's **plenty** [a lot] to do in the evening.❞

❝St Petersburg has lots of **historic monuments** [important places built a long time ago] but the Hermitage Museum was the main **attraction** for me. [something that makes people come to a place or want to do a particular thing]❞

❝If you go to Poland, it's definitely **worth** visit**ing** Kraków.❞

> ### Language help
>
> We use **worth** + noun/-*ing* to say that it is a good idea to do something or go somewhere.
> It's **worth hiring** a car if you go to Scotland. Glasgow is **worth a visit** as well.

Exercises

50.1 **Tick (✓) the words which refer to religious places.**

castle	church ✓	temple
statue	market	cathedral
fountain	mosque	palace

50.2 **Complete the email.**

● ● ●   ✉   <u>Reply</u>   <u>Forward</u>

From   John H. x   ▼   7:03 AM (3 hours ago)

Hi everyone,
I've been in Paris for over a week now and I'm having a great ¹ [*time*]. I did quite a lot of
² [   ] in the first few days – the Eiffel Tower, Notre-Dame, and all the usual tourist
³ [   ]. Most places are absolutely ⁴ [   ] with tourists at the moment, so
yesterday I decided to ⁵ [   ] one or two shopping areas. I got ⁶ [   ] on my
way back to the hotel, but it didn't matter because I discovered a really fascinating street
⁷ [   ] selling just about everything from apples to antiques.

I ate in the hotel the first night but I usually ⁸ [   ] for dinner – the restaurants are great
and I can get a set meal for €20.

I hope you're all well. I'll write again in a few days.
All the best,
John

50.3 **Complete the dialogues, but without using a word from the question.**

1 A: It's a fabulous city, isn't it?
   B: Yes, it's a wonderful ...*place*........................ .
2 A: It was very crowded, wasn't it?
   B: Yes, it was absolutely ....
3 A: It's lively in the evening, isn't it?
   B: Yes, there's ....
4 A: Did you enjoy yourselves?
   B: Yes, we had a ....
5 A: Kyoto is a good place to go to, isn't it?
   B: Yes, Kyoto is definitely ....
6 A: You know a lot about this castle, don't you?
   B: Yes, I bought a ....
7 A: St Petersburg has got many famous old places to see, hasn't it?
   B: Yes, lots of historic ....
8 A: The Taj Mahal was impressive and so beautiful.
   B: Yes, it was ....
9 A: Did you explore the town centre?
   B: Yes, we had a ....

50.4

Over to you

Think about your own country and write answers. If possible, compare your answers with someone else.

1 Write down a place that is worth visiting and a place that is not worth visiting and say why.

2 Is there a place that is particularly famous for its historic monuments? What are they?

3 What typical souvenirs do tourists buy when they visit?

4 What are the main attractions for tourists to your country? Do you think they are worth seeing?

A The beach

Many people **spend** their holiday at the **coast** [the land close to the sea], where there are a lot of **seaside resorts** [towns by the sea for tourists] and they can go to the beach every day. Generally people prefer beaches that are **sandy** [with lots of sand], where you can go for a **stroll** [a casual walk] along the **shore** [the place where the sea meets the land] in the **sunshine** [when it is sunny]. On the beach, you also sometimes get a **breeze** [a nice gentle wind] that blows off the sea.

B Beach activities

surfing	**windsurfing**	**diving**	**playing volleyball**	**sunbathing**

Volleyball is a popular beach game and some people enjoy water sports such as **surfing**, **windsurfing** or **diving**. If the sea is **calm**[1], you can **go for a swim**, but a lot of people just want to lie on the beach and **sunbathe** and get a nice **(sun)tan**[2]. However, there are now worries about the dangers of **sunbathing**. People who lie in the sun without any **protection**[3] can get **sunburn**[4], and worse still, they are **at risk of**[5] getting skin cancer. Doctors now **recommend**[6] that people do not sit in the sun without using **sunscreen**[7]. It may be safer just to sit in the **shade**[8].

[1] without waves (does not move very much); *opp* **rough**
[2] when the skin becomes brown
[3] something to keep someone safe
[4] when the skin becomes red and very sore
[5] if you are at risk of something, there is a danger that something bad may happen to you

[6] say what someone should do
[7] cream that gives protection from the sun; *syns* **sunblock**, **sun cream**
[8] an area where there is no light from the sun, so it is darker and less hot

Language help

We can **go for a walk**, a **drive** (a journey in the car for pleasure), **a swim**, **a coffee** [drink some coffee], **a drink** (often an alcoholic drink, e.g. wine, beer). We can also **have a swim**, **a coffee**, **a drink**.
*We **went for a drive** along the coast. I **had a coffee** at Caffé Nero. Let's **go for a drink** tonight.*

Exercises

51.1 **Write down four more words beginning with *sun*.**

sun *shine* ....   sun.......................   sun.......................   sun.......................   sun.......................

51.2 **Match the words on the left with the words on the right.**

1	sun	d	a	shade
2	wind	☐	b	sea
3	seaside	☐	c	surfing
4	sit in the	☐	d	tan
5	sandy	☐	e	resort
6	rough	☐	f	beach

51.3 **Cover the opposite page. What are these people doing?**

1 *playing volleyball*   2 ....   3 ....   4 ....   5 ....

51.4 **Cross out the wrong answer.**

		a	b	c	d
1	The beach was	lovely	~~calm~~	sandy	dirty
2	We went for a	drive	shop	drink	stroll
3	The sea was	sandy	calm	rough	cold
4	I enjoy	surfing	diving	getting sunburn	windsurfing
5	We walked	along the beach	by the shore	on the waves	on the sand
6	The beach was	near the cliffs	by the breeze	by the rocks	very sandy

51.5 **Complete the sentences.**

1 I love sunbathing, so I can get a nice ...*suntan*........................ .
2 Doctors .... that you stay out of the sun completely in the middle of the day.
3 We used to sunbathe for hours, but then we didn't know we were at .... of getting skin cancer.
4 I always take a beach umbrella to give me .... from the sun when it is very hot.
5 In the city it feels like there's no air, but you often get a nice .... by the sea.
6 I love going for a .... along the beach, especially in the evening when it's quiet.
7 I don't like sitting in the sun; I prefer to sit in the ....
8 We decided to .... a swim before lunch.

51.6 `Over to you`

Answer the questions. If possible, ask someone else the same questions.

1 Do you ever spend time at seaside resorts? Where do you go, and how often?

2 Do you enjoy any of the beach activities on the opposite page? Which ones?

3 Do you like sunbathing? Why? / Why not?

4 Do you get a suntan easily? Have you ever had sunburn? Do you often use sunscreen?

5 What do you like to do in the evening after a day on the beach?

52 Newspapers and television

A Newspapers

Most **papers** [newspapers] are **daily**, which means that they **come out** [appear in shops; *syn* **are published**] every day. Some are **national** [for the whole country], others are **regional** [for a part of the country]. Some newspapers are published online; these are called **e-papers**. You can also get **mobile editions** [you read a newspaper on your phone]. Magazines are usually **weekly** or **monthly**.

B Contents of* newspapers

Reports [pieces of writing about news items, written by **reporters/ journalists**, e.g. a **report in** *The Times* **on/about** a crime]
Articles [pieces of writing about an important subject, e.g. an **article on/ about** drugs]
Headlines [titles written in large letters above reports/articles, e.g. GOVERNMENT LOSES VOTE]
Reviews [pieces of writing giving an opinion, e.g. **a review of** a new book]
Advertisements or **adverts** [words and pictures about a product, to make people buy it, e.g. **an advert for** shampoo]

*information in

C Television

If you **broadcast** something, you send it out on TV, radio or the Internet. There are now many broadcasting companies and many programmes. People watch:

- **the news** [information about world events]
- **the weather forecast** [a description of what the weather will be like in the next few days]
- **documentaries** [programmes that give facts about real situations and real people]
- **chat shows** [programmes where famous people are asked questions about themselves]
- **a series** [a number of programmes that have the same characters or deal with the same subject]
- **soap operas** [a regular series of programmes, often two or three times a week, about a group of characters who live in the same area]
- **reality TV shows** [programmes which follow ordinary people or **celebrities** [famous people] through a number of situations or challenges. **Well-known** [famous] examples include: *Pop Idol*, *The X Factor* and *Strictly Come Dancing*].

Language help

We usually use **channel** to talk about television broadcasting, e.g. *The news is on Channel 4*; and **station** to talk about radio broadcasting, e.g. *A: What **station** are you listening to? B: Radio 1 – it's mostly pop music.*

D Media reporting*

Many newspapers also have online **forums** where people can leave messages and discuss topics. News is also reported online through **podcasts** [a radio programme that you download from the Internet and play on your computer or phone], e.g. Have you heard the latest business **podcast** on the CNN website?

Common mistakes

It says in the paper / **According to** the paper … (NOT ~~It's written in the paper …~~)

When we refer to something that someone has said or written, we do it in these ways:
It said in *The Times* that the plane crashed in the sea.
According to the news on TV last night, the plane crashed in the sea.

*reporting in newspapers, on TV or the Internet

Exercises

52.1 **Tick (✓) the words which describe a type of TV programme.**

the news ✓   documentary   headline   soap opera
chat show   review   article   series

52.2 **Complete the dialogues.**

1 A: Have you heard of 'Radio Five Live'?
   B: Yes, it's a very popular ..*station*.............. .
2 A: Is the magazine published every day?
   B: No, it .... monthly.
3 A: Is it a national paper?
   B: No, it's a .... paper for the south-west.
4 A: Can we watch the news now?
   B: Yes, it's on .... Four.
5 A: Are they mostly famous people?
   B: Yes, they're all ....

52.3 **Complete the crossword. What is the vertical word in grey?**

1 a famous person
2 a number of programmes with the same characters
3 a piece of writing about a news item
4 programmes several times a week about the same people
5 happening every day
6 a factual programme about real people and situations
7 relating to the whole country
8 a programme that interviews famous people
9 a piece of writing about an important subject

52.4 **Complete the sentences.**

1 Did you read that ..*article*.............. in the paper yesterday about space?
2 The manager was interviewed for the paper by one of their well-known ....
3 Do you understand this ....? '*200 WOMEN GIVEN WRONG DIAGNOSIS*'
4 Rock FM is the name of a radio ....
5 It .... in the paper that the interest rate is likely to go up soon.
6 I read a .... of his latest film. It doesn't sound very good.
7 You often see .... in the paper which promise that you can learn a language in ten hours with this method. It isn't true.
8 .... to the weather .... last night, it's going to rain today.
9 I never watch .... operas.
10 I love *The X Factor*; in fact, I love all .... TV shows!

52.5   **Over to you**

Answer the questions. If possible, compare your answers with someone else.

1 How many daily national newspapers are there?

2 How many newspapers only come out on Sunday in your country?

3 What parts of the newspaper do you read?

4 What types of TV programme do you watch?

53 Phoning and texting

A Starting a phone conversation

The call on the left is between two friends: Joe and Lily. When British people answer the phone at home, they usually just say 'hello'. The call on the right is a more formal business call.

JOE: Hello?
LILY: **Is that** Joe?
JOE: Yeah.
LILY: Hi. **It's** Lily.

RECEPTIONIST: Good morning. Chalfont Electronics.
PAUL SHARP: Oh, **could I speak to** Jane Gordon, please?
RECEPTIONIST: Yes. **Who's calling,** please?
PAUL SHARP: **My name is** Paul Sharp from Bexel Plastics.
RECEPTIONIST: Right, Mr Sharp. **I'm putting you through** [I'm connecting you] … (*pause*) …
JANE GORDON: Hello?
PAUL SHARP: Mrs Gordon?
JANE GORDON: **Speaking**. [Yes, this is Mrs Gordon.]

Common mistakes

We say: **Is that** Joe? (NOT ~~Are you~~ Joe? or ~~Is it~~ Joe?)

And we say: **It's** Lily. (NOT ~~I am~~ Lily or ~~Here is~~ Lily.)

B Problems on the phone

I tried to **ring** you this morning [phone you] but I think you were **on the phone** to your mother [using the phone].

I think I **dialled** [made a phone call to a particular number] **the wrong number** (e.g. 451 and not 351) this morning – I got a very angry person on the phone!

I **gave her a ring** this morning [phoned her], but I couldn't **get through** [make contact / speak to her]; the line was **engaged** [being used, someone was on the phone].

I **left a message** (e.g. Please ring me) on Dan's **answerphone** as he was **out** [not there; *syn* **not in**], but he never **phoned** me **back** [returned my phone call], so I don't know if he got my message.

C Phone numbers

Q: What's your **home** phone number? (also **landline**)   A: 603 884
Q: What's your **mobile number**?   A: 07723 259369
Q: What's the **emergency number** for the police, fire or ambulance?   A: 999
Q: What's the **dialling code** for the UK when you are phoning from Hungary?   A: 0044

D Mobile phones and texting

Many people use their mobile **mostly/mainly** [most of the time] for **texting** [sending short written messages from one phone to another]. Do you **text** your friends and family all the time?

These are common text **abbreviations** [letters which represent words].

ASAP = as soon as possible
BF = boyfriend (GF = girlfriend)
B4 = before
2DAY = today
2MORO = tomorrow
Y = why?
PLS = please

CU = see you
IMO = **in my opinion** [this is what I think]
FYI = for your information
U = you
THX = thanks
LOL = laughing out loud
X = kiss

Exercises

53.1 **Answer the questions.**

1 What are two more ways of saying *I called him*?
I phoned him. ....

2 You phoned Tom but weren't able to speak to him. What are three possible reasons for this?
....
....
....

3 You can ring a phone number. What are three other numbers you can ring?
.... number .... number .... number

53.2 **Complete the phone conversations.**

A: Hello?
B: Good morning. Could I [1] *speak to* .... Luke James?
A: Who's [2] .... , please?
B: [3] .... Liam Matthews.
A: One moment, please. I'm [4] .... you through.
C: Hello?
B: [5] .... Mr James?
C: [6] ....

A: Good morning. Boulding Limited. Can I help you?
B: Yes. I'm trying to contact Oliver Fallow. He left a [7] .... on my [8] ....
A: I see. Well, I'm afraid Mr Fallow's [9] .... at the moment. Can I ask him to
[10] .... you .... later?

A: Hello.
B: Hi. [11] .... Carlos?
A: Yeah, speaking.
B: Hi Carlos. [12] .... Serena.
A: Oh hello. I was expecting you to ring last night.
B: I did, but I couldn't get [13] .... ; the line was [14] ....
A: Oh yes, I'm sorry about that. I was [15] .... the phone to my brother for about
an hour.

53.3 **What do these text abbreviations mean?**

1 GRT = *great* ....
2 X = ...
3 CU = ...
4 IMO = ...
5 ASAP = ...

6 FYI = ...
7 LOL = ...
8 THX = ...
9 BF = ...
10 U = ...

53.4 `Over to you`

Answer the questions. If possible, compare your answers with someone else.

1 How often do you use a mobile phone? What do you use it for? How often do you text people?
Who do you text?

2 In your country, what is the emergency number for the police, fire brigade or ambulance?

3 From your country, what's the international dialling code for the United Kingdom?

4 How do you feel about people who use their mobile phone on a train?

A The computer

webcam

screen

printer

microphone

escape key

spacebar

keyboard

mouse mat

mouse

memory stick

CD-ROM

B Using a computer

After you have **switched on** [turned on] your computer, you may need to **log in/on** (*opp* **log out/off**) with your **username** and **enter** your **password** [put a special word into the computer that only you know]. If you then **double-click** on an **icon** [a small picture on the screen], you can open an **application** [email, Internet browser, etc.].

Computers can **store** [keep] large amounts of information, but when you're working it is important to **back up** the **files** you are working on [make an extra copy of the files; *syn* **make a backup**], so you don't lose the files if something goes wrong.

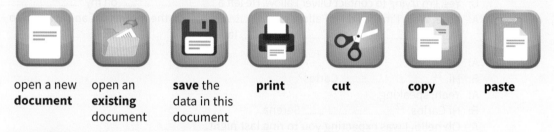

| open a new **document** | open an **existing** document | **save** the data in this document | **print** | **cut** | **copy** | **paste** |

To **create** [make or start] a new document, select NEW from the **File menu**.
You can **copy** and **paste** information from one file into another.
If you save the document, you can **print** it **out** later (OR you can get a **hard copy / a printout** later). It is also important to save the document in case the computer **crashes** [suddenly stops working]. Press the Escape key to **exit** [stop using an application].

C FAQs* about computers

example question	explanation
• Do you have a **PC** or a **laptop**?	PC is short for personal computer; a laptop is a small computer that you can carry around.
• What **hard drive** do you have?	the part inside the computer that stores large amounts of information (also **hard disk**)
• What **operating system** are you using?	computer software, e.g. Windows or Mac OS, that controls how the computer works
• Have you **installed** any new **software**?	put new programs onto your computer
• What software applications are you **running**?	What software applications are you using?
• Do you have **anti-virus software**?	A **virus** is a program put on a computer to destroy or steal the information on it. Anti-virus software is a program to stop a virus entering your computer.

*frequently asked questions

Exercises

54.1 **Match the words on the left with the words on the right.**

1	CD-	`e`	a	system
2	memory	☐	b	on
3	operating	☐	c	key
4	hard	☐	d	software
5	log	☐	e	ROM
6	anti-virus	☐	f	mat
7	mouse	☐	g	copy
8	escape	☐	h	stick

54.2 **Complete these words.**

1 soft *ware*   3 key   5 user
2 lap   4 space   6 pass

54.3 **Test your knowledge. Can you remember what these icons mean without looking at the opposite page?**

1 *open a new document*   3 ....   5 ....   7 ....

2 ....   4 ....   6 ....

54.4 **Complete the definitions.**

1 Computer software that controls how different parts work together is the *operating system* .
2 The part inside the computer that stores large amounts of information is the ....
3 A program secretly put on a computer to destroy the information on it is a ....
4 A small computer that you can carry round with you is a ....
5 The special word you type into your computer that only you know is your ....

54.5 **Complete the dialogues.**

1 A: What do I do when I finish?
  B: You can press the escape key to *exit* .
2 A: How often do you .... your files?
  B: At the end of every day if I can remember.
3 A: Is the data .... on the hard disk?
  B: Yes, but I always make a ....
4 A: Did you .... the software yourself?
  B: No, I don't understand anything about computers. My wife did it for me.
5 A: How do I .... a new document?
  B: Just select NEW from the File ....
6 A: There was a warning on the news this morning about a new computer ....
  B: Well, I should be OK. I've got .... software.

54.6 **Over to you**

Do you have a computer? If so, can you answer all the questions in section C on the opposite page?

A   Using email

Think about the way you use email.

- How often do you **check your email** [look to see if you have any messages]?
- How many emails do you send a week? Are they all **essential** [important/necessary]?
- How many emails do you get every week? Do you read them **immediately** [without waiting]?
- How quickly do you **reply to** [answer] the emails you receive?
- Do you **delete** emails **regularly** [remove them from your computer often]?
- Do you get much **spam** [emails that you do not want, usually adverts; also called **junk mail**]?
- Have you got **anti-virus software** [a program that stops a virus entering your computer]?
- How often do you send or receive **attachments**?

> **Language** help
>
> In English an email address may be written as pd@freeserve.co.uk, but we say it like this: pd **at** freeserve **dot** co **dot** uk.

B   Getting started on the Internet

To go **on the Internet**, you need an **ISP** (Internet service provider) that will **connect** [join or link] your computer to the Internet and give you **access to** [the ability to use] email and other services. When you **go online** [use the Internet], you can then send and receive emails, or you can **browse** the Internet [look at websites]; you do this using a **browser** such as Internet Explorer or Firefox. Many **websites** also have **links**: if you **click on** a link, it will take you to a different website, or move you from one part of the website to another.

C   Using the Internet

Many people now have Internet **access** and Internet use is changing all the time. These are common uses.

- Students **search** the Internet [look for information on the Internet; also **do an Internet search**] to help with their studies.
- People **download** [copy onto their computer; *opp* **upload**] information, pictures, music, **video clips** [small parts of a video recording], etc.
- People buy books, clothes and food online, book their holidays online, take out insurance online, etc. People go to a website, select the **item** [product, e.g. a book] they want and click **add to basket/bag**. When they have finished shopping they go to **checkout** and pay for their items, usually with a credit card.
- Some people have a personal website to provide news about a particular subject, or just write about events in their life. These are called **blogs**, and people who write them are **bloggers**.
- Some people just like to spend hours **surfing the web** [looking at different websites].
- Some people spend a lot of time on **social networking sites** [places on the Internet where you can have a discussion with other people, e.g. Facebook, Twitter, etc.]. On these sites people **post** comments [leave messages] to their friends.
- Some people do a lot of **instant messaging** [send and receive messages in real time].

Exercises

55.1 **Match the words on the left with the words on the right.**

1	go	b	a	the web
2	do	☐	b	online
3	surf	☐	c	emails
4	delete	☐	d	on a link
5	download	☐	e	an Internet search
6	click	☐	f	music

55.2 **Answer the questions.**

1 What can you do when you
   go online? ......*Send emails and use the Internet*......
2 What does ISP stand for? ....
3 What does an ISP give you? ....
4 What are Safari, Internet Explorer and Firefox? ....
5 What do bloggers write about? ....
6 What is spam? ....
7 How do you say this: Zac@hotmail.com? ....
8 What do people do on social networking sites? ....

55.3 **Complete the dialogues. The first letter of each answer has been given to help you.**

1 A: A friend of mine has got his own b.....*log*.................... .
   B: Oh yeah. What does he write about?
2 A: Do you always reply to emails i..................................... ?
   B: Yes. I think it's rude if you don't reply as soon as you receive an email. Don't you do that?
   A: No. I don't reply at once unless it's really e.................................... .
3 A: How can I view information about the computers they sell?
   B: Just c..................................... on that l..................................... , and it will take you to the website which has
      the details.
4 A: Do you have Internet a..................................... at your school?
   B: We do in school hours, but not before or after school.
5 A: I sent you an email earlier with an a..................................... . Did you get it?
   B: Oh, I'm afraid I haven't c..................................... my email today yet. I'll do it now.
6 A: Do you d..................................... much stuff from the Internet?
   B: Well, music naturally, and I also d..................................... a few video c..................................... .
7 A: I keep getting viruses on my computer.
   B: Ah, you will need to get some a.....................................- v..................................... software.
8 A: Do you delete emails r..................................... ?
   B: Yes, every day. I have to, because I receive so many, and most of them aren't important.

55.4

Over to you

Answer the questions. If possible, ask someone else the same questions.

1 Do you go on the Internet? If so, what are your favourite websites?

2 Do you have a blog or read other people's? Whose blog do you read?

3 Do you download material from the Internet? What do you download?

4 Do you watch video clips on the Internet? What video clips do you watch?

5 Do you use social networking sites or instant messaging? Which websites do you use?
   Who do you talk to?

A Different crimes

A **crime** is an activity that is wrong and not allowed by law. A person who **commits a crime** is a **criminal**.

crime	person	verb
theft [stealing something, e.g. a car]	**thief**	**steal/take** (something)
robbery [stealing from a person or place, e.g. a bank]	**robber**	**rob** (someone, a place)
burglary [getting into a building, usually someone's home, and stealing something]	**burglar**	**steal** something **burgle** (a place)
murder [killing someone]	**murderer**	**murder**

Someone's **stolen/taken** my handbag.
I don't know who **robbed** me.
Our flat was **burgled**, but they only took money.

There's been another **burglary** in the area.
Did you hear about the **bank robbery** yesterday?
Do they know who **murdered** the boy?

B Reporting crimes in the media

Two women robbed a jeweller's shop in West London early this morning. They broke in[1] around 7 o'clock and stole jewellery worth[2] over £10,000.

[1] entered the building using force, e.g. broke a window
[2] with a value of

BREAKING NEWS
Detectives[5] arrested[6] a man this morning in connection with the murder of shop assistant, Tracey Miles.

➜ *Read full story*

The two men **attacked**[3] Mr Crawford while he was walking home yesterday afternoon. Police say the two men hit him in the face several times, then took his money and **escaped**[4] through Bushy Park.

[3] used physical violence to hurt him
[4] left the place to avoid danger; *syn* **got away**
[5] police officers who try to find information to solve crimes
[6] If you *arrest* someone, you take them to the police station because you believe they committed a crime. That person is then **under arrest**.

C Punishment*

If you commit a crime and the police **catch** you [find you and arrest you], you will be **punished**. For **minor offences** [crimes that are not very important; *opp* **serious**], the punishment may only be a **fine** [money you have to pay], but for serious crimes, you will have to go to **court**. If you are found **guilty** [the **judge**, or a **jury** of 12 people, decides you committed the crime; *opp* **innocent**], you may be sent to **prison** (*syn* **jail**).

judge

court

prison

* what a person must suffer if they do something wrong

Exercises

56.1 **Test your knowledge. Can you complete this table without looking at the opposite page?**

noun	person	verb
crime	*criminal*	
murder		
theft		
robbery		
burglary		

56.2 **Find five more pairs of words that have a similar meaning.**

> ~~catch~~   theft   crime   jail   prison   ~~arrest~~   get away
> steal   offence   hit   escape   attack

catch – arrest ....

....

56.3 **Complete the dialogues.**

1 A: Is it being decided by a judge?
   B: No, there will be a *jury* ....
2 A: Have the police caught the man?
   B: Yes, he's under ....
3 A: Is she guilty?
   B: No, the jury found her ....
4 A: He killed his wife?
   B: Yes, he's under arrest for ....
5 A: Was it a serious crime?
   B: No, just a minor ....

6 A: Will she go to prison?
   B: No, she just has to pay a ....
7 A: Have you ever broken the law?
   B: Yes, but I've never committed a serious
   ....
8 A: How do you think he will be
   .... ?
   B: Well, it wasn't a very serious crime, so it'll
   probably be a fine.

56.4 **Complete the news report.**

NEWS   World | Politics | Finance | Tech | Sports

TODAY
BRISTOL FASHION THEFT
Two men are [1] *under* arrest for [2] _____ clothes from a warehouse* in Bristol. The two men [3] _____ into the warehouse late yesterday evening, [4] _____ the guard and tied him up, then [5] _____ a collection of expensive designer outfits [6] _____ over £40,000. A passer-by saw lights on in the warehouse and rang the police, but the two men managed to [7] _____ through a back door and then drove off with the stolen clothes. However, one of the men was later caught and [8] _____ at his home, and [9] _____ caught the second man just hours later hiding at a friend's house. Both men have now been charged with [10] _____ and will appear before a judge in [11] _____ on Monday. If they are found [12] _____, the two men will go to [13] _____ for a number of years. The guard who was attacked has now been released from hospital.

* A warehouse is a large building for storing goods that are going to be sold.

57 Politics

A Elections in the UK

When you **vote for** someone, you choose them by putting a cross (X) on an official piece of paper (called a **secret ballot** because no one knows who you vote for), or by putting up your hand. In the UK, a **general election** is when the people **elect**[1] the next **government**[2]. These **elections** are **held**[3] at least every five years. Each **constituency**[4] elects one person from one **political party**. That person then becomes the **MP** (Member of Parliament) for that area, and the political party with the most MPs – there are 650 at the moment – forms the next government. The **leader**[5] of the party **in power**[6] is the **Prime Minister**.

[1] choose by voting
[2] the group of people who control the country
[3] organised
[4] an area where people vote
[5] the person in control
[6] in control (of the country)

B Political policies

People usually vote for a political party because they **believe in** the party's ideas [think the ideas are good or right], and these ideas become **policies** [sets of plans and ideas that a political party has agreed on].

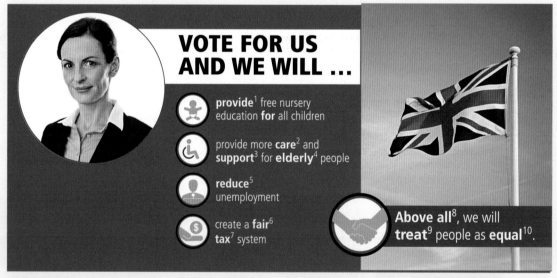

VOTE FOR US AND WE WILL …

- **provide**[1] free nursery education **for** all children
- provide more **care**[2] and **support**[3] for **elderly**[4] people
- **reduce**[5] unemployment
- create a **fair**[6] **tax**[7] system

Above all[8], we will **treat**[9] people as **equal**[10].

[1] give something to those who need it (also **provide** someone **with** something)
[2] looking after people, especially old people
[3] help (sometimes in the form of money)
[4] old
[5] make less; *syn* **cut**
[6] dealing with everyone in the same way; *opp* **unfair**
[7] money people must pay the government
[8] most importantly
[9] behave or deal with someone in a particular way
[10] having the same importance; *adv* **equally**

Exercises

57.1 **Complete the sentences using the correct form of the word on the right.**

1 Have they set the date for the *election*....................... ?   ELECT
2 Employment is an important .... issue.   POLITICS
3 My political .... are important to me.   BELIEVE
4 The president is a very .... man.   POWER
5 I hope there will be a .... in my tax.   REDUCE
6 Do you believe what .... say?   POLITICS

57.2 **Complete the crossword. What is the vertical word in grey?**

1 Most importantly
2 Person in control of a political party
3 Another word for 'old'
4 A synonym for 'reduce'
5 Money people must pay to the government
6 A set of plans and ideas that a group agree on
7 Help, often in the form of money
8 Not fair

57.3 **Rewrite the sentences on the left starting with the words given. Keep a similar meaning.**

1 They are in control of the country.   They are in *power*............................ .
2 They elected her.   They voted ....
3 Elections take place every five years.   Elections are ....
4 They will give hospitals more money.   They will provide ....
5 No one knows who you vote for.   It's a secret ....
6 It's a fair system for everyone.   The system treats ....
7 Our policy is to look after old people.   Our policy is to provide ....

57.4 **Complete the text.**

In Canada, [1] *elections*.................... work in a similar way to the UK. Canada is divided into 308 political [2].................................... , but they are called 'ridings' in Canada, and altogether there are 19 registered [3]........................ parties in the country. [4]...................................... are held every five years, and people [5].......................... for just one person in each riding to become their member of [6].................................. . The [7]...................................... that wins the most ridings is then asked by the Governor-General to form the next [8]............................... , and the leader of that party becomes [9].......................... Minister.

57.5 **Over to you**

Answer the questions. If possible, ask someone else the same questions.

1 How many major political parties are there in your country?

2 Which party is in power at the moment?

3 When were they elected?

4 Who is the leader of this party?

5 Did you vote in this election?

57.6 **Over to you**

Look at the policies in section B on the opposite page. What do you think of them? If you were in power, would you have these policies? What policies would you have? If possible, compare your answers with someone else.

A   The problem

WHAT IS THE GREENHOUSE EFFECT?

Many **greenhouse gases**, e.g. carbon dioxide, methane and ozone, **exist**[1] naturally and are needed to **create**[2] **the greenhouse effect** that keeps the Earth warm enough to **support**[3] human life. However, the use of **fossil fuels**, e.g. oil, natural gas and coal, has produced **excessive**[4] amounts of greenhouse gases, and the **result**[5] is **global warming**: an increase in the average temperature on Earth. Of the 15 warmest years **on record**[6], 14 have **occurred**[7] since 2000.

The **effects**[8] of **climate change** can already be seen in our everyday lives. Summers are getting hotter and winters are getting wetter, so **drought**[9] and **floods**[10] are becoming more common. With it, animal and plant life is **suffering**[11] – some species will disappear altogether – and certain illnesses, e.g. hay fever, asthma and skin cancer, are becoming more common.

To stop global warming from **destroying**[12] our **environment**[13], we need to act now.

[1] are real or present
[2] make something happen or exist
[3] help (human life) to continue
[4] more than you want or need
[5] something that happens because of something else that has happened
[6] If information is *on record*, it has been written down or kept on a computer.
[7] happened; *fml*

[8] a change or result that is caused by something
[9] a long time without rain when people do not have enough water
[10] when water covers an area that is usually dry, often from too much rain
[11] experiencing something which is unpleasant
[12] damaging something so badly that it does not exist or cannot be used
[13] the air, land and water around us

B   The solution* – or part of it

To **reduce** global warming [make it less], the nations of the world will have to **act** together [do something to solve a problem; *syn* **take action**]. In the meantime, individuals can also help.

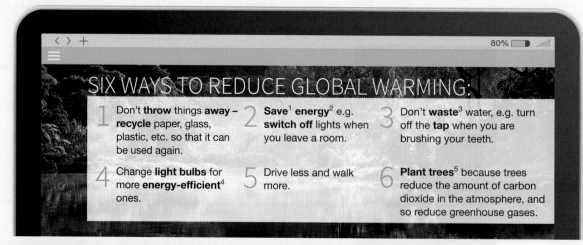

SIX WAYS TO REDUCE GLOBAL WARMING:

1 Don't **throw** things **away** – **recycle** paper, glass, plastic, etc. so that it can be used again.

2 **Save**[1] **energy**[2] e.g. **switch off** lights when you leave a room.

3 Don't **waste**[3] water, e.g. turn off the **tap** when you are brushing your teeth.

4 Change **light bulbs** for more **energy-efficient**[4] ones.

5 Drive less and walk more.

6 **Plant trees**[5] because trees reduce the amount of carbon dioxide in the atmosphere, and so reduce greenhouse gases.

* the answer to a problem
[1] don't waste
[2] gas and electricity
[3] use it badly

[4] working well and not wasting energy
[5] put a new tree in the ground

Exercises

58.1 **How do you pronounce the underlined letters? Use the index to help you.**

1 gl<u>o</u>bal   Is it like g<u>o</u> or g<u>o</u>t? *go*
2 fl<u>oo</u>d   Is it like f<u>oo</u>t or f<u>u</u>n?
3 f<u>ue</u>l   Is it like f<u>oo</u>d or f<u>ew</u>?
4 dr<u>ou</u>ght   Is it like n<u>o</u> or n<u>ow</u>?
5 s<u>u</u>ffer   Is it like s<u>o</u>n or s<u>oo</u>n?
6 clim<u>a</u>te   Is it like educ<u>a</u>te or comfort<u>a</u>ble?

58.2 **Match the words on the left with the words on the right.**

1 the greenhouse   [c]   a warming
2 global   [ ]   b change
3 fossil   [ ]   c effect
4 greenhouse   [ ]   d fuels
5 climate   [ ]   e gases

58.3 **How can we help with global warming? Cover the opposite page and complete the text.**

- Don't [1] *throw away* .... paper, glass and plastic; [2] .... it.
- Don't [3] .... water: turn off the [4] .... when you brush your teeth.
- [5] .... energy by [6] .... off lights when you leave a room.
- [7] .... trees in order to [8] .... the amount of carbon dioxide.
- [9] .... action now, before it's too late.

58.4 **Complete the explanations.**

1 We don't have to create greenhouse gases; they ..*exist*.................... naturally.
2 Greenhouse gases in the atmosphere .... the greenhouse effect.
3 Global warming is the .... of an increase in the amount of greenhouse gases.
4 Two .... of climate change have been hotter summers and wetter winters.
5 A .... is often the result of too much rain when the rivers are full.
6 A .... is a long period without rain, and they are .... more frequently now.
7 The .... is the air, land and water around us.
8 If you .... something, it is so badly damaged, it cannot be used again.
9 If something is .... , it works well and doesn't waste energy.
10 .... is the power that comes from gas, electricity, etc.

58.5 **Complete the tables. Use a dictionary to help you.**

verb	noun
recycle	*recycling*
waste	
destroy	
exist	

verb	noun
	solution
reduce	
support	
suffer	

58.6 `Over to you`

Answer the questions. If possible, talk to someone else about the problems.

1 Can you see the effects of global warming and climate change in your country? What do you see?

2 What things do people recycle every week?

3 Do you think you often waste water and energy? How?

4 What more could you do to solve the problem? Does it worry you?

A The job of the army

These men are **soldiers**, and they are **carrying guns**[1]. They are members of an **army**, and part of the responsibility of an army is to **defend** their country from **attack**[2] and to **protect** the people[3]. Sometimes this means they have to **fight** the **enemy**[4]. A long period of fighting is called a **war**, e.g. the First World War, 1914–1918, and during a war there will be a number of **battles**[5].

[1] have guns with them
[2] stop others who use violence against their country
[3] keep them safe
[4] the people they are fighting against
[5] fights between two armies

Language help

Violence is when someone tries to hurt or kill someone; the adjective is **violent**.
*The **violence** has increased in recent weeks; There have been a number of **violent** attacks.*

B Reporting in war

BREAKING NEWS
Recent Bombing

Ten people were **killed** and many more were injured when a **bomb exploded** (see picture) in **the heart of**[1] the city. The attack happened just before midday, and **destroyed**[2] several buildings. The army are now **searching**[3] the area where the attack **took place**[4]. Most of the attackers **escaped**[5], but the army believe they may still be **hiding**[6] in other parts of the city.

During the attack, one soldier was **shot**[7] and later died. It also appears that another soldier is **missing**[8]. The number of **deaths**[9] is expected to rise.

[1] the centre of
[2] damaged them so badly that they don't exist now; NOT ~~completely damaged~~
[3] trying to find someone or something
[4] happened
[5] left the place without being caught; *syn* **get away**

[6] staying in a place where you cannot be seen or found
[7] injured by a gun
[8] It isn't known where someone or something is.
[9] people who are dead / have **died**

Language help

Several words in the unit can be used as verbs and nouns with a similar meaning.

They're **searching** for them.   They're continuing their **search** for them.
He can't **escape**.   There is no **escape**.
When did they **attack**?   Where did the **attack** take place?

Exercises

59.1 **Are these words *nouns*, *verbs*, or *nouns* and *verbs*?**

protect	*verb*	shoot	....
search	*noun and verb*	war	....
die	....	defend	....
attack	....	escape	....
death	....	hide	....

59.2 **Complete the sentences with the correct verb.**

1 The soldiers have been ..*fighting*.................. for days, and so far three have been injured.
2 The woman was .... with a small handgun, but wasn't seriously injured.
3 One of the soldiers managed to .... under the house where no one could find him.
4 There are 20 soldiers surrounding the house, so the men inside cannot ....
5 The bomb .... inside the café. Nobody was .... but several people were injured.
6 I understand the army are .... houses in an effort to find the gunman.
7 The bomb completely .... the building, but fortunately no one was inside at the time.
8 My men had to .... the village from outside attacks.
9 Were the police .... guns when they saw the men?

59.3 **Choose the correct word to complete the sentences. Sometimes both are correct.**

1 One man was found but the other is still *lost* / *missing*.
2 The *battle* / *war* lasted for two hours.
3 The attack happened in the *heart* / *centre* of the city.
4 One of the buildings was completely *damaged* / *destroyed*.
5 Three of the men are *died* / *dead*.
6 One woman *escaped* / *got away*.
7 The boy was badly injured and later *died* / *killed*.
8 Some of the policemen are not allowed to *hold* / *carry* guns.
9 They don't know who *shoot* / *shot* the man.

59.4 **Complete the text.**

The [1] ..*attack*.................. happened early this morning. The [2] .... were out on patrol when they saw the [3] .... about half a mile away. Moments later a [4] .... exploded quite close to them, and was followed by a [5] .... gun battle which lasted two hours. Two soldiers were [6] .... and several were injured. An [7] .... captain said that they have now taken control of the area where the attack [8] ....

59.5 **Use a dictionary to develop these word families, and write example sentences for the new words.**

verb	noun	example
protect	*protection*	*The army gave the families protection.*
destroy		
explode		
defend		

60 Time

A Phrases with *time*

We got to the meeting **in time** [before the meeting started].
My brother is always **on time** [not early or late].
It's time (**for** us) **to** go. [used to say that something should happen now]
Do you **have time for** a cup of coffee? [have enough time to do something]
Call me **the next time** you're in London. [on the next occasion]
The weather was wonderful **the last time** we were there. [on the last occasion]
Sophie and I arrived **at the same time**, 9 o'clock exactly.

B Time prepositions often confused

I'll be here **until** 4.30. [I won't leave before 4.30]
I'll be there **by** 8.15. [not later than 8.15]

I've worked here **for** six months. (*for* + a period of time, e.g. a week, ten days, two years)
I've worked here **since** May. (*since* + a point in time in the past, e.g. last Friday, March, 2011)

I worked on a farm **during** the summer. (this tells you 'when')
I worked on a farm **for** a month. (this tells you 'how long') (NOT ~~during~~ a month)

I'm going back to Brazil **in** ten days' **time** [ten days from now]. (NOT ~~after~~ ten days)

C Approximate periods of time – past, present and future

Past
I've known Lucia **for ages** [for a long time, e.g. many years].
I haven't been to the dentist **recently/lately** [e.g. in the last few months].
I saw Tom **recently** [e.g. a few weeks ago / not long ago].
I used to go skiing, but that was **a long time ago** [e.g. 5–10 years ago; *syn* **ages ago**].
My sister went to the zoo **the other day** [e.g. a few days ago, perhaps a week].

Present
I don't see my brother much **these days** [a period including the past and now; *syn* **nowadays**].

Future
This dictionary's fine **for the time being** [for now / the near future – but not for a long time].
I'm sure I'll go to America **one day** [in the future but I don't know when].

D Counting time

There are 60 **seconds** in a minute; 60 minutes in an hour; 24 hours in a day; 7 days in a week; 2 weeks in a **fortnight**; 52 weeks in a year; 10 years in a **decade**; 100 years in a **century**.

E *Take* and *last*

We use **take** to say how long we need to do something.
It takes me half an hour to get to school.
We can walk, but it'll **take (us)** a long time.

We use **last** to talk about how long something continues, from the beginning to the end.
The course **lasts for** ten weeks.
How long does the film **last**?
The battery in my camera didn't **last long** [continue for a long time].

Exercises

60.1 **Complete the sentences.**

1 I'll see you the ..*next*............ time I come to London.
2 The shop closes at 5.30. If we don't hurry, we'll never get there .... time.
3 I always get to meetings .... time; I hate it when people are late.
4 I'm afraid I won't .... time to see you this week.
5 I'll have to go soon. It's time .... me to pick up the children from school.
6 Julian and I got to the station at the .... time.

60.2 **Choose the correct word to complete the sentences.**

1 I'll see you (in)/ *after* ten days' time.
2 The teacher told us to finish our homework *by* / *until* Monday.
3 We can't leave *by* / *until* the others get back.
4 I've been in the army *for* / *since* I was eighteen.
5 They've worked here *for* / *since* / *during* six months.
6 I visit my uncle every week *for* / *since* / *during* the winter.
7 I was at university *for* / *since* / *during* three years.
8 She's going back to France *in* / *after* three months' time.
9 I haven't seen them *for* / *since* last Thursday.

60.3 **Replace the underlined words with more 'approximate' time expressions.**

1 I had my hair cut <u>two weeks ago</u>. *recently*..............
2 I went to Egypt with my parents but that was <u>ten years ago</u>. ....
3 I went to the library <u>three days ago</u>. ....
4 I haven't been to the cinema <u>for the last three weeks</u>. ....
5 I haven't been to a concert <u>for three or four years</u>. ....
6 This computer will be fine <u>for the next year</u>. ....

60.4 **Test your general knowledge. Can you complete these sentences with the correct number or period of time?**

1 Michael Jackson died in ..*2009*.............. .
2 The Olympic Games usually last about a ....
3 Picasso was born in the ....th century, and died in the ....th century.
4 President Kennedy died in .... That's over .... years ago.
5 It takes approximately .... hours to fly from London to New York.
6 The best athletes can run 100 metres in less than .... seconds.
7 The .... was the decade in which the USA and USSR were trying to be the first country to put a man on the moon.

60.5

Over to you

Complete the sentences about yourself. If possible, compare your answers with someone else.

1 I've been in my present school/university/job for ....
2 It takes me .... to get to school/university/work.
3 A typical school/college/working day for me lasts ....
4 I've been studying English since ....
5 I haven't actually spoken English since ....
6 I saw .... the other day.
7 Nowadays I don't ....
8 One day I hope ....

A Cardinal numbers

379 = three **hundred** and seventy-nine
5,084 = five thousand and eighty-four
2,000,000 = two **million**

2,860 = two **thousand**, eight hundred and sixty
470,000 = four hundred and seventy thousand
3,000,000,000 = three **billion**

Language help

There is no plural 's' after *hundred*, *thousand*, *million* and *billion* when they are part of a number. When we are talking generally, they are plural, e.g. **thousands** of people, **millions** of insects.

B Dates

With dates, we write them and say them in a different way.
We can write **4 June** or **June 4th**, but say **the fourth of June** or **June the fourth**.
We can write **21 May** or **May 21st**, but say **the twenty-first of May** or **May the twenty-first**.
1997 = **nineteen ninety-seven**; 2016 = **two thousand and sixteen** or **twenty sixteen**

Common mistakes

The **seventh** of April (NOT The seven April); the **fourth** question (NOT the four question)

C Fractions and decimals

1¼ = one and **a quarter**
1½ = one and **a half**
1¾ = one and **three quarters**

1.25 = one **point** two five
1.5 = one point five
1.75 = one point seven five

D Percentages

26% is spoken as twenty-six **per cent**. More than 50% of something is the **majority of** it, less than 50% of something is the **minority**:
The **vast majority** of the students (e.g. 95%) agreed with the new plan, only a **small minority** (e.g. 5%) were unhappy.

E Calculations

There are four basic processes. Notice how they are said when we are **working out** [trying to **calculate**] the answer.

+ = **addition**   e.g. 6 + 4 = 10 (six **plus/and** four **equals/is** ten)
− = **subtraction**   e.g. 6 − 4 = 2 (six **minus** four is two)
x = **multiplication** e.g. 6 x 4 = 24 (six **multiplied by / times** four is twenty-four)
÷ = **division**   e.g. 8 ÷ 2 = 4 (eight **divided by** two is four)

Some people are not very good at **adding up** numbers [putting numbers together to reach a total], and often **get stuck** [have a problem] if they have to work out something quite difficult. The easiest way is to use a **calculator** [a small electronic machine for working out numbers].

F Saying '0'

'0' can be spoken in different ways in different situations:
telephone number: 603449 = six **oh** three, **double** four nine OR six **zero** three, **double** four nine
mathematics: 0.7 = **nought** point seven; 6.02 = six point **oh** two OR six point **nought** two
temperature: −10 degrees = ten degrees below **zero** OR **minus** ten degrees

Exercises

61.1 **How do you say these numbers in English? Write the answers in words, then practise saying them.**

1 462   *four hundred and sixty-two* ....
2 2½ ....
3 2,345 ....
4 0.25 ....
5 1,250,000 ....
6 10.04 ....
7 47% ....
8 10 September ....
9 940338 (phone number) ....
10 -5 Celsius ....
11 in 1996 ....
12 2012 ....

61.2 **Correct the mistakes.**

1 Two thousand and five hundred.   *Two thousand, five hundred* ....
2 After the game, I heard that the crowd was over twenty thousands. ....
3 We arrived on the seven June. ....
4 There were two hundred twenty altogether. ....
5 My birthday is the thirty-one August. ....
6 My phone number is seven twenty-three, six nought nine. ....

61.3 **Complete the sentences.**

1 Eight *multiplied* .... by seven is fifty-six.
2 The .... were in favour of the new airport; about 80%, I think.
3 A small .... did not support the idea, but it was only 5%.
4 I'm not very good at arithmetic. I always have to use a ....
5 When I tried to add .... all the numbers, I couldn't .... it out.
6 I can do simple calculations, but I get .... if the numbers are very big.

61.4 **Can you work out the answers? If you find it difficult, use paper or a calculator.**

1 23 and 36 is *fifty-nine* ....
2 24 times 3 is ....
3 80 minus 20 is ....
4 65 divided by 13 is ....
5 Add 10 and 6, multiply by 3, then subtract 15 and divide by 11. What number is left?
   ....
6 Divide 33 by 11, multiply by 7, add 10, and subtract 16. What number is left? ....

61.5   **Over to you**

Answer the questions. Write your answers in words.

1 When were you born? ....

2 How tall are you? ....

3 What's the number of the flat or house where you live? ....

4 When's your birthday? ....

5 What's the approximate population of your town? ....

6 What's your body temperature? ....

A   Distance: how far …

British people buy most things in metres, centimetres and millimetres, but they still often talk about distance using the old system of **miles** [1 mile = about 1.6 kilometres], **yards** [1 yard = almost 1 metre], **feet** [1 foot = 30 centimetres], and **inches** [1 inch = 2.5 centimetres].

About a mile **away** [a mile from here].

The **nearest** one is half a mile. [the one at the shortest distance from here]

How far's the post office?

It's **just round the corner** [very near].

About a hundred yards **up/down** the road. [further along the road]

About **ten minutes' walk**.

At least [not less than] a **couple of** miles. [two, perhaps three]

Is it far?

Yes, it's (**quite**) **a long way**.

B   Dimensions: how long or wide …

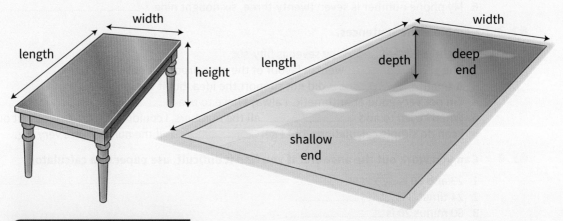

width
length
height

width
length
depth
deep end
shallow end

We can ask about the dimensions like this:

What's the **length** of the garage? OR How **long** is the garage?	It's five metres (**long**).
What's the **width** of the path? OR How **wide** is the path?	It's a metre (**wide**).
What's the **height** of the wall? OR How **high** is the wall?	It's two metres (**high**).
What's the **depth** of the pool? OR How **deep** is the pool?	It's three metres (**deep**).

C   Size: how big or small …

We use a range of adjectives to describe the size of something.

It was a very **thick** book – over 500 pages. (*opp* a **thin** book)
Their living room is **huge** [very big; *syn* **enormous**; *opp* a **tiny** room].
We caught a **giant** crab. [very large or bigger than other similar things]
It was a very **narrow** road for a bus. (*opp* a **wide** road)

Exercises

62.1 **Disagree with the speaker in each dialogue.**

1 A: It's only a thin book, isn't it?
B: No, *it's quite thick.*

2 A: The water's deep in the middle, isn't it?
B: No, ...

3 A: Is the road very wide at that point?
B: No, ...

4 A: James is quite short, isn't he?
B: No, ...

5 A: They only live in a small place, don't they?
B: No, ...

6 A: Is it a really huge pool?
B: No, ...

62.2 **Complete the questions (in two ways) about the lake, the mountain, the woman and the football pitch.**

1 How ...*deep*........................... is the lake?
2 What's .... the lake?
3 How .... is the mountain?
4 What's .... the mountain?

5 How .... is she?
6 What's her .... ?
7 How .... is the pitch?
8 What's .... the pitch?

62.3 **Over to you**

Think about the building you are in now, and answer the questions using expressions from the opposite page.

1 How far is it to the nearest shop? ....

2 How far is it to a bank? ....

3 Is it very far to the nearest bus stop? ....

4 Is it very far to a post office? ....

5 Is it a long way to the nearest swimming pool? ....

6 Is it a long way to the next big town? ....

7 How far is the nearest train station? ....

8 Is it far to the centre of town? ....

A Objects¹ and materials²

¹ things you can see or touch   ² what something is made of or from

object	material	description
1 a **bell**	**metal**	used in hotel receptions
2 a chair	wood	an **antique** [an object that is old and often rare or beautiful]
3 a hat	**fur**	made from a **real** animal
4 a **bone**	**rubber**	a **toy** for dogs
5 a **flag**	cloth, e.g. cotton	the Italian **national** flag
6 a shirt	**cotton**	it has red **stripes**
7 a top	**silk**	beautifully soft and stylish
8 a sofa	**leather**	**stylish** [fashionable and attractive]
9 a **ladder**	metal	light and easy to carry
10 a **tissue**	paper	a soft piece of paper that you use for cleaning your nose
11 a **bucket**	**plastic**	used to clean floors

Language help

Most of the materials above can be adjectives or nouns, e.g. *a cotton shirt*, or *a shirt made of cotton*; *a leather sofa*, or *a sofa made of leather*. The exception is wood: a chair made of wood is *a **wooden** chair*.

B Shapes and colours

a **grey square**   a **pink star**   a **navy blue circle**   a **green semi-circle**   a **purple heart**

a **round** ball   a **square** box   shoes with **pointed** toes

Language help

When we want to say that a shape is 'almost round' or a colour is 'a sort of green', we can also express this idea with the suffix **-ish**, e.g. *She had a **roundish** face*; *He wore a **greenish** tie.*

Exercises

63.1 **Put the words into the correct columns.**

| bell | circle | pink | silk | flag | grey | cotton | purple |
| plastic | bucket | fur | ladder | square | navy blue | | |

objects	materials	shapes	colours
bell			

63.2 **Match the words on the left with the words on the right.**

1 a plastic   [d]   a scarf
2 a silk   [ ]   b hat
3 a rubber   [ ]   c belt
4 a fur   [ ]   d toy
5 a cotton   [ ]   e tyre (on the wheel of a car)
6 a leather   [ ]   f T-shirt

63.3 **Label the objects, and their shape or colour.**

1 *a grey sofa* ....

3 ....

5 ....

2 ....

4 ....

6 ....

63.4 **Which object is being described?**

1 It's got a point at one end and that's the end you write with.   *a pencil* ....
2 It's a shellfish. It is usually grey, but it goes pink when you cook it.   ....
3 It can be metal or plastic and you often put water in it to wash floors.   ....
4 It is usually made of wood or metal, and you climb up it.   ....
5 At certain times of the month it's round; at others, it's closer to a semi-circle.   ....
6 An adult human body has 206 of these.   ....

63.5 `Over to you`

> **Answer the questions. If possible, compare your answers with someone else.**
>
> **1** Do you wear shoes with pointed toes?
>
> **2** What clothes do you have that are pink, purple or navy blue?
>
> **3** Do you wear anything that has stripes? If so, what?
>
> **4** Do you have any clothes that are made from silk or fur?
>
> **5** What things do you own that are made of leather?

A Containers and contents*

a **bag of** shopping

a **bottle of** apple juice

a **jar of** jam

a **bowl of** sugar

a **jug of** water

a **box of** chocolates

a **packet of** biscuits

a **packet of** crisps

a **can of** cola

a **carton of** orange juice

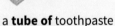
a **tube of** toothpaste

a **vase of** flowers

a **tin of** fruit

a **bar of** chocolate

* the things inside something

> **Language help**
>
> A **tin** usually has something we eat inside it; a **can** has something we drink.

B Quantities*

Just a **drop of** milk [a very small amount] and no sugar in my coffee, please.

I've cut three **slices of** beef; that should be enough for the sandwiches. (Or three **pieces of** beef)

I took my boss a **bunch of** flowers when I visited her in hospital.

I need a **sheet of** paper. (Or a **piece/bit of** paper)

Andrew bought two **pairs of** trousers and a pair of shoes yesterday.

I bought **a couple of** books. [two, perhaps three]

We saw **several** churches on our way here. [some but not a lot, e.g. between three and eight]

I bought **half a dozen** eggs at the supermarket. [six]

There are a **dozen** students in the class. [twelve]

Could I have **a spoonful of** sugar in my tea?

We've got **plenty of** time. [a lot of]

The company is now making the toys **in large quantities**.

* the amount or number of something

three **slices of** beef

two **sheets of** paper

a **spoonful of** sugar

a **bunch of** keys

> **Language help**
>
> We can usually use **slice** when talking about pieces of bread, cakes and meat. We can use **bunch** to talk about flowers, grapes, bananas and keys.

Exercises

64.1 **How do you pronounce the underlined letters? Use the index to help you.**

1 t<u>i</u>n   Is it like f<u>i</u>ne or w<u>i</u>nd? *wind*
2 p<u>ai</u>r   Is it like c<u>a</u>r or c<u>a</u>re?
3 v<u>a</u>se   Is it like f<u>a</u>r or f<u>a</u>ce?
4 t<u>u</u>be   Is it like n<u>oo</u>n or n<u>ew</u>?

5 c<u>ou</u>ple   Is it like p<u>oo</u>l or c<u>u</u>p?
6 d<u>o</u>zen   Is it like r<u>u</u>n or r<u>o</u>b?
7 qu<u>a</u>ntity   Is it like r<u>a</u>n or w<u>a</u>nt?

64.2 **Complete the phrases below.**

1   3   5   7   9

2   4   6   8

1   a *bottle* .... of water
2   a .... of spaghetti
3   a .... of fruit
4   a .... of coffee
5   a .... of milk

6   a .... of water
7   a .... of matches
8   a .... of soap
9   a .... of apples

64.3 **Correct the mistake with the container.**

1   a ~~packet~~ of chocolate *bar* ....
2   a vase of jam ....
3   a tube of cigarettes ....
4   a tin of cola ....

5   a can of milk ....
6   a carton of toothpaste ....
7   a jar of flowers ....
8   a jug of biscuits ....

64.4 **Complete the sentences with one word.**

1   I need two *pairs* .... of socks inside these shoes.
2   I gave her a big .... of flowers from my garden.
3   I cut about six .... of bread and put them on a plate.
4   Could you get half a .... more chairs?
5   The teacher told us to take out a blank .... of paper.
6   I like to put a .... of cream in my coffee.
7   There's no need to hurry – we've got .... of time.
8   I met a .... of friends – Stefan and Julia – on the way to the station.
9   She opened her bag on the table, turned it upside down, and all the .... fell out.
10   Tennis is quite popular in our office. I know .... people who play.

64.5 **Cross out the wrong answer.**

1   Could you get a carton of *milk / juice / ~~coffee~~*?
2   I bought a bunch of *grapes / bananas / apples*.
3   There were *a couple of / a pair of / several* people waiting at the bus stop.
4   Would you like a slice of *cake / bread / biscuit*?
5   It's nice with a spoonful of *sugar / jam / crisps*.
6   I bought two pairs of *socks / shirts / jeans*.
7   Have you got a *piece / bunch / sheet* of paper I could borrow?

65 Apologies, excuses and thanks

A Apologies with common replies

We can **apologise** [say sorry] in different ways in different situations.

 A: **I'm (terribly/really) sorry** – I've forgotten your book.

Terribly/really makes you sound 'more sorry'.

 B: **Never mind.** That's OK.

 A: **I beg your pardon** – I didn't see you there.

I beg your pardon is a more formal apology, often used if you walk into someone.

 B: **That's all right.** (also **That's OK.**)

 A: **(I'm) sorry to disturb you.**

We use this phrase when we **interrupt** / speak to someone who is busy working.

 B: **Don't worry.** Come on in. I can finish this later.

 A: **(I'm) sorry to keep you waiting** – I won't be long.

We use this phrase when someone is waiting for us. *I won't be long* = I will be with you very soon.

 B: OK. Fine.

 A: **Excuse me**, I won't be a minute.

We use this phrase when we have to leave a room or go somewhere.

 B: OK. Fine.

 A: **I must apologise for** the noise last night.

This is a more formal apology, and it is often used in business letters.

 B: That's all right. I understand.

 A: **I'm (really) sorry I'm late.**

 B: Don't worry.

> **Common mistakes**
>
> I'm sorry I'm late. (NOT I'm sorry ~~for be~~ late. OR I'm sorry ~~to be~~ late.)

B Excuses

We often give an explanation or **excuse** after an apology. An **excuse** is a *reason* for the apology, which may or may not be true. These are excuses students might give for being late for class.

I'm sorry I'm late for class …
- There was a **delay** / **hold-up** on the underground. [when a train, plane, etc. leaves or arrives later than you expect]
- I was **held up** in traffic. [**hold up** – cause a delay and make someone late – is often used in the passive]
- My train **was cancelled** [the train company decided not to run the train], and I had to wait half an hour for the next one.
- I **overslept** [slept longer than I planned or wanted to].

C Thanks and replies

These are some common ways of **thanking** people, with typical replies.

A: **Thanks (very much).**
B: **Not at all.** (also **That's OK.**)

A: I've brought your books.
B: Oh, **cheers.** (*infml*)
A: **No problem.** (*infml*)

A: I'll post those letters for you.
B: Oh, thank you. **That's very kind of you.** (This is polite and slightly more formal.)

Exercises

65.1 **Find three more pairs of phrases that have a similar meaning.**

> ~~thanks very much~~   I'm terribly sorry   don't worry   never mind
> I was held up   ~~cheers~~   I beg your pardon   there was a delay

thanks very much / cheers ....

....

65.2 **Complete the dialogues with one word. Contractions (e.g. *I'm*) count as one word.**

1 A: I'm *terribly* .... sorry.
   B: That's OK.

2 A: Thanks very much.
   B: .... at all.

3 A: Sorry to .... you waiting. I won't be ....
   B: That's all ....

4 A: I'm sorry .... late. The 7:30 train was .... , so I had to wait for the
       next one.
   B: That's OK. No ....

5 A: I gave your parents a lift to the station.
   B: Oh, thanks. That's very .... of you.

6 A: I must .... for missing the meeting yesterday afternoon.
   B: .... mind. I'll ask Claire to tell you what happened.

7 A: I .... your pardon. I thought the room was empty.
   B: That's OK.

65.3 **What could you say in these situations? If it is an apology, give an explanation.**

1 You walk into someone by accident and he/she almost falls over.
   I'm terribly sorry. OR I beg your pardon. I didn't see you.

2 You arrange to meet some friends in town at 9 am but you are twenty minutes late.
   ....

3 Your car has broken down. You're pushing it to the side of the road and a man offers to help.
   ....

4 You need to speak to your boss but she's working. What do you say when you enter her office?
   ....

5 You have to leave a meeting to take an important phone call. What do you say to the others?
   ....

6 You are on the phone but a customer is waiting to talk to you. What can you say to them?
   ....

7 You are late for an appointment because you had to wait half an hour in traffic.
   ....

8 Your company promised to send some information to a customer last week. You still haven't sent the
   information and you must now write to explain. Write the first sentence of your letter.
   ....

65.4
Over to you

Answer the questions. If possible, compare your answers with someone else.

1 Are you ever late for class or work? If so, do you have to apologise to anyone? Do you normally
give a reason why you are late? If so, what reasons are most common?

2 What other things have you apologised for recently? What did you say? Did you give an excuse?

66 Requests, permission and suggestions

A Requests and replies

 A: Could you pass the salt?

 B: Sure. / No problem.

 A: Could you possibly help me?

 B: Yes, **of course**.

 A: Naomi, **I wonder if you could** help me?

 B: Sure.

 A: I was wondering if you could lend me some money until tomorrow.

 B: No, **I'm afraid I can't**. [I'm sorry but I can't.]

> **Language help**
>
> As the requests become bigger it is normal to use longer phrases which sound more **polite**.

B Asking permission and replies

 A: Could I possibly have a look at your magazine?

 B: Yes, **help yourself**.

 A: May / Could I open the window?

 B: Sure, **go ahead**.

 A: Do you mind if I watch TV?

 B: No, go ahead.

> **Language help**
>
> When we answer **go ahead** or **help yourself**, we are giving someone permission to do the thing they have asked.

C Suggestions and replies

We could try that new restaurant.

How about go**ing** to a club?

What **shall we** do tonight?

I don't mind. You choose.

Let's go to the café in the square.

Why don't we go and see a film?

Do you fancy listen**ing** to some music?
[do you want to; *infml*]

We can reply with different answers, from positive to negative.

Yeah, **(that's a) great idea**.   Yes, **if you like**.   No, **I don't fancy that**.
That **sounds good**.   Yeah, **I don't mind**.   Mm, **I'd rather** do something else.
[I would prefer to do something else.]

Exercises

66.1 **Correct six more mistakes in the dialogue.**

A: ~~Do~~ you like to go out this evening?   *Would*
B: I'm afraid but I haven't got any money.
A: That's OK. I'll pay. How about go to see a film?
B: No, I think I'd rather to stay in. I have to do some homework.
A: Why you don't do your homework this afternoon?
B: I'm busy this afternoon.
A: Well, we could to go tomorrow.
B: Yeah, it's a great idea.

66.2 **Match 1–6 with a–f.**

1 Could you close the door?	c	a a suggestion
2 May I close the window?	☐	b a negative reply
3 We could go to the cinema.	☐	c a request
4 Yeah, great idea.	☐	d asking for permission
5 I wonder if you could close the door?	☐	e a positive reply
6 I don't fancy that.	☐	f a polite request

66.3 **Complete the dialogues with one word. Contractions (e.g. *don't*) count as one word.**

1 A: What ....*would*.............. you like to do this weekend?
   B: I don't .... You decide.
2 A: Could you .... open that window? It's very hot in here.
   B: Yes, of ....
3 A: I was .... if you could give me a lift to Luke's this evening.
   B: Sure, no ....
4 A: What do you .... doing this evening?
   B: I don't .... Any ideas?
   A: Why .... we go to the cinema? We haven't been for ages.
   B: Yeah, that's a great ....
5 A: Do you .... if I use your phone?
   B: No, go ....
6 A: OK. Where .... we go on Saturday?
   B: How .... going to the beach if the weather's nice?
   A: Yeah. Or we .... try that new sports centre just outside town.
   B: Mmm. I think I'd .... go to the beach.
   A: Yes, OK, if you ....

66.4 **Reply to the questions. Try to give a different answer each time.**

1 Could I borrow your pen for a minute?   *Yes, sure*..........................
2 Could you possibly post a letter for me?   ....
3 I was wondering if you've got a suitcase you could lend me?   ....
4 Do you mind if I take this chair?   ....
5 I've got some tickets for a concert. Do you fancy going?   ....
6 How about going to a football match at the weekend?   ....
7 Why don't we meet this afternoon and practise our English?   ....

67 Opinions, agreeing and disagreeing

A Asking someone for their opinion

What do you think of his new book / Tom's girlfriend? (asking about a specific thing or person)
What do you think about global warming / cosmetic surgery? (asking about a general topic)
How do you feel about working with the others?

B Introducing your own opinion

Personally, I think Helena was probably right.
Personally, I feel that we should increase the price.
In my opinion [I think], we need to change the direction of the company.
My view/feeling is [my opinion is] that we need to wait a bit longer.

> ### Common mistakes
>
> Personally, I **don't think it's** a good idea. (NOT I think it's not a good idea.)
> **In** my **opinion**, motorbikes are dangerous. (NOT On my opinion OR In my meaning)
> In most situations, it is probably easier and more natural to use **personally**.

C Giving the opinion of others

The newspaper **says** that his death was not an accident. (NOT It's written in the newspaper)
According to the paper [the paper says], the government didn't know about it.

D Agreeing and disagreeing (with someone)

I **totally agree (with you)** [agree completely, 100%].
I **partly agree (with you)** [agree but not completely].
I **agree (with you) to a certain extent** [partly agree].

> ### Common mistakes
>
> I **agree** with you. (NOT I'm agree with you.)
> **Do you** agree? (NOT Are you agree?)

In British English, it is common to agree with someone before giving a different opinion.
That's true, **but** I think …
I see what you mean, [I understand what you are saying] **but** …
I agree to some extent, but …
I think that's a good **point** [idea or opinion], **but** …
I **take your point** [I understand and partly agree with your opinion], **but** …

E Giving a strong opinion

I feel very strongly about military service.
I think everyone should do it.

 I think you're **absolutely right/ wrong** [100% correct/wrong].

 I don't agree **at all** [I completely disagree].

 I **disagree completely** [100% don't agree].

Exercises

67.1 **Complete the questions in different ways to ask people their opinion.**

1 What do you think *about* .... sending people to Mars?
2 .... these shoes? Do you like them?
3 .... having more responsibility?

67.2 **Complete the dialogues.**

1 A: Did you think he was right in what he said?
  B: Not completely, but I *partly* .... agreed with him.
2 A: What did you think .... the film?
  B: Well, ... I didn't like it.
3 A: Do you agree with her?
  B: Yes, to a certain ....
4 A: She feels very .... about protecting the environment.
  B: Yes, I know, and I think she's absolutely ....
5 A: .... , I think all politicians tell lies.
  B: Sorry, but I .... completely.
6 A: We can't send everyone to university.
  B: Yes, that's .... , but we should give everyone a chance to go.
7 A: My .... is that we should make all chocolate and sweets more expensive, and then people couldn't afford to eat so many things that are bad for them.
  B: That's a good .... , but it seems unfair on people who don't eat too many sweet things.
8 A: I see what you .... about spending more money, but can we afford it?
  B: Well, in my .... we have no choice.

67.3 **Rewrite the sentences using the words in capitals. Keep a similar meaning.**

1 I think you're right. AGREE   *I agree with you.* ....
2 I think the club needs new players. OPINION ....
3 I completely disagree with you. AT ALL ....
4 The newspaper says the fire was started on purpose. ACCORDING ....
....
5 I partly agree with her. EXTENT ....
6 I see what you mean, but I'm not sure I agree. POINT ....
....

67.4 `Over to you`

Respond to the statements with your own opinion. If possible, compare your answers with someone else.

1 I think most women are happy to stay at home and be a mother and housewife.

....

2 Personally I don't think the government should give so much money to people who don't work.

....

3 My feeling is that we should give more money to poor countries in other parts of the world.

....

4 I think we should make it more expensive to drive a car in order to reduce the number of cars.

....

68 Likes, dislikes, attitudes and preferences

A Likes and dislikes

	agree	disagree
I **love** rock music. I'**m really into** dance music. [like it very much; *infml*] I like a lot of pop music.	**So do I. / Me too.** **So am I. / Me too.** So do I. / Me too.	**Really?** I don't. Really? I'm not. Do you? I hate it.
I **quite** like salsa and samba. I **don't mind** jazz. [it's OK]	So do I. / Me too. Yeah, it's OK.	Oh, I'm not very keen. Oh, I can't stand it.
I'm **not very keen on** folk music. I **can't stand** classical music. [dislike it very much; *infml*] I **hate** opera.	**Neither am I. / Me neither.** **Neither can I. / Me neither.** So do I. / Me too.	Really? I love it. Really? I quite like it.

Language help

Many of these verbs can be followed by a noun or an *-ing* form, e.g. *I love driving, I like singing, I don't mind work, I dislike driving, I can't stand getting up early, I hate cold weather.*

B Attitudes and interests

My **attitude to** a lot of things has changed over the years. [how you think or feel about something]
I **used to** like chips. [I liked chips in the past but not now.]
I used to play computer games, but now they **don't interest** me. [I don't find them interesting.]
I'm very **interested in** modern architecture, but I used to think it was awful.
I used to go swimming a lot, but now I don't go **at all** [*at all* makes a negative stronger].
Mark and I used to have the same **interests** [things we enjoy doing], but now it seems we **have nothing in common** [have no interests that are similar; *opp* **have a lot in common**].

Common mistakes

I'm **interested in** see**ing** that. (NOT I'm ~~interest~~ in seeing that; OR I'm interested ~~to see~~ that.)

It takes time to **get used to** [become familiar with] liv**ing** in a different country.
I didn't like my new glasses at first, but now I've **got used to** them.
I found the winters very cold at first, but you **get used to** it.

C Which do you, or would you, prefer?

A: Which do you **prefer** in general, tea or coffee? [like more]

B: Well, I **prefer** coffee **to** tea in the morning, but in the afternoon I usually drink tea.

A: Tonight, we can go to the cinema or the theatre. Which **would you prefer**?

B: I think **I'd prefer to** go to the cinema. (*syn* **I'd rather**)

Exercises

68.1 **Correct the mistakes in B's replies.**

1 A: I can drive.
   B: So ~~do~~ I. ....*can*................

2 A: I love modern art.
   B: Yes, so I do. ....

3 A: Do you like chocolate?
   B: Yes, I like very much. ....

4 A: Do you like it in England?
   B: Yes, I'm getting used to live
   here. ....

5 A: I don't like shopping.
   B: Me too. ....

6 A: Do you like football?
   B: Yes, but I prefer rugby than football.
   ....

7 A: Do you like this?
   B: No, I'm not interest in music.
   ....

68.2 **Complete each sentence with one word.**

1 My sister loves Robbie Williams, but I can't ....*stand*.............. him.
2 The two boys have nothing in .... ; they're completely different.
3 The others enjoyed the film, but I didn't like it at ....
4 I love the cinema, but this particular film doesn't .... me.
5 Carole is really .... modern art at the moment. Personally, I hate it.
6 I .... to love cheese, but I never eat it now.
7 A: Would you like to go out? B: I'd .... stay here, actually. Is that OK with you?
8 I didn't like raw fish at first, but I'm .... used to it now.

68.3 **Agree with the statements using *so* or *neither* and the correct verb. Then agree using *Me too* or *Me neither*.**

1 I love this ice cream.   *So do I.* ....   *Me too.* ....
2 I like strawberries.   ....
3 I don't like cold tea.   ....
4 I can't work with music on.   ....
5 I'm single.   ....
6 I'm not married.   ....
7 I've got a cat.   ....

68.4 **Rewrite the sentences using the word in capitals. Keep a similar meaning.**

1 He likes salsa. INTO *He's into salsa.* ....
2 I hate these new shoes. STAND ....
3 She'd prefer to go home. RATHER ....
4 I don't like James Bond films very much. KEEN ....
5 I think the new building is alright. MIND ....
6 I went riding a lot in the past, but not now. USED ....
7 We have a lot of the same interests. COMMON ....
8 I'm becoming familiar with this new computer. USED ....
9 I don't feel the same way about work now. ATTITUDE ....

68.5 `Over to you`

Complete the sentences. If possible, compare your answers with someone else.

I really like ....   I prefer .... to ....
I don't mind .... doesn't interest me.
I can't stand ....   I used to ....

69 Greetings, farewells and special expressions

A Greetings*

When we are **introduced to** a **stranger** [told the name of someone we have never met] in a formal **situation**, we usually **shake hands** and say *hello*, or perhaps **hello, nice to meet you**. In an informal situation, we usually just say *hello* or *hi*.

When we **greet** friends, there are no real rules in Britain. Men may kiss **female** friends [girls/women] on one **cheek** [side of the face], on both cheeks, or not at all. Women may kiss **male** friends and female friends **once**, **twice**, or not at all. We usually say things like this:

A: Hello. How are you?   B: Fine, thanks. **How about** you?
A: Hi. **How's it going? / How are things**? (*infml*)   B: **Not (so) bad**, thanks. And you?

* saying hello

B Farewells*

To someone we have just met for the first time we can say **Goodbye. Nice to meet you.**

With friends we can say **bye**, **cheers** (*infml*), **take care** (*infml*), or **see you** (soon/later/tomorrow, etc.).

When we say goodbye to a school or work friend on Friday afternoon we usually say:
A: Have a nice weekend.
B: Yeah, **same to you**. (NOT same for you)

* saying goodbye

C Expressions for special situations

Excuse me, could I just **get past**?

Yes, of course.

It's your exam today, isn't it? **Good luck**.

Thanks, I'll need it.

Cheers.

Sue found my wallet and my credit cards.

Oh, **thank goodness** for that.

Achoo!

Bless you.

I hear you passed your exam. **Congratulations**.

Thanks.

Language help

We use **Thank goodness** when we are happy that something bad did not happen. A synonym is **Thank God** (*infml*), but there are some people who may not like the use of this expression. We can use *Goodness* on its own to express surprise, e.g. *Goodness, is it ten o'clock already?*

Exercises

69.1 **Find five more phrases.**

~~good~~	take	excuse	bless	~~luck~~	you
thank	me	goodness	not	care	bad

good luck ....

....

69.2 **Complete the dialogues.**

1 A: How are you?
   B: Fine. How *about* .... you?

2 A: How's it .... ?
   B: Not .... And you?

3 A: Have a nice weekend.
   B: Yeah, ... you.

4 A: Nobody was hurt in the accident.
   B: Oh, ... for that.

5 A: I'll see you tomorrow.
   B: Yeah, ... care.

6 A: I've just passed my exam.
   B: .... !

7 A: I'm fine, thanks.
   B: Good. And .... Sarah?

69.3 **What could you say in these situations?**

1 A friend says, 'Have a good weekend'. What do you reply? *Yeah, same to you.* ....
2 You met a new business client for the first time fifteen minutes ago, and now you are leaving. What do you say? ....
3 You are on a crowded bus. It is your stop and you want to get off. What do you say to other passengers as you move past them? ....
4 A friend tells you they have just won some money. What do you say? ....
5 A friend is going for a job interview this afternoon. What do you say? ....
6 You are having a drink with friends. What do you say when you hold up your glasses to drink?
   ....
7 Someone sneezes next to you. What do you say? ....

69.4 **Complete the sentences.**

1 When you meet someone for the first time in a formal *situation* .... , what do you say?
2 When you are .... to someone in a formal situation, do you normally
   .... hands?
3 What do you do and say when you .... friends?
4 Do you usually kiss friends? If so, is it on one .... or both .... ?
5 When you say goodbye to friends, do you use informal expressions like *Cheers*, or *Take*
   .... ? If so, what are they?

69.5 **Over to you**

> Answer the questions in Exercise 69.4 about your country. If possible, ask someone from
> a different country the same questions.

A With adjectives

Prefixes, e.g. **un-**, **dis-**, **im-**, can be added to some adjectives to give the opposite meaning.

happy	**un**happy
possible	**im**possible
regular	**ir**regular

honest [tells the truth]	**dis**honest
correct [right ✓]	**in**correct
legal [allowed by law]	**il**legal

Dan used all the milk but said he didn't; he's very **dishonest**.
I got eight answers right, but two were **incorrect**.
It's **illegal** in the UK to ride a motorbike without a helmet.

B un-

Of the prefixes above, **un-** is the most common, and appears in a number of adjectives.

This chair is incredibly **uncomfortable**.
It was **unnecessary** for them to wait for us.
Xerxes – that's a very **unusual** name. [different, not common or ordinary]
I won the game; it was completely **unexpected**. [I didn't think I was going to win]
Marsha's hat is **unbelievable**. [surprising because it is either very good or very bad]
We tried to open the door, but we **were unable to** get in. [could not]
I need to do more exercise; I'm very **unfit**. [not healthy and not in good condition]
Declan played well, and I thought he was **unlucky** to lose.
They're **unlikely** to get here before midday. [They probably won't get here before midday.]
The test was **unfair** because some of the students had more time to do it than others. [If something is *unfair*, it does not treat people equally.]

> ### Language help
>
> Adding a negative prefix does not usually change the pronunciation; the stress stays the same.
> She was un'lucky. It's unbe'lievable. (NOT She was ~~'unlucky~~. It was ~~'unbelievable~~.)

C With verbs

With some verbs, these prefixes can have particular meanings.

dis- [the opposite of something]	I **disagree** with the others. [don't agree / have the same opinion] The plane **appeared** in the sky, then it **disappeared** behind a cloud.
un- [the opposite of an action]	I couldn't **unlock** the door this morning. [open the door using a key; opp **lock**] We had to **get undressed** in the cold. [take off our clothes; opp **get dressed**] I **unpacked** the bags. [took everything out of the bags; opp **pack**]
over- [too much]	The bank **overcharged** me. [asked me to pay too much money]
mis- [do something incorrectly]	I **misunderstood** what he said; I'm afraid my English isn't very good. I **misheard** her. I thought she said *Rita*, not *Brita*.
re- [again]	The teacher has asked me to **rewrite** my essay.

Exercises

70.1 **Write the opposite.**

1 ....*un*....happy
2 ....able
3 ....correct
4 ....usual
5 ....possible
6 ....comfortable

7 ....agree
8 ....necessary
9 ....regular
10 ....honest
11 ....fair
12 ....lucky

70.2 **Which sentence on the right logically follows each sentence on the left?**

1 She arrived home. | *b* |
2 Her essay was terrible. | ☐ |
3 She decided to go to bed. | ☐ |
4 He called her name. | ☐ |
5 She's not here now. | ☐ |
6 He thought he was right. | ☐ |
7 She got to the hotel. | ☐ |
8 After I paid, I looked at the price. | ☐ |

a She unpacked her suitcase.
b She unlocked the front door.
c She has disappeared.
d She had overcharged me.
e She had to rewrite it.
f She misheard it.
g She disagreed.
h She got undressed.

70.3 **Complete the dialogues so that B agrees with A using different words. You only need one word for each gap.**

1 A: Adera is a strange name.
   B: Yes, very *unusual* .

2 A: It's against the law, isn't it?
   B: Oh yes, it's ....

3 A: You mean he took off all his clothes!
   B: Yes, he got completely ....

4 A: He probably won't get back in time for the meeting.
   B: I agree. It's very ....

5 A: A lot of the answers were wrong.
   B: Yes, I'm afraid they were nearly all ....

6 A: He doesn't look in very good condition; he's a bit overweight.
   B: I know. He looks terribly ....

7 A: Nobody thought this would happen.
   B: Yes, it was completely ....

8 A: They never tell the truth.
   B: I know. They're both ....

9 A: His business always seems to lose money, and it's not his fault.
   B: I know. He's very ....

10 A: Ann always gives more attention to Sarah than she does to Lucas.
   B: Yes, it's very .... on poor Lucas.

70.4 **These words all appear in other units of the book. Do you know how to form the opposites?**

pleasant	*unpleasant*	fashionable	....
kind	....	reliable	....
patient (adj)	....	friendly	....
suitable	....	tidy	....
like (v)	....	ability	....
do up	....	sociable	....

71 Suffixes: forming nouns

A Verb + noun suffix

Suffixes are used at the ends of words; they often tell you if a word is a noun, a verb, an adjective or an adverb. Two suffixes which form nouns from verbs are **-ion** and **-ment**.

verb	noun
invent [produce or design something completely new]	**invention**
discuss [talk about something seriously]	**discussion**
translate [change from one language to another]	**translation**
relax [rest, and feel calm and comfortable]	**relaxation**
improve [get better]	**improvement**
govern [control the affairs of a city or country]	**government**
manage [direct or control a business]	**management**
develop [grow or change and become more advanced]	**development**

His latest **invention** is a new board game.
Relaxation will help you to sleep better.
We had a **discussion about** politics.

The **management** has to change.
I need money for more **development**.
We need an **improvement in** the weather.

B Adjective + noun suffix

The suffixes **-ness** and **-ity** often form nouns from adjectives.

adjective	noun
weak (*opp* strong)	**weakness**
happy	**happiness**
ill [sick, not well]	**illness**
fit [in good condition, usually because of exercise]	**fitness**
stupid (*opp* intelligent, clever)	**stupidity**
popular [liked by a lot of people]	**popularity**
similar [almost the same; *opp* different]	**similarity**
able	**ability** (*opp* **inability**)

What is his main **weakness** as a manager?
Snowboarding is growing in **popularity**.
I'm frustrated by my **inability to** use computers.

Fortunately it wasn't a serious **illness**.
There is a **similarity between** them.
Her **happiness** is all that matters to me.

C -er, -or and -ist

These suffixes can be added to nouns or verbs. They often describe people and jobs.

-er	-or	-ist
ballet **dancer**	company **director**	**artist**, e.g. Picasso
pop **singer**	**translator**	**economist**
professional **footballer**	film **actor**	**scientist**

Language help

Adding a suffix to a verb, adjective or noun may change the position of the main stress, e.g. re'lax – relax'ation, 'stupid – stu'pidity, eco'nomics – e'conomist.
(The ' symbol is before the syllable with the main stress.)

Exercises

71.1 Complete the tables and mark the stress on each word. (Stress is marked on the pronunciation of a word in a dictionary.) The last two in each column are not on the opposite page, but do you know or can you guess the noun formed from them?

verb	noun
dis'cuss	*dis'cussion*
improve	
invent	
relax	
hesitate	
arrange	

adjective	noun
stupid	
happy	
similar	
popular	
sad	
active	

71.2 Write down the names of the people who do these things as a job.

1 sing opera music *opera singers*.............................
2 act in films ....
3 important managers in a company ....
4 change words from one language into another ....
5 play football ....
6 dance in ballets ....
7 paint pictures ....
8 work in science ....

71.3 Complete the text using words from the box with the correct suffix and spelling. One word also needs a prefix.

~~weak~~   improve   govern   economics   able   manage   discuss

"In his speech last night, the prime minister said that the present [1] *weakness*................. of the economy was caused by the bad [2]................................... of the last [3].................................. and their [4].......................... to give the right kind of help for industry. He said he was now involved in detailed [5].............................. with ministers, bankers and [6].................................. about a range of different financial measures, and he hoped the people would be able to see a big [7].................................. in the economy by the end of the year. "

71.4 Complete the dialogues.

1 A: He hasn't been well at all, has he?
   B: No, it's quite a serious *illness*........................ .
2 A: Are they almost the same?
   B: Yes, the .... is amazing.
3 A: Has anyone made anything like this before?
   B: No, it's a brand-new ....
4 A: Is her new novel going to be published in other languages?
   B: Yes, someone is working on a .... right now.
5 A: Does your daughter enjoy drawing too?
   B: Yes, she's a very good ....
6 A: Javier gets tired after he's been playing for about ten minutes.
   B: I know. If he wants to be in the team, he'll have to improve his ....
7 A: Do you think the organisation can still grow?
   B: Yes, I think there is an opportunity for further ....

72 Suffixes: forming adjectives

Common suffixes that form adjectives include: **-able** (comfortable), **-al** (musical), **-y** (cloudy), **-ous** (famous) and **-ive** (attractive).

A -al

Adjectives ending **-al** are usually formed from nouns, and often mean 'relating to the noun', e.g. a **musical** instrument (from music), a **political** issue (from politics), an **electrical** fault (related to electricity), a **personal** opinion (the opinion of one person).

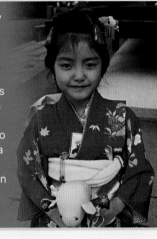

SHICHI-GO-SAN

Shichi-Go-San (meaning 7, 5, 3) is an **annual** ceremony in Japan for three- and seven-year-old girls, and three- and five-year-old boys. It is on November 15, but it is not a **national**[1] holiday, so people often have it on the nearest weekend. Seven, five and three are seen as important years in the growth of a child, and the numbers also have **cultural significance**[2] because odd numbers (1, 3, 5, 7, 9, etc.) are lucky in Japan. This is one of the special days when the older boys and girls are allowed to wear **traditional**[3] clothes: a kimono for girls and hakama trousers for boys. Now it is quite **normal**[4] for children to wear western-style clothes at this ceremony. The children visit a shrine and are then given special sweets called *Chitose-Ame* by their parents.

[1] a holiday for the whole country
[2] they are important in Japanese culture
[3] in a style that has continued for many years
[4] usual

B -able /əbl/

This suffix forms adjectives from nouns *and* verbs, and the prefix **un-** often forms the opposite:
an **enjoyable** party [something that you enjoyed]
a **comfortable** chair (*opp* **uncomfortable**)
a **suitable** word or phrase [right/correct for a particular situation; *opp* **unsuitable**]
a **reliable** service; reliable information [able to be trusted or believed; *opp* **unreliable**]
fashionable clothes [popular now with many people; *opp* **unfashionable**]
a **reasonable** decision or price [fair; not a bad decision or price; *opp* **unreasonable**]
a **sociable** person [enjoys being with people; *opp* **unsociable**]

Sometimes the opposite form is the more common adjective:
an **unforgettable** experience [something that cannot be forgotten]
an **unbelievable** story [something that is very surprising and very difficult to believe]

C -ful and -less

The suffix **-ful** often means 'full of' or 'having the quality of the noun', e.g. a **colourful** room has a lot of colour in it; a **helpful** person gives a lot of help; a **peaceful** place is calm and quiet. The opposite meaning is sometimes formed by adding the suffix **-less** to the noun.
a **useful** machine [having a lot of uses; *opp* a **useless** machine]
a **painful** injection [giving pain and being unpleasant; *opp* a **painless** injection]
a **careful** driver [drives with care and attention; *opp* a **careless** driver]

Common mistakes

The suffix is **-ful** (NOT ~~full~~), so **useful** and **careful** (NOT ~~usefull~~ or ~~carefull~~).

Exercises

72.1 **Correct the spelling mistakes. Be careful: one word is correct.**

1 enjoiable *enjoyable* ....
2 carful ....
3 relyable ....

4 peacefull ....
5 confortable ....
6 anual ....

7 unforgetable ....
8 reasonable ....
9 unbeleivable ....

72.2 **Match the words on the left with the words on the right.**

1 a national [d]
2 a useful [ ]
3 a painful [ ]
4 fashionable [ ]
5 a careless [ ]
6 an electrical [ ]
7 an unsociable [ ]
8 a reasonable [ ]

a injection
b mistake
c price
d holiday
e man
f bit of advice
g clothes
h fault

72.3 **Write an adjective formed from these nouns or verbs. 11–15 are not on the opposite page, but you can find them in the index if you don't know them.**

1 tradition *traditional* ....
2 attract ....
3 person ....
4 cloud ....
5 colour ....

6 fame ....
7 electricity ....
8 politics ....
9 enjoy ....
10 nation ....

11 wind ....
12 danger ....
13 create ....
14 emotion ....
15 fog ....

72.4 **Tick (✓) the words which form opposites with the suffix *-less*.**

wonderful *No (wonderless)*

careful

useful

painful

beautiful

peaceful

72.5 **Complete the sentences.**

1 You must be very ....*careful*.......... when you drive in wet weather.
2 She told us an .... story about a dog that could speak.
3 The tourist information office was very .... , and told us everything we needed to know.
4 The festival is an .... event, held on the first Monday in September.
5 It was very .... when I hit my leg against the corner of that table.
6 This bag is .... ; it's too small for me to put anything in it.
7 We've never had any problems with our TV in ten years; it's been very ....
8 Most people agreed with it, so I think it was a .... decision.
9 This is just my .... opinion; others may not agree.
10 Travelling round China and the Far East was an .... experience.
11 Children perform .... dances at the ceremony, as they have done for hundreds of years.
12 Do you think this dress is .... for a wedding?

72.6 **Choose three adjectives from the opposite page which could describe these people or things.**

1 a village: *attractive* .... , *famous* .... , *peaceful* ....
2 a jacket: .... , ... , ...
3 an event: .... , ... , ...
4 a person you know: .... , ... , ...
5 an opinion: .... , ... , ...
6 a room: .... , ... , ...

A   Formation

We form compound nouns by putting two words together (or three) to create a new idea. Compound nouns are very common in English.

Ice hockey is a game of hockey played on ice.
Public transport is transport that can be used by the public.
A **campsite** is a **site** for camping. [a place used for a special purpose]
A **babysitter** is someone who looks after young children when their parents go out.
Income tax is money you pay to the government out of your **income** [the total amount of money you receive every year from your work and other places].
Your **mother tongue** is the first language you learn as a child.
A **travel agent** is someone whose job is to make travel arrangements for you.
A **film-maker** is someone who makes films for the cinema or television.
A **full stop** is a punctuation mark at the end of a sentence.
A **haircut** is the act of cutting someone's hair, e.g. *That boy needs a haircut.*

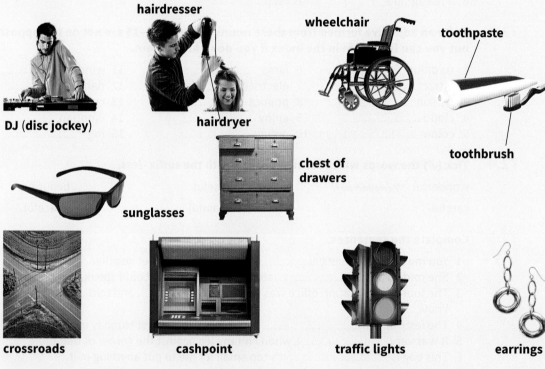

hairdresser

wheelchair

toothpaste

DJ (disc jockey)

hairdryer

toothbrush

chest of drawers

sunglasses

crossroads   **cashpoint**   **traffic lights**   **earrings**

B   One word or two?

Some compound nouns are written as one word, e.g. **wheelchair**; a few are written with a hyphen, e.g. **T-shirt**; many are written as two words, e.g. **credit card**, **bus stop**. Use a dictionary to check if necessary.

C   Pronunciation

The main stress is usually on the first part, e.g. **'haircut** or **'income tax**, but sometimes it is on the second part, e.g. **public 'transport**, **full 'stop**. Use a dictionary to check if necessary.

D   Forming new compounds

One part of a compound often forms the basis for a number of compound nouns.

airport e.g. Heathrow	**bus driver**	**ID card (identity card)**
airline e.g. Lufthansa, KLM	**bus stop**	**credit card**
aircraft e.g. Airbus A380	**bus station**	**birthday card**

Exercises

73.1 Complete the circles with compound nouns from the opposite page.

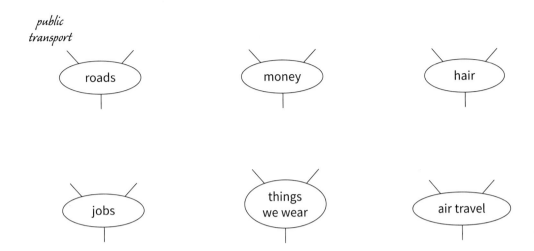

73.2 Complete the sentences.

1 I got some money from the *cashpoint* .
2 I booked our holiday through a ....
3 We stayed on a very nice .... , but unfortunately our tent wasn't really big enough.
4 He can't walk at all now, so he has to use a .... to move around.
5 I sent her a .... but she never received it; it must have got lost in the post.
6 Liz and Mark wanted to go out, but they couldn't find a .... for the children.
7 When I'm driving I always wear .... if it's very bright and sunny.
8 Most people have to pay .... on their salary; the more you earn, the more you pay.
9 I washed my hair, then discovered that the .... wasn't working.

73.3 Which words are being defined?

1 A substance that you use to clean your teeth. *toothpaste*
2 A piece of furniture for keeping clothes in. ....
3 Someone who plays music on the radio or at discos. ....
4 A card with your name, photograph and information to prove who you are. ....
5 The first language you learn as a child. ....
6 A game played on ice using sticks. ....
7 A punctuation mark at the end of a sentence. ....
8 A card you use to pay for things. ....

73.4 Make new compounds using one part of the compounds below. Answers for 1–6 are on the opposite page, answers for 7–12 are in other parts of the book.

1 airport   *airline*
2 full stop   ....
3 hairdresser   ....
4 credit card   ....
5 toothpaste   ....
6 bus driver   ....

7 living room   ....
8 brother-in-law   ....
9 sunglasses   ....
10 traffic lights   ....
11 wheelchair   ....
12 film-maker   ....

A What do we mean by word partners?

If you want to use a word naturally, you often need to know other words that are commonly used with it. These are called word partners or collocations, and they can be different from language to language. For example:

I **spent time** in Paris. (NOT I passed time in Paris.) I **missed the bus**. (NOT I lost the bus.)
We **have** children. (NOT We get children.)

I **made** a mistake. (NOT I did a mistake.)
It was a **serious injury**. (also a **serious illness**)
It's **quite likely** that we'll stay here.
[we'll probably stay here]
It **depends on** my parents. (NOT It depends of my parents. See Unit 77.)

> ### Language help
> More *word partners* can be found in the *Cambridge Learner's Dictionary* for intermediate learners and the *Cambridge Advanced Learner's Dictionary*.

B Verbs and nouns

There are many verbs and nouns that are often used together.

Pavel **told** me a **joke** but I can't remember it. [told me a funny story]
I need to **lose weight**. [become less heavy; *opp* **put on weight**]
The doctor told my father that he should **go on a diet**. [eat less in order to lose weight]
It's very difficult to **predict the future**. [say what will happen in the future]
We won the game 2–1, and my brother **scored** the first **goal**[1].
My neighbour's **alarm went off**[2] in the middle of the night.
They **fell in love** and got married. Now Emily is **expecting a baby**[3].

C Adjectives and nouns

Many adjectives and nouns are often used together. These are all examples where the meaning is 'big' or 'a lot', but where we usually use a particular adjective.

We've got a **large number** of students/tourists this year. (*opp* a **limited/small** number)
I will need a **large amount** of money.
There's a **wide choice** of food available. (*opp* a **limited/narrow** choice)
Sergio has a **wide vocabulary** in English. (*opp* a **limited vocabulary**)
It's only a toy gun but it makes a very **loud noise**.
Her family is of **great importance** to her.
We went to a party last night and it was **great fun** [very enjoyable; we enjoyed it a lot].
There was **heavy traffic** on the motorway going out of town. (*opp* **light** traffic)

D Adverbs and adjectives

The adverbs in the first three sentences mean *very*, the adverbs in the last sentence mean *fully/completely*. In each case, the adverbs and adjectives are common word partners.

I'm **terribly sorry** I'm late.
She's **well aware** of the problem. [She knows all about the problem.]
It's **vitally important** that we get the right person for the job.
Ava is **fast asleep**, but the other two are still **wide awake**.

Exercises

74.1 **Correct the mistakes.**

1 Why does she ~~do~~ so many mistakes? ....*make*....
2 My sister got a baby last month. ....
3 I'm sorry I'm late; I lost the bus. ....
4 There was an accident and Tommy has a grave head injury. ....
5 I don't know if I can come – it depends of the weather. ....
6 We passed three days in Amsterdam. ....
7 I wouldn't like to try and say the future. ....
8 My sister is waiting for a baby next month. ....
9 Axel said me a very funny joke. ....
10 She gave us a big amount of money. ....

74.2 **Complete the text.**

My mum went to see the doctor, and he told her to go on a [1] ....*diet*.... . I think she knows that she needs to [2] .... weight, but she's not happy about giving up chocolate. Anyway, I told her it's [3] .... important that she keeps to the diet, because if she [4] .... any more weight, it's quite [5] .... that she'll end up with a more [6] .... illness. Fortunately, I think she's [7] .... aware of that.

74.3 **Replace *big* or *little* with a more suitable adjective.**

1 You won't need a ~~big~~ amount of money. ....*large*....
2 Why are they making such a *big* noise? ....
3 I've got quite a *big* vocabulary in French. ....
4 There is only a *little* choice of things we can buy. ....
5 We had a very *big* number of tourists this year. ....
6 I think the event had *big* importance for her. ....
7 Isabel only has a *little* vocabulary in English. ....

74.4 **Complete the sentences and dialogues.**

1 A: Why were they late?   B: They got stuck in ....*heavy*.... traffic.
2 When I went into her bedroom, she was .... asleep.
3 A: Did you enjoy last night?   B: Yes, it was .... fun.
4 I met Sasha in town. She told me she's .... a baby in June. Isn't that fantastic news?
5 A: We won 1–0.   B: Who .... the goal?
6 Mathis .... me a joke, but I'm afraid I didn't understand it.
7 A: Are the boys asleep?   B: No, they're still .... awake.
8 My neighbour's burglar alarm .... at 2 o'clock this morning and woke me up.
9 A: Why is she staying in Paris? B: She .... in love with a French guy.
10 I'm .... sorry, but I've lost your book – I'll buy you a new one.

74.5 ███ Over to you ███

Look at the verbs and nouns in section B, and the adjectives and nouns in section C on the opposite page. Are they the same in your language? If possible, compare with someone else who speaks your language.

A What are fixed phrases?

There are many groups of words which you need to learn as complete phrases, because they often have a meaning which is different from the words on their own. Many of these are called idioms.

They arrived **out of the blue** [I didn't know they were coming; it was unexpected].
Does the name Merchant **ring a bell** [sound familiar]?
You'll have to **make up your mind** soon. [make a decision]

Some fixed phrases are easier to understand, but the same idea may be expressed in a different way in your language.

I think we'll have to **get rid of** some of this furniture.
[remove it, e.g. sell it, throw it away, give it away, etc.]
I'm afraid I can't talk to you now; I**'m (just) about to**
leave. [I am going to leave very soon]
I don't know what Martin said, but Natalie **burst into
tears** [suddenly started crying]. She was very upset.
Everyone was there **apart from** Yasmine.
[not including Yasmine; *syn* **except for**]

B Time phrases

He's leaving **in four days' time** [four days from now; also in three weeks'/six months'/two years' time, etc.].
I got here **the week before last** [during the week/month, etc. before the previous one].
The course is fine **so far** [up until now].
I rang our local doctor and fortunately she was able to come **at once** [now, immediately; *syns* **right away / straight away**].
He's so busy at work; he comes home late **night after night** [every night; also **day after day**, etc.].

C Pairs of words

A number of fixed phrases consist of two words, usually joined by **and**, and sometimes **or**.

I go to the theatre **now and again** [occasionally; *syns* **now and then**].
Andy had **one or two** [a few] suggestions.
I've got a house in the country, and I like to go there whenever possible for a bit of **peace and quiet** [a calm situation without noise].
I've been **up and down** the street, but I can't find their house. [first in one direction, then the other]
I've been to Paris **once or twice** [a few times].
I'll finish this report **sooner or later** [I don't know when, but I'll finish it].

D Introducing advice, opinions, etc.

Many fixed phrases are used to introduce advice, an opinion, an example, etc.

If I were you [in your situation], I'd accept the job they offered you.
In general [usually, or in most situations; *syn* **on the whole**] the summers are quite warm in this part of the country.
There were lots of questions. **For instance** [for example], how much will it cost?
I'm sure you'll have a great holiday. **By the way**, what time does the train leave? (used to introduce a new subject to the conversation)
To be honest, I didn't like her boyfriend very much. (used to say what you really think)

Exercises

75.1 **Using all the words in the square, find eight more phrases.**

~~ON~~	DAY	SOONER	~~AND~~	RIGHT
SO	AND	NOW	TWO	LATER
UP	OR	~~OFF~~	PEACE	AFTER
FAR	AND	ONE	AWAY	AGAIN
AND	DAY	QUIET	OR	DOWN

on and off ....

....

....

75.2 **Complete the sentences with one word, then underline the full fixed phrase in each sentence.**

1 She's been working on that essay <u>night after</u> .... *night* ....
2 I'm arranging everything for next week. By the .... , is your sister coming this evening?
3 My parents always turn up at my flat out of the ....
4 Some people enjoyed the book, but to be .... , I thought it was boring.
5 I'd like to get .... of these CDs because I don't listen to them any more.
6 In .... , people are much happier when they have jobs that they enjoy.
7 I don't know what to do at the moment but I'll have to make up my .... soon.
8 It's a flexible ticket. For .... , you can use it during the week or at weekends.
9 Can I ring you later? I'm just .... to have lunch.
10 If I .... you, I'd get a new dictionary.

75.3 **Complete the fixed phrase in each dialogue.**

1 A: Do you go there much?
   B: Now .... *and again* ....

2 A: Have you had any ideas?
   B: Yeah. One ....

3 A: Was she very upset?
   B: Yes. She burst ....

4 A: You arrived ten days ago?
   B: Yeah, the week ....

5 A: Should I accept the job?
   B: Yes, I would if ....

6 A: Will they get here?
   B: Yeah, sooner ....

7 A: Have you been there often?
   B: Once ....

8 A: Do you need me there now?
   B: Yes. Could you come at .... ?

9 A: When are you going back?
   B: In two weeks' ....

10 A: How's the course?
   B: It's good so ....

11 A: I spoke to Chris Myler. Do you know him?
   B: No, the name doesn't ring ....

12 A: Have you done all the housework?
   B: Yes, apart .... the washing.

75.4 **Here are more idioms. Can you underline one in each sentence, and guess what it means?**

1 I've been in the job a few days, but I already <u>feel at home</u>.   *feel comfortable and relaxed* ....
2 I've just bought these shoes and they cost a fortune. ....
3 Could you keep an eye on my bag for me? ....
4 The answer's on the tip of my tongue. ....
5 We had a night on the town last night. ....
6 I could do with a new computer; mine's quite old now. ....

A   Common responses

A large number of fixed phrases are used as common responses in everyday conversation.

A: What time did he get here? — B: **I've no idea**. [I don't know]

A: Are you going tonight? — B: **That depends**. [used to say you are not sure because other things affect your answer; also **It depends**]

A: Shall we go out tonight? — B: Yeah, **why not** [OK]?

A: Did you like the film? — B: **Not really**. [used to say *no* but not strongly]

A: I'm going to Sweden next week. — B: Really. **What for**? [why?]

A: Can I borrow your car? — B: **No way**. [that's impossible; *infml*; *syn* **no chance**]

A: They're coming tonight, aren't they? — B: **I suppose so**. [used to say *yes* but not strongly]

A: Jason has grown a beard. — B: I know. **I couldn't believe my eyes**! [I was very surprised when I saw it]

A: We have to work tonight. — B: **You must be joking**.

A: Eli got top marks. — B: **I don't believe it**! [used to express great surprise]

Language help

We can use **you must be joking** (*syns* **you're joking/kidding**) when someone has just said something that is a surprise. It may be an unpleasant surprise (as above), or a nice surprise, e.g.
A: My father said he would pay for all of us to go on holiday.
B: You're kidding. Fantastic!

B   In conversation

Notice how fixed phrases can form an important part of an everyday conversation.

A: I had to **have a word with** Vince and Milan today. [speak to them without others listening]

B: Oh yeah? Are they causing trouble again?

A: Well, **you know**, [used to fill a pause in conversation] they just keep talking to each other, and they don't **pay attention** [listen] – **that sort of thing**.

B: Why don't you make them sit in different places?

A: I tried that, but they still talked to each other.

B: Well, **in that case** [because of the situation described], you'll have to move one of them.

A: Maybe, but I'd **feel bad about** that [be unhappy about]. They're quite nice boys, you know, they just **can't help it** [can't control some actions or behaviour].

B: Sure … but you can't let **that kind of thing** continue.

A: No, you're right. But I've given them a final warning today, so let's **wait and see** what happens. [wait to discover what will happen]

B: OK. But **what if** they don't improve? [what will you do if they don't improve?]

A: I think it'll be OK.

B: Well, if you **change your mind** [change your decision], come and see me again, and I'll arrange for one of them to be moved to another class.

Language help

We use **sort/kind** in several common phrases in informal speech.
(and) that sort/kind of thing [examples of that type]
e.g. *I grow onions and carrots – that sort/kind of thing*.
sort/kind of [approximately/more or less] e.g. *Her new top is sort of blue; I thought he was kind of strange*.

Exercises

76.1 **Put the responses in the most suitable column below.**

~~no way~~	not really	I suppose so	why not
you're kidding	that depends	I don't believe it	

positive	negative	not sure *or* either
	no way	

76.2 **Choose the correct word. Sometimes both are correct.**

1 I need to have a (word) / speak with Catalina.
2 I don't know what they plan to do; we'll have to wait and *see / watch*.
3 He usually wears jeans, trainers, and that *sort / kind* of thing.
4 Little children shout and scream all the time; they can't *help / leave* it.
5 A: I went to Cambridge last week.   B: Really? *What / Why* for?
6 The trouble with Mark is that he doesn't *pay / give* attention.
7 A: Are you working tonight?   B: *It / That* depends.

76.3 **Complete the dialogues with a suitable fixed phrase.**

1 A: Did you hear that Daniel's getting married?
   B: Yeah. ..*I don't believe it!*..................................
2 A: Sofia doesn't listen.
   B: No. She never ....
3 A: Did you speak to Nathalie?
   B: Yes, I ....
4 A: Dad wasn't happy about forgetting my birthday.
   B: No, he felt ....
5 A: Do you know what time he'll be here?
   B: No, I'm afraid I've ....
6 A: Are you still planning to sell the flat?
   B: No, I've .... I'm going to keep it now.

76.4 **Where could you add the phrases in the box to the dialogues below?**

~~you know~~	I couldn't believe my eyes	kind of	in that case
that sort of thing	you must be joking	why not	

1 A: What did you say to him?
   B: Well, ∨ it was quite difficult. *you know*
2 A: What colour was it?
   B: Blue.
3 A: He's not coming this evening, so you won't be able to ask him.
   B: Well, I'll phone him and ask him.
4 A: Jerry says we'll have to walk all the way to the campsite.
   B: That's ten miles!
5 A: Do you want to get a takeaway?
   B: Yeah.
6 A: What do they sell?
   B: Oh, burgers, pizzas, …
7 A: Did you see Chloe wearing those high-heeled shoes?
   B: Yes.

A   Verb + preposition

Pay special attention to prepositions that are different in your language.

Paul doesn't like the manager's decision and I **agree with** him. [have the same opinion as]
Don't **worry about** your exam. [be nervous about]
His teachers were **satisfied with** his progress. [pleased with]
Many people **spend** a lot of money **on** clothes.
I'**m thinking of** going to China. [it's my plan to go] (used in the continuous form)
This land **belongs to** the company. [it is the company's land]
I **translated** the letter **into** French. [changed from one language into another]
She **complained to** the manager **about** the food. [said she wasn't happy/satisfied with]
I can't **concentrate on** [think about] my work when the radio is playing.
We can **rely on** this photocopier. [trust it; it will not go wrong]
I may go but it **depends on** the weather. [used to say you are not sure about something]

> ### Language help
>
> **Depend (on)** has other meanings:
> *Martha **depends on** her son for money.* [she <u>needs</u> his money]
> *We can **depend on** the others for support.* [we can <u>trust</u> the others to support us]
> Remember: it **depends on** something or someone (NOT it depends ~~of~~ something or someone)

B   Prepositions that change the meaning

She **shouted to** me. [spoke in a loud voice to be heard]   He **shouted at** me. [spoke in a loud voice because he was angry]

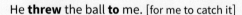

He **threw** the ball **to** me. [for me to catch it]   He **threw** the ball **at** me. [in order to hit me]

C   Adjective + preposition

I've never been very **good at** maths. (*opp* **bad at**)
She's **afraid of** flying. [frightened of]
The neighbours **are fond of** the children. [like]
She's **similar to** her sister [the same as her in some ways], but very **different from** her brother.
He's very **interested in** photography.
I think she'**s aware of** the problem. [knows about]
I'm **tired of** people telling me what to do. [bored or a bit angry about]
Katya **is mad about** Brad Pitt. [likes him very much; *infml*]
We'**re short of** coffee at the moment. [we don't have much]
There's **something wrong with** this TV. [the TV is not working correctly]

Exercises

77.1 **Match the sentence beginnings on the left with the best endings on the right.**

1 He's tired	c	a me, but it missed.
2 She wasn't aware	☐	b to the manager.
3 He threw the pen to	☐	c of working at weekends.
4 She complained	☐	d his friend on the other side of the lake.
5 He shouted at	☐	e me, but I dropped it.
6 He shouted to	☐	f with them.
7 He threw the book at	☐	g us to get out of his garden.
8 I don't agree	☐	h of her mistakes.

77.2 **Complete the questions with the correct preposition, then write an answer for each one.**

1 A: What is she worried ....*about*.......... ? B: *Her exams.*.................................
2 A: What subjects is she good ....? B: ....
3 A: Who does this belong .... ? B: ....
4 A: What does he spend all his money ....? B: ....
5 A: What are you afraid ....? B: ....
6 A: What kind of films are you interested ....? B: ....
7 A: What does the decision depend ....? B: ....
8 A: I know he's angry, but who's he shouting ....? B: ....
9 A: Who can we rely ....? B: ....
10 A: What language is the book being translated ....? B: ....

77.3 **Complete the dialogues.**

1 A: Are you going to the exhibition?
   B: Yes, I'm very .....*interested*. in art.
2 A: Is she .... to her sister?
   B: No, they're completely different.
3 A: What did she .... about?
   B: She wasn't happy with the food.
4 A: Angel is very good-looking.
   B: That's why I'm .... about him!
5 A: What's .... with the radio?
   B: I don't know, but it's not working.

6 A: Did you like the course?
   B: No, I wasn't very satisfied .... it.
7 A: What's the matter?
   B: I can't .... on this with the TV on.
8 A: It's a big problem.
   B: Yes, but we're .... of that.
9 A: We're a bit .... of milk.
   B: OK. I'll buy some when I go out.
10 A: Do Max's children have jobs?
   B: No, they still .... on their parents.

77.4 **Do you know which preposition follows the words below? They are all in this book. If you don't know, use the index to help you. A good dictionary will tell you if a verb or adjective is usually followed by a special preposition.**

keen ....   succeed ....   apply ....
suffer ....   get married ....   apologise ....

77.5
Over to you

Complete the sentences about yourself. If possible, compare your answers with someone else.

1 I'm not very good ....

2 I've always been interested ....

3 I'm not very fond ....

4 I spend most of my money ....

5 For my next holiday, I'm thinking ....

A   *By*, *on* or *in* + noun

I took his pen **by mistake** [I thought it was my pen].
These shoes are made **by hand** [not using a machine].
I met them **by chance** [it wasn't planned; it was luck].

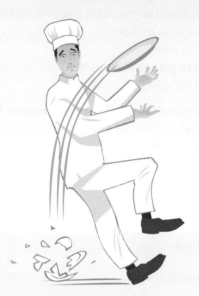

He broke the plate **by accident** [he did not want or plan to do it].

He broke the plate **on purpose** [he wanted to do it; it was his intention].

My boss is **on the phone** at the moment. [using the phone]
The workers are **on strike** [they refuse to work because of a problem over pay, hours, etc.].
The books were **on display** in the window. [in the window for people to look at]
Part of the building was **on fire** [burning].
Most of the passengers are now **on board** [on the train, boat, plane, etc.].
Why are they always **in a hurry** [needing to do something or go somewhere very quickly]?
I explained everything **in detail** [including all the important information].
She won't make that mistake again **in future**.
The poor little girl was **in tears** [crying].

B   Phrases easily confused

Sometimes two prepositions can be used with the same noun, but the meaning is different.

Lessons begin at 8.30 and the students are usually here **on time** [at 8.30].
If we hurry, we'll be there **in time** [before the time we need to be there].

We were tired of waiting, so **in the end** we went home. [finally, after a lot of time or thought]
At the end of the book they get married. [in the last part]

To be successful **in business** it's important to get on well with people. [working as businesspeople]
They're both in Germany **on business** [they are there for work, not a holiday].

I'm afraid this book's a bit **out-of-date** [old and not useful, or not correct in its information].
I try to keep **up-to-date** with all the changes. [knowing all the most recent ideas and information]

I'll see you **in a moment** [not now, but very soon; *syn* **in a minute**].
I can't speak to you **at the moment** [now; *syn* **right now**].

Common mistakes

I'm busy **at the moment**. (NOT I'm busy ~~in this~~ moment.)

Exercises

78.1 **Put the nouns into the correct columns.**

~~board~~   hand   accident   display   detail
fire   future   mistake   tears   strike

on	in	by
board		

78.2 **Choose the correct word to complete the sentences.**

1 I'm afraid I deleted your email *on / in /(by)* accident.
2 Did she hit him *on / by / in* purpose?
3 I just saw them *with / by / on* chance.
4 Most of these files are *out-of- / out-from- / out-for-* date.
5 My wife is away *in / on / by* business at the moment.
6 I'm afraid I'm busy *on / in / at* the moment.
7 I've got to go; I'm *in / on / at* a hurry.
8 I won't go there again *on / in / at* future.

78.3 **Complete the missing noun in these prepositional phrases.**

1 I saw smoke coming out of the window, and I realised the house was on ....*fire*............ .
2 Nobody is at the factory. The workers are all on ....
3 These chocolates are expensive because they are all made by ....
4 I'm just going to the shop but I'll be back in a ....
5 I'm sure she broke that vase on .... ; she never liked it.
6 I'm sorry I can't stop to talk now – I'm in a ....
7 She never thanked me for the present, so I won't buy her another one in ....
8 You can't trust things you read on the Internet; a lot of the information there is out-of- ....
9 I told them everything they wanted to know. I explained it all in ....
10 I went to the exhibition, and some of Katya's paintings were on ....
11 The manager can't speak to you at the .... ; I'm afraid she's on the ....
12 It was a terrible journey but we got there in the ....

78.4 **Replace the underlined word(s) with a prepositional phrase.**

1 The meeting was planned for 11 am and we got there <u>at 11 am</u>. ....*on time*.................
2 Did you get to the cinema <u>before the film started</u>? ....
3 Most of the factory is <u>burning</u>. ....
4 I had great difficulty finding the camera I wanted, so <u>finally</u> I bought one on the Internet.
   ....
5 He gets killed <u>in the last scene</u> of the film. ....
6 I'm afraid I'm very busy <u>right now</u>. ....
7 I saw her yesterday <u>but we didn't plan to meet</u>. ....
8 I'm writing an email, but I'll be with you <u>very soon</u>. ....
9 Most of these books are <u>old and the information is wrong</u>. ....
10 I explained the system <u>with all the important information</u>. ....

A   Formation

A phrasal verb is a verb + adverb *or* preposition, and sometimes a verb + adverb *and* preposition.

He **fell over** [fell to the ground] and hurt his knee.
I'll try to **find out** [learn/discover] the quickest way to get there.
He didn't like his coat, so he **gave** it **away** [gave it to someone for no money].
If you don't understand the meaning, **look** it **up** [find the meaning in a book/dictionary].
Who's going to **sort out** the problem? [deal with it successfully; solve it]
He doesn't **get on with** [have a good relationship with] his parents. (verb + adv. + prep.)

B   Meaning

The adverb or preposition does not always change the meaning of the verb, and is not always used.
I didn't **wake** (**up**) until 7 o'clock.   She's **saving** (**up**) for a new computer.
Hurry (**up**) or we'll be late.   I went to **lie** (**down**) on the bed.

Sometimes an adverb adds a particular meaning to the verb. For example, **back** can mean *return*.
I bought this jacket yesterday, but I'm going to **take** it **back** to the shop; it's too small.
You can look at the books, but remember to **put** them **back** on the shelf.
They liked Greece so much they want to **go back** next year.

Often, the adverb or preposition changes the meaning of the verb: *give up* doesn't mean the same as *give*, and *carry on* doesn't mean the same as *carry*.
My wife has decided to **give up** [stop] smoking.
We'll take a short break and then **carry on** [continue] with the meeting.
The shops are going to **put up** [increase] the price of bread.
When the hotel gets busy, we have to **take on** [employ] more staff.

C   Multiple meanings

Many phrasal verbs have more than one meaning.

go away
I was busy, so I told him to **go away** [leave].
We try to **go away** in August. [go on holiday]

Pick something / someone up
I **picked up** most of the rubbish. [lifted it from the floor]
I'm going to **pick** Jane **up** at the station. [collect someone, usually in a car]

Put something on
Could you **put** the light **on** [make a piece of equipment work by pressing a switch; *syn* **switch sth on**]?
I **put on** my best suit. [put clothes on your body]

Exercises

79.1 **Choose the correct adverb or preposition to complete the sentence.**

		a	b	c
1	I can't see. Could you put the light .... ?	a in	(b on)	c out
2	If he doesn't want it, he can give it	a out	b away	c up
3	Have they sorted it .... ?	a out	b over	c up
4	It was broken, so I had to take it	a over	b on	c back
5	I went to the airport to pick her	a up	b down	c over
6	What time did you wake .... ?	a to	b up	c for
7	I get married next year. I need to start saving	a out	b on	c up
8	Could you switch the TV .... ?	a down	b on	c in

79.2 **Replace the underlined word(s) with a phrasal verb that keeps a similar meaning.**

1 We never <u>discovered</u> what it means.   *found out*
2 I'd like to <u>return</u> next year.   ....
3 We <u>collected</u> Mia from the station.   ....
4 We'll have to <u>increase</u> the price this year.   ....
5 I've decided to <u>stop</u> eating chocolate.   ....
6 Is Hana going to <u>continue</u> with her English course?   ....
7 I told them to <u>leave</u>.   ....
8 I <u>have a good relationship</u> with my parents.   ....
9 We are planning to <u>employ</u> ten new drivers next year.   ....

79.3 **Look at the dictionary entry for *go off* and match the meanings with the sentences below.**

a When the light goes off, the machine has finished. ..*3*..
b My alarm clock went off early this morning. ....
c I think this meat has gone off. ....
d The bomb went off without any warning. ....
e Beatriz went off early; she had to meet a friend. ....

79.4 **Complete the dialogues.**

1 A: Can you afford that bike?
  B: No, I'll have to .....*save up*..... for it.

2 A: Is there still a problem?
  B: Don't worry. I'll .... it ....

3 A: Can we look at some books?
  B: Yes, but .... them .... afterwards.

4 A: Did you feel unwell?
  B: Yes, I had to .... on the bed.

5 A: What's the matter?
  B: I .... and cut my knee.

6 A: I don't know what this means.
  B: Well, ... it .... in a dictionary.

7 A: Does he look smart?
  B: Yes. He's .... his suit.

8 A: .... or we'll be late.
  B: OK, I'm coming.

---

go off

1 Leave
to leave a place and go somewhere else
She's gone off to the cafe with Tony.

2 Food *UK informal*
If food goes off it is not good to eat anymore because it is too old.

3 Stop
If a light or machine goes off, it stops working.
The heating goes off at 10 o'clock.

4 Explode
If a bomb or gun goes off, it explodes or fires.

5 Make noise
If something that makes a noise goes off, it suddenly starts making a noise.
His car alarm goes off every time it rains.

80 Phrasal verbs 2: grammar and style

A Phrasal verbs with no object

Some phrasal verbs don't have an object. We cannot put other words between the parts of the verb.

When does your train **get in** [arrive]?

Hold on [wait a moment], I just need to get my coat.

The car **broke down** on my way to work. [stopped working]

I'll **call for** them at 8 o'clock. [go to collect them]

We **set off** [started the journey] about 7.30.

B Phrasal verbs with an object

Many phrasal verbs need an object. We can usually put the object in different positions.

Put on your shoes.	**Turn on** the TV.	**Take off** your coat.
Put your shoes **on**.	**Turn** the TV **on**.	**Take** your coat **off**.

These are separable phrasal verbs, but if the object is a long phrase, it usually goes at the end, e.g. I **turned off** <u>the lights in the living room</u>. If the object is a pronoun, it must go in the middle, e.g. **Turn** <u>it</u> **off**.

> **Common mistakes**
>
> **Put** them **on**. (NOT Put ~~on them~~.); **Take** it **off**. (NOT Take ~~off it~~.)

There are some phrasal verbs where the object must come after the phrasal verb.

I will **look after** <u>the children</u> for you. [take care of them]

How did the two men **break into** <u>the shop</u>? [enter the shop using force, e.g. breaking a window]

C In dictionaries

Dictionaries usually show the grammar of a phrasal verb like this:

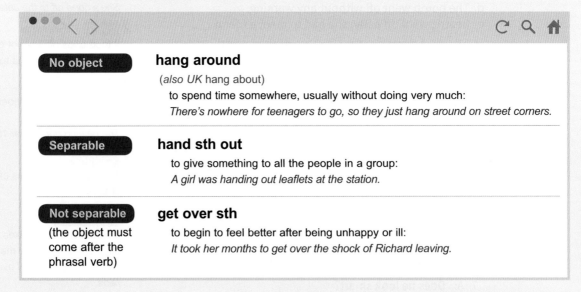

No object

hang around

(*also UK* hang about)

to spend time somewhere, usually without doing very much:
There's nowhere for teenagers to go, so they just hang around on street corners.

Separable

hand sth out

to give something to all the people in a group:
A girl was handing out leaflets at the station.

Not separable

(the object must come after the phrasal verb)

get over sth

to begin to feel better after being unhappy or ill:
It took her months to get over the shock of Richard leaving.

D Style

Phrasal verbs are commonly used in spoken and written English. Many phrasal verbs are quite informal, and sometimes there is a single word with the same meaning as a phrasal verb, which sounds more formal. We use this word instead of the phrasal verb in more formal situations.

leave sb/sth out [not include sb/sth; *syn* **omit**], e.g. He made a list of people but left me out.

make sth up [create sth from your imagination; *syn* **invent**], e.g. We had to make up a story.

put sth off [put sth back to a later date; *syn* **postpone**], e.g. They put the game off till Friday.

turn sth/sb down [refuse an offer or request; *syn* **reject**], e.g. I offered her a job but she turned it down.

Exercises

80.1 Correct any mistakes with word order in the sentences. Be careful: some are correct.

1 She asked me to hand ~~out them~~. *hand them out*
2 I've got some boots but I'll put on them later.
3 Could you turn the light on?
4 My boots were tight and I couldn't take off them.
5 We set off very early this morning.
6 Why did they turn down it?
7 The boys were hanging the station around.

80.2 Replace the underlined word with a phrasal verb that makes the sentence more informal.

1 Could you <u>wait</u> a minute, please? ....*hold on*.................
2 As so many people are ill, I've had to <u>postpone</u> the meeting till next week. ....
3 The teacher told us to <u>invent</u> a story to go with the picture in our books. ....
4 They <u>omitted</u> a number of the names from my list. ....
5 I don't know why he <u>rejected</u> my offer of help. ....
6 The train should <u>arrive</u> by ten o'clock. ....

80.3 Write a sentence to describe what is happening or what has happened in the pictures.

1 *He's putting on his jacket.*   3 ....   5 ....

2 ....   4 ....   6 ....

80.4 Complete the phrasal verbs.

1 I'm not stopping, so I won't take ....*off*............... my coat.
2 We didn't think Mike was good enough, so we left him ....
3 He told me he was 25, but I don't believe him. I think he's making that ....
4 We'll get there by seven if we set .... now.
5 I'll call .... you a bit later. I should be at your house by 7 o'clock.
6 They offered him the job but he turned it ....

80.5 Complete these sentences in a suitable way.

1 It was cold so I put on ...*my gloves/coat/scarf.*...............
2 Inma is still getting over ....
3 I'm not very good at making up ....
4 She asked me to turn on ....
5 Two men tried to break into ....
6 She's going out, so I said I'd look after ....

A Things we *make*, *do* and *take*

> **Common mistakes**
>
> We use all three of these common verbs with particular nouns. These word partners (collocations) are often different in other languages, so look at them carefully.

I've **made** a **mistake**.
She **took** a **photo** of me this morning.
They **made** a big **effort** to finish the work.

I'm afraid I haven't **done** my **homework**.
I haven't **done** the **housework** yet.
The children are **making** too much **noise**.

Sometimes two different verbs are possible.
I'm just going to **take/have** a **shower**.
Take/Have a look at these pictures.
We must **make/take** a **decision**.

I'm **doing/taking** a Spanish **course** next month.
I don't **do/take** much **exercise**.

B *Make*

Make can mean 'to cause something to happen or cause a particular state'.
  I like Boris – he **makes me** laugh.
  It **made them** angry when Karen refused to help with the washing-up.
Make can also mean 'to force someone to do something'.
  My parents **made me** do my homework when I was a child.
  The police **made us** wait outside the main gates.

If you **make friends with** someone, you get to know them and like them.
  I **made friends with** a couple of guys from Canada when I was on holiday.
If you **make up your mind**, you decide something.
  He's **made up his mind** to leave work at the end of next month.

C *Do*

We use **do** to describe a general action when we don't know what it is, or there's no noun.
  What shall we **do** this afternoon?
  Don't just stand there, **do** something.

If you **do your hair** / **make-up**, you make it look nice.
  I'll just **do my hair**, then we can go out.

If you **do your best**, you try as hard as possible.
  I'm not a good student, but I always **do my best**.

D *Take*

Take can mean to:
- remove something from a place/person, e.g. I **took** the key **out of** my pocket.
- remove something without permission, e.g. Someone has **taken** my pen.
- accept something, e.g. Did he **take** the job they offered him? Do they **take** credit cards there?
- write something down, e.g. I **took** notes during the meeting. The man **took** my name and address.
- wear a particular size in clothes, e.g. I **take** size 43 shoes.

If you **take it** / **things easy**, you relax and don't do very much.
  I'll **take things easy** today.

If you **take a break**, you stop work and rest for a short period.
  Let's **take a** ten-minute **break**.

Exercises

81.1 **Choose the correct verb(s). Sometimes both are correct.**

1 Did he *do* / *make* many mistakes?
2 I couldn't *do* / *make* the homework.
3 We must *take* / *make* a decision soon.
4 I want to *do* / *make* a course in English.
5 Could you *take* / *have* a look at this letter?
6 How many photos did they *make* / *take*?
7 I don't often *make* / *do* the housework.
8 They *did* / *made* a lot of noise at the party.

81.2 **What are the people doing in the pictures?**

1 *She's taking a photo.* 3 .... 5 ....

2 .... 4 .... 6 ....

81.3 **Replace the underlined word or phrase with a phrase including the verb in capitals. Keep a similar meaning.**

1 I clean the flat at the weekend. DO   *I do the housework at the weekend.*
2 They forced us to go. MAKE   ....
3 I'm trying as hard as possible. DO   ....
4 OK, let's stop work and relax for a bit. TAKE ....
5 He is definitely trying. MAKE   ....
6 When are they going to decide? MAKE   ....
7 I'm going to relax and do nothing this weekend. TAKE ....

81.4 **Complete the sentences.**

1 Someone *took* my coat. It was here a minute ago and now it's gone.
2 I'm tired of writing this report. I'm going to .... a break for ten minutes.
3 We .... friends with Andrés when we were in the same class last year.
4 I've .... nothing today.
5 If they offered him a job with more money, why didn't he .... it?
6 Could you take a .... at my essay? I think there are lots of mistakes in it.
7 When he shouted out the wrong answer, it .... him look stupid.
8 What size do you .... ?
9 I'm putting on weight because I don't .... enough exercise.
10 I've .... up my mind. I'm going to go to Thailand for my holiday.

81.5

Answer the questions. If possible, ask someone else the same questions.

1 What things make you happy, make you sad, and make you angry?
2 What things do your parents, or your boss, or your teachers make you do (or made you do in the past)?

A Give

We can use **give** when someone or something causes a certain effect.

All that noise has **given me a headache**.
The walk this morning **gave me an appetite** [made me hungry].
Listening to Wai Sin has **given me an idea**.

We often use **give** with different nouns to express an action.

He **gave** me some **advice** [advised me].
Valentina **gave** us a **shock** when she shouted like that. [shocked us]
I had to **give** a **speech** at the wedding. [talk formally to a group of people; also **give a lecture**]
I'll **give** her a **ring** [ring/phone her].
I had lots of work to do, but fortunately Ollie **gave** me **a hand** [helped me].

She **gave** me a **hug**.

He **gave** the car a **push**.

B Keep

Keep can mean to stay or cause someone to stay in a particular state or condition.

Keep right [stay on the right side].   She asked us to **keep quiet**.
This coat will **keep you warm**.   Going to the gym **keeps me fit**.

Keep (on) doing something means to repeat doing something, and often it is something you don't want to do or happen.

I **keep losing** my glasses.   I **keep getting** backache.
She **keeps on interrupting** me. [talks to me / disturbs me when I am doing something]

If you **keep in touch**, you continue to communicate with someone, especially by phone or email.
I met Mara on holiday and we've **kept in touch** ever since.
If you **keep a secret**, you don't tell other people something that you know.
Tom told me not to tell anyone about his new job, but I'm not very good at **keeping a secret**.
If you **keep something up**, you continue doing something at a high level.
You're working hard and your English is improving. That's good – **keep it up**.

C Miss

If you **miss** a person, you feel sad because that person is not there.
When I went to work in Hungary, I really **missed my girlfriend**.
If you **miss** what someone says, you don't hear it.
I'm sorry, I **missed that**. What did you say?
If you **miss a chance** / **opportunity**, you don't use an opportunity to do something.
Lily's been chosen for the team, but now she's injured, she might **miss her chance** to play.
If you **miss** something, you manage to avoid it or not experience it.
I left home early in order to **miss the rush hour**.

Exercises

82.1 **Match each verb with three phrases on the right.**

give   *a speech* ....   in touch
        ....   ~~a speech~~
        ....   an opportunity
                                                         on doing something
miss   ....   someone a hug
        ....   a person
        ....   someone a hand
keep   ....   what someone says
        ....   a secret
        ....

82.2 **Complete the sentences with a suitable adjective or -ing form.**

1 I never drink coffee at night; it keeps me ...*awake*............. .
2 This umbrella should keep you ....
3 I don't know why she keeps .... – it wasn't a very funny story.
4 If you do lots of exercise, it'll keep you ....
5 It's really stupid, but I keep .... to lock the doors and windows when I go out.
6 They're making a lot of noise in there. Could you tell them to keep .... ?
7 I know his name is Stuart, but I keep .... it's Stephen.
8 I keep .... up early in the morning because it's so light in my bedroom.

82.3 **Complete the dialogues using a verb + noun. Don't repeat the underlined phrases.**

1 A: He's <u>sad without Harper</u>.
    B: I know. He ...*misses her*............. .
2 A: Did you <u>phone</u> her?
    B: Yes, I .... her a .... last night.
3 A: He didn't <u>put his arms round her</u>, did he?
    B: Yes. He .... her a big ....
4 A: Have you <u>stayed in contact</u> with your old school friends all this time?
    B: Yes, I've tried to .... in .... as much as possible.
5 A: Could anyone <u>help me</u> with this?
    B: Yeah, I'll .... you a ....
6 A: It's his own fault. He <u>had a chance to go and he didn't take it</u>.
    B: I know. He .... his ....
7 A: I expect <u>you're hungry</u> after all that work.
    B: Yes, it's .... me an ....

82.4 **Complete the sentences with the correct verb and a word from the box.**

| ~~shock~~ | fun | headaches | secret | push | up | dog | idea | rush hour |

1 She *gave*............... me a *shock*............... when she broke that window.
2 If we leave the party early, we'll .... all the ....
3 The guys are working really hard, but I don't know if they can ....
   it ....
4 I couldn't get the car started, but fortunately someone .... me a ....
5 We left before seven because we wanted to .... the ....
6 She doesn't know what the problem is, but she .... getting ....
7 I saw a fascinating programme on TV, and that's what .... me the ....
8 When I go on holiday alone, I really .... my ....
9 I didn't say anything to Annie about the wedding because she can't .... a
   ....

83 *Get*: uses, phrases and phrasal verbs

A Uses

Get is an informal word and is very common in spoken English. It can have many different meanings.

OBTAIN	I **got** a ticket from my brother.	I need to **get** some help.
RECEIVE	I **got** a new phone for my birthday.	Did you **get** my email?
BUY	Where did you **get** that watch?	I went to **get** a magazine.
ARRIVE	What time did you **get** here?	I'll phone when I **get** home.
BECOME	It **gets** dark very early in winter.	My hands are **getting** cold.
FETCH	Could you (**go and**) **get** my glasses from the kitchen for me?	
ANSWER the door/phone	A: Is that the door?	B: Yes, I'll **get** it.

I need to get my hair cut.

DO a task, or arrange for someone to do it for you, using get + past participle

I'll never **get** this essay <u>finished</u>; it's too difficult.
I need to **get** my hair <u>cut</u>.
I **got** my watch <u>repaired</u> today.

B Phrases

You can **get in touch with** me via email. [make contact by email, phone or letter]
A bedtime story helps children **get to sleep** [start sleeping].
The salsa classes are a chance for us to **get together** [meet and spend time together].
I'm sorry I **got** the number **wrong** [said or wrote something that was not correct].
My cold is **getting worse** [becoming more unpleasant; *opp* **getting better**].
I'd like to **get rid of** my old CDs. [throw them away, give them away, or sell them]
I **got to know** lots of Americans when I stayed in San Francisco. [met and became friends with]

C Phrasal verbs

He stopped the car and I **got out** [left the car; also leave a building].
I gave her £25, but I'll **get** it **back** tomorrow. [have it returned to me]
The door was locked so we couldn't **get in** [enter a place, especially when it is difficult].
Our train should **get in** around midnight. [arrive]
What time did you **get up** this morning? [get out of bed]

172   *English Vocabulary in Use Pre-intermediate and Intermediate*

Exercises

83.1 **Write a synonym for *get* in each of these sentences.**

1 I usually get about five emails a day. *receive*.................
2 Where can I get something to eat round here? ....
3 I'm just going to get some paper from the office. I'll be back in a minute. ....
4 What time did they get here last night? ....
5 He got very angry when I told him what you did with his CDs. ....
6 I couldn't get a room; all the hotels were full. ....
7 The phone's ringing. Could you get it for me? ....
8 Molly sent me a card but I never got it. ....

83.2 **Complete the dialogues using *getting* + a suitable adjective. Add other words if necessary.**

1 A: It's .*getting cold in here*............ .
   B: Yes, it is. I'll turn on the heating.
2 A: I'm ....
   B: Me too. Let's have something to eat.
3 A: I'm ....
   B: Yes, me too. I'll open the window.
4 A: It's ....
   B: Yes, it is. I'll put the lights on.
5 A: It's ....
   B: Yes, it is. I think I'll go to bed.
6 A: My English is ....
   B: No, it isn't – it's much better now.

83.3 **Rewrite the sentences using a phrase or phrasal verb with *get*. Keep a similar meaning.**

1 Will the books be returned to you?
   Will you .*get the books back?*...........
2 We must meet up and have a meal.
   We must ....
3 How do you meet people and make friends in this country?
   How do you ....
4 I must contact the travel company.
   I must ....
5 I'd like to throw away these old magazines.
   I'd like to ....
6 The train won't arrive before 10 o'clock.
   The train won't ....
7 The doors were locked; we couldn't leave.
   The doors were locked; we couldn't ....
8 I was awake for hours last night.
   I couldn't ....

83.4 **Continue these statements in a suitable way.**

1 The window is broken. We .*need to get it repaired*..........
2 My hair is getting long. I ....
3 This essay is taking me hours. I ....
4 My watch isn't working. I ....
5 Lola has still got my CDs. I ....

83.5 **Write down examples of *get* that you see or hear, and try to group your sentences according to the different meanings. This will help you to understand how this important word is used in English.**

A Different meanings of *go*

- When we leave a place in order to do an activity, especially for enjoyment, we often express it with **go** + **-ing** or **go** (**out**) **for a** + noun.
  We could **go shopping** / **sightseeing** / **swimming** / **clubbing** [to a nightclub] tomorrow.
  Why don't we **go** (**out**) **for a walk** / **drive** / **drink** / **meal** / **picnic** at lunchtime?

- **Go** can also describe a changing state (usually to a bad one) with certain adjectives.
  My dad's **going grey** [his hair is becoming grey] and my uncle is **going bald** [losing his hair].
  My grandmother is **going deaf** [deaf = cannot hear].
  Our 12-year-old dog is **going blind** [blind = cannot see].
  He'll **go mad** if you wear his jacket. [become very angry; *infml*]

going bald

- We use **go** when we want to ask/say if a road or form of transport takes you somewhere.
  Does this bus **go** to the National Gallery?
  I think this road **goes** through the village.

- **Go** can also mean 'disappear'.
  When I looked in the drawer, my watch **had gone** [it was there before, but not now].

- **Go and get** means **fetch** [go to a place and bring something back with you].
  You stay here, and I'll **go and get** the bags from the car.

B Phrasal verbs and expressions

A: What's **going on** in here? [happening]

B: I don't know. I touched this switch and the lights **went out** [stopped working].

A: Shall we wait for George or **go on to** the theatre? [continue or move to another place/thing]

B: Er, I'm not sure of the way; let's wait for George.

A: How's the business?

B: Well, it was **going well** [successful; *opp* **going badly**] up until the summer, but since then a few things have **gone wrong** [there have been problems], and we've lost a few customers.

A: Are you **going away** this year? [going on holiday]

B: Yes. We had a lovely time in Italy last year, so we've decided to **go back** in June. [return]

A: I think I'll have the chicken. How about you?

A: **How's it going**? [How are you? *infml*]

B: I'm **going for** the roast beef. [choosing]

B: Not bad. And you?

Exercises

84.1 **Complete the sentences with an *-ing* noun, e.g. riding, or *(out) for a* + noun, e.g. (out) for a walk.**

1 I went *shopping* .... this morning and bought some new clothes.
2 It was a lovely day, so we made some sandwiches and decided to go ....
3 Why don't we go .... in that nice new café near the square?
4 I wanted to go .... because it was my first time in Rome.
5 My brother has just got a new sports car. We could go .... at the weekend.
6 The pool is at the end of the road, so we often go ....
7 I'm just going to take the dog ....
8 We went .... last night and didn't get home until three this morning.
9 It was my father's birthday, so we decided to go ....

84.2 **Replace the underlined words with a different word or phrase. Keep a similar meaning.**

1 He <u>went mad</u> when he saw me. *got angry* ....
2 Hi Sue. How<u>'s it going</u>? ....
3 Could you <u>go and get</u> my handbag from the other room? ....
4 Do you want to <u>go on</u> and do the next exercise? ....
5 What's <u>going on</u> in the next classroom? ....
6 When I got back, the others had <u>gone</u>. ....
7 I can't stay for the weekend; I have to <u>go back</u> on Friday. ....
8 Excuse me. Does this road <u>go</u> to the bus station? ....
9 My girlfriend had fish but I <u>went for</u> the chicken dish. ....

84.3 **Complete the dialogues with a phrasal verb or expression using *go*.**

1 A: I hear you had problems with your exam?
   B: Yes, everything *went wrong* .... I couldn't answer any of the questions.

2 A: Can't he see very well?
   B: No, I'm afraid he's ....

3 A: Your uncle's just opened a new restaurant, hasn't he? How's it doing?
   B: Great. It's ....

4 A: I imagine your parents were angry that you had a party when they were away.
   B: They were. My dad ....

5 A: Simon isn't losing his hair already, is he?
   B: Yes, I'm afraid he's ....

6 A: Are the books downstairs in the staffroom?
   B: Yes. Could you .... them for me?
   A: Yeah, sure.

7 A: Are you having a holiday this year?
   B: Yes, we're hoping to .... in the summer.

8 A: What have you done?!
   B: I don't know. The lights just ....

84.4
Over to you

Answer the questions. If possible, ask someone else the same questions.

Do you often go swimming in the summer?   Do you often go for a walk on your own?
Do you go clubbing most weekends?   Do you like going out for a meal?
Do you often go shopping with a friend?   Do you often go sightseeing on holiday?
Did you often go for picnics as a child?   Do you enjoy going out for a drive in the country?

85 The senses

A The five basic senses

sight   **hearing**   **taste**   **smell**   **touch**

To express it another way, the ability to see, hear, taste, smell and feel.

B Sense verbs with adjectives

You **look** tired this evening. [from what I can see]
That man **sounded foreign**. [from another country, from what I could hear]
This cake **tastes** a bit strange.
Fresh bread **smells** wonderful.
This shirt **feels damp**. [slightly wet, often
in an unpleasant way]

> ### Language help
> The verbs above can all be used as nouns.
> *I like* **the look of** *this hotel.* [the appearance of it]
> *I love* **the sound of** *his voice.*

C Sense verbs with *like* or *as if/though*

We can describe things using sense verbs with **like** + noun or **as if / though** + clause, but *not*
like + adjective (NOT She looks ~~like~~ nice). When we use **like** + noun, we are often describing
how similar two things are.

Have you ever had a nectarine? They **look
like** peaches.
Did you hear that noise? It **sounded like** an alarm.
That shampoo **smells like** coconut. (also **smells
of** coconut)
Don't you think this material **feels like** silk?

nectarine   **alarm**

That boy **looks as if** he's trying to get over
the wall.
I spoke to Isobel. It **sounded as though** they had
a good time on holiday.

coconut   **silk**

> ### Language help
> We also use **seem** and **appear** to describe a sense or feeling about someone or something, after
> we have seen them, talked to them, etc. Before **like** + noun, we usually use **seem**.
> *I saw Will and he* **seemed/appeared** *quite happy.*   *The shop* **appears/seems** *to be very busy.*
> *Amelia said she wanted to travel a bit, which* **seems like** *a good idea.*

D Verbs easily confused

If you **look** [look carefully] at the map, you can **see** [are able to see] the church on the left.
They've been **watching** that man for weeks. [paying attention to something, often for a
long time]
He ran into me because he wasn't **looking** [paying attention].
I **watched/saw** a film on TV. I **saw** a film at the cinema. (NOT I ~~watched~~ a film at
the cinema.)
I **heard** [was able to hear] what she said but I wasn't **listening** [paying attention].
Don't **touch** the oven [put your hand on it]. It's hot!
Just **feel** my feet [put your hand on them to discover something about them]. Aren't they cold?

Exercises

85.1 **Cover the opposite page. What are the five basic senses?**

sight ....

85.2 **Choose the correct word to complete the sentences.**

1 I was very angry with Tom – he just wasn't *hearing* /(*listening to*)what I was saying.
2 I was *listening to / hearing* the radio when I *listened to / heard* a terrible noise outside.
3 She turned up the volume but I still couldn't *listen to / hear* it.
4 There's a good film on at the cinema. Have you *watched / seen* it?
5 Quick. Come and *watch / look at* this man walking by.
6 We *watched / looked at* the birds while they were eating food from the bird table.
7 If you stand near the fire, you can *touch / feel* how hot it is.
8 You mustn't *touch / feel* the paintings in the museum.
9 If you *see / look* carefully, you can *look / see* how the man does the magic trick.
10 Anya wants to get a parrot, which *seems / appears* like a strange thing to do.

85.3 **Complete the sentences with a different sense verb and a word from the box. Add *like* where necessary.**

| ~~delicious~~ a church an alarm very nice |
| damp coconut calm and relaxed silk |

1 Abigail has just taken the cakes out of the oven and they *smell delicious* ....
2 The sheets on her bed looked expensive, and when I touched them, they
....
3 I could see something quite tall in the distance. It ....
4 When I heard the noise I jumped out of bed because it ....
5 Have you tried these biscuits? They ....
6 I've just met my new class; they ....
7 I don't want to sit on the grass. It ....
8 I saw her before the exam and she ....

85.4 **Complete the middle part of the sentences.**

1 Alexei said that Lola was doing well, so it ...*sounds as if/though*.............................. she'll pass the exam.
2 Erin told me about the accident. It .... it was quite serious.
3 Put your hand on the radiator. Does it .... it's getting warm?
4 I've just spoken to Tom. He .... he's got a cold.
5 Have you tried the soup? It .... it needs a bit more salt to me.
6 Is that your little boy on the floor? It .... he's fallen over.
7 Alina didn't ask any questions. It .... she wasn't interested.

85.5 **Over to you**

Complete the sentences about your own likes and dislikes. If possible, ask someone else the same questions.

I love the smell of ....
I hate the smell of ....
I love the sound of ....
I hate the sound of ....
I love the taste of ....
I hate the taste of ....

A   Common uncountable nouns

One of the problems with uncountable nouns is that many of them are countable in other languages.

Common mistakes

I need information. (NOT I need ~~an~~ information.) (no indefinite article)
I need some information. (NOT I need ~~informations~~.) (no plural form)
The homework was difficult. (NOT The homework ~~were~~ difficult.) (use with a singular verb)

- You can put all that **rubbish** in the bin over there. [things that you throw away because you do not want them]
- Is there any more **news** about the man who was injured?
- She gave me some good **advice** about buying a car. [what you think someone should do]
- Do the children get **pocket money** [money that parents give regularly to their children]?
- You need a lot of **equipment** for camping, e.g. tent, sleeping bag, torch, things for cooking, etc. [the things that are used for a particular activity]
- We sold the **furniture** [tables, chairs, armchairs, etc.].
- The **scenery** is really beautiful. [the natural beauty you see around you]
- My **knowledge of** Russian is limited. [what I know about it]
- She's worked very hard and I believe she is **making progress** [improving / getting better].
- Can you take the dog? We haven't got any **room** in our car. [empty space]
- Would anyone like some more **toast**?
- The children's **behaviour** was terrible: they were climbing all over the furniture and making a lot of noise. [the way you do and say things]

bin

tent

sleeping bag

torch

toast

B   Uncountable nouns in dictionaries

Dictionaries show countable nouns with a (C) and uncountable nouns with a (U). Some nouns can be countable with one meaning, and uncountable with another.

experience (U) [the knowledge you get from doing a particular job or activity]
She's got a lot of **experience of** working with children.
experience (C) [something that happens to you that affects the way you feel]
I had so many fantastic **experiences** on my trip to Thailand and Japan.

chance (U) [luck]
Lotto is a game of **chance**.
chance (C) [the opportunity to do something]
He's had several **chances** to go abroad, but he's just not interested.

C   Making uncountable nouns countable

You can make some uncountable nouns singular. Sometimes we do this with a word like **piece** (for advice, equipment, toast, furniture, news), but in spoken English we often use **a bit** (*infml*) with most uncountable nouns.

a good **piece of** advice   an interesting **bit of** news
another piece of toast   just **a bit of** rubbish

Exercises

86.1 **Correct the mistakes.**

1 I need some ~~informations~~. *information* ....
2 Our teacher has a news about the trip. ....
3 She gave me some good advices. ....
4 Her progress are very good. ....
5 We had a lot of homeworks yesterday. ....
6 The furnitures were very old. ....
7 I have no experiences of using these equipments. ....
8 I need to improve my knowledges of this new technology. ....

86.2 **Make the uncountable nouns countable.**

1 I did some homework.   I did *a bit of homework.* ....
2 It's useful equipment.   It's ....
3 It was good advice.   It was ....
4 Do you want some more toast?   Do you want ....
5 She's making progress.   She's making ....
6 There's some rubbish on the floor.   There's ....
7 I gave them some pocket money.   I gave them ....
8 I heard some news this morning.   I heard ....

86.3 **Complete the dialogues.**

1 A: Have you been given all the details?
    B: No, I need more *information* ....
2 A: She hasn't worked there long enough.
    B: No, she needs more ....
3 A: Is your flat big enough?
    B: No, we need more ....
4 A: Does she know what to do when she leaves school?
    B: No, she needs some ....
5 A: Don't you think the room looks empty?
    B: Yes, we need more ....
6 A: Is his English getting better?
    B: No, he isn't making any ....

86.4 **Complete the sentences. The first letter has been given to help you.**

1 I asked my teacher for some a*dvice* .... about grammar books.
2 I've had some great e........................ when I've travelled on my own.
3 If we give him another c........................ , I'm sure he'll be able to do it.
4 That stuff over there is r........................ ; just throw it in the bin.
5 We camped on the hill above the lake because the s........................ is so beautiful.
6 I don't know what's wrong with Celia, but her b........................ was very strange this morning.
7 Do you have any e........................ of working with computers?
8 I don't have any k........................ of this subject; you'd better ask Fariah.

86.5 **Use a dictionary to find out if these nouns are countable or uncountable. Keep a record of them in your notebook.**

transport   luggage   suitcase   pasta   traffic   accident

A Verb + -ing form

A number of verbs are commonly followed by an -ing form.

QUESTIONNAIRE

QUESTIONS	ANSWERS
• Do you **enjoy** studying?	Yes, I do.
• Do you **mind** getting up early? [Is it OK for you, or not?]	No, I don't mind at all.
• Do you **like** or **dislike** having your photograph taken?	I **hate** having my picture taken.
• Do you usually **avoid** speaking to strangers at parties? [try not to do something]	Yes. I prefer to talk to people that I already know.
• Can you **imagine** being without a car? [think of yourself in a situation with no car]	No, I can't. I need my car.
• Have you ever **considered** [thought about] living in another country?	Yes, many times. I'd like to live abroad.
• Would you **recommend** [advise] having a holiday in the capital city of your country? If so, would you **suggest** going at a particular time of the year?	Yes, I would, and I would suggest going in spring or autumn.

Common mistakes

I enjoy going there. (NOT I enjoy to go there.) They suggested leaving early. (NOT They suggested to leave early.) He recommended staying there. (NOT He recommended to stay there.)

B Verb + to infinitive

I **hope** to see them next week. [want to see them and believe I will see them]
They **agreed** to help me. [said they will help]
I **intend** to leave next month. [plan]
I **offered** to help them. [said I was happy to help]
I **attempted** to cook the dinner, but it was terrible. [tried]
I **promised** to bring her book back. [said I would definitely bring it back]
The shop assistant was very rude, so I **demanded** to see the manager. [said in a firm way]

C Verb + (object) + preposition + noun/-ing

A: Jo has just rung and **asked** me **for** advice about Greece. They're **thinking of**[1] going there.

B: Well, be careful. They went to India last year on your advice and then **blamed**[2] you **for** the terrible holiday they had.

A: That was their fault. They **insisted on**[3] going in the summer when it was far too hot.

[1] thinking about going to Greece (often used in the continuous and followed by a noun/-ing form; NOT I'm thinking to go there.)
[2] said you were responsible for something bad, in this case the terrible holiday
[3] said they must go (in the summer)

Exercises

87.1 **Choose the correct word(s) to complete the sentences.**

1 I hope *seeing / (to see)* them.
2 They agreed *helping / to help* me.
3 We enjoy *staying / to stay* by the sea.
4 I suggested *going / to go* on the train.
5 She insisted *in / on* paying for our meal.
6 We must attempt *getting / to get* there on time.
7 Have you considered *working / to work* in a bank?
8 I demanded *speaking / to speak* to the doctor in charge.
9 I asked *him help / him for help*.
10 They blamed me *for / of* it.
11 I don't mind *waiting / to wait* for you.
12 I try to avoid *travelling / to travel* in the rush hour.

87.2 **Complete the sentences with the most suitable verb.**

1 Have you ...*asked*........... the waiter for the bill?
2 My sister is .... of spending the summer in France if she can afford it.
3 I've had a computer for about 20 years; I can't .... being without one.
4 We always try to .... driving into town in the rush hour.
5 The accident wasn't my fault but they .... me for it.
6 We're .... to see my parents later this week. We had .... to go last week, but Madison was ill and we couldn't go.
7 I .... meeting your friends; they were really nice.
8 Have you ever .... moving out of a town and going to live in the country?
9 I offered to drive, but Mason .... on taking his car because he said he .... being a passenger.
10 Ella's parents weren't happy with the school, and they .... to see the head teacher.

87.3 **When you learn new verbs, you may need to know the constructions that are used with them. A good dictionary will give you this information, usually with examples. Using a good English dictionary, find the constructions that commonly follow these verbs.**

> *FORMAL*
>   *Might I suggest a white wine with your salmon, sir?*
> **[+ (that)]**
>   *I suggest* **(that)** *we wait a while before we make any firm decisions.*
>   *Liz suggested* **(that)** *I try the shop on Mill Road.*
> **[+ -ing** VERB]
>   *I suggested put**ting** the matter to the committee.*

fancy + ...   pretend + ... or ....

decide + ... or ....   accuse + ...

87.4   `Over to you`

Answer the questions in the questionnaire on the opposite page. If possible, ask someone else the same questions. Then complete the sentences about yourself using the correct construction after each verb.

I like ....
I dislike ....
I don't mind ....
I'm thinking ....
I can't imagine ....
I hope ....
I intend ....

A   A great opportunity

"I'm 24 years old, and I work in a photography studio. It's not a very exciting job but I love photography and the pay isn't bad. But, two months ago, I was given the chance to go to Italy and work on a film by a famous director. My best friend thought that it was a fantastic opportunity and **advised**[1] **me to go**. Dad wasn't so sure. He didn't try and **persuade**[2] **me** not **to go**, but he **warned**[3] **me that** it would be hard work, and **reminded**[4] **me that** it was only three months, then I'd be out of a job. I **realised**[5] **that** my girlfriend wasn't happy about it either, but I **promised**[6] **her that** I would phone every day, and **suggested**[7] **that** she could come out to Italy for a holiday while I was there. I didn't **mention**[8] **that** I was part of a small team with three other women. Anyway, I'm going."

[1] say what you think someone should do   advise + obj + inf
[2] make someone agree to do something by talking a lot   persuade + obj + inf
[3] tell someone that something bad may happen, to stop it happening   warn + obj + (that) …
[4] tell someone something so that they don't forget it   remind + obj + (that) …
[5] understand something (that) you didn't understand before   realise + (that) …
[6] say (that) you will certainly do something   promise + (obj) + (that) …
[7] tell someone about a possible idea or plan   suggest + (that) …
[8] say something, often briefly or quickly   mention + (that) …

> ### Language help
>
> Some verbs can be followed by different constructions. We can also say, for example:
>
> | | |
> |---|---|
> | *I suggested going there.* | suggest + -ing |
> | *She warned me not to go.* | warn + obj + inf |
> | *He reminded me to post the letter.* | remind + obj + inf |

B   Other verbs

Here are some more verbs which are used with the same constructions.

Verb + (*that*) …: *say, hope, notice, recommend* and *expect.*
I **said** that I was busy. (NOT I said ~~him~~ that I was busy.)
I **hope** (that) you'll come and see us soon.
When I left, I **noticed** that the door was open. [could see]
I **recommended** that we all go together, so no one gets lost.
I **expect** (that) he'll ring us later. [think or believe that something will happen]

Verb + object + (*that*) …: *tell, show* and *convince.*
I **told** them (that) they could leave early.
He tried to **convince me** that I needed some new clothes. [make me believe]

Verb + object + *to* infinitive: *ask, tell, want, allow, expect, remind, help* and *encourage.*
Tracey **asked** me to look after her cat.
They **told** us to wait outside.
They **want** us to stay at school.
I **expected** them to be here by now.
I had to **remind** him to buy the food. [tell somebody so that they do not forget]
She **helped** me to write the report. (You can also say: She helped me write the report.)
My parents **encouraged** me to read. [gave me support and confidence to make it possible]

Exercises

88.1 **Correct the mistakes.**

1 She encouraged me going. *She encouraged me to go.*
2 He told it's impossible. ....
3 I asked that Chloe stay with me. ....
4 She suggested us to go to an Italian restaurant. ....
5 I warned them not going. ....
6 He helped me buying my suit. ....
7 She allowed us go. ....
8 He said me the film was terrible. ....
9 She advised me buy a dictionary. ....
10 I recommended to stay there. ....
11 He reminded me go to the bank. ....
12 I want that he leaves. ....

88.2 **Complete the sentences with a verb from the box in the correct form.**

| ~~realise~~ | warn | expect | remind | convince | encourage |
| help | persuade | mention | recommend | notice | hope |

1 She couldn't breathe easily, so I ....*realised*.... that something was wrong.
2 When we went in, I .... that people were looking at us.
3 Martin knew the area was dangerous but he didn't .... me not to go there.
4 I didn't want the job but my mother .... me to take it. It was a mistake.
5 I wasn't sure about the plan, but my boss .... me that it would work.
6 My uncle .... that we try the new Chinese restaurant.
7 When I spoke to Jodie, I .... that we were busy tonight.
8 Our teacher has always .... us to practise our English outside of class.
9 Fortunately Aidan .... me that it was Marsha's birthday; I'd forgotten.
10 I said I would .... Ian to put up the shelves.
11 They said they'd come, so I .... that they'll be here soon.
12 I .... that I pass my exams.

88.3 **Complete the sentences in a suitable way.**

1 He was given some money and I recommended ....*that he put it in the bank.*....
2 Some of them were getting hungry so I suggested ....
3 She said there were strange noises outside her flat, so I advised ....
4 When I saw her face, I noticed ....
5 When I was young, my parents sometimes allowed ....
6 As soon as I put on the coat, I realised ....
7 It was only a few minutes to the beach, but I still couldn't persuade ....
8 Her train was delayed, so I expect ....
9 The water can make you ill and I warned ....
10 I borrowed his laptop yesterday but promised him that ....

88.4 **Over to you**

Look at the verbs on the opposite page again and translate them into your own language.
Do you use the translated verbs with the same constructions? If not, these are the verbs that
may cause you the most problems when you are speaking English.

89 Adjectives

A Extreme adjectives

There are many 'extreme' adjectives we use to say that something is very good, or very small, or very surprising, etc.

We were lucky – the weather was **marvellous** [very good; *syns* **terrific**, **wonderful**, **amazing**].
Don't go and see that film – it's **awful** [very bad; *syn* **dreadful**].
I was **delighted** she passed her exam. [very pleased]
It's a nice modern flat, but it's absolutely **tiny** [very small].

I wasn't very hungry, but they gave us a **huge** meal. [very big; *syn* **enormous**]
You should watch that programme; you'll find it absolutely **fascinating** [very interesting].
Everyone was really **exhausted** by the end of the day. [very tired]
Bungee jumping is the most **terrifying** thing I've ever done. [very frightening]
Computers are an **essential** part of modern life. [very important and necessary]
The food was **delicious** [very good; but usually only for food].

Language help

The food was **absolutely marvellous**. (NOT The food was ~~very marvellous~~.) We can use **absolutely** or **really** before extreme adjectives, e.g. *absolutely awful, really terrific*, but we can't use **very**.
We use **very** or **really** with gradable adjectives which do not have an extreme meaning, e.g. *very big, very good, very nice, very tired, really good, really tired*, etc. (NOT ~~absolutely big~~)

B Adjectives ending in *-ing* and *-ed*

A large group of adjectives can have an **-ing** or **-ed** ending. The **-ing** ending describes a person, thing or situation; the **-ed** ending describes the effect on someone of this person, thing or situation.

I don't know if other people were **bored**, but I thought it was a very **boring** lesson.
The weather is so **depressing** at the moment; it's making everyone feel **depressed**.

Common mistakes

I was bored by that film. (NOT I was ~~boring~~ by that film.)
We're very interested in the new designs. (NOT We're very ~~interesting~~ in the new designs.)

These adjectives can all end in **-ing** or **-ed**, depending on the meaning.

It was really **tiring** going up that hill. [making you feel tired]
I was **amazed** she could climb that wall. [very surprised]
My exam results were very **disappointing** [not as good as I expected].
She was **annoyed** that I forgot to tell her. [angry]
I kept calling her Emma, so I was **embarrassed** when Ben told me her name was Angela.
[feeling a bit stupid because of something you have said or done]
The map he gave us was very **confusing** [difficult to understand].
We were **shocked** by the violence in the film. [very surprised in an unpleasant way]

Exercises

89.1 **Put the words into the correct column.**

| bad   dreadful   important   small   exhausted |
| terrified   tired   essential   frightened   tiny |

gradable adjectives	extreme adjectives
bad	*dreadful*

89.2 **Change the adjectives where possible to give the email a more positive and/or more extreme effect. Include *absolutely* or *really* two or three times.**

● ● ●   Reply   Forward

From   Benita S. x ▾   4:35 PM (1 hour ago)

Dear Sandy
                                    an (absolutely) exhausting
Arrived on Sunday evening after a very tiring journey. We're very pleased with the hotel: our room is very big, and the food is very nice. We've been lucky with the weather as well. The first day was wet but the last three days have been very nice.

Tomorrow we're going to walk the coastal path to Dartmouth Castle. It's quite a difficult route and people tell us it's very important to take a map, but it sounds very interesting, so I'm looking forward to it.

I'll write again in a couple of days and tell you all about it.

love

Benita

89.3 **Complete the dialogues so that B agrees with A, using a suitable adjective from the opposite page.**

1 A: I was <u>very interested</u> in her talk.
   B: Yes, it was ...*fascinating*........... .
2 A: Were you <u>very frightened</u>?
   B: Yes, it was absolutely ....
3 A: It was <u>surprising</u> to see the children behave so badly.
   B: I know. We were ....

4 A: Did you have a <u>nice</u> holiday?
   B: Yes, absolutely ....
5 A: I expect you were <u>very pleased</u> with your score.
   B: Yes, I was absolutely ....
6 A: I expect you were a bit <u>angry</u> when they arrived an hour late?
   B: Yes, I was very ....

89.4 **Write an adjective to describe how the people felt in these situations.**

1 They walked ten miles, then spent the afternoon cutting down trees. *exhausted*..............
2 From the description on the travel website, they expected a beautiful big villa by the sea. In actual fact it was quite small, not very nice, and miles from the beach. ....
3 I arrived in jeans, but everyone else was wearing very formal clothes. ....
4 One person told them the street was on the left, another told them to turn right, and a third person said they had to go back to the station. ....
5 My brother has a flat and it's usually in a terrible mess – he's very untidy. But yesterday when I visited him, the place was incredibly tidy. In fact, everything looked new. ....
6 I got my results yesterday and I passed every exam with a grade A. ....

A · At, *on* and *in*

At a point or place, e.g. I met her **at** the bus stop. He's **at** work at the moment.
On a surface, e.g. The book's **on** the desk. They sat **on** the floor. I put the picture **on** the wall.
In an area, space, or inside something, e.g. He's **in** the kitchen. She lives **in** Warsaw/Poland. The knife's **in** the top drawer.

Common mistakes

I met them **at** the airport. (NOT I met them ~~on~~ the airport.)
There's a computer **on** my desk. (NOT There's a computer ~~in~~ my desk.)
The conference is being held **in** Delhi. (NOT The conference is being held ~~at~~ Delhi.)

B · Where exactly?

 I know they live **in** Danvers Street, and I think they're **at** number twenty-three.

 I'm sure there's a chemist on the left **before** the bank. [first there is a chemist, and then a bank; *opp* **after**]

 Their house is **beyond** the farm [on the other side of the farm], **by** [near] the old church.

 I saw your bike in the back garden **against** the wall. [touching the wall]

 They've just bought a house **right** [exactly] **beside/by** [next to] the river.

 I found your phone on the sofa **beneath/underneath** a pile of cushions. [under]

 Their office is **above** the shop (*opp* **below**).

 You can just see the top of the building **among** the trees. [somewhere in the middle of the trees]

C · Movement

We came **over** the bridge (*opp* **under**), then **through** the tunnel and **round** the lake.

The mouse ran **out of** the back door (*opp* **into**), **towards** the gate, then disappeared **down** a hole.

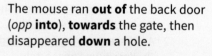

The woman came **after** us [followed in order to catch us], but we managed to climb **into** the back of my dad's van. Fortunately she went **past** the van and didn't see us.

Exercises

90.1 **Complete the sentences.**

1 I put the milk .....*in*.......... the fridge.
2 They live .... the next road.
3 They live .... 34 Lawrence Street.
4 Your clothes are .... the floor.
5 I met her .... a party.
6 She works .... Moscow.
7 The dictionary is .... my desk.

8 I sat .... the bed and wrote the letter.
9 I left my books .... school.
10 There was snow .... the ground when I arrived.
11 The key is .... my jacket pocket.
12 Mausha's .... work this morning.

90.2 **Put the prepositions in the box under the correct picture.**

| beside   towards   out of   ~~down~~   among   into   up   underneath |

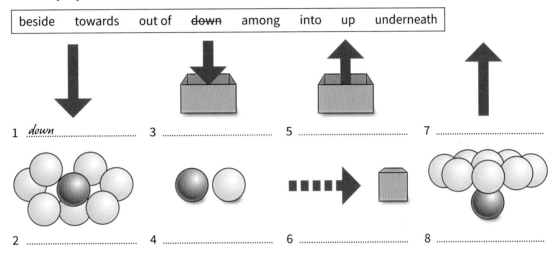

1 *down* ....
2 ....

3 ....
4 ....

5 ....
6 ....

7 ....
8 ....

90.3 **Complete the dialogues so that B says the opposite to A.**

1 A: Did you go up the hill?
   B: No, *down the hill.* ....
2 A: Did you climb over the fence?
   B: No, we went ....
3 A: Did you see her get into the car?
   B: No, but I saw her ....
4 A: Did you say we had to turn left before the bridge?
   B: No, turn left ....
5 A: Does she live in the flat above you?
   B: No, she's in the flat ....
6 A: Did you say the bed was in the middle of the room?
   B: No, it's .... the wall.

90.4 `Over to you`

> **Answer the questions, and give reasons for your answers. If possible, compare your answers with someone else.**
>
> **1** Is it a good idea to live right beside a hospital?
>
> **2** Would you like to live above a restaurant?
>
> **3** Are you happy to drive on icy roads?
>
> **4** Do you like putting lots of things on your bedroom wall?
>
> **5** In a plane or train, do you like sitting by the window?
>
> **6** Would you like to live among lots of rich and famous people?

91 Adverbs

A Adverbs of frequency: how often

always   often   **quite often**   sometimes   **occasionally**   **hardly ever**   never
        frequently   **rarely**
                                                                 seldom (fml)

She **hardly ever** plays tennis now.
I **occasionally** go to the theatre.
We see them quite **frequently**.

I am **often** late.
He **rarely** works at weekends.
I have **never** been to America.

> **Language help**
>
> Remember that frequency adverbs usually go before the main verb, with the exception of the verb *be*. Notice the position of the adverb when the present perfect is used.

B Adverbs of degree: how much

I was **a bit** tired. (*infml*)   The flat was **a little** (**bit**) small.   She was **slightly** nervous.

> **Language help**
>
> **A bit**, **a little** and **slightly** have the same meaning and are mostly used before adjectives that express negative ideas, e.g. *We were **a bit bored**. / I was **slightly upset**.* (NOT *I was a bit happy*.)
> *A bit* and *a little* cannot be used with adjectives before a noun.
> *It was a **slightly small flat**.* (NOT *It was a bit small flat*.)

The next four adverbs all mean 'more than *a bit* but less than *very*'.
The hotel was **quite** busy.
The food was **fairly** boring.
I was **rather** annoyed I missed the film.
The weather was **pretty** good. (*infml*)

We had **quite a** nice room. (NOT *a quite nice* room)
It was **a fairly** wet day.
It was **a rather** good party. OR **rather a** good party.
We had **a pretty** difficult journey.

The restaurant was **completely/totally** empty.   I **totally/completely** agree with you.

We had an **extremely** interesting trip. [very interesting]
It's an **incredibly** good book.

C Adverbs of manner

These adverbs describe the way in which someone does something, or the way that something happens.

Nora had **secretly**[1] put all of the letters into her bag.

Penelope was in pain, and I could see she needed help **urgently**[3].

I went in and shut the door **quietly**. The curtains were closed and the room was dark, but I **suddenly**[2] realised I wasn't alone.

I spoke to Charles **briefly**[4] this morning. I asked him very **politely** if he could work an extra hour this evening, but he reacted quite **angrily** and walked off.

[1] in a way that others couldn't know about
[2] quickly

[3] very quickly because of something important
[4] for a short time

Exercises

91.1 **Form sentences from the words.**

1 get occasionally I early up   *I occasionally get up early.*
2 me ever phones she hardly
3 have leg my broken never I
4 frequently them I at visit weekends
5 brother often me Sunday calls quite on my
6 summer saw I him rarely the during
7 office always in she the is eight before

91.2 **Replace the underlined adverb with a different adverb that has a similar meaning.**

1 The film was <u>pretty</u> good.   *rather*
2 She <u>hardly ever</u> goes to conferences now.
3 The shops were <u>quite</u> busy.
4 They are two sisters, but they look <u>totally</u> different.
5 I thought the film was <u>a bit</u> disappointing, didn't you?
6 I'm afraid I'm <u>extremely</u> busy next week.
7 We <u>often</u> ask them to turn their music down.

91.3 **Put the two ideas into one sentence by using a suitable adverb.**

1 I walked up the path. I didn't make a noise.   *I walked up the path quietly.*
2 I must speak to her. It's important.
3 I asked him to move his car. I did it in a nice and correct way.
4 I spoke to her. I made sure the others didn't know.
5 He ran out of the room. It was very quick and unexpected.
6 I spoke to her this morning. It was only for a few minutes.

91.4 **Change the underlined adverbs in 1–4 to make them more positive. Change the underlined adverbs in 5–7 to make them less negative.**

1 The play was <u>quite</u> interesting.   *very*
2 I thought they were <u>very</u> good.
3 He's been getting <u>quite</u> good marks in his exams.
4 It's a <u>pretty</u> nice house.
5 John said the flat was <u>very</u> small.
6 They said it was <u>fairly</u> boring.
7 His clothes were <u>very</u> dirty.

91.5

Over to you

Make the sentences true for you by adding a suitable adverb, in the correct place.

1 I clean my teeth after breakfast. *I always clean my teeth after breakfast.*

2 I buy clothes I don't like.

3 I lose things.

4 I forget things.

5 I remember my dreams.

6 I speak to strangers on buses and trains.

7 I give money to people in the street if they ask me.

Now think about each of your answers to the sentences above. Do you think they are:

a) fairly typical?   **b)** slightly unusual?   **c)** quite unusual?

If possible, compare your answers with someone else.

92 Time and sequence

A When / As soon as

The meaning of these two time expressions is almost the same, but **as soon as** suggests something more immediate or important.

I'll phone my uncle **when** / **as soon as** I get home.
As soon as / **When** you've finished this exercise, you can go home.

> **Common mistakes**
>
> I'll see you **when** I **get** there. (NOT I'll see you when I ~~will~~ get there.)
> We don't use a future form after *when / as soon as*.

B Two things happening at the same time

Violet got ready **while** I cooked the dinner. [two long actions]
The accident happened **while** I was on my way to work. [a longer action 'on my way to work' and a short action 'the accident'; we can also use **when** or **as** here.]
I saw him (**just**) **as** I came out of the office. [two short actions happening at the same time; we can also use **when** here]

C One thing after another

We met the others in the café, and **then** / **after that** / **afterwards** we went to the match.
I talked to Joe, and **afterwards** [at a later time but usually the same day] I came home.
I was in Caracas for three months, and **then** / **after that** I went to Colombia.
After my visit to New York, I decided to have a rest.
We had something to eat **before** going out.

> **Common mistakes**
>
> After **seeing** the film, we went home.
> (NOT After ~~see~~ the film, we went home.)

D A sequence* of actions

We had a really nice holiday. **First of all** / **First** we spent a few days in St Moritz. **After that** / **Then** we drove down the coast and stayed in Portofino for a week. **Finally**, we went back to Switzerland to stay with my uncle. (*Finally* is used here to introduce the last thing in a list.)

* one action after another, and so on

E At first … eventually

To begin with, the two girls got on very well when they shared the flat. But after **a while** [a period of time], they started arguing about various things, and **eventually** [finally, after a long time or a lot of problems] Lauren walked out and found a new place.

At first I enjoyed the classes, but after a while it got a bit boring, and **in the end** [finally, after a period of time or thought] I left.

F A list of reasons

We can use **firstly** / **for one thing** / **for a start** to introduce a first reason for something, and then **secondly/besides/anyway** to add a further reason.

A: What's wrong with her new dress?
B: **Firstly**, it's a horrible colour, and **secondly**, I don't think it suits her.

A: Why can't we go out tonight?
B: Well, **for one thing** / **for a start**, I've got a lot of work – and **besides/anyway**, I can't afford it.

Exercises

92.1 **Find five more pairs of words/phrases that are similar in meaning.**

> ~~then~~   for one thing   when   besides   finally   at first   for a start
> in the end   ~~after that~~   to begin with   as soon as   anyway

then / after that ....

....

....

92.2 **Choose the correct word to complete the sentences. Sometimes both are correct.**

1 I rang my mum (when / while) I was waiting for my train.
2 I'll give them your message as soon as I *get / will get* there.
3 Maria cleaned the kitchen *as / while* I did the bathroom.
4 Before *leave / leaving* they went to an exhibition in a little gallery.
5 We can have lunch *when / as soon as* we've finished this.
6 The phone rang *while / just as* I was shutting the front door.
7 We spent the morning in the park and *after that / afterwards* we went home for lunch.
8 The letter arrived *while / just as* we were having lunch.
9 I met the others *when / as* I was on my way to the station.
10 After *to clean / cleaning* my room, I was exhausted.

92.3 **Complete the dialogues.**

1 A: Why do you want to stay in this evening, when we could go to Karl's party?
   B: Well, *for one thing* .... , I'd like to watch a programme on TV, and .... , I don't
       think it'll be a very good party.
2 A: What did you do in Portugal?
   B: Well, ... we flew to Lisbon and spent a few days there. .... we took
       the train down to Lagos and spent a week on the Algarve with a couple we met in London. And
       .... we went to Faro and flew back from there.
3 A: Did Matt enjoy his time in India?
   B: Well, ... I think he found it difficult because the food and weather are so
       different. But after a .... he got used to it, and didn't want to come home.
4 A: Why can't the company pay for me to go to the conference?
   B: Well, ... the boss doesn't seem to think it's very important, and ....
       we're too busy at the moment to give anyone time off work.
5 A: Did the new company do well?
   B: Yeah, ... it did very well. But then the manager left, and after a ....
       they started losing money. .... , they had to close down.

92.4 **Complete the sentences in a suitable way.**

1 We had a game of table tennis and afterwards *we went for a drink* ....
2 I'll give you the answers to this exercise when ....
3 I'll text you as soon as ....
4 I must remember to lock the back door before ....
5 He thinks he dropped the letter as ....
6 I worked with a partner in class. I looked up half of the words while ....
7 We were in a traffic jam for hours but eventually ....
8 If we phone his home, he probably won't be there. Anyway, ...

A | As well (as), what's more, in addition (to), besides

We often link ideas using *and*, e.g. The food's nice **and** very good value. There are other words and phrases we also use to add more information. Sometimes we still include *and* or *also*.

The restaurant has excellent food; it's **also** very good value.
You always get a good view, *and* the seats are comfortable **as well**. (*syn* **too**)
As well as getting cheaper tickets, I *also* got the opportunity to buy them in advance.
The clothes are nice, *and* **what's more**, the shop is open every day of the week.
The scheme gives young people experience. **In addition**, companies can afford to employ them.
In addition to the new food department, they're *also* planning to open a café.
Besides being a mum with four children, she's *also* a successful designer.

B | Although, despite, in spite of

We use these link words when there are two ideas in a sentence, and the second is surprising or not expected. They can be used at the beginning or in the middle of the sentence.

Although / **Even though** the sun was shining, it wasn't very warm.
We found the place quite easily, **although** / **even though** we didn't know where it was.
They went for a walk **despite the fact that** it was raining.
Despite having no money, he **still** seemed very happy.
They got there on time **in spite of** the delay.
In spite of all the problems, we **still** enjoyed the trip.

> ### Language help
>
> We can use **still** to emphasise that we didn't expect something to happen or be true, e.g. *He didn't do any work but he **still** passed the exam*; *The work is very hard, but he **still** enjoys it.*

C | However, yet, though

We can use **however** and **yet** when the second part of an idea is surprising after the first part. *However* is often used to link ideas in two separate sentences. **Though** can be used in a similar way in spoken English, but usually comes at the end of the sentence. Notice the use of commas (,) here, and the different positions of *however*.

I don't agree with a lot of his methods. **However**, he is a very good teacher.
We didn't particularly like the house. The garden, **however**, was wonderful.
It was warm and sunny when we were there. Most of the time, **however**, it's quite cold.

We went in the autumn, **yet** it was still quite warm.
I didn't like the film much. I'm glad I went to see it, **though**.
They told us the shop was next to the station. We never found it, **though**.

D | While and whereas

We can use **while** and **whereas** to compare two different facts or situations.

Alex is very quick to understand, **whereas/while** the others are quite slow.
I get £20 an hour, **while** Josh only gets £12.
The speed limit on this road is 80kph, **whereas** it's 130kph on the motorway.
I was very keen on the film, **whereas** Christoph didn't like it at all.

Exercises

93.1 **Put the words into the correct column.**

in addition	although	in spite of	as well	however	also	what's more	despite

words that add more information	words that introduce surprising information
in addition	

93.2 **Choose the correct word(s) to complete the sentences. Sometimes both are correct.**

1 *(Although)* / *In spite of* we left late, we still got there in time.
2 She's going on holiday with friends. Her parents, *however* / *whereas,* are not very happy about it.
3 We decided to work *in spite of* / *despite* the fact we were on holiday.
4 They enjoyed the course, *even though* / *as well* it was very difficult.
5 I told John the car was too expensive. *However* / *Although*, he still bought it.
6 Most people tried to help us. They were very friendly *too* / *as well*.
7 Ethan spends his time in the library, *while* / *whereas* the others are always playing football.
8 It was a fantastic evening, *although* / *despite* the terrible food.

93.3 **Combine parts from each column to form five short texts.**

She went to school today — in spite of — she was never happy in the job.
She always worked hard in class, — although — she is very experienced.
She has the ability to do the job. — However, — the help I gave her.
She didn't pass the exam — whereas — she didn't feel very well.
She worked there for ten years. — What's more, — most of her classmates were lazy.

She went to school today although she didn't feel very well.
....
....
....
....

93.4 **Complete the sentences.**

1 People say the hotel is very good. It's *also* .... quite cheap.
2 .... the fact that they were busy, they .... helped us.
3 It's not the best dictionary you can buy. .... , it's better than nothing.
4 She managed to get there, ... she didn't have a map like the others.
5 .... heavy rain, they've also had very strong winds.
6 She's the youngest in the group, and she's better than most of them ....
7 I think you can do it. It won't be easy, ...
8 I was right at the back at the concert, ... I could ....
   hear everything.

93.5 **Complete the sentences in a suitable way.**

1 Although it's an old skirt, *I still like it. (OR it still looks nice.)* ....
2 My parents get up at 7.30, whereas ....
3 We enjoyed the holiday in spite of ....
4 If you buy a season ticket, you can travel as often as you like. What's more, ...
5 The exam was very difficult. However, ...
6 I understood what she was saying, although ....
7 My uncle is nearly 70, but he still ....

94 Reason, purpose, result, condition

A Reason

I went home early **because** I was feeling tired.
As/Since I was feeling tired, I went home early. (We don't usually start a sentence with *because*.)
I was feeling tired, **so** I went home early. (This is very common in spoken English.)
The reason I went home early **was that** I was feeling tired.

We can also use **because of** with a different construction. Compare:
They go there **because** the weather is wonderful. (because + noun + verb)
They go there **because of** the wonderful weather. (because of + (adjective) + noun)

Due to means the same as **because of**, and is often used to explain the reason for a problem.
The plane was late **due to** bad weather. (**Due to** is often used after the verb *be*.)

> ### Common mistakes
>
> It's a pity you can't go on holiday **because** Chiclayo is very nice. (NOT It's a pity you can't go on holiday because of Chiclayo is very nice.)
> We moved house **because of** my father's work. (NOT We moved house because my father's work.)

B Purpose

A **purpose** is an intention or reason for doing something.
The **purpose of** the meeting is to plan next year's timetable. [the reason *for* the meeting]

We often introduce a purpose using **so** (**that**) or (**in order**) **to**:
I bought this book **so** (**that**) I **could** improve my English.
They went home early (**in order**) **to** watch the match on television.
We moved house **so** (**that**) we **could** send our children to this school.
She went into town (**in order**) **to** do some shopping.

C Result

These link words/phrases are used when one thing happens because another thing has happened. **Therefore** and **as a result** are more formal than **so**, and less common in spoken English.
I left my ticket at home, **so** I had to buy another one.
They've got more money, and **therefore** they can afford to buy the best football players.
I forgot to send the email. **As a result,** no one knew about the meeting.

D Conditions

We sometimes use **whether** [if] when we are not sure about something.
I didn't buy it because I wasn't sure **whether** you'd like it.
I spoke to the others, but I don't know **whether** they're coming.

We'll be late **unless** we leave now. [if we don't leave now]
Unless the weather improves [if the weather doesn't improve], we won't be able to go.

I have to go now, **otherwise** [because if I don't] I'll miss the last bus.
You'll have to turn up the music, **otherwise** [because if you don't] they won't be able to hear it.

You can borrow it **as long as** you bring it back by Thursday. [but you *must* bring it back]
You can wear what you like **as long as** you look quite smart. [but you *must* look quite smart]

I'm taking my umbrella **in case** it rains. [I'm doing A because B might happen later.]
Take some money **in case** you need to get a taxi.

Exercises

94.1 **Rewrite the sentences using *because of*. Make any necessary changes.**

1 I couldn't play because my arm was broken. *I couldn't play because of my broken arm.*
2 Teresa got the job because her exam results were good. ....
3 The weather was terrible, so we couldn't eat outside. ....
4 As she had a cold, she didn't go to school. ....
5 The light was bad, so the referee stopped the game. ....
6 The traffic was terrible; I was late. ....
7 He's only 17, and therefore he can't vote. ....

94.2 **Complete the sentences.**

1 I must write that letter now, *otherwise* .... I'll forget to do it.
2 I'll take some sandwiches with me .... I get hungry.
3 We agreed to buy my daughter a dog .... she takes it for a walk every day.
4 I left early .... miss the rush-hour traffic.
5 My girlfriend didn't feel very well. .... , we left the party quite early.
6 .... there's a problem, I won't disturb you.
7 You can borrow my dictionary .... you bring it back on Monday.
8 You'd better tidy your room, ... your mother will be angry.
9 I sent Luiza an invitation, but I don't know .... she's coming.
10 The .... I didn't ring you was that I'd lost your phone number.

94.3 **Complete the memo.**

● ● ●   Reply   Forward

To	All Staff ⊗		CC BCC
From	Daniel Myers ⊗		09 August

Subject Temporary roadworks

From next Monday, the council are closing both approach roads to the factory. The [1] | *purpose* | of this, I believe, is to install new gas pipes. [2] | _____ | this will create long delays, could I please ask staff to leave home a few minutes early in the morning [3] | _____ | everyone gets here on time. The roadworks also mean that you won't be able to park on the street, and [4] | _____ | it may be a good idea to leave your cars at home [5] | _____ | it is absolutely impossible for you to use public transport.

I haven't been told [6] | _____ | the roadworks will continue for the whole week, but I will let you know as soon as possible, and I apologise for the inconvenience.

Daniel Myers
Office manager

94.4

Over to you

Complete the sentences in a way that is true for you.

I want to improve my English because ....

I don't know whether my English ....

I often need to write words down, otherwise I ....

I don't get many opportunities to practise my English, therefore ....

Speaking English may be important in order to ....

A Formal English

Formal English is more common in writing, but you will also hear examples in more formal spoken English, e.g. announcements, speeches, television news, or discussions.

NOTICE IN A CAFE: Only food **purchased** [bought] here may be eaten **on the premises** [here].

POLICE STATEMENT: The man is being questioned **regarding** [about] the robbery last night.

BUSINESS LETTER: I **regret to inform you** [I am sorry to say] that we are unable to …

THEATRE ANNOUNCEMENT: The play will **commence** [start] in two minutes.

INFORMATION NOTICE: If you **require** [need] **further assistance** [more help], please contact the above address.

STATION ANNOUNCEMENT: The next train to **depart** [leave] from platform 7 will be the 7:22 to Reading.

FORMAL LETTER: We are not in a position to **grant** [give or allow] you a visa to this country.

AIRPORT ANNOUNCEMENT: Will passengers for Miami please **proceed to** [go to] gate 36.

B Informal English

Informal language is more common in spoken English, and also in most emails or letters to friends. The words and phrases in **bold** in these dialogues are all informal.

A: Who's Callum?
B: A **mate** [a friend] of mine.
A: Really?
B: Yeah, I see him **quite a bit** [often]; he's a nice **bloke** [man].

A: Toby, I'm afraid I can't **make it** [come] this evening.
B: Oh, that's a shame.
A: Yeah, I'm sorry, but **the thing is** [the problem is], Ella's not well, so I'll have to look after the **kids** [children].
B: OK, don't worry. There will still be twelve **or so** [about twelve] at the meeting, and I'll ring you later and let you know what happens.
A: **Cheers** [thanks]. That would be great.

A: **I bet** [I'm sure] you're hungry.
B: Yes, **I'm dying for** something to eat. [want to eat something very much]
A: Well, I think you'll find some **stuff** in the fridge.

A: What **are** you **up to** this evening? [What are you doing?]
B: Nothing much. Why?
A: Well, would you like to see the new Coen Brothers film? I've heard it's **great** [very good; *syn* **terrific**].
B: Really? My brother saw it and said it was **a load of rubbish** [terrible].

Language help

We often use the uncountable noun **stuff,** especially in spoken English, to refer to an uncountable noun or a group of things. We do this when others know what we are talking about, or if we don't need to be exact.
Put this **stuff** in the cupboard. [e.g. plates, food, toys]
We carried our camping **stuff** [equipment].
What's this **stuff** in the fridge in the blue bottle? [liquid]

Exercises

95.1 **Put the words into the correct column on the right.**

depart	mate
cheers	commence
regarding	terrific
purchase	bloke
proceed to	kids

(depart is crossed out)

formal	informal
depart	

95.2 **Now write a synonym for each of the words in 95.1.**

depart	*leave*	mate	
cheers		commence	
regarding		terrific	
purchase		bloke	
proceed to		kids	

95.3 **Replace the underlined words and phrases with more informal words or phrases.**

1 <u>I'm sure</u> your parents are pleased?   *I bet* ....
2 I'd love to come, but the <u>problem</u> is, my mother wants us to go and see her. ....
3 I watched that new series on TV last night. It was <u>absolutely terrible</u>. ....
4 What are you <u>doing</u> this weekend? ....
5 <u>I really want</u> something to drink. ....
6 None of them can <u>come</u> on Monday. ....
7 Jamie is a <u>friend</u> of mine. ....
8 We go there <u>often</u>. ....
9 You can leave all <u>those books, files and papers</u> on the desk. ....
10 We should be able to get <u>approximately 40</u> on the coach. ....

95.4 **Rewrite the underlined parts of this letter in more suitable formal English.**

1 *regarding* ....
2 ....
  ....
3 ....
4 ....
  ....

● ● ●   <u>Reply</u>   <u>Forward</u>

To   [M. Collins x ▾]   7:03 AM (3 hours ago)

Dear Mr Collins

We are writing <u>about</u>[1] your application to the council for a disabled parking space outside your home. <u>We're sorry to say</u>[2] that we are unable to <u>allow</u>[3] this request as parking is the sole responsibility of the Highways Agency.

We suggest that if you <u>need more help</u>[4], you should contact them on 01727 717 317.

95.5 **Dictionaries will tell you if a word is *formal* or *informal/spoken*. Use your dictionary to find out if the underlined words here are *formal* or *informal/spoken*. What do they mean?**

1 I thought the film was <u>a drag</u>.
2 Smoking isn't <u>permitted</u>.
3 It's a <u>scary</u> film.
4 This watch cost fifty <u>quid</u>.

A Types of form

- a **registration form** — where you enter your name on an official list, e.g. at a school or college (also called an **enrolment form** when you are applying to do a course of study)

- an **entry form** — if you want to enter for an exam, e.g. Cambridge English: First
- a **landing card** — for people from some countries when they enter the UK
- a **visa application form** — when you make an official request to enter or leave some countries

B Language of forms

When you **fill in** [complete] a form, you will see that they often have more formal expressions. In spoken English, ideas may be expressed differently.

written	spoken
date of birth	= When were you born?
place of birth	= Where were you born?
country of origin	= Where do you come from?
marital status	= Are you single or married?
date of arrival	= When did you arrive?
date of departure	= When are you leaving? OR When did you leave?
signed	= Write your **signature** [the special way you have of writing your own name]

C Curriculum vitae

If you **apply for** a job, you need to send a letter and a **CV** (**curriculum vitae** or **résumé** in American English), which should give:

- **personal details** [information about you such as your name, address, email address, etc.]
- details about your **education** and **qualifications**, e.g. university degree, teaching certificate, etc.
- your **work experience** [the jobs you have done]
- your **interests** [what you enjoy doing]
- **skills** [abilities you have learned and practised, e.g. ability to speak a foreign language]
- **career aims** [what you want to do in your future working life]
- names of people who will give you a **reference** [a letter written by someone who knows you which says if you are suitable for a particular job]

If you **apply to** university, they **require** [need; *fml*] a **personal statement** in which you must explain why you want to go to this university; why you want to follow this particular course; details of your educational background; your skills; your interests.

D Tips for writing a CV or personal statement

A **tip** is a useful piece of advice. Here are some tips for writing a CV or personal statement.

- A CV should be no longer than two pages; a personal statement no more than 45 lines of text.
- **Type** your CV or personal statement (**handwriting** is not suitable).
- Keep it simple. Don't make it **complicated** [difficult to understand].
- Check there are no mistakes.
- Make sure the information you give is **relevant** [connected to and useful for the particular job]. For example, if you are going to be working **on your own** [without others], don't say that you are good at working **in a team** [with a group of people].

Exercises

96.1 **What forms do you have to complete in these situations?**

1 You are just arriving in Britain and you come from a country outside the European Union. *A landing card*
2 You are applying to do an English course at a school in Britain. ....
3 You are going to do a Cambridge exam. ....
4 You want to travel to the United States this summer. ....

96.2 **Write these sentences in more informal English.**

1 What was your date of arrival? *When did you arrive/get here?*
2 What's your date of birth? ....
3 What's your country of origin? ....
4 What's your marital status? ....
5 What's your date of departure? ....

96.3 **Match the words on the left with the information on the right.**

1 personal details   [c]   a I would like to become a radio producer.
2 education   [ ]   b Trainee at Northern Radio Station, Jan–June 2007
3 qualifications   [ ]   c Leona Phillips, 18 Mansion Road, Beckington BE2 3RJ
4 work experience   [ ]   d I direct plays for a theatre group, and help with a children's charity.
5 career aims   [ ]   e letter from Mr J. Tobin BA, MA (University tutor)
6 interests   [ ]   f BA Honours degree in Media Studies
7 references   [ ]   g Kent University 2007–2010, Ainslie Grammar School 1999–2006

96.4 **Answer *correct* or *incorrect*.**

1 It's OK to make one or two mistakes in my CV. *incorrect*
2 I need to type my CV. ....
3 It's OK if my CV is three pages long. ....
4 My CV should be complicated. ....
5 For an admin job, it is relevant to say I have computer skills. ....
6 I can put down a driving licence as one of my skills. ....
7 I can put down travelling abroad as a career aim. ....

96.5 **Replace the underlined words with a word or phrase that has a similar meaning.**

1 Do I have to complete this form? *fill in*
2 Monica gave me a useful piece of advice about shopping in America. ....
3 I shall be alone most of the time. ....
4 They sent the form back to me because I didn't write my signature at the bottom. ....
5 Please contact us if you need any more help. ....
6 I think I'm good at working as part of a group of people. ....

96.6 **Over to you**

Answer the questions. If possible, ask someone else the same questions.

1 Have you ever written a CV? If so, what information did it include?

2 Have you had to write a personal statement? If so, why?

3 On a CV, what would you put as your interests, your skills, and your career aims?

A The basis of a discursive essay*

In a discursive essay you have to express your own ideas and **point of view** [opinion]. It is also important to show that you understand **both sides of an argument** [reasons **for** something and reasons **against** something]. This means you need to understand and use different link words and phrases such as **in addition**, **however**, etc. (See Unit 93.)

* an essay that discusses a subject

B Expressing a point of view

Some people believe [Some people think] that no one should be sent to prison under the age of 18.
There is **an argument** [a reason to think] that everyone should have a university education.

Language help

You can express a personal point of view with phrases such as **I believe** / **think that ...** or **It seems to me that ...** but you can also use less personal and direct ways of expressing a point of view, as in the phrases on the left. Many people think it is better not to use *In my opinion* in written essays.

C Giving both sides of an argument

One of the advantages of being an only child is that you have more attention from your parents. **However**, it can be lonely without the company of brothers and sisters.

On the one hand, computers can do so many things faster than human beings. **On the other** (**hand**), some people are becoming dependent on them, which is not a good thing.

D Comparing and contrasting*

We often **make comparisons** between groups of people, or between the past and the present.
Compared with / to my grandparents, I have had much more opportunity to travel abroad.
In the past people didn't have computers, **but nowadays** there is one in almost every home.
Most parts of the developed world have become richer in the last thirty years. **In contrast**, many countries in Africa have become much poorer.

* saying how two things are similar and how they are different

E Making generalisations

Sometimes a simple statement is not accurate, e.g. *Young people prefer to watch American films*. This is not true for *all* young people, so we use certain words and phrases to show that we are **making a generalisation** [saying that something is true most of the time or in most situations].
In general, Japanese society is more focused on groups than individuals. (*syn* **on the whole**)
Teenagers **tend to** have [usually have] more freedom than in the past.

F Cause and effect*

Poor diet and lack of exercise are the main **causes of obesity** [reasons for being very fat].
Obesity is often the **result of** a bad diet and not enough exercise.
People don't eat the right food or get enough exercise, and **consequently** [because of this; *syn* **as a result**] they put on weight.
Poor diet can cause obesity, and this can have a bad **effect on** people's health.

* how something happens, and then makes something else happen

Language help

Don't confuse the verb **affect** and the noun **effect**.
*Pollution can **affect** people's breathing.*
*Pollution can **have an effect on** people's breathing.*

Exercises

97.1 **Match the definitions on the left with the examples on the right.**

1 expressing a point of view
2 making a comparison
3 describing the result of something
4 showing both sides of an argument
5 making a generalisation

c	a Canada has a smaller population than the USA.
	b People tend to retire at a later age.
	c Some people believe we should never go to war.
	d Animals die because we're cutting down the forest.
	e Television can make children lazy. However, there are many programmes with real educational value.

97.2 **One word is missing in each sentence. What is it, and where should it go?**

1 It seems∕me that there is a problem. *to*
2 One of the advantages studying law is that it should lead to a good career.
3 It is important to give sides of the argument.
4 Too much time spent in front of a television can have a bad effect children.
5 People like to have freedom of choice. On the other, too much choice can be a bad thing.
6 Time tends go faster as you get older.

97.3 **Choose the correct word to complete the sentences. Sometimes both are correct.**

1 There is not enough food, and ⟨consequently⟩ / *on the other hand* people are dying.
2 Advertising is so powerful that it *causes* / *affects* people to buy things they don't want.
   In addition / *However*, it can help them make the right choice when they buy things.
3 *In general* / *On the whole* people have more access to education than fifty years ago.
4 Supermarkets are very convenient because you can buy almost everything you want.
   On the other *side* / *hand*, they are putting small shops out of business.
5 The north of the country is much richer compared *with* / *to* the south.

97.4 **Complete part of this essay on the advantages and disadvantages of the Internet for children.**

One of the [1] *advantages*.............. of the Internet is that children have access to so much knowledge and information. [2]............................. , many children can access this knowledge from their own homes; they don't have to go to libraries. [3]............................. , some of the information on the Internet is unreliable and out-of-date, and there are some websites we would not want our children to look at. [4]............................. , we need to control the way that our children use the Internet, and there is certainly an [5]............................. for much stricter controls on the websites that people are allowed to create. If we don't do this, the Internet could have a bad [6]............................. on children.

97.5 **Rewrite the sentences following the instructions in (brackets).**

1 People who drink and drive should go to prison. (*Show that this is a personal opinion.*)
   I believe that people who drink and drive should go to prison...........................
2 People are conservative. (*Make this statement a generalisation.*)
   ....
3 Cars should not be allowed in town centres. (*Make this opinion less personal.*)
   ....
4 Children played on their bikes. Children spend most of their time in front of a computer. (*Make this a comparison between the past and the present in one sentence.*)
   ....
5 Many people work longer and longer hours. They don't have time for hobbies. (*Show the connection between these two statements in one sentence.*)
   ....

A   A formal letter

> 10 Baldwyn Gardens
> Ealing
> London W5 8PR
> 8 August
>
> Dear **Sir or Madam**[1]
>
> **I am writing**[2] **in response to**[3] your advertisement about job opportunities for **graduates**[4]. I have just completed a degree in Economics at Durham University, and **I would be grateful if you could**[5] send me further **details**[6] of the graduate training schemes you mention. I am **available**[7] for interview at any time.
>
> **I look forward to hearing from you**.[8]
>
> **Yours faithfully**[9]
>
> *Nicole Drew* [10]
>
> Nicole Drew

[1] use this beginning if you don't know the person's name
[2] This is a common way to start a letter.
[3] in reply to
[4] people with a university degree
[5] this is slightly more polite/formal than **Please could you** …
[6] information about something (plural noun)
[7] free
[8] This sentence is often used to close a letter when you expect a reply.
[9] Use this ending if you don't know the name of the person you are writing to. If you know the name, end the letter with **Yours sincerely**, or **Kind regards**.
[10] Writing your name like this in a particular way is a **signature**. It is normal at the end of a formal letter to **sign** your name first [write your signature], and then print it, e.g. Nicole Drew.

B   Useful words and phrases

Thank you for your letter **regarding** [about] the damage to your vehicle.
I regret to inform you [I am sorry to say] that your **application** [official request for something] has not been successful.
I am pleased to inform you that your application has been successful. [I am happy to say]
I am writing to **enquire about** English courses at your school. [ask about]
You will need to **confirm** the booking **in writing** [write to say that the booking is certain].
We would like to **thank you for** offering your **support** [say thank you for offering your help].
We would like to **apologise for** [say sorry for] the **delay** [when something arrives later than expected]. OR **Please accept our apologies for** the delay.
I **enclose** a cheque for £100. [I am sending a cheque for £100 in the same envelope as this letter.]

Exercises

98.1 **Correct seven more mistakes in the email.**

> Reply   Forward
>
> From   Michael Ridley x ▾   7:03 AM (3 hours ago)
>
> _____Sir_____
> Dear ~~sir~~ or Madame
>
> I write with response to your advertisement for trainees in yesterday's newspaper, and I would be greatful if you could send me further detail.
>
> I look forward to hear from you.
>
> Kind regards,
>
> Michael Ridley

98.2 **Finish the sentences.**

1 If you don't know the person you are writing to, you start *Dear Sir or Madam* ....
2 If you would like more information, you ask for further ....
3 A common way of closing a letter is *I look forward* ....
4 If you don't know the person you are writing to, you end *Yours* ....
5 If you know the name of the person, you can end *Yours* ....
6 Another way of ending a letter is *Kind* ....
7 At the end of the letter you also write your ....

98.3 **Rewrite the phrases and sentences in more formal English, starting with the words given. Keep a similar meaning.**

1 Thanks for the letter about the fire.   Thank you for your letter *regarding the fire.* ....
2 I'm sorry to tell you …   I ....
3 I'm happy to tell you …   I am ....
4 Are you free on Wednesday?   Are you ....
5 I want to ask about the dates of the course. I would like to ....
6 We want to say sorry for the delay.   Please accept ....
7 Please send me the details.   I would be ....
8 Could you say that's definite in a letter?   Could you ....
9 I'm sending a copy of my CV.   I ....

98.4 **Complete the letter.**

> [1] *Dear* .... Mr Wilkinson,
>
> I am [2] .... in [3] .... to your letter of 10 February [4] .... the delivery of the Maxwell dining table and four chairs that you ordered.
>
> In the middle of January there was a fire at the factory and it had to close down for almost a week. The recent heavy snow has caused further problems, and coming so soon after the busy Christmas period, we [5] .... to inform you that there are [6] .... of up to four weeks on most orders.
>
> We promise to do everything we can to speed up deliveries, but in the meantime we would like to [7] .... for the obvious inconvenience this has caused.
>
> Yours [8] .... ,
>
> *James Porter*
> James Porter
> Customer services manager

99 Informal emails and messages

A An email

¹ We can begin an informal email or letter with **Hi** Beth, **Hello** Beth, or **Dear** Beth.

² a funny person

³ planning or intending to

⁴ make contact, e.g. by phone, email or text

⁵ want (to see) *infml*

⁶ say hello to Conrad from me; also **send my regards to** Conrad. With family members and very close friends we also say **give** / **send my love to**.

⁷ again, as before (here it is used to say thank you one more time)

⁸ We can end an informal email/letter to a close friend or family member with **Love** or **Lots of love**. We also often use **Best wishes** or **All the best** when we end a letter or email to a friend.

From Sophie C. x ▼   9:47 AM (2 hours ago)

Hi¹ Beth

Just a quick message to thank you for dinner last night. Absolutely delicious, as always, and I really enjoyed meeting your friend Alice. She's **a laugh**², isn't she?

I'm **hoping to**³ get tickets for the film festival next week, so **I'll be in touch**⁴ to see if there's anything you **fancy**⁵ seeing.

Give my regards to⁶ Conrad when he gets back from Poland, and **once again**⁷, thanks for last night.

Love⁸
Sophie

B Messaging

Hi Emma
Sorry it's been **ages**¹ **since**² I last got in touch, but I just wanted to **let you know**³ that I'm coming to Birmingham **in two weeks' time**⁴ – **actually**⁵ just before your birthday.

Sounds great, when exactly?

12 March. Could we **get together**⁶ and go out for a meal? Maybe Mark could **join us**⁷ as well?

That's perfect. Can you contact Mark and I'll book a restaurant?

Great! **Anyway**⁸, better get back to work. See you soon!

Language help

We can use **actually** to give more exact information, as in the letter (*syn* **in fact**). We also use it a great deal in spoken English to say something which is surprising or different from what you expect, e.g. He looks Italian, but **actually** he's not. (*Syn* **in fact**) **Actually** does *not* mean *at the moment*, e.g. *The land is **currently** for sale* (NOT *The land is ~~actually~~ for sale*).

¹ a long time
² from a time in the past until now
³ tell you
⁴ two weeks from now
⁵ (see Language help)
⁶ meet for a social reason
⁷ come with us
⁸ used to change the subject or end a conversation/letter

Exercises

99.1 **Find five more phrases using words from the box.**

~~in~~	give	~~be~~	once	best	let	in	to	again	you
week's	~~touch~~	my	a	regards	time	wishes	know

be in touch ....

....

....

99.2 **Write these phrases in different ways. The phrases can be similar but don't repeat exactly the same words.**

1 Hello Julie   *Hi* .... Julie
2 Hello Mark   .... Mark
3 Give my love to Patricia   .... Patricia
4 Love, Evelyn   .... , Evelyn
5 Best wishes, Sam   .... , Sam

99.3 **Rewrite the sentences using the word in capitals. Keep a similar meaning.**

1 Do you want to come with us?   JOIN   Do you want to *join us?* ....
2 Do you want to go?   FANCY   Do you ....
3 I'll write soon.   TOUCH   I'll ....
4 It looks new, but actually it isn't.   FACT   It looks new, but ....
5 I'll tell you as soon as possible.   LET   I'll ....
6 I'm going three weeks from now.   IN   I'm going ....
7 Jamie is very funny.   LAUGH   Jamie is ....
8 Let's meet for lunch.   GET   Let's ....
9 I haven't written for ages.   SINCE   It's ....

99.4 **Complete the email with words from the box.**

~~touch~~	join	fact	together	hoping	in
let	since	give	ages	actually	anyway

Dear Gilberto

I haven't been in ¹ [*touch*] for ² [_____] – I'm sorry about that. In
³ [_____] , I've been really busy ⁴ [_____] I last wrote because
I've got a new job in TV – ⁵ [_____] it's with the BBC. I'm doing research
for various documentary programmes and I'm ⁶ [_____] to go to Brazil
⁷ [_____] three months' time. If so, I'll obviously get in touch.
It would be great if we could get ⁸ [_____] , and maybe Filipe could
⁹ [_____] us if he's free. ¹⁰ [_____] , I'll write again soon. I hope
things are going well with you, and ¹¹ [_____] me know when the baby
arrives. And, of course, ¹² [_____] my love to Teresa.

All the best,
Jonny

A Letters or words?

Most abbreviations are spoken as individual letters.

EU	European Union
UN	United Nations
PM	Prime Minister
MP	Member of Parliament
BBC	British Broadcasting Corporation
ID	identification, e.g. Do you have an ID card?
PC	personal computer
CV	curriculum vitae [a history of your job experience]
ISP	Internet Service Provider

Occasionally abbreviations are spoken as words, e.g. **AIDS** /eɪdz/ and **PIN** /pɪn/ [personal identification number, especially used with a bank/credit card]

> ### Language help
>
> We use the verb **stand for** to ask about the meaning of an abbreviation.
> A: **What does** EU **stand for**?
> B: European Union.

B Written forms only

Some abbreviations are written forms only, but pronounced as full words.

Mr Scott (mister Scott)   **St** Mark's Church (Saint Mark's Church)
Mrs Bryant (misses Bryant)   Dean **St** (Dean Street)
Dr Chapman (doctor Chapman)

C Abbreviations as part of the language

Some abbreviations (from Latin) are used as part of the language.

Latin	abbreviation	pronunciation	meaning
et cetera	**etc.**	/et ˈsetərə/	**and so on**
exempli gratia	**e.g.**	/iːˈdʒiː/	**for example**
id est	**i.e.**	/aɪˈiː/	**that's to say / in other words**

D Shortened words

Some common English words can be shortened, especially in spoken English. In some cases, the shorter form is more common and the full form sounds quite formal, e.g. refrigerator, influenza, gymnasium and veterinary surgeon.

phone (telephone)   **fridge** (refrigerator)
maths (mathematics)   **exam** (examination)
board (whiteboard/smartboard/blackboard)   **plane** (aeroplane)
case (suitcase)   **photo** (photograph)
ad/advert (advertisement)   **flu** (influenza) [illness like a cold but more serious]
gym (gymnasium)   **lab** (laboratory) [special room where scientists work]
bike (bicycle)   **sales rep** (sales representative; *syn* **salesperson**)
TV/telly (television)   **vet** (veterinary surgeon)
paper (newspaper)

Exercises

100.1 **Are these sentences correct or incorrect? If a sentence is incorrect, change it to make it correct.**

1 ISP stands for Internet Service Player. *Incorrect. It's Internet Service Provider.*
2 BBC stands for British Broadcasting Company. ....
3 MP stands for Minister of Parliament. ....
4 PC stands for personal computer. ....
5 UN stands for Unified Nations. ....
6 ID stands for identification. ....
7 CV stands for curricular vitae. ....

100.2 **What abbreviations in written English are often used for these words or phrases?**

1 Mister   *Mr* ....
2 for example   ....
3 and so on   ....
4 Street   ....
5 in other words   ....
6 Saint   ....
7 Doctor   ....

100.3 **Rewrite this note, making it more informal by using short forms where possible.**

Luke

                maths
Olly had a ~~mathematics~~ examination this afternoon and then had to take his
bicycle to the repair shop, so he'll probably be a bit late home. You can watch
television while you're waiting for him, and please help yourself to anything
in the refrigerator. If there's a problem — for example, if Doctor Brown
rings about the influenza vaccination, my telephone number is next to the
photographs on the dining room table. I should be home myself by about five.
Pam (Olly's mum)

100.4 **Complete the sentences with suitable words, shortened words or abbreviations.**

1 It was a warm day, so I put the milk and butter in the ....*fridge*............ .
2 He didn't want to walk, so he went on his ....
3 If you go to Mediterranean islands, ... Sardinia or Corsica, it's a good idea to hire
a car.
4 If you want to apply for the job, you'll need to send your .... with a letter
of application.
5 The dog was sick, so we had to take her to the ....
6 In that shop on the corner you can get books, pens, writing paper, ...
7 I took my large bag with me on the plane, but I didn't have a ....
8 When I sold my CDs, I put an .... in the paper and had three replies the same day.
9 If you use the cashpoint, remember you'll need your .... number.
10 What does MP .... for?
11 We did some experiments in the chemistry ....
12 My uncle is a sales ....

100.5 **Here are some more abbreviations. What does each one stand for, and where will you
see them?**

PTO ....   RSVP ....   asap ....

IMO ....   DOB ....   PS ....

Answer key

Unit 1

1.1 *Your own answers*

1.2 *Your own answers*

1.3 *Your own answers*

1.4 2 temporary   3 cruel/unkind   4 rough   5 exit/way out   6 alive   7 refuse

1.5 2 argument   4 choose   6 difference; differ
       3 revision   5 expansion   7 communication; communicative

1.6 *Your own answers*

Unit 2

2.1

food	garden	numbers
diet, lay the table, flour, raw, butcher, frozen, e.g. *frozen peas*	branch, dig, ground, leaf, butterfly, frozen, e.g. *the ground is frozen*	count, add up, minus, thousand, zero

2.2 *Possible answers:*
2 translation
3 a person who sells meat
4

5 translation
6 put plates, knives, forks, etc. on a table before a meal
7 translation is probably the easiest way
8 six minus four is two (6- 4 = 2)

2.3 2 (synonym) A synonym for *awful* is *dreadful.*
       3 (opposite) The opposite of *necessary* is *unnecessary.*
       4 (word partner and part of speech) You *translate* something *into* another language; the noun is *translation.*
       5 (meanings) *Tip* has two meanings: a piece of advice, and money you give a waiter for serving you.
       6 (grammar and part of speech) *Enjoy* is followed by an *-ing* form; the noun is *enjoyment,* the adjective is *enjoyable.*

2.4 *Your own answers*

Unit 3

3.1 2 really   5 clothes   8 beautiful
       3 unfortunately   6 comfortable   9 unbelievable
       4 especially   7 accommodation   10 necessary

3.2 1 knee (k)   2 comb (b)   3 castle (t)   4 salmon (l)   5 receipt (p)

3.3 2 amount   3 behave   4 official   5 emphasise   6 relating to

3.4 2 The 'z' spelling is usual in American English, but both are possible in British English.
       3 an adverb
       4 uncountable
       5 on
       6 She's an **old** friend; he's my **best** friend; you **make** friends with people. You may also have found these common word partners (a **close** friend, a friend **of mine**)

3.5 1 definition 3   2 definition 1   3 definition 4   4 definition 2

Unit 4

4.1

parts of speech	punctuation	pronunciation
noun, adjective, adverb, preposition	comma, question mark, full stop	phonemic symbol, stress, syllable

4.2 2 **in** Seville (preposition)   7 wonderful **hotel/place** (noun)
3 **took/got** a train (verb)   8 **to** Spain (preposition)
4 **a** beautiful city (indefinite article)   9 **never** stays (adverb)
5 **expensive** hotel (adjective)   10 if **I** have (pronoun)
6 **of** money (preposition)

4.3 2 a capital letter   7 phrasal verbs
3 a full stop   8 punctuation
4 a question mark   9 with (phonemic) symbols
5 a comma   10 late
6 uncountable noun

4.4 in'formal 3   'opposite 3   'syllable 3   de'cide 2
'adjective 3   edu'cation 4   pronunci'ation 5

4.5 2 cheaply; dangerously   3 find   4 un-   5 -ness

Unit 5

5.1 2 Thai   7 Arabic
3 Spanish   8 German
4 Israel   9 England/the UK, the USA, Australia
5 China   10 (Swiss) German, French, Italian
6 Portuguese

5.2 2 Asia / the Far East   5 the Caribbean
3 the Middle East   6 South America
4 Europe

5.3 Chinese; Japan; Portuguese; Egyptian; Australia; Arabic; Saudi Arabia; Scandinavia

5.4 2 Turkey   3 South Korea   4 Russia   5 Argentina   6 Greece

5.5 2 Germans   5 Brazilians   7 The Swiss
3 the Japanese   6 the British   8 Russians
4 Israelis

5.6 *Possible answers:*

1 I'm French.
2 The capital of France is Paris. I think the population of France is about 60 million.
3 French.
4 I can speak Italian and English.
5 I have visited Germany, Spain, Italy and the UK.
6 I don't know the Far East, so I would like to visit China and Japan.

Unit 6

6.1 2 in the west   4 in the north-east   6 in the north-east
3 in the south-west   5 in the north-west   7 in the south

6.2 2 coldest place on Earth / in the world   6 waterfall
3 hottest place on Earth / in the world   7 rainforest in the world
4 Cave   8 ocean
5 Canal   9 planet

English Vocabulary in Use Pre-intermediate and Intermediate   **209**

6.3
2 covered
3 regions
4 contrasts
5 covers
6 landscape
7 temperature
8 consists
9 Earth
10 climate
11 distance; distance
12 minus; degrees

6.4 *Possible answers:*

1 In England, 30 °C is about the highest; minus 5 degrees is about the lowest during the day.
2 I like the fact it isn't too hot or too cold, but I would like more sun and less rain.
3 It's flatter in the east, and there are more hills in the west. There is also an area in the north of England with some large lakes. There are more mountains in Scotland.
4 We have a number of long canals, and lots of caves. We don't have any famous waterfalls.
5 It's very hilly, with several large rivers nearby.
6 I live in a medium-sized town which is ten miles from Bristol.

Unit 7

7.1   2 f   3 g   4 c   5 a   6 b   7 d

7.2   2 It's snowing.   3 It's cloudy.   4 It's raining.   5 It's icy.   6 It's sunny.

7.3
2 False. It's not nice to sit outside when it's freezing. / It's nice to sit outside when it's warm.
3 True
4 False. A shower is a short period of rain.
5 True
6 False. If it's humid, the air will feel warm and wet.
7 False. A mild winter means it is warmer than usual.
8 True

7.4
2 cold
3 shower
4 pouring
5 degrees; zero; extremely
6 thunderstorm
7 came
8 temperature
9 cool

7.5 *Possible answers for England:*

We sometimes get humid weather in the summer. We occasionally get thick fog in the winter, especially in the morning. We sometimes get storms in winter. Thunderstorms sometimes occur in the summer at the end of a period of hot weather. Temperatures below zero are not common during the day, but do occur at night in the winter. We sometimes get strong winds in the autumn and winter, and showers can be frequent at any time of the year, but especially in the spring.

Unit 8

8.1

farm animals	wild animals	insects
horse, goat, bull, pig, donkey	monkey, elephant, tiger, camel, leopard	fly, bee, mosquito, ant, butterfly

8.2
3 different
4 different
5 same
6 different
7 same
8 different
9 different
10 different

8.3   2 wild   3 cage   4 insects   5 rare   6 protect

8.4
2 Monkeys
3 Camels
4 Whales
5 Giraffes
6 Snakes
7 Elephants
8 Parrots

8.5 *Possible answers:*

1 Yes. I've got a dog called Max.
2 No.
3 I don't like seeing birds in cages, but I can understand why we need to keep some wild animals in zoos.
4 I'm not frightened of animals, but I don't like it when birds get inside the house and fly around the rooms; it's scary!

Unit 9

9.1 *DOWN:* heel, knee, chest, ankle, chin

ACROSS: cheek, hip, elbow, lip(s), skin

9.2 2 c   3 a   4 f   5 b   6 d

9.3 2 lips   3 chin   4 shoulder   5 waist   6 cheek   7 neck   8 chest

9.4 *Possible answers:*

2 running
3 when someone says something funny
4 when they see someone they know or say goodbye to someone
5 when they have a cold

6 when they mean 'no'
7 when they mean 'yes'
8 when they're sad
9 when they're tired

Unit 10

10.1 2 looking   3 hair   4 shoulders   5 smart   6 height   7 dark

10.2 Your **height** is how **tall** you are.
Your **weight** is how much you **weigh**.
Roughly and **approximately** are similar in meaning.
Medium and **average** are similar in meaning.
Broad and **narrow** are opposite in meaning.
Wavy and **curly** are similar in meaning, and describe hair.

10.3 2 gorgeous
3 attractive/handsome
4 athletic

5 pretty
6 overweight
7 ordinary

8 roughly/approximately
9 tallish

10.4 *Possible answers from a man:*

1 I'm about one metre 78.
2 It's dark brown and quite wavy.
3 My girlfriend is about one metre 68. She's very attractive in my opinion, and she's got short blonde hair, which is straight. I don't know how much she weighs; I wouldn't ask her that.

Unit 11

11.1

positive	negative
nice	unpleasant
generous	mean
sensible	silly
hard-working	lazy
calm	nervous

11.2 2 **un**friendly   3 **un**pleasant   4 **im**patient   5 **dis**honest   6 **un**reliable

11.3 2 mean
3 unreliable
4 patient

5 shy
6 sensible
7 serious

8 calm
9 creative
10 talented

11.4   2 nervous   5 humour   8 character
         3 wish   6 clever/intelligent   9 stupid
         4 lazy   7 trust   10 kind

11.5   *Possible answers:*

I think I am quite positive (2), very reliable (1), not very confident (3), a bit lazy (4), have quite a good sense of humour (2) and am quite impatient (5).
I would like to be creative and more patient; I would hate to be mean.

Unit 12

12.1   Nouns: jealousy, confusion, disappointment, anxiety
Adjectives: proud, curious, emotional

12.2   2 f   3 d   4 b   5 a   6 e

12.3   scared 6   cheerful 5   upset 3   confused 2   depressed 4

12.4   2 feelings/emotions   6 mood
         3 energetic   7 hopeful
         4 effect   8 frightened/scared
         5 stress

12.5   *Possible answers:*

1 I'm not sure that colour does, but the weather certainly affects me. I feel more positive when the sun is shining, and rain makes me depressed.
2 I think I suffer from stress sometimes at work, or if I have too many things on my mind.
3 I don't think my mood changes much from day to day.
4 I feel more energetic in the evening.

Unit 13

13.1   2 niece   5 brother-in-law   8 only
         3 nephew   6 elder
         4 sister-in-law   7 cousin

13.2   2 Remarry   6 Twins
         3 Relatives/Relations   7 Mate
         4 best   8 Friendship
         5 old   9 stepfather

13.3   2 married   3 altogether   4 since   5 get on (well)   6 ex

13.4   *Possible answers for Laura, aged 20:*

1 I have an elder sister called Rosie.
2 Yes, very well.
3 No, not especially close, but we all get on well.
4 My cousin Daniel; he got married last year.
5 Anita.
6 I've known her for nine years.
7 We started secondary school at the same time.

Unit 14

14.1   2 early twenties   5 middle-aged   8 an adult
         3 mid-thirties   6 elderly   9 teens
         4 teenager   7 retired   10 toddler

14.2   2 True   5 False. At first life wasn't easy.
         3 False. Her parents were very strict.   6 False. She managed to get a job in Cardiff.
         4 True

14.3
2 in the end I did it
3 roughly/about my age
4 nearly thirty now
5 strict
6 allowed to stay up and watch TV
7 brought up in Scotland
8 managed to pass my exams
9 stayed out late
10 let me wear what I liked
11 childhood
12 retired

14.4 *Possible answers:*

1 I was brought up in a town called Dartmouth.
2 It's on the coast and I remember going to the beach a lot with my family and friends.
3 My mum was quite strict, but not my dad. They didn't let me swim in certain places because they thought it was dangerous.
4 Up to the age of 17, I had to be home on the last bus, which was about 11:15. When I learnt to drive, I stayed out later than that.

Unit 15

15.1
I went out with Gabriel.	3
We got married.	5
I got pregnant three months later.	8
We got engaged.	4
I got to know Gabriel.	2
Our son was born just after our first anniversary.	9
We went on our honeymoon.	7
I met Gabriel at a party.	1
We had a big reception.	6

15.2
2 date
3 marriage
4 pregnant
5 anniversary
6 bride; (bride)groom
7 give

15.3
1 couple
2 to know; wedding
3 ceremony; honeymoon
4 left; wrong; his own; divorced / a divorce

15.4 *Possible answers:*

1 I was 14 or 15 and I went to a party with a girl called Yvonne.
2 Yes, it was at university when I was about 20. Her name was Liz and we were together for almost three years.
3 The last wedding I went to was my cousin's, who got married to a man I had never met.
4 I went to a friend's 30th birthday party.

Unit 16

16.1 *Possible answers:*
have a late night / an early night / a sleep / a wash / a shower / a bath / a snack / a light lunch
do the washing / the ironing / the housework / the shopping

16.2 2 h   3 e   4 c   5 f   6 b   7 a   8 d

16.3
2 usually *wakes* me up
3 have a *snack* in the afternoon
4 go *out* on Friday
5 friends *come* round
6 eat *out* at the weekend
7 don't *bother* with a full meal
8 have *cereal* for breakfast
9 housework; *fortunately/luckily* I have a husband
10 I try to reply to them straight *away*

16.4
2 instead
3 stay in
4 early
5 come round
6 takeaway
7 chat

16.5   *Possible answers:*

Similar
1 I usually have a light lunch.
2 I have my main meal in the evening.
3 I sometimes have a bath instead of a shower in the winter.

Different
1 I usually wake up before 7.00 am.
2 I have a shower in the morning.
3 I do my own washing because I don't have a cleaner.

Unit 17

17.1   2 False. They used to live in the centre of town.   7 False. A French couple live upstairs.
3 False. They rent their flat.   8 False. The parents own a cottage.
4 True   9 True
5 False. They live on the second floor.   10 True
6 True

17.2   Positive: air conditioning, character, charming
Negative: dark, no central heating

17.3   2 a lift   3 a balcony   4 a cottage   5 front door   6 steps

17.4   2 on; downstairs   5 outskirts   8 floor; lift
3 space   6 balcony   9 moved
4 location   7 heat   10 light

17.5   *Possible answers:*
I live in a house, which I own, and it's near the centre of town. I've lived here for seven years now.
I used to live in a house in London, but I moved because I didn't need to be in London for my job.
I've got central heating where I live, but I haven't got air conditioning or a balcony.

Unit 18

18.1   2 in the microwave   4 in the washing machine   6 in a cupboard
3 in the oven   5 in the dishwasher (or sink)   7 in the freezer

18.2   2 sink, in the kitchen
3 curtains, in the living room or the bedroom
4 cushions, in the living room
5 kettle, in the kitchen
6 washbasin, in the bathroom
7 carpet, in the living room or the bedrooms
8 pillow, in the bedroom
9 washing machine, in the utility room or the kitchen
10 cooker, in the kitchen
11 armchair, in the living room
12 tiles, in any room, though more likely in the kitchen or bathroom

18.3   2 wooden   5 share; own   8 blanket; duvet
3 choice   6 spare   9 en suite
4 study   7 tap(s)   10 utility

18.4   *Possible answers:*

1 tiles   2 tiles   3 carpet and a couple of rugs   4 curtains   5 a duvet

18.5   *Possible answers:*
I like big sofas with lots of cushions.
I prefer a wooden floor with rugs.
I have no preference – it depends on the blinds and the curtains.
I prefer a duvet.
I must have two pillows. I can't stand only one pillow.

Unit 19

19.1 2 No 3 No 4 No 5 Yes 6 Yes 7 Yes 8 No 9 Yes 10 Yes

19.2 2 a bank loan 3 fee(s) 4 cash 5 rent 6 cashpoint 7 currency

19.3 2 She **wasted** the money. 5 He **charged** us £25.
3 I **can't afford** to go. 6 I **owe** a lot of money.
4 We could **hire** a car. 7 I always **check** my account carefully.

19.4 2 account 3 amount 4 earn 5 owe 6 pay (them) back 7 accommodation

19.5 *Possible answers:*

1 Yes, I've had an account for about fifteen years.
2 I don't check my account very often. (see next answer)
3 I get money from a cashpoint about once a week, and I always ask for a receipt so that I know how much is in my account.
4 I had a bank loan to buy my first car – that's all.
5 Yes, I'm saving up for a holiday.
6 Yes, I rent a flat with a friend. We had to pay a deposit of one month's rent.

Unit 20

20.1 3 different 4 different 5 same 6 different 7 same 8 different

20.2 3 a 4 a 5 a 6 – 7 – 8 a 9 – 10 a

20.3 2 sick 5 bleeding 8 serious
3 hurts 6 suffer
4 bandage 7 aches

20.4 *people have* **heart attacks**
surgeons *perform* **operations**
tablets/pills *are common forms of* **medicine**
hepatitis *affects the* **liver**
people have **sore throats**

20.5 *Possible answers:*

1 I take tablets such as aspirin.
2 I hardly ever get a cough or sore throat.
3 No, I haven't been a patient.
4 I had to go into hospital for a minor operation, but I didn't have to stay overnight.
5 We have various tablets for pain, e.g. paracetamol or Ibuprofen. We usually have different medicines for colds and flu, or for stomach problems.

Unit 21

21.1

items of clothing	jewellery	parts of clothing
boots, top, jumper, scarf, cap, tights	earrings, ring, bracelet, necklace	button, zip, pocket, sleeve, collar

21.2 2 The first woman is wearing a necklace; the second isn't.
3 The first woman has four pockets on her jacket; the second has two.
4 The first woman has two buttons on her jacket sleeve; the second has one.
5 The second woman is wearing earrings; the first isn't.
6 The second woman is wearing a bracelet; the first isn't.

21.3 2 in 5 suit 8 undid
3 dressed 6 up 9 rucksack
4 on 7 into 10 dressed

21.4 *Possible answers for an English woman:*

1 I always wear earrings, and I sometimes wear a ring and a necklace. I don't wear a bracelet very often.
2 I think dark colours suit me best.
3 I prefer to wear casual clothes, but I have to wear smart clothes for work.
4 I hope I look quite stylish, but I'm not sure I do.
5 I never wear a cap, but I sometimes wear a hat.
6 I often wear T-shirts, but I never wear trainers.

21.5 *Possible answers for an English boy:*

1 I hardly ever wear a suit.
2 I don't like wearing ties – but I have to wear one for school.
3 I almost always undo the top button of my shirt – unless I'm cold.
4 I always change into jeans after school.
5 I don't wear a cap or a hat.
6 I wear T-shirts a lot, and I always wear trainers.

Unit 22

22.1 2 different   3 different   4 similar   5 different   6 different   7 similar

22.2
2 fashion
3 with your skirt
4 got on
5 good on you
6 fit
7 tight
8 dresses

22.3
2 reasonable
3 wardrobe
4 fashionable / in fashion
5 changing room
6 designer labels / designers
7 shop assistant
8 serve

22.4
2 try
3 changing
4 served
5 fit
6 tight
7 shame/pity
8 size
9 suited/suits
10 leave

22.5 *Possible answers for a young man:*

I occasionally shop with a friend but usually on my own.
I always try on shoes and trousers before I buy them, but not shirts.
I sometimes buy clothes that don't suit me, but that's just a mistake. I never buy clothes just because they're fashionable.
If I buy trousers, I don't usually buy a shirt to go with it. But if I buy a jacket, I might buy a shirt to go with it.
My wardrobe does have quite a few things that I hardly ever wear.
I don't buy designer labels unless they're reduced in the sales; the price has to be reasonable.
I like casual clothes. I don't really care whether they're fashionable.
I'm not always happy with what I've got on, but if I'm honest, I don't think about it much.

Unit 23

23.1
2 True
3 True
4 False. Expensive items are on the middle shelves.
5 True
6 True
7 True
8 False. Sometimes you buy more than you need and throw some of it away.

23.2 con'venient   'checkout   'entrance   a 'refund   re'place   'item

23.3
2 shopping centres
3 street markets
4 street markets
5 shopping centres
6 both, but probably more true of shopping centres

23.4
2 makes; replace	5 offer	8 atmosphere
3 throw	6 entrance	9 likely
4 queue	7 range	

23.5 *Possible answers:*

1 I go to a supermarket once a week. I don't like shopping there, but it is convenient.
2 I hardly ever go to shopping centres. I don't like them very much.
3 I go to a small food market once a week. I really like it because you get to know the people who have the stalls and they often sell things which are a bit different.
4 I don't often haggle for things; I'm not very good at it.
5 I take things back to shops if there is something wrong with them, and usually I get a refund.

Unit 24

24.1
1 vegetable: *pea(s)*	fruit: peach, pear, pineapple
2 vegetable: garlic	fruit: grapes
3 vegetable: mushroom	fruit: melon
4 vegetable: spinach	fruit: strawberry
5 vegetable: onion	fruit: olive

24.2 lett<u>u</u>ce/ch<u>i</u>cken, <u>au</u>bergine/tomat<u>o</u>, <u>o</u>nion/m<u>u</u>shroom, pr<u>aw</u>n/p<u>o</u>rk, s<u>a</u>lmon/l<u>a</u>mb

24.3
2 cabbage, the others are all used in salad
3 crab, the others are all meat
4 peach, the others are all vegetables
5 broccoli, the others are all types of seafood
6 chicken, the others are all vegetables

24.4 *These are the most likely answers:*

melon: NO   grapes: YES   peaches: YES or SOMETIMES
pears: YES or SOMETIMES   lemon: NO

24.5
1 lamb; veal; pork	4 a vegetarian
2 lettuce	5 bunch
3 oil and vinegar (oil and lemon is also possible)	

24.6 *Possible answers for the UK:*

1 Strawberries and pears are more common than pineapple.
2 Lamb and beef are more expensive than pork or chicken.
3 lettuce, tomato and cucumber; sometimes onion and red pepper as well
4 aubergine, red pepper, pineapple, melons, grapes or peaches
5 veal
6 Peaches are my favourite fruit. / Lamb is my favourite meat.

Unit 25

25.1 fry, grill, roast, bake, barbecue

25.2 raw – door; sour – hour; oven – love; pie – lie; saucepan – four

25.3
2 ~~cooker~~ cook	5 ~~good in~~ good at
3 ~~fry pan~~ frying pan	6 ~~tastes~~ flavours
4 ~~sour~~ bitter	

25.4
2 chef	5 sour
3 tasty	6 raw
4 cooker	7 delicious; horrible/terrible/unpleasant

25.5
2 ingredients	5 chopped	8 stirred
3 peeled	6 fried	9 tasted
4 boiled	7 added	

25.6 *Possible answers for a British person:*

1 We eat a lot of roast beef, baked potatoes and barbecued chicken in the UK. We sometimes eat fried rice but we don't usually eat raw fish unless we go to a Japanese restaurant.
2 I like bitter chocolate, I like spicy food, and I like the taste of garlic. I don't like chocolate-flavoured ice cream very much – I prefer vanilla.
3 The weather isn't good enough in the UK to cook outside on a barbecue very often.
4 I'm not a great cook but I'm quite good at making desserts.

Unit 26

26.1   2 f   3 g   4 a   5 c   6 b   7 h   8 e

26.2   2 It was quiet.   5 There are disadvantages.
3 It's very dirty.   6 There's nowhere to park.
4 It was very dull/boring.

26.3   2 cultural   3 variety   4 night   5 stuck   6 value

26.4   2 exhausted   5 pollution   8 going on
3 stressed   6 hurry   9 get poverty
4 lively   7 park

26.5 *Possible answers for a town in the south of England:*

1 It's quite bad from 8.00 to 9.00 in the morning, and then again from 4.30 to 6.00 pm.
2 It's very good for a medium-sized town: lots of restaurants and bars, a few nightclubs, two or three cinemas, two or three theatres, several concert halls, etc.
3 Yes it is. As well as cinema, theatre and concerts, we have a number of festivals: a literature festival, a jazz festival, a food festival, and lots of cultural talks and lectures you can go to.
4 There is pollution in the town centre because it's between two hills.
5 The crime rate isn't bad because it is quite a rich town, and I feel safe at night.
6 Living in my town has lots of advantages. There are lots of things to do, like go to the cinema, theatre, etc. There are plenty of shops too, and a train station. But some of the disadvantages are that there are too many cars and traffic jams and this means there is pollution too.

Unit 27

27.1   2 grass   3 leaves   4 woods   5 plants   6 roots   7 branches   8 crops

27.2   2 countryside (also country)   4 own   6 ground/grass
3 up   5 season   7 keep

27.3   2 gate   3 tractor   4 footpath   5 field   6 valley   7 woods   8 farmhouse

27.4   2 spaces   5 surrounded   8 public   11 away
3 air   6 worst   9 hopeless
4 pick   7 get   10 much

27.5 *Possible answers:*

I agree with most of the ideas in the text. I also think that life in the country is probably less stressful than in a big city, and probably healthier too. One of the disadvantages of living in the country is that you become totally dependent on having a car.

Unit 28

28.1   2 ride   5 run   8 fares
3 get in   6 fly   9 driver
4 journey   7 missed   10 off; stop

28.2   2 van   4 lorry (also truck)   6 bicycle/bike
3 motorbike   5 coach

28.3
2 journey
3 convenient; away
4 corner
5 reliable
6 queue
7 return
8 complaining
9 season
10 platform

28.4 *Possible answers:*

1 Generally yes.
2 Prices vary a great deal in England. Sometimes a return is twice the price of a single, but sometimes it is not much more than a single.
3 Where I live is very convenient for the train station if I need to travel out of town.
4 I don't take taxis very often; only if I need to get home late at night.
5 I usually ride my bike once a week.

Unit 29

29.1
2 pedestrians
3 pavement
4 pedestrian crossing
5 (road) junction
6 brake
7 road sign

29.2
2 lane
3 traffic light(s)
4 overtaking
5 motorway
6 bridge
7 bend
8 (road) junction

29.3
2 lost
3 direct
4 via
5 way
6 ended
7 turning

29.4
2 accident
3 approaching
4 overtake
5 speed
6 swerve
7 crashed
8 damaged
9 injuries

29.5 *Possible answers for England:*

1 Yes, it's 70 mph. (about 115 kph)
2 There are usually three lanes.
3 Yes, they do.
4 Not very often, but it sometimes happens if the road is very narrow.

Unit 30

30.1
2 Mind the step
3 Admission free
4 Out of order
5 No vacancies/entry/exit
6 Do not lean out of the window / leave bags unattended
7 Please queue other side
8 Mind your head
9 Please do not disturb / Please do not feed the animals
10 Keep off the grass
11 Keep right/left
12 Silence examination in progress

30.2
2 In a hotel window
3 In a bank or post office
4 On a vending machine (a machine selling drinks and snacks)
5 At a theatre
6 On a parcel
7 In a zoo

30.3 2 Do not leave bags unattended
3 Please do not disturb
4 No parking
5 Do not lean out of the window
6 Mind your head
7 Admission free
8 SILENCE – examination in progress

30.4 No exit, Silence – examination in progress, out of order, keep right, mind the step, no entry

30.5 *Possible signs in English you might see are:*

English spoken here
Entrance [you go in here]
Flat to let [advertising a flat that you can rent]
Cyclists dismount here [people on bicycles must get off their bikes here]
No through road [there is no way out for cars at the other end of this road]

Unit 31

31.1 2 c   3 h   4 a   5 f   6 d   7 e   8 b

31.2 2 to look up the meaning of words
3 a plug
4 to rub something out
5 because you haven't got one (or someone else hasn't got one)
6 to highlight something
7 to sharpen a pencil
8 to measure something, or perhaps to underline something

31.3 2 How do you pronounce 'swap'?   4 How do you use the word 'swap' in a sentence?
3 How do you spell 'swap'?

31.4 2 Could you turn up the DVD player?
3 Could you lend me a dictionary?
4 Could you repeat that, please?
5 Could you explain the difference between *lend* and *borrow*?
6 Could I borrow your ruler?
7 Could we swap places?

31.5 *Your own answers*

Unit 32

32.1 2 f   3 g   4 b   5 h   6 d   7 c   8 a

32.2 2 primary   3 secondary   4 take; vocational training   5 stay   6 go (on)

32.3 2 timetable   3 into   4 both are correct   5 break   6 break up
7 get   8 dress (you can wear what you want = you can dress the way you want)

32.4 2 wear   3 male; female   4 trouble   5 punished   6 atmosphere

32.5 *Your own answers*

Unit 33

33.1 2 both are correct   3 up   4 revise for   5 do   6 both are correct   7 failed

33.2 2 grade
3 candidates
4 essay
5 work
6 increase; basic
7 vowels; consonants
8 hard work
9 willing

33.3 2 revision   3 my best   4 exam preparation   5 things wrong   6 ear for language

33.4   2 accent   4 accurate   6 through
       3 fluent   5 understood   7 well

33.5   *Your own answers*

Unit 34

34.1   2 engineering   3 medicine   4 economics   5 law   6 architecture

34.2

I did a degree course.	5
I passed with good grades.	2
I got a Master's.	8
I did a postgraduate course.	7
I did my final exams at school.	1
I became an undergraduate.	4
I got a place at university.	3
I got a degree in business studies.	6

34.3   2 False. You have to get good grades in your school exams.
       3 True
       4 False. Most degree courses last three years.
       5 True
       6 False. If you are successful, you get a degree.
       7 False. Students studying for their first degree are called undergraduates.
       8 False. Science students do not write a lot of essays. (They spend their time in laboratories.) Arts students have to write a lot of essays.
       9 True
     10 False. If you study arts subjects you work in a library. / If you study science subjects you work in a laboratory.

34.4   2 degree   3 went on   4 lasted   5 into   6 research   7 qualification

34.5   *Your own answers*

Unit 35

35.1   2 d   3 f   4 e   5 a   6 b

35.2   2 sailor   6 accountant
       3 mechanic   7 plumber, carpenter, electrician, builder, mechanic and surgeon
       4 vet   8 doctor, surgeon, dentist, vet, pilot, electrician
       5 pilot or builder   9 police officer, soldier, sailor, firefighter, pilot, doctor, vet

35.3   2 A vet treats animals.
       3 An architect designs buildings.
       4 An electrician installs and repairs electrical things.
       5 A lawyer represents people with legal problems.
       6 A surgeon operates on people.
       7 A mechanic repairs cars.
       8 A dentist looks after people's teeth.
       9 An engineer plans the building of roads, bridges, etc.

35.4   2 Really? When did he join the navy?   4 Really? When did she join the army?
       3 Really? When did he join the air force?   5 Really? When did he join the fire brigade?

35.5 *Possible answers:*

My father is an accountant.
I have an uncle who is a doctor, and another who is retired. (He is 63 and no longer works.)
The man next door is a police officer, and his wife is a teacher.
I have another neighbour who is a journalist.
I have a friend in the army, another friend who is training to be a doctor, and a third friend who is an electrician.

Unit 36

36.1 Words which are connected with money: earn, wages, salary, income

36.2 2 e 3 d 4 f 5 c 6 a

36.3
2 I work in marketing.
3 I work for the government.
4 My income is £34,000.
5 What does your job involve?
6 I'm in charge of the reception area.
7 What do you do for a living?
8 My job involves reading government reports.
9 I give advice to clients.
10 I made a complaint about the service.

36.4
2 runs / is in charge of
3 responsible
4 involves
5 day
6 five
7 overtime
8 earn/make
9 conditions
10 tax
11 a
12 off
13 advises
14 dealing
15 fixed
16 do/work

36.5 *Your own answers*

Unit 37

37.1 2 e 3 d 4 a 5 f 6 b

37.2

verb	noun	adjective
employ	(un)employment	(un)employed
promote	promotion	
retire	retirement	retired
resign	resignation	
succeed	success	successful
own	owner	

37.3
2 abroad
3 part time
4 quit; rise
5 experience; courses
6 work
7 succeed
8 apply
9 sack
10 own
11 own; success
12 application

37.4 *Possible answers:*

1 Yes, I was promoted to hotel manager last year.
2 I get a pay rise, but not always a good one.
3 Yes, I went on a computer course last year.
4 I would like to do a course on financial planning to help me with my current job.
5 I have never been given the sack, but I resigned from my last job when I was given the opportunity to work for my present employer.

Unit 38

38.1 2 rubbish bin 3 filing cabinet 4 paperwork 5 noticeboard

38.2 2 colleagues 3 calendar 4 diary 5 invoice 6 calculator 7 loads

38.3 2 arranged; appointment   4 attend / go to   6 involve; organise/arrange
3 run out   5 show (them) round

38.4 2 The photocopier isn't working.   5 We've run out of paper.
3 We've got loads of work today.   6 Why is he absent this morning?
4 I have to attend a meeting.

38.5 *Possible answer:*

In my job as a dentist, I have to do quite a lot of paperwork, I send a few emails, I attend a few meetings, and I never use a photocopier. I don't show people round, I don't have to organise events or type letters, and I don't send out invoices. The only things I repair are people's teeth.

Unit 39

39.1 *Words which refer to people: expert, accountant, client, contacts*

39.2 2 demand   5 employees   8 job
3 aim   6 set up   9 expanding
4 firm/business   7 headquarters   10 a great deal

39.3 2 take up   5 set up   8 take over
3 clients   6 customer   9 a former
4 ex-   7 currently

39.4 2 They achieved a lot / a great deal.
3 I have a lot of contacts in banking.
4 They were formerly (called) BMG.
5 It's always been my ambition to fly a plane.
6 She's an expert in finance.
7 The adverts attracted (a lot of) attention.

39.5 2 firm/business/company   4 branch   6 expanded
3 achieved/had   5 run   7 ambition/aim

Unit 40

40.1 2 by   3 from   4 of   5 in   6 in   7 of

40.2 2 a loan   3 interest   4 inflation   5 profit   6 trade   7 trend

40.3 1 loan; charges; interest; pay back. ANSWER €600
2 rate; % (per cent); pay back. ANSWER €575.

40.4 2 figures   6 sharp   10 quarters
3 increased / went up / rose   7 fall/decrease   11 risen / gone up
4 made   8 loss   12 sharply
5 raise/increase   9 stayed

40.5 *Possible answers:*

1 About 2%   2 7–8%   3 Badly   4 2010–1   5 One British pound is 1.4 US dollars.

Unit 41

41.1

sport	person	place	verb	equipment
swimming, motor racing, basketball, skiing	golfer, athlete, goalkeeper, racing driver	court, track, pitch, rink	jump, box, race, sail	net, stick, skis, swimming costume

41.2 2 do   3 play   4 ski   5 did   6 go   7 do   8 keep   9 work out

41.3 2 swimming/swimmer   3 boxing/boxer   4 sailing/sailor   5 athletics/athlete

41.4
2 hockey	5 costumes	8 climbing
3 courses	6 racing	9 tent
4 fun/pleasure	7 fit	10 jogging

41.5 *Possible answers:*

1 In the winter I play football, and in the summer I play tennis and go swimming. It's not serious; I just do it for fun.

2 I watch a lot of sport on the TV: football, tennis, ice hockey, motor racing. In fact, I'll watch almost any sport if I have nothing else to do.

Unit 42

42.1
2 lose / lost / have lost
3 beat / beat / have beaten
4 draw / drew / have drawn
5 break / broke / have broken
6 give up / gave up / have given up

42.2
2 both are correct	4 tournament	6 beat
3 score	5 both are correct	7 competition

42.3
2 score; result (score is also possible)		7 league
3 beat/defeated		8 took
4 drew		9 leading
5 championship/tournament		10 against
6 record		

42.4

```
¹R A C E
  ²L O S E
³T E A M
  ⁴S U P E R B
⁵G I V E U P
⁶C A P T A I N
    ⁷W I N N E R
⁸V I C T O R Y
    ⁹F I N A L
   ¹⁰L O S E R
¹¹T O U R N A M E N T
```

42.5 *Possible answers:*

1 I've taken part in lots of competitions: football, cricket, rugby, swimming and athletics.
2 I won a cup competition at secondary school in football.
3 I was captain of the rugby team at secondary school.
4 I came first in a backstroke (swimming) race when I was at primary school, and at secondary school I won the 100 and 200 metres (athletics) on several occasions.
5 I've watched lots of finals on TV: the FA Cup, the World Cup, the UEFA Cup, Wimbledon, the French Open, the Olympics, and so on. I also went to Twickenham to see the rugby team I support in an important final of a cup competition. Unfortunately we lost.

Unit 43

43.1
across: literature, author, actor, fiction, novel, poetry, comedy
down: poem, thriller, star, film, review

43.2
2 ~~year~~ century	5 ~~article~~ review
3 ~~past~~ future	6 ~~autobiography~~ biography
4 ~~happening~~ on	7 ~~frightened~~ laugh; or ~~Comedies~~ Horror films

43.3
2	entertainment	5	acting	8	director
3	actors	6	entertainer		
4	poem	7	reviewer		

43.4
2	latest	4	(film) director	6	on	8	novel
3	directed	5	complicated	7	comedies	9	fancy

43.5 *Possible answers:*

1 I don't read poetry but I read lots of novels. I enjoy thrillers and I like the English writer William Boyd.
2 Yes, I go to the cinema quite a lot. There are certain directors whose films I always see, but usually I go and see films that have had good reviews, or films that friends recommend.
3 I read reviews in the Sunday paper.
4 My favourite films are *Godfather* 1 and 2, and part of the reason I like them is that they have three of my favourite actors: Robert De Niro, Al Pacino and Marlon Brando.

Unit 44

44.1   2 e   3 a   4 f   5 b   6 d

44.2   2 single   3 album; comes   4 live   5 recorded   6 advertised

44.3 *Suggested answers:*

Ballet *is a form of* **dancing** *that tells a story to music.*
Audiences *listen to* **concerts**.
Albums *are made in a* **recording studio**.
The **conductor** *stands in front of an* **orchestra**.
A **composer** *is someone who writes* **classical music**.

44.4
2	orchestra; conductor	5	album	8	composer
3	opera singers (tenors)	6	guitarist	9	operas
4	single	7	cellist	10	solo; Michael Jackson

44.5
1 I like rock music, pop and R&B. My taste in music is very different from my parents – they hate rock music!
2 My favourite artist is Beyoncé. I really like her song, *Formation*.
3 I bought Iggy Azalea's latest album earlier this year.
4 The last time I saw someone perform live was last year.
5 I'm interested in both the tune and the lyrics.
6 I play the guitar, but very badly!

Unit 45

45.1   2 included   3 maximum   4 exciting   5 ships/boats   6 move/walk

45.2
2 The children dress up.
3 People come from all over Japan.
4 The event is held every year.
5 Do you celebrate your birthday? OR Do you do anything (special) to celebrate your birthday?
6 The festival is an annual event. OR The festival happens annually.

45.3
2	festival	5	celebrates	8	gather
3	lasts	6	consists	9	Firework
4	takes	7	spectacular		

45.4 *Your own answers*

Unit 46

46.1 2 e   3 b   4 f   5 a   6 d

46.2
2 reviews	3 B&B (or bed and breakfast)
4 accommodation	5 package holiday

46.3
2 destination	3 package holiday	4 listing
5 iron	6 central heating	

46.4
2 recommend	3 nearest	4 password
5 nearby	6 switch on	

46.5 *Your own answers*

Unit 47

47.1
2 excess baggage	6 duty free	10 cabin crew
3 check-in desk	7 flight number	11 baggage reclaim
4 hand luggage	8 overhead locker	12 passport control
5 terminal building	9 boarding card	

47.2
2 passengers	5 destination	8 hand luggage
3 luggage/suitcases	6 check your passport	9 runway
4 boarding card	7 gate	

47.3
2 announcement	5 take off	8 landed
3 delay	6 fasten	9 terminal
4 boarded	7 crew	10 flight

47.4 *Possible answers:*

1 The worst part of the flight for me is the take-off, and the best part is the landing because I'm just pleased when it's over. I don't like flying much.
2 There are often delays in the winter when the weather is bad.
3 I often think about the place I'm going to or the place I've just been to. Other than that, I read a book or watch a film. Occasionally I talk to the person sitting next to me.
4 I try to get through customs quickly, so I can go home or start to enjoy my holiday!
5 I never have anything to declare because I rarely buy things when I travel.

Unit 48

48.1

steak	facilities	courses	*water*
rare, medium, well-done	mini-bar, room service, safe	starter, main course, dessert	still, sparkling

48.2 2 e   3 a   4 c   5 h   6 b   7 d   8 f

48.3
2 reception	5 'll have	8 heart/centre
3 double/twin	6 facilities	9 mixed; course
4 service	7 tip	10 stay; check

48.4
2 reservation	4 included (in the price)	6 parking
3 available	5 advance	7 to order

48.5 *Possible answers:*

If I go to a hotel in my own country, I usually drive, so parking is very important. I also like to have satellite TV.
A restaurant is only important if there are no other good restaurants in the area.
A mini-bar and air conditioning are great if it's in the summer and it is quite hot.
I usually carry my money and credit cards with me, so I don't need a safe.
I never use room service or need Internet access, so they're not important at all.

Unit 49

49.1
1 latte, milkshake, hot chocolate, smoothie
2 bagel, panini, toastie, baguette, wrap
3 cupcake, muffin, waffle

49.2
2 cappuccino   3 croissants   4 decaf
5 milkshake   6 smoothie   7 vegetarian

49.3   2 e   3 a   4 c   5 d

49.4   2 large   3 panini   4 muffin   5 take away

49.5   *Your own answers*

Unit 50

50.1   Religious places are: temple, cathedral, mosque

50.2
2 sightseeing   4 packed   6 lost   8 go out
3 attractions/sights   5 explore/visit   7 market

50.3
2 packed   4 great/lovely time   6 guidebook   8 magnificent
3 plenty to do   5 worth seeing/visiting   7 monuments   9 look round

50.4   *Your own answers*

Unit 51

51.1   Any four of these: sunbathe, suntan, sunburn, sunscreen, sunblock, sun cream

51.2   2 c   3 e   4 a   5 f   6 b

51.3   2 sunbathing   3 surfing   4 diving   5 windsurfing

51.4   2 b   3 a   4 c   5 c   6 b

51.5
2 recommend   4 protection/shade   6 stroll/walk   8 go for / have
3 risk   5 breeze   7 shade

51.6   *Possible answers:*

1 I go to seaside resorts in the south-west of England, and sometimes the south of France, or the coast of Spain near Barcelona. I usually go once or twice a year.
2 I go for a swim; that's all.
3 No, I don't like sunbathing. It's boring and I get sunburn easily.
4 No, I don't get a suntan easily and I have had sunburn in the past. I might use sunscreen on my face. I usually wear a T-shirt or sit in the shade if it is very hot.
5 I like to go for a drink and then have a meal.

Unit 52

52.1   Types of TV programme: documentary, soap opera, chat show, series

52.2
2 comes out / is published   4 Channel
3 regional   5 celebrities / well-known

52.3

¹C	E	L	E	B	R	I	T	Y	
	²S	E	R	I	E	S			
³R	E	P	O	R	T				
	⁴S	O	A	P	O	P	E	R	A
		D	A	I	L	Y			
⁶D	O	C	U	M	E	N	T	A	R	Y
	⁷N	A	T	I	O	N	A	L	
⁸C	H	A	T	S	H	O	W		
	⁹A	R	T	I	C	L	E		

52.4
2 reporters/journalists   5 says/said   8 According; forecast
3 headline   6 review   9 soap
4 station   7 adverts/advertisements   10 reality

52.5   *Possible answers:*

1 I think there are about ten national newspapers in England.
2 At least two only come out on Sunday: *The Observer* and *The People*.
3 I read the front-page stories, the sports pages, the reviews, and anything that looks interesting.
4 I watch the news and the weather forecast every day. Programmes I enjoy are documentaries and some drama series. I never watch soap operas.

Unit 53

53.1
1 I gave him a ring; I rang him
2 *Possible answers:* the line was engaged, you rang the wrong number, Tom was out / wasn't in
3 Any three of these: a mobile number, an emergency number, the wrong number, a home phone / landline number

53.2
2 calling   7 message   12 It's
3 My name is   8 answerphone   13 through
4 putting   9 out / not in   14 engaged
5 Is that   10 phone/ring/call (you) back   15 on
6 Speaking   11 Is that

53.3
2 kiss   5 as soon as possible   8 thanks
3 see you   6 for your information   9 boyfriend
4 in my opinion   7 laughing out loud   10 you

53.4   *Your own answers*

Unit 54

54.1   2 h   3 a   4 g   5 b   6 d   7 f   8 c

54.2   2 laptop   3 keyboard   4 spacebar   5 username   6 password

54.3   2 paste   3 copy   4 print   5 cut   6 open an existing document
7 save

54.4   2 hard drive/disk   3 virus   4 laptop   5 password

54.5   2 back up   3 stored; backup/copy   4 install   5 create/open; menu   6 virus; anti-virus

54.6   *Possible answer:*
I have a PC and I use the operating system Windows 10 on it. My computer has a 500GB hard drive so I can store lots of data, particularly photos. I've recently installed software that will help me make my family tree. I have anti-virus software too, which is very important. I'm currently running Microsoft Word.

Unit 55

55.1   2 e   3 a   4 c   5 f   6 d

55.2
2 Internet Service Provider   6 Emails that you do not want, usually advertisements
3 Access to email and other services   7 Zac at hotmail dot com
4 Browsers   8 They discuss things and share information about
5 A particular subject or their everyday lives   themselves.

55.3
2 immediately; essential   5 attachment; checked   8 regularly
3 click; link   6 download; download; clips
4 access   7 anti-virus

Possible answers:

1 I use the Internet a lot for my work. I use the BBC website a lot, and I read newspapers online.
2 I don't have a blog, but I occasionally read other people's.
3 I don't download much stuff from the Internet.
4 I watch video clips on Youtube: sporting events, comedy clips, etc. I also watch TV on the Internet.
5 I don't use social networking sites at all.

Unit 56

56.1

noun	person	verb
crime	*criminal*	commit a crime
murder	murderer	murder
theft	thief	steal/take
robbery	robber	rob
burglary	burglar	burgle

56.2 theft/steal; crime/offence; jail/prison; get away/escape; hit/attack

56.3 2 arrest 3 innocent 4 murder 5 offence 6 fine 7 crime 8 punished

56.4
2 stealing
3 broke
4 attacked/hit
5 stole

6 worth
7 escape / get away
8 arrested
9 detectives / the police

10 robbery
11 court
12 guilty
13 prison/jail

Unit 57

57.1 2 political 3 beliefs 4 powerful 5 reduction 6 politicians

57.2

```
¹A B O V E A L L
      L E A D E R
      E L D E R L Y
      C U T
      T A X
  ⁶P O L I C Y
⁷S U P P O R T
      ⁸U N F A I R
```

57.3
2 They voted for her.
3 Elections are held every five years.
4 They will provide hospitals with more money. OR They will provide more money for hospitals.
5 It's a secret ballot.
6 The system treats everyone equally / fairly / the same way.
7 Our policy is to provide care for old people / the elderly.

57.4
2 constituencies
3 political
4 Elections

5 vote
6 parliament
7 party

8 government
9 Prime

57.5 *Your own answers*

57.6 *Your own answers*

Unit 58

58.1   2 fun   3 few   4 now   5 son   6 comfortable

58.2   2 a   3 d   4 e   5 b

58.3
2 recycle		5 Save		8 reduce	
3 waste		6 switching/turning		9 Take	
4 tap		7 Plant			

58.4
2 create		7 environment	
3 result		8 destroy	
4 effects		9 efficient	
5 flood		10 Energy	
6 drought; occurring/happening			

58.5

verb	noun		verb	noun
recycle	*recycling*		solve	solution
waste	waste		reduce	reduction
destroy	destruction		support	support
exist	existence		suffer	suffering

58.6   *Possible answers:*

1 You can certainly see changes in the climate. The weather seems more extreme: more hot weather, more wet weather, etc.
2 We have to put our household rubbish in different containers every week so that more things are recycled, e.g. one container for newspapers; one for bottles, tins and plastic; one for garden rubbish, etc.
3 Yes, I waste energy. I leave lights on and taps running; but I only use the car for essential journeys.
4 I could turn off taps and lights, drive a smaller car, and do things to the house to make it more energy-efficient. Climate change worries me when I think about it.

Unit 59

59.1
die is a verb	war is a noun
attack is a noun and verb	defend is a verb
death is a noun	escape is a noun and verb
shoot is a verb	hide is a verb

59.2
2 shot		5 exploded; killed		8 defend (protect is also possible)
3 hide		6 searching		9 carrying
4 escape / get away		7 destroyed		

59.3
2 battle		5 dead		8 carry
3 both are correct		6 both are correct		9 shot
4 destroyed		7 died		

59.4
2 soldiers (army is possible)		6 killed
3 enemy		7 army
4 bomb		8 took place
5 violent		

59.5   destruction, e.g. The bomb caused a huge amount of destruction.
explosion, e.g. The explosion happened outside the main gates.
defence, e.g. The army are responsible for the defence of the nation.

Unit 60

60.1 2 in   3 on   4 have   5 for   6 same

60.2 2 by   3 until   4 since   5 for   6 during   7 for   8 in   9 since

60.3 2 a long time ago / ages ago   4 recently/lately   6 for the time being
3 the other day   5 for ages

60.4 2 fortnight   4 1963; 50   6 10
3 19; 20   5 7   7 1960s

60.5 *Possible answers (from a Spanish man):*

1 I've been in my present job for a year.
2 It takes me half an hour to get to work.
3 A typical working day for me lasts about seven hours. I work from 9.30 am to 1.30 pm, then I have a long lunch break (siesta) and work again from 5 pm to 8 pm.
4 I've been studying English since 2009, but I stopped for three years during 2011–2014.
5 I haven't spoken English since 11 o'clock this morning.
6 I saw my cousin Rafa the other day.
7 Nowadays I don't go to the gym as much as I used to.
8 One day I hope to be a very successful architect.

Unit 61

61.1 2 two and a half
3 two thousand, three hundred and forty-five
4 nought point two five
5 one million, two hundred and fifty thousand
6 ten point nought/oh four
7 forty-seven per cent
8 the tenth of September (OR September the tenth)
9 nine four oh/zero, double three eight
10 minus five degrees Celsius (OR five degrees below zero)
11 in nineteen ninety-six
12 twenty twelve (OR two thousand and twelve)

61.2 2 twenty thousand   5 the thirty-first of August / August the thirty-first
3 the seventh of June / June the seventh   6 seven two three, six oh/zero nine
4 two hundred and twenty

61.3 2 majority   3 minority   4 calculator   5 up; work   6 stuck

61.4 2 seventy-two   3 sixty   4 five   5 three   6 fifteen

61.5 *Possible answers:*

1 Nineteen eighty eight   4 June the sixth
2 One metre eighty   5 About eighty thousand
3 My building is number twenty-one,   6 I think it's about thirty-seven degrees.
and I live in flat three.

Unit 62

62.1 2 it's (quite) shallow.   5 it's huge/enormous.
3 it's (quite) narrow.   6 it's tiny.
4 he's (quite) tall.

62.2 2 What's the depth of the lake?   6 What's her height?
3 How high is the mountain?   7 How long/wide is the pitch?
4 What's the height of the mountain?   8 What's the length/width of the pitch?
5 How tall is she?

62.3 *Possible answers:*

1 It's just round the corner.
2 It's about a mile away.
3 It's just down the road.
4 No, not far.
5 No, it isn't far.
6 Yes, (it's) quite a long way – about twenty miles.
7 About fifteen minutes' walk.
8 About ten minutes' walk.

Unit 63

63.1

objects	materials	shapes	colours
bell, flag, bucket, ladder	silk, cotton, plastic, fur	circle, square	pink, grey, purple, navy blue

63.2 2 a   3 e   4 b   5 f   6 c

63.3
2 a red chair
3 a round mirror
4 a purple shirt
5 a square table
6 a navy blue hat

63.4 2 a prawn   3 a bucket   4 a ladder   5 the moon   6 bones

63.5 *Possible answers:*

1 No. I don't think they look nice.
2 I have a pink top, a purple skirt, a navy blue jumper and navy blue jeans.
3 I've got a T-shirt with different-coloured stripes and a skirt with thin blue and black stripes.
4 I've got nothing made from fur, but I have got two silk dresses.
5 I've got several pairs of leather shoes and some leather bags.

Unit 64

64.1 2 care   3 far   4 new   5 cup   6 run   7 want

64.2
2 a packet of spaghetti
3 a bowl of fruit
4 a jar of coffee
5 a carton of milk
6 a jug of water
7 a box of matches
8 a bar of soap
9 a bag of apples

64.3
2 a jar of jam
3 a packet of cigarettes
4 a can of cola
5 a carton of milk (or a bottle of milk)
6 a tube of toothpaste
7 a vase of flowers
8 a packet of biscuits

64.4
2 bunch
3 slices/pieces/bits
4 dozen
5 sheet/piece/bit
6 drop/spoonful
7 plenty/lots
8 couple
9 contents
10 several

64.5 2 apples   3 a pair of   4 biscuit   5 crisps   6 shirts   7 bunch

Unit 65

65.1
I'm terribly sorry / I beg your pardon
I was held up / there was a delay
don't worry / never mind

65.2
2 Not
3 keep; long; right
4 I'm; cancelled; problem
5 kind
6 apologise; Never
7 beg

65.3 *Possible answers:*

2 I'm sorry I'm late but I overslept.
3 Oh, thank you very much. That's very kind of you.
4 I'm sorry to disturb you.
5 Excuse me, I have to take an important phone call.
6 I'm sorry to keep you waiting. I won't be long.
7 I'm sorry I'm late but I got held up / delayed in traffic.
8 I must apologise for not sending the information we promised you. Unfortunately....

65.4   1 I'm sometimes late for class. I have to apologise to my teacher and say why I'm late. Ususaly it's because I miss the bus.
    2 I apologised to my friend as I spilt water on one of her books. I said that I was sorry and offered to buy her a new one. I didn't give an excuse.

Unit 66

66.1   A: ~~Do~~ you like to go out this evening? *Would*
    B: I'm afraid ~~but~~ I haven't got any money.
    A: That's OK. I'll pay. How about ~~go~~ to see a film? *going*
    B: No, I think I'd rather ~~to~~ stay in. I have to do some homework.
    A: Why ~~you don't~~ do your homework this afternoon? *don't you*
    B: I'm busy this afternoon.
    A: Well, we could ~~to~~ go tomorrow.
    B: Yeah, ~~it's~~ a great idea. *that's*

66.2   2 d   3 a   4 e   5 f   6 b

66.3   1 mind   3 wondering; problem   5 mind; ahead
    2 possibly; course   4 fancy; mind; don't; idea   6 shall; about; could; rather; like

66.4   *Possible answers:*
    2 Yes, of course.
    3 No, I'm afraid I haven't.
    4 No, help yourself / go ahead.
    5 Yeah, (that's a) great idea.
    6 No, I don't fancy that. OR Yes, if you like. / Yeah, I don't mind.
    7 I'd rather go out somewhere. OR Yes, if you like.

Unit 67

67.1   2 What do you think of   3 How do you feel about

67.2   2 of; personally   4 strongly; right   6 true   8 mean; opinion
    3 extent   5 Personally; disagree   7 view/feeling; point/idea

67.3   2 In my opinion the club needs new players.
    3 I don't agree with you at all.
    4 According to the newspaper, the fire was started on purpose.
    5 I agree with her to some extent.
    6 I take your point / I think that's a good point, but I'm not sure I agree.

67.4   *Possible answers:*

    1 I completely disagree. Lots of women want to have a career *and* children.
    2 Yes, I agree to a certain extent, but most people want to work. It's not their fault they haven't got a job.
    3 Yes, that's true, but you have to remember there are lots of poor people in *our* country.
    4 Yes, I take your point, but what about people who need cars for their work but don't have a lot of money?

Unit 68

68.1   2 so do I   4 to living   6 prefer rugby *to* football
    3 I like *it* very much   5 Me neither. / Neither do I.   7 not interest*ed* in music

68.2   2 common   3 all   4 interest   5 into   6 used   7 rather   8 getting

68.3   2 So do I.   Me too.   4 Neither can I.   Me neither.   6 Neither am I.   Me neither.
    3 Neither do I.   Me neither.   5 So am I.   Me too.   7 So have I.   Me too.

68.4
2 I can't stand these new shoes.
3 She'd rather go home.
4 I'm not very keen on James Bond films.
5 I don't mind the new building.
6 I used to go riding a lot.
7 We have a lot (of things) in common.
8 I'm getting used to this new computer.
9 I don't have the same attitude to work now. OR My attitude to work has changed.

68.5 *Possible answers:*

I really like Italian food.
I don't mind getting up early.
I can't stand waiting for buses or trains.

I prefer classical music to pop music.
Opera doesn't interest me.
I used to have a beard, but not any more.

Unit 69

69.1 take care; excuse me; bless you; thank goodness; not bad

69.2
2 going; bad	4 thank goodness	6 Congratulations	
3 same to	5 take	7 how about	

69.3
2 Goodbye. Nice to meet you.
3 Excuse me. (Could I just get past?)
4 Congratulations.
5 Good luck.
6 Cheers.
7 Bless you.

69.4 2 introduced; shake   3 greet   4 cheek; cheeks   5 care

69.5 *Your own answers*

Unit 70

70.1
2 **un**able
3 **in**correct
4 **un**usual
5 **im**possible
6 **un**comfortable
7 **dis**agree
8 **un**necessary
9 **ir**regular
10 **dis**honest
11 **un**fair
12 **un**lucky

70.2 2 e   3 h   4 f   5 c   6 g   7 a   8 d

70.3
2 illegal
3 undressed
4 unlikely
5 incorrect
6 unfit
7 unexpected
8 dishonest
9 unlucky
10 unfair

70.4 unkind; impatient; unsuitable; dislike; undo; unfashionable; unreliable; unfriendly; untidy; inability; unsociable

Unit 71

71.1

verb	noun	adjective	noun
im'prove	im'provement	'stupid	stu'pidity
in'vent	in'vention	'happy	'happiness
re'lax	relax'ation	'similar	simi'larity
'hesitate	hesi'tation	'popular	popu'larity
ar'range	ar'rangement	sad	'sadness
		'active	ac'tivity

71.2
2 actors
3 directors
4 translators
5 footballers
6 ballet dancers
7 artists
8 scientists

71.3
2 management	4 inability	6 economists
3 government	5 discussions	7 improvement

71.4
2 similarity	4 translation	6 fitness
3 invention	5 artist	7 development

Unit 72

72.1
2 careful	5 comfortable	8 correct
3 reliable	6 annual	9 unbelievable
4 peaceful	7 unforgettable	

72.2 2 f 3 a 4 g 5 b 6 h 7 e 8 c

72.3
2 attractive	7 electrical	12 dangerous
3 personal	8 political	13 creative
4 cloudy	9 enjoyable	14 emotional
5 colourful	10 national	15 foggy
6 famous	11 windy	

72.4 Words with an opposite with the suffix *-less*: useful/useless; careful/careless; painful/painless

72.5
2 unbelievable	6 useless	10 unforgettable
3 helpful	7 reliable	11 traditional
4 annual	8 reasonable	12 suitable
5 painful	9 personal	

72.6 *Possible answers:*

2 a jacket: (un)comfortable, (un)fashionable, useful, attractive, (un)suitable
3 an event: annual, enjoyable, traditional, political, cultural, famous
4 a person you know: (un)reliable, sociable, helpful, attractive, famous, normal
5 an opinion: political, personal, (un)reasonable
6 a room: (un)comfortable, peaceful, colourful, attractive

Unit 73

73.1 Roads: *public transport*, traffic lights, crossroads, bus stop, bus station
Money: income tax, cashpoint, credit card
Hair: haircut, hairdresser, hairdryer
Jobs: hairdresser, travel agent, film-maker, DJ, bus driver, (babysitter)
Things we wear: earrings, T-shirt, sunglasses
Air travel: airport, airline, aircraft

73.2
2 travel agent	5 birthday card	8 income tax
3 campsite	6 babysitter	9 hairdryer
4 wheelchair	7 sunglasses	

73.3
2 chest of drawers	4 ID/identity card	6 ice hockey	8 credit card
3 DJ (disc jockey)	5 mother tongue	7 full stop	

73.4 *Possible answers:*

2 bus stop	8 sister-in-law, mother-in-law, father-in-law
3 hairdryer	9 suntan, sunshine, sunblock, sunburn, sunscreen
4 birthday card, ID card	10 traffic jam
5 toothbrush	11 armchair
6 bus station	12 film director
7 dining room	

Unit 74

74.1
2 had a baby
3 missed the bus
4 a serious head injury
5 it depends on the weather
6 spent three days
7 predict the future
8 expecting a baby
9 told me a very funny joke
10 a large amount of money

74.2 2 lose   3 vitally   4 puts on   5 likely   6 serious   7 well

74.3 2 loud   3 wide   4 limited   5 large   6 great   7 limited

74.4
2 fast
3 great
4 expecting
5 scored
6 told
7 wide
8 went off
9 fell
10 terribly

74.5 *Your own answers*

Unit 75

75.1 sooner or later; one or two; peace and quiet; day after day; now and again; up and down; so far; right away

75.2
2 By the way
3 out of the blue
4 to be honest
5 get rid of
6 In general
7 make up my mind
8 For instance
9 I'm just about to
10 If I were you

75.3
2 One or two
3 burst into tears
4 the week before last
5 if I were you
6 sooner or later
7 Once or twice
8 at once
9 In two weeks' time
10 so far
11 ring a bell
12 apart from

75.4
2 cost a fortune = cost a lot of money
3 keep an eye on = watch (and make sure something is safe)
4 on the tip of my tongue = I know it but I can't remember it at the moment
5 a night on the town = a night out
6 could do with = need

Unit 76

76.1

positive	negative	not sure *or* either
why not; I suppose so	*no way;* not really	you're kidding; that depends; I don't believe it

76.2
2 see
3 both are correct
4 help
5 What
6 pay
7 both are correct

76.3
2 pays attention
3 had a word with her
4 felt bad about that/it
5 no idea
6 changed my mind

76.4
2 *Kind of* blue
3 Well, *in that case* …
4 *You must be joking.* That's ten miles!
5 Yeah. *Why not?*
6 Oh, burgers, pizzas, *that sort of thing.*
7 Yes. *I couldn't believe my eyes.*

Unit 77

77.1 2 h   3 e   4 b   5 g   6 d   7 a   8 f

77.2
2 at; e.g. maths and history
3 to; e.g. me, Carl
4 on; e.g. clothes, himself
5 of; e.g. heights, nothing
6 in; e.g. thrillers, serious films
7 on; e.g. my parents, the time
8 at; e.g. the children, I don't know
9 on; e.g. all of them, none of them
10 into; e.g. German

77.3
2 similar
3 complain
4 mad
5 wrong
6 with
7 concentrate
8 aware
9 short
10 depend

77.4 keen on; suffer from; succeed in; get married to; apply for; apologise for

77.5 *Possible answers:*
1 at languages
2 in sport
3 of flying
4 on food, clothes, rent and my car
5 of going to Turkey

Unit 78

78.1

on	in	by
board, display, fire, strike	detail, future, tears	hand, accident, mistake

78.2
2 on purpose
3 by chance
4 out-of-date
5 on business
6 at the moment
7 in a hurry
8 in future

78.3
2 strike
3 hand
4 minute/moment
5 purpose
6 hurry
7 future
8 date
9 detail
10 display
11 moment; phone
12 end

78.4
2 in time
3 on fire
4 in the end
5 at the end
6 at the moment
7 by chance
8 in a minute/moment
9 out-of-date
10 in detail

Unit 79

79.1 2 away   3 out   4 back   5 up   6 up   7 up   8 on

79.2
2 go back
3 picked up
4 put up
5 give up
6 carry on
7 go away
8 get on (well)
9 take on

79.3 b meaning 5   c meaning 2   d meaning 4   e meaning 1

79.4
2 sort (it) out
3 put them back
4 lie down
5 fell over
6 look (it) up
7 putting on / put on
8 Hurry up

Unit 80

80.1
2 put them on
3 correct
4 take them off
5 correct
6 turn it down
7 hanging around the station

80.2 2 put off   3 make up   4 left out   5 turned down   6 get in

80.3
1 ALSO: He's putting his jacket on.
2 She's turning the light on. / She's turning on the light.
3 The car has broken down.
4 He's breaking into a shop.
5 They're hanging around (a street corner).
6 The teacher is handing out books. / The teacher is handing books out.

80.4 2 out   3 up   4 off   5 for   6 down

80.5 *Possible answers:*
2 a cold/flu
3 stories/excuses
4 the light/TV
5 the shop/flat
6 her children/dog

Unit 81

81.1
2 do
3 both are correct
4 do
5 both are correct
6 take
7 do
8 made

81.2
2 She's having/taking a shower.
3 She's taking it/things easy.
4 She's taking something out of her pocket.
5 They're making a noise.
6 She's doing her hair.

81.3
2 made us go
3 doing my best
4 take a break
5 making an effort
6 make up their minds
7 take things/it easy

81.4
2 take
3 made
4 done
5 take
6 look
7 made
8 take
9 do (take is also possible)
10 made

81.5 *Your own answers*

Unit 82

82.1
give: *a speech*; someone a hug; someone a hand
miss: an opportunity; a person; what someone says
keep: in touch; on doing something; a secret

82.2
2 dry   3 laughing   4 fit   5 forgetting   6 quiet   7 thinking   8 waking

82.3
2 gave her a ring
3 gave her a big hug
4 keep in touch
5 give you a hand
6 missed his opportunity
7 given me an appetite

82.4
2 miss all the fun
3 keep it up
4 gave me a push
5 miss the rush hour
6 keeps getting headaches
7 gave me the idea
8 miss my dog
9 keep a secret

Unit 83

83.1
2 buy/obtain   3 fetch   4 arrive   5 became   6 obtain/find   7 answer   8 received

83.2
2 getting hungry
3 getting hot
4 getting dark
5 getting late
6 getting worse

83.3
2 get together and have a meal.
3 get to know people in this country?
4 get in touch with the travel company.
5 get rid of these old magazines.
6 get in before 10 o'clock.
7 get out.
8 get to sleep for hours last night.

83.4
2 need to get it cut.
3 need to get it finished.
4 need to get it fixed/repaired.
5 need to get them back.

83.5 *Your own answers*

Unit 84

84.1
2 (out) for a picnic
3 (out) for a drink/meal
4 sightseeing
5 (out) for a drive
6 swimming
7 (out) for a walk
8 clubbing
9 (out) for a meal / for a picnic / for a drink

84.2
2 are you?
3 fetch
4 continue
5 happening
6 disappeared
7 return
8 take me
9 chose

84.3
2 going blind
3 going (very) well
4 went mad
5 going bald
6 go and get
7 go away
8 went out

84.4 *Your own answers*

Unit 85

85.1 hearing; taste; smell; touch

85.2
2 listening to; heard	5 look at	8 touch
3 hear	6 watched	9 look; see
4 seen	7 feel	10 seems

85.3
2 felt like silk	6 seem/appear very nice
3 looked like a church	7 feels/looks damp
4 sounded like an alarm	8 seemed/appeared/looked calm and relaxed
5 taste like/of coconut	

85.4
2 sounds as if/though	5 tastes as if
3 feel as if/though	6 looks as if/though
4 sounds as if	7 seemed/appeared as if/though (*also* looked as if/though)

85.5 *Your own answers*

Unit 86

86.1
2 a news news / some news / a bit of news
3 advices advice
4 are is
5 homeworks homework
6 furnitures were furniture was
7 experiences experience these equipments this equipment
8 knowledges knowledge

86.2
2 a useful piece/bit of equipment.
3 a good piece/bit of advice.
4 another piece/bit of toast?
5 a bit of progress. (piece is not possible here)
6 a bit of rubbish on the floor. (piece is not possible here)
7 a bit of pocket money. (piece is not possible here)
8 a bit/piece of news this morning.

86.3 2 experience   3 room/space   4 advice   5 furniture   6 progress

86.4
2 experiences	4 rubbish	6 behaviour	8 knowledge
3 chance	5 scenery	7 experience	

86.5 transport U   luggage U   suitcase C   pasta U   traffic U   accident C

Unit 87

87.1
2 to help	5 on	8 to speak	11 waiting
3 staying	6 to get	9 him for help	12 travelling
4 going	7 working	10 for	

87.2
2 thinking	5 blamed	8 considered
3 imagine	6 hoping; intended/planned	9 insisted; hates
4 avoid	7 enjoyed/liked	10 demanded

87.3
fancy + -ing
decide + infinitive or decide + (that)
pretend + infinitive or pretend + (that)
accuse + (obj) + of

87.4 *Possible answers:*

I like reading. I dislike sport. I don't mind doing homework. I'm thinking of going to the mountains this weekend to ski. I can't imagine living without my two dogs. I hope to go to university next year. I intend to buy myself a motorbike when I go to university.

Unit 88

88.1
2 He told me it's / it was impossible.
3 I asked Chloe to stay with me.
4 She suggested that we go to an Italian restaurant. OR She suggested going to …
5 I warned them not to go.
6 He helped me to buy my suit.
7 She allowed us to go.
8 He said the film was terrible. OR He told me …
9 She advised me to buy a dictionary.
10 I recommended that they stay there. OR I reccomend staying there.
11 He reminded me to go to the bank.
12 I want him to leave.

88.2

2 noticed	5 convinced	8 encouraged	11 expect
3 warn	6 recommended	9 reminded	12 hope
4 persuaded	7 mentioned	10 help	

88.3 *Possible answers:*
2 (that) we have something to eat.
3 her to ring the police.
4 (that) something was wrong / she looked ill / she was smiling, etc.
5 me to stay up late / watch TV, etc.
6 (that) it wasn't mine.
7 them to go.
8 (that) she'll be late.
9 them not to drink it.
10 I would look after it / bring it back tomorrow, etc.

88.4 *Your own answers*

Unit 89

89.1

gradable adjectives	extreme adjectives
bad, important, small, tired, frightened	*dreadful*, essential, tiny, exhausted, terrified

89.2
~~very pleased~~ (really/absolutely) delighted
~~very big~~ (really/absolutely) huge/enormous
food is ~~very nice~~ (really/absolutely) delicious
last three days have been ~~very nice~~ (really/absolutely) wonderful/marvellous/terrific
~~very important~~ (absolutely/really) essential
~~very interesting~~ (absolutely/really) fascinating

89.3
2 terrifying	4 amazing/terrific/wonderful/marvellous	6 annoyed
3 shocked	5 delighted	

89.4 2 disappointed/annoyed   3 embarrassed   4 confused   5 amazed/surprised   6 delighted

Unit 90

90.1 2 in   3 at   4 on   5 at   6 in   7 on   8 on   9 at   10 on   11 in   12 at

90.2 2 among   3 into   4 beside   5 out of   6 towards   7 up   8 underneath

90.3
2 under the fence	4 after the bridge	6 (right) against
3 get out of the car	5 below/beneath me	

90.4 *Possible answers:*

1 No, because it will be noisy at night due to the ambulances.
2 No, because of the smell and the noise.
3 No, because it's dangerous.
4 No. I like one or two things on the wall, but not lots of things because it looks untidy.
5 No. I prefer the aisle seat because I can move around easily without disturbing anyone else.
6 Well, that sounds nice, but it really depends who the people are.

Unit 91

91.1
2 She hardly ever phones me.
3 I have never broken my leg.
4 I frequently visit them at weekends. OR I visit them frequently at weekends.
5 My brother quite often calls me on Sunday.
6 I rarely saw him during the summer.
7 She is always in the office before eight.

91.2
2 rarely/seldom
3 fairly/pretty/rather
4 completely
5 a little / slightly
6 incredibly
7 frequently

91.3
2 I must speak to her urgently.
3 I asked him politely to move his car.
4 I spoke to her secretly.
5 He suddenly ran out of the room.
6 I spoke to her briefly this morning.

91.4
2 extremely/incredibly
3 very
4 very
5 quite/fairly/pretty/rather
6 a bit / a little / slightly
7 quite/fairly/pretty/rather

91.5 *Possible answers:*

2 I sometimes buy clothes I don't like. I buy them because they are fashionable. I think that's fairly typical.
3 I hardly ever lose things; I'm very careful. I think that's slightly unusual.
4 I often forget things – my glasses, people's names, etc. I expect that's fairly typical.
5 For some reason, I hardly ever remember my dreams. I think that's quite unusual.
6 I often speak to strangers on buses and trains. That's probably quite unusual.
7 I sometimes give money to people in the street; it depends how I feel. That's fairly typical, I think.

Unit 92

92.1
for one thing / for a start
when / as soon as
besides/anyway
finally / in the end
at first / to begin with

92.2
2 get
3 while
4 leaving
5 both are correct
6 just as
7 both are correct
8 while
9 both are correct
10 cleaning

92.3
1 besides/anyway/secondly
2 first of all; Then / After that; finally
3 at first / to begin with; while
4 firstly / for a start / for one thing; secondly/besides/anyway
5 at first / to begin with; while; Eventually / In the end

92.4 *Possible answers:*

2 you finish / you've finished
3 I get there/home
4 leaving
5 he opened the door / he got out of the car
6 he/she looked up the other half
7 we got there
8 it's not important / we can phone him later

English Vocabulary in Use Pre-intermediate and Intermediate   **241**

Unit 93

93.1

words that add more information	words that introduce surprising information
in addition, as well, also, what's more	although, in spite of, however, despite

93.2
2 however   5 However   8 despite
3 both are correct   6 both are correct
4 even though   7 both are correct

93.3
She always worked hard in class, whereas most of her classmates were lazy.
She has the ability to do the job. What's more, she is very experienced.
She didn't pass the exam in spite of the help I gave her.
She worked there for ten years. However, she was never happy in the job.

93.4
2 In spite of / Despite; still   6 as well / too
3 However   7 though
4 although / even though   8 yet; still
5 In addition to / As well as / Besides

93.5   *Possible answers:*
2 I get up much later   5 I think I'll pass
3 the bad weather   6 she spoke very quickly
4 it's cheaper (with a season ticket)   7 goes jogging / plays tennis / works, etc.

Unit 94

94.1
2 Teresa got the job because of her good exam results.
3 We couldn't eat outside because of the terrible weather.
4 She didn't go to school because of her cold.
5 The referee stopped the game because of the bad light.
6 I was late because of the terrible traffic.
7 He can't vote because of his age.

94.2
2 in case   5 As a result / Therefore   8 otherwise
3 as long as   6 Unless   9 whether/if
4 in order to / so that I would   7 as long as   10 reason

94.3   2 As/Since   3 so that   4 as a result / therefore   5 unless   6 whether

94.4   *Possible answers:*

I want to improve my English because *I need good English for my job.*
I don't know whether my English *is good enough.*
I often need to write words down, otherwise I *forget them.*
I don't get many opportunities to practise my English, therefore *my speaking is not very good.*
Speaking English may be important in order to *get a better job in the future.*

Unit 95

95.1

formal	informal
depart, regarding, purchase, proceed to, commence	cheers, mate, terrific, bloke, kids

95.2

depart	*leave*	mate	**friend**
cheers	**thanks**	commence	**start**
regarding	**about**	terrific	**fantastic** (marvellous, wonderful, etc.)
purchase	**buy**	bloke	**man**
proceed to	**go to**	kids	**children**

95.3
2 thing
3 a load of rubbish
4 up to
5 I'm dying for
6 make it
7 mate
8 quite a bit
9 that stuff
10 40 or so

95.4 2 We regret to inform you   3 grant   4 require further assistance

95.5
1 a drag *informal* = boring; it can also mean unpleasant, e.g. Housework is a drag.
2 permit *formal* = allow
3 scary *informal* = frightening
4 quid *informal* = pounds (£)

Unit 96

96.1
2 a registration form or an enrolment form
3 an entry form
4 a visa application form

96.2
2 When were you born?
3 Where do you come from?
4 Are you single or married?
5 When are you leaving?

96.3 2 g   3 f   4 b   5 a   6 d   7 e

96.4 2 correct   3 incorrect   4 incorrect   5 correct   6 correct   7 incorrect

96.5 2 tip   3 on my own   4 sign it   5 require   6 team

96.6 *Your own answers*

Unit 97

97.1 2 a   3 d   4 e   5 b

97.2
2 advantages *of* studying   4 effect *on* children   6 tends *to* go
3 give *both* sides   5 On the other *hand*, too

97.3 2 causes; However   3 both are correct   4 hand   5 both are correct

97.4 2 In addition   3 However   4 Consequently   5 argument   6 effect

97.5
2 People tend to be conservative. OR In general / On the whole people are conservative.
3 There is an argument that cars should not be allowed in town centres. OR Some people believe that cars should not be allowed in town centres.
4 In the past children played on their bikes, but nowadays they spend most of their time in front of a computer.
5 Many people work longer and longer hours, and consequently / as a result they don't have time for hobbies.

Unit 98

98.1
Dear Sir or **Madam**
I am writing in response to your advertisement for trainees in yesterday's newspaper, and I would be **grateful** if you could send me further **details**.
I look forward to **hearing** from you.
Yours faithfully

98.2
2 details
3 to hearing from you
4 faithfully
5 sincerely
6 regards
7 signature

98.3
2 I regret to inform you …
3 I am pleased to inform you …
4 Are you available on Wednesday?
5 I would like to enquire about the dates of the course.
6 Please accept our apologies for the delay.
7 I would be grateful if you could send me the details.
8 Could you confirm that in writing?
9 I enclose a copy of my CV.

98.4   2 writing   4 regarding/about   6 delays   8 sincerely
3 response/reply   5 regret   7 apologise

Unit 99

99.1   in a week's time; once again; let you know; best wishes; give my regards to

99.2   2 Dear Mark   4 Lots of love, Evelyn
3 Send/Give my regards/love to Patricia   5 All the best, Sam

99.3   2 Do you fancy going?   6 I'm going in three weeks' time.
3 I'll be/get in touch soon.   7 Jamie is a laugh.
4 It looks new, but in fact it isn't.   8 Let's get together for lunch.
5 I'll let you know as soon as possible.   9 It's ages since I wrote.

99.4   2 ages   6 hoping   10 Anyway
3 fact   7 in   11 let
4 since   8 together   12 give
5 actually   9 join

Unit 100

100.1   2 British Broadcasting Corporation   4 correct   6 correct
3 Member of Parliament   5 United Nations   7 curriculum vitae

100.2   2 e.g.   3 etc.   4 St   5 i.e.   6 St   7 Dr

100.3   Luke
Olly had a **maths exam** this afternoon and then had to take his **bike** to the repair shop, so he'll probably be a bit late home. You can watch **TV/telly** while you're waiting for him, and please help yourself to anything in the **fridge**. If there's a problem, **e.g.** if **Dr** Brown rings about the **flu** vaccination, my **phone** number is next to the **photos** on the dining room table. I should be home myself by about five.
Pam (Olly's mum)

100.4   2 bike   5 vet   8 ad/advert   11 lab
3 e.g. / for example   6 etc. / and so on   9 PIN   12 rep
4 CV   7 case   10 stand

100.5   PTO = Please turn over (you see it at the bottom of a page)
RSVP = Répondez s'il vous plaît, which is French for 'please reply' (you see it on letters of invitation, which means they want a reply to the invitation)
asap = as soon as possible (in emails and text messages)
IMO = in my opinion (also in emails and text messages)
DOB = date of birth (on forms)
PS = postscript. It is used at the end of a letter (after you have signed your name) to add extra information, or something you have forgotten to say in the letter.

Phonemic symbols

Vowel sounds

Symbol	Examples
/iː/	sleep me
/i/	happy recipe
/ɪ/	pin dinner
/ʊ/	foot could pull
/u/	casual
/uː/	do shoe through
/e/	red head said
/ə/	arrive father colour
/ɜː/	turn bird work
/ɔː/	sort thought walk
/æ/	cat black
/ʌ/	sun enough wonder
/ɒ/	got watch sock
/ɑː/	part heart laugh
/eɪ/	name late aim
/aɪ/	my idea time
/ɔɪ/	boy noise
/eə/	pair where bear
/ɪə/	hear cheers
/əʊ/	go home show
/aʊ/	out cow
/ʊə/	pure fewer

Consonant sounds

Symbol	Examples
/p/	put
/b/	book
/t/	take
/d/	dog
/k/	car kick
/g/	go guarantee
/tʃ/	catch church
/dʒ/	age lounge
/f/	for cough photograph
/v/	love vehicle
/θ/	thick path
/ð/	this mother
/s/	since rice
/z/	zoo surprise
/ʃ/	shop sugar machine
/ʒ/	pleasure usual vision
/h/	hear hotel
/m/	make
/n/	name now know
/ŋ/	bring
/l/	look while
/r/	road
/j/	young
/w/	wear

ˈ This shows that the next syllable is the one with the stress.

ˌ This is used when some longer words have a second stress, less strong than on the main stressed syllable.

Index

The numbers in the Index are **unit** numbers not page numbers.
The pronunciation provided is for standard British English.

a bit [slightly]   ə bɪt   91
a great deal   ə greɪt diːl   39
a laugh   ə lɑːf   99
a little (bit)   ə ˈlɪtəl   91
a load of rubbish   ə ləʊd ɒv
   ˈrʌbɪʃ   60
a long time ago   ə lɒŋ taɪm
   əˈgəʊ   59
a paper   ə ˈpeɪpə   100
a piece of sth   ə piːs ɒv
   ˈsʌmθɪŋ   86
a return   ə rɪˈtɜːn   28
a week/month/year (etc.) [every]
   ə wiːk mʌnθ jɪə   36
abbreviation   əˌbriːviˈeɪʃən   53
ability   əˈbɪləti   71
able   ˈeɪbəl   71
above   əˈbʌv   90
above all   əˈbʌv ɔːl   57
abroad   əˈbrɔːd   37
absent   ˈæbsənt   38
absolutely   ˌæbsəˈluːtli   89
accent   ˈæksənt   33
accept   əkˈsept   1
access (to sth)   ˈækses   48, 55
accident   ˈæksɪdənt   29
accommodation
   əˌkɒməˈdeɪʃən   46
according to   əˈkɔːdɪŋ tuː   52, 67
accountant   əˈkaʊntənt   35
accurate(ly)   ˈækjərət   33
ache   n, v   eɪk   20
achieve   əˈtʃiːv   39
achievement   əˈtʃiːvmənt   39
act [do sth]   ækt   58
act [perform]   ækt   43
acting   ˈæktɪŋ   43
active   ˈæktɪv   1
actor   ˈæktə   43, 71
actually   ˈæktʃuəli   99
ad/advert   æd ˈædvɜːt   100
add   æd   25
add sth up   æd ˈsʌmθɪŋ ʌp   61
add to basket/bag   æd tuː ˈbɑːskɪt/
   bæg   55
addition   əˈdɪʃən   61
adjective   ˈædʒɪktɪv   4
admin   ˈædmɪn   36
admission   ədˈmɪʃən   30
adult   ˈædʌlt   14
advantage   ədˈvɑːntɪdʒ   26
adventure holiday   ədˈventʃə
   ˈhɒlədeɪ   46
adverb   ˈædvɜːb   4
advert   ˈædvɜːt   44, 52, 100
advertisement   ədˈvɜːtɪsmənt   52
advice   ədˈvaɪs   1, 86
advise   ədˈvaɪz   36, 88
afford   əˈfɔːd   19
afraid (of)   əˈfreɪd   77

Africa   ˈæfrɪkə   5
after [follow sb/sth]   ˈɑːftə   90
after [time/event]   ˈɑːftə   92
after that   ˈɑːftə ðæt   92
afterwards   ˈɑːftəwədz   92
against [compete]   əˈgenst   42
against [touching]   əˈgenst   90
ages   ˈeɪdʒɪz   99
ages ago   ˈeɪdʒɪz əˈgəʊ   60
agree [have the same
   opinion]   əˈgriː   67, 77
agree [say yes]   əˈgriː   87
aim   eɪm   39
air conditioning   eə
   kənˈdɪʃənɪŋ   17
air force   eə fɔːs   35
aircraft   ˈeəkrɑːft   47, 73
airline   ˈeəlaɪn   73
airport   ˈeəpɔːt   73
alarm   əˈlɑːm   74
album   ˈælbəm   44
alive   əˈlaɪv   14
all over [everywhere]   ɔːl
   ˈəʊvə   45
all the best   ɔːl ðə best   99
allow   əˈlaʊ   14
almost   ˈɔːlməʊst   14
alone   əˈləʊn   15
aloud   əˈlaʊd   1
alphabet   ˈælfəbet   33
also   ˈɔːlsəʊ   93
although   ɔːlˈðəʊ   93
altogether   ˌɔːltəˈgeðə   13
amazed   əˈmeɪzd   89
amazing [very good]
   əˈmeɪzɪŋ   89
amazing [very
   surprising]   əˈmeɪzɪŋ   89
ambition   æmˈbɪʃən   39
American   əˈmerɪkən   5
among   əˈmʌŋ   90
amount   əˈmaʊnt   3, 19
and so on   ænd səʊ ɒn   100
anger   ˈæŋgə   12
angrily   ˈæŋgrɪli   91
ankle   ˈæŋkəl   9
anniversary   ˌænɪˈvɜːsəri   15
announcement   əˈnaʊntsmənt
   47
annoyed   əˈnɔɪd   89
annoying   əˈnɔɪɪŋ   89
annual   ˈænjuəl   45, 72
answerphone   ˈɑːnsəfəʊn   53
ant   ænt   8
antique   n   ænˈtiːk   63
anti-virus software   ˈænti ˈvaɪrəs
   ˈsɒftweə   55, 54
anxiety   æŋˈzaɪəti   12
anxious   ˈæŋkʃəs   11, 12

anyway [more
   importantly]   ˈeniweɪ   92
anyway [returning to an earlier
   subject]   ˈeniweɪ   99
apart from   əˈpɑːt frɒm   75
apartment   əˈpɑːtmənt   17
apologise for sth   əˈpɒlədʒaɪz fɔː
   ˈsʌmθɪŋ   65, 98
apology   əˈpɒlədʒi   65
appear [become visible]   əˈpɪə   70
appear [seem]   əˈpɪə   85
appearance   əˈpɪərəns   10
application (computer)
   ˌæplɪˈkeɪʃən   54
application (job)   ˌæplɪˈkeɪʃən
   37, 98
apply for sth   əˈplaɪ fɔː ˈsʌmθɪŋ
   37
appointment   əˈpɔɪntmənt   38
approach   əˈprəʊtʃ   29
approximately   əˈprɒksɪmətli
   10, 14
Arabic   ˈærəbɪk   5
architect   ˈɑːkɪtekt   34, 35
architecture   ˈɑːkɪtektʃə   34
Argentina   ˌɑːdʒənˈtiːnə   5
Argentinian   ˌɑːdʒənˈtɪniən   5
argue   ˈɑːgjuː   1
argument [angry discussion]
   ˈɑːgjəmənt   1
argument [reason to think]
   ˈɑːgjəmənt   97
armchair   ˈɑːmtʃeə   18
army   ˈɑːmi   35, 59
arrange   əˈreɪndʒ   38
arrangement   əˈreɪndʒmənt   38
arrest   əˈrest   56
arrival   əˈraɪvəl   96
article   ˈɑːtɪkəl   52
artist   ˈɑːtɪst   71
arts   ɑːts   34
as [because]   æz   94
as [when]   æz   92
as a result   æz ə rɪˈzʌlt   94, 97
as if/though   æz ɪf/ðəʊ   85
as long as   æz lɒŋ æz   94
as soon as   æz suːn æz   92
as well (as)   æz wel   93
Asia   ˈeɪʒə   5
ask sb for sth   ɑːsk ˈsʌmbɒdi fɔː
   ˈsʌmθɪŋ   87
ask sb the way   ɑːsk ˈsʌmbɒdi ðə
   weɪ   29
assistance   əˈsɪstəns   95
at [place]   æt   90
at [@]   æt   55
at all   æt ɔːl   67
at first   æt ˈfɜːst   14, 92
at home   æt həʊm   19
at least   æt liːst   1, 62

at night ˌæt naɪt 27
at once ˌæt wʌns 75
at risk of ˌæt 'rɪsk əv 51
at the end ˌæt ði end 78
at the moment ˌæt ðə 'məʊmənt 78
at the same time ˌæt ðə seɪm taɪm 60
athlete 'æθliːt 41
athletic æθ'letɪk 10
athletics æθ'letɪks 41
atmosphere 'ætməsfɪə 22, 32
attachment ə'tætʃmənt 55
attack n ə'tæk 59
attack v ə'tæk 56
attempt n, v ə'tempt 87
attend ə'tend 32, 38
attendance ə'tendəns 38
attitude 'ætɪtjuːd 68
attract attention ə'trækt ə'tenʃən 39
attraction ə'trækʃən 50
attractive ə'træktɪv 10
aubergine 'əʊbəʒiːn 24
audience 'ɔːdiəns 44
Australia ɒs'treɪliə 5
Australian ɒs'treɪliən 5
author 'ɔːθə 43
available ə'veɪləbəl 47, 98
average [typical] 'ævərɪdʒ 10
avoid ə'vɔɪd 87
aware of ə'weər ɒv 77
away [distance] ə'weɪ 26, 28, 62
awful 'ɔːfəl 2, 89
B&B ˌbiː ənd biː 46
babysitter 'beɪbiˌsɪtə 73
back up sth ˌbæk ʌp 'sʌmθɪŋ 54
backache 'bækeɪk 20
backpack 'bækpæk 21
backup 'bækʌp 54
bag bæg 64
bagel 'beɪgl 49
baggage reclaim 'bægɪdʒ rɪ'kleɪm 47
baguette bæg'et 49
bakery 'beɪkəri 39
balcony 'bælkəni 17
bald bɔːld 84
ballet (dancer) 'bæleɪ 44
ballot 'bælət 57
bandage 'bændɪdʒ 20
bank (of a river) bæŋk 27
bank account bæŋk ə'kaʊnt 19
bank loan bæŋk ləʊn 19
bar (of chocolate) bɑː 64
barbecue n, v 'bɑːbɪkjuː 25
basic 'beɪsɪk 33
basket 'bɑːskɪt 23
bass guitar beɪs gɪ'tɑː 44
bass guitarist beɪs gɪ'tɑːrɪst 44
bath bɑːθ 16
bathroom 'bɑːθruːm 18
battle 'bætəl 59
BBC ˌbiːbiː'siː 100
be (just) about to biː ə'baʊt tuː 75
be delayed biː dɪ'leɪd 65

be dying for sth biː 'daɪɪŋ fɔː 'sʌmθɪŋ 95
be held up biː held ʌp 65
be in touch biː ɪn tʌtʃ 99
be into sth [like sth] biː 'ɪntə 'sʌmθɪŋ 68
beach biːtʃ 51
beach holiday biːtʃ 'hɒlədeɪ 46
beans biːnz 24
bear beə 8
beat biːt 42
beauty 'bjuːti 10
because bɪ'kɒz 94
because of bɪ'kɒz ɒv 94
bee biː 8
beef biːf 24
before [place] bɪ'fɔː 90
before [time] bɪ'fɔː 92
behave bɪ'heɪv 3
behaviour bɪ'heɪvjə 86
belief bɪ'liːf 57
believe [think] bɪ'liːv 97
believe in bɪ'liːv ɪn 57
bell bel 63
belong to bɪ'lɒŋ tuː 77
below bɪ'ləʊ 90
bend n, v bend 29
beneath bɪ'niːθ 90
beside [next to] bɪ'saɪd 90
besides [giving another reason] bɪ'saɪdz 92
besides [in addition] bɪ'saɪdz 93
best friend best frend 13
best wishes best 'wɪʃɪz 99
beyond bɪ'jɒnd 90
bicycle 'baɪsɪkəl 28
bike baɪk 28, 100
bilingual baɪ'lɪŋgwl 3
billion 'bɪliən 61
bin bɪn 38, 86
biography baɪ'ɒgrəfi 43
birth bɜːθ 14
birthday card 'bɜːθdeɪ kɑːd 73
(a) bit of sth bɪt ɒv 'sʌmθɪŋ 86
bitter 'bɪtə 24
black blæk 10
black coffee blæk 'kɒfi 49
blame sb for sth bleɪm 'sʌmbɒdy fɔː 'sʌmθɪŋ 87
blanket 'blæŋkɪt 18
bleed bliːd 20
bless you bles juː 69
blind blaɪnd 84
blinds blaɪndz 18
block of flats blɒk ɒv flæts 17
blog blɒg 55
blogger 'blɒgə 55
bloke bləʊk 95
blond(e) blɒnd 10
blow (ing) v bləʊ 7
blow your nose bləʊ jɔː nəʊz 9
board n, v bɔːd 47
board [blackboard] n bɔːd 100
boarding card 'bɔːdɪŋ kɑːd 47
boil bɔɪl 25
boiling 'bɔɪlɪŋ 7
bomb bɒm 59

bone bəʊn 63
book v bʊk 48
book online bʊk ɒn'laɪn 46
boots buːts 21
bored bɔːd 89
boring 'bɔːrɪŋ 89
borrow 'bɒrəʊ 31
both sides of an argument bəʊθ saɪdz ɒv æn 'ɑːgjəmənt 97
bother 'bɒðə 16
bottle 'bɒtəl 64
bottom 'bɒtəm 9
bowl bəʊl 64
box bɒks 64
boxing 'bɒksɪŋ 41
bracelet 'breɪslət 21
brake n, v breɪk 29, 72
branch (of a company) brɑːntʃ 39
branch (of a tree) brɑːntʃ 27
Brazil brə'zɪl 5
Brazilian brə'zɪliən 5
break [rest] n breɪk 32
break a record breɪk ə 'rekɔːd 42
break down breɪk daʊn 38, 80
break in(to sth) breɪk ɪn 56, 80
break the rules breɪk ðə ruːlz 32
break up [end a relationship] breɪk ʌp 15
break up [end of term] breɪk ʌp 32
breast brest 9
breathe (in/out) briːð 9
breeze briːz 51
brick brɪk 35
bride braɪd 15
(bride)groom gruːm 15
bridge brɪdʒ 29
briefly 'briːfli 91
bright braɪt 21
bring sb luck brɪŋ 'sʌmbɒdi lʌk 45
bring sb up brɪŋ 'sʌmbɒdi ʌp 14
British 'brɪtɪʃ 5
broad brɔːd 10
broadcast 'brɔːdkɑːst 52
broccoli 'brɒkəli 24
broken down 'brəʊkən daʊn 38
brown braʊn 10
browse braʊz 55
browser 'braʊzə 55
brush your teeth brʌʃ jɔː tiːθ 16
bucket 'bʌkɪt 63
build bɪld 35
builder 'bɪldə 35
bull bʊl 8
bunch bʌntʃ 24, 64
burglar 'bɜːglə 56
burglary 'bɜːgləri 56
burn v bɜːn 19
burst into tears bɜːst 'ɪntə tɪəz 75
bus bʌs 28
bus driver bʌs 'draɪvə 73
bus station bʌs 'steɪʃən 73

bus stop bʌs stɒp 28, 73
business studies 'bɪznɪs 'stʌdiz 34
businessman/woman 'bɪznɪsmæn/'wʊmən 34
butterfly 'bʌtəflaɪ 8
button 'bʌtən 21
by [how much] baɪ 40
by [near] baɪ 90
by [next to] baɪ 90
by [not later than] baɪ 60
by accident baɪ 'æksɪdənt 78
by chance baɪ tʃɑːns 78
by hand baɪ hænd 78
by mistake baɪ mɪ'steɪk 78
by the way baɪ ðə weɪ 75
cabbage 'kæbɪdʒ 24
cabin crew 'kæbɪn kruː 47
cage keɪdʒ 8
calculate 'kælkjəleɪt 61
calculation ˌkælkjə'leɪʃən 61
calculator 'kælkjəleɪtə 38, 61
calendar 'kælɪndə 38
calf kɑːf 24
call [describe sb] kɔːl 32
call [phone] kɔːl 53
call for sb kɔːl fɔː 'sʌmbɒdi 80
calm (person) kɑːm 11
calm (sea) kɑːm 51
camel 'kæməl 8
camping 'kæmpɪŋ 41
campsite 'kæmpsaɪt 73
can (of cola) kæn 63
can't afford (it) 19
can't help it kɑːnt help ɪt 76
can't stand kɑːnt stænd 67
canal kə'næl 6
cancel 'kænsəl 64
cancer 'kænsə 20
candidate 'kændɪdət 33
Cantonese ˌkæntə'niːz 5
cap kæp 21
capital [city] 'kæpɪtəl 5
capital letter 'kæpɪtəl 'letə 4
cappuccino kæpu'tʃiːnəʊ 49
captain 'kæptɪn 42
car park kɑː pɑːk 25
cardinal number 'kɑːdɪnəl 'nʌmbə 61
care keə 57
career aim kə'rɪər eɪm 96
careful 'keəfəl 72
careless 'keələs 72
Caribbean ˌkærɪ'biːən 5
caring 'keərɪŋ 12
carpenter 'kɑːpɪntə 35
carpet 'kɑːpɪt 18
carrot 'kærət 24
carry guns 'kæri ɡʌnz 59
carry on (with sth) 'kæri ɒn 79
carton 'kɑːtən 64
case keɪs 100
cash kæʃ 19
cashpoint 'kæʃpɔɪnt 19, 73
castle 'kɑːsəl 50
casual 'kæʒjuəl 21
catch (a bus/train) kætʃ 28

catch (a criminal) kætʃ 56
cathedral kə'θiːdrəl 50
cause kɔːz 97
cave keɪv 6
CD player ˌsiː'diː 'pleɪə 31
celebrate 'seləbreɪt 15, 47
celebration ˌselə'breɪʃən 15
celebrity sə'lebrəti 52
cellist 'tʃelɪst 44
cello 'tʃeləʊ 44
central heating 'sentrəl 'hiːtɪŋ 17
century 'sentʃəri 42, 60
cereal 'sɪəriəl 16
ceremony 'serɪməni 15
certificate sə'tɪfɪkət 3, 34
champion 'tʃæmpiən 42
championship 'tʃæmpiənʃɪp 42
chance [opportunity] tʃɑːns 86
chance [possibility that sth will happen] tʃɑːns 86
change into sth tʃeɪndʒ 'ɪntə 'sʌmθɪŋ 21
change your mind tʃeɪndʒ jɔː maɪnd 76
changing room 'tʃeɪndʒɪŋ ruːm 22
channel [TV] 'tʃænəl 52
character [good qualities] 'kærəktə 17
character [personality] 'kærəktə 11
charge v tʃɑːdʒ 19, 40
charming 'tʃɑːmɪŋ 17
chat n, v tʃæt 16, 72
chat show tʃæt ʃəʊ 52
check [examine] tʃek 20, 47
check out tʃek aʊt 48
checkout [online shopping] 'tʃekaʊt 55
checkout [supermarket] 'tʃekaʊt 23
check your email tʃek jɔːr 'iːmeɪl 55
check-in (desk) 'tʃekɪn 47
cheek tʃiːk 9, 68
cheerful 'tʃɪəfəl 12
cheers [a toast] tʃɪəz 69
cheers [goodbye] tʃɪəz 69
cheers [thanks] tʃɪəz 65, 95
chef ʃef 25
chest tʃest 9
chest of drawers tʃest ɒv drɔːz 73
childhood 'tʃaɪldhʊd 14
chilly 'tʃɪli 7
chin tʃɪn 9
China 'tʃaɪnə 5
Chinese tʃaɪ'niːz 5
choice tʃɔɪs 1, 18
chop tʃɒp 25
circle 'sɜːkəl 63
city break sɪti breɪk 46
classical music 'klæsɪkəl 'mjuːzɪk 44
clean kliːn 1, 25
clean your teeth kliːn jɔː tiːθ 16

cleaner 'kliːnə 16
clear (sky) klɪə 7
clever 'klevə 11
click on (a link) klɪk ɒn 55
client 'klaɪənt 39
cliff klɪf 51
climate 'klaɪmət 6
climate change 'klaɪmət tʃeɪndʒ 58
close family kləʊs 'fæməli 13
clothes kləʊðz 22
cloud klaʊd 7
cloudy 'klaʊdi 7
coach kəʊtʃ 28
coast kəʊst 51
coconut 'kəʊkənʌt 24
coin kɔɪn 19
cold kəʊld 7
collar 'kɒlə 21
colleague 'kɒliːɡ 38
colourful 'kʌləfəl 71
comb your hair kəʊm jɔː heə 9
come from kʌm frəm 5
come out [be available] kʌm aʊt 44, 52
come out [sun] kʌm aʊt 7
come round [visit] kʌm raʊnd 16
comedy 'kɒmədi 43
comfortable 'kʌmftəbəl 72
comma 'kɒmə 4
commence kə'mens 95
commit a crime kə'mɪt ə kraɪm 56
communicate kə'mjuːnɪkeɪt 1
compare kəm'peə 97
compared with/to kəm'peəd wɪð/tuː 97
comparison kəm'pærɪsən 97
competition ˌkɒmpə'tɪʃən 42
complain kəm'pleɪn 28, 36
complaint kəm'pleɪnt 28, 36
completely kəm'pliːtli 91
complicated 'kɒmplɪkeɪtɪd 43, 96
composer kəm'pəʊzə 44
concentrate 'kɒnsəntreɪt 77
conditions kən'dɪʃənz 36
conductor kən'dʌktə 44
confident 'kɒnfɪdənt 11
confirm kən'fɜːm 98
confused kən'fjuːzd 12, 89
confusing kən'fjuːzɪŋ 89
confusion kən'fjuːʒən 12
congratulations kənˌɡrætʃʊ'leɪʃənz 69
conjunction kən'dʒʌŋkʃən 4
connect kə'nekt 55
connected to/with kə'nektɪd tuː/wɪð 3
consequently 'kɒntsɪkwəntli 97
consider kən'sɪdə 87
consist of kən'sɪst ɒv 6, 45
consonant 'kɒnsənənt 33
constituency kən'stɪtjuənsi 57
consultant kən'sʌltənt 36
contacts 'kɒntækts 39

container kən'teɪnə 64
contents 'kɒntents 52, 64
continent 'kɒntɪnənt 5
contrast n 'kɒntrɑːst 6
contrast v 'kɒn'trɑːst 97
convenient kən'viːniənt 23, 28
convince kən'vɪns 88
cook n kʊk 25
cooker 'kʊkə 18, 25
cool kuːl 7
copy 'kɒpi 54
correct adj kə'rekt 70
correct v kə'rekt 31
cottage 'kɒtɪdʒ 17
cotton 'kɒtən 63
cough kɒf 20
Could I speak to …? kʊd aɪ spiːk
   tuː 53
(I) could not believe my eyes
   kʊd nɒt bɪ'liːv maɪ aɪz 76
Could you (possibly) …?
   kʊd juː 66
countable (noun) 'kaʊntəbəl 4
country of origin 'kʌntri ɒv
   'ɒrɪdʒɪn 96
countryside 'kʌntrɪsaɪd 27
couple [several] 'kʌpəl 15, 62, 64
courgette kɔː'ʒet 24
course [sport] kɔːs 41
course (of a meal) kɔːs 48
court (of law) kɔːt 56
court [sport] kɔːt 41
cousin 'kʌzən 13
cover v 'kʌvə 6
crab kræb 24
crash [computer] kræʃ 54
crash into sth kræʃ 'ɪntə
   'sʌmθɪŋ 29
create kri'eɪt 54, 58
creative kri'eɪtɪv 11, 12
creature 'kriːtʃə 8
credit card 'kredɪt kɑːd 73
crime kraɪm 56
crime rate kraɪm reɪt 26
criminal 'krɪmɪnəl 56
crisps krɪsps 49
croissant 'kwæs.ɒ̃ 49
crop krɒp 27
crossroads 'krɒsrəʊdz 73
crowded 'kraʊdɪd 26
cruise kruːz 46
cry kraɪ 9
cucumber 'kjuːkʌmbə 24
cultural 'kʌltʃərəl 26, 72
culture 'kʌltʃə 26
cup [sport] kʌp 3
cupboard 'kʌbəd 18
cupcake 'kʌpkeɪk 49
cure n, v kjʊə 72
curiosity ˌkjʊəri'ɒsəti 12
curious 'kjʊəriəs 12
curly 'kɜːli 10
currency 'kʌrənsi 19
current 'kʌrənt 13
currently 'kʌrəntli 39
curtains 'kɜːtənz 18
cushion 'kʊʃən 18

custom 'kʌstəm 45
customary 'kʌstəməri 45
customs 'kʌstəmz 47
cut [computer] v kʌt 54
cut [injure] v kʌt 20
cut [reduce] v kʌt 57
CV ˌsiː'viː 37, 96, 100
cycle 'saɪkəl 28
cyclist 'saɪklɪst 28
daily 'deɪli 1, 39, 52
damage n, v 'dæmɪdʒ 29
dangerous 'deɪndʒərəs 25
dancer 'dɑːntsə 71
dark dɑːk 17
dark (hair) dɑːk 10
date [day] deɪt 2
date [romantic meeting] deɪt 15
date of arrival/departure
   deɪt ɒv ə'raɪvəl/dɪ'pɑːtʃə 96
date of birth deɪt ɒv bɜːθ 96
day after day deɪ 'ɑːftə deɪ 75
day-to-day ˌdeɪtə'deɪ 36
dead ded 1, 14, 59
deaf def 84
deal with diːl wɪð 36
Dear Sir/Madam dɪə
   sɜː/'mædəm 98
death deθ 59
decade 'dekeɪd 60
decaf diːkæf 49
decimal 'desɪməl 61
decrease n 'diːkriːs 40
decrease v diː'kriːs 40
defeat n, v dɪ'fiːt 42
defend dɪ'fend 59
definite article 'defɪnət 'ɑːtɪkəl
   4
definition ˌdefɪ'nɪʃən 3
degree [amount] dɪ'griː 91
degree [university] dɪ'griː 34
degree(s) [temperature] dɪ'griː
   6, 7
delay dɪ'leɪ 47, 65, 98
delete dɪ'liːt 55
delicious dɪ'lɪʃəs 25, 89
delighted dɪ'laɪtɪd 89
deliver dɪ'lɪvə 39
demand n dɪ'mɑːnd 39
demand v dɪ'mɑːnd 87
dentist 'dentɪst 35
depart dɪ'pɑːt 95
departure dɪ'pɑːtʃə 47
departures board dɪ'pɑːtʃəz
   bɔːd 47
depend (on sth) [not sure about
   sth] dɪ'pend 74, 77
depend on sb [need sb to support
   you] dɪ'pend ɒn 'sʌmbɒdi 77
deposit dɪ'pɒzɪt 19
depressed dɪ'prest 12, 89
depressing dɪ'presɪŋ 89
depth depθ 60
design dɪ'zaɪn 35
designer label dɪ'zaɪnə
   'leɪbəl 22
despite dɪ'spaɪt 93
dessert dɪ'zɜːt 48

destination ˌdestɪ'neɪʃən 46, 47
destroy dɪ'strɔɪ 58, 59
details 'diːteɪlz 98
detective dɪ'tektɪv 56
develop dɪ'veləp 71
development dɪ'veləpmənt 71
dial 'daɪəl 53
dialling code 'daɪəlɪŋ kəʊd 53
diary 'daɪəri 38
die daɪ 59
different 'dɪfərənt 1
different from 'dɪfərənt frɒm 77
direct (a film) dɪ'rekt 43
direct sb dɪ'rekt 'sʌmbɒdi 29
directing dɪ'rektɪŋ 43
director (of a company) dɪ'rektə
   70
director (of a film) dɪ'rektə 43
dirty 'dɜːti 1, 26
disadvantage ˌdɪsəd'vɑːntɪdʒ
   26
disagree ˌdɪsə'griː 67, 70
disappear ˌdɪsə'pɪə 70
disappointed ˌdɪsə'pɔɪntɪd
   12, 89
disappointing ˌdɪsə'pɔɪntɪŋ 89
disappointment ˌdɪsə'pɔɪntmənt
   12
disc jockey (DJ) dɪsk 'dʒɒki 73
discuss dɪ'skʌs 71
discussion dɪ'skʌʃən 71
disease dɪ'ziːz 20
dishonest dɪ'sɒnɪst 11, 70
dishwasher 'dɪʃwɒʃər 18
dislike n, v dɪ'slaɪk 68
display dɪ'spleɪ 45
distance 'dɪstəns 6, 62
disturb dɪ'stɜːb 30
divide [maths] dɪ'vaɪd 61
divide [separate] dɪ'vaɪd 32
diving 'daɪvɪŋ 51
division dɪ'vɪʒən 61
divorce dɪ'vɔːs 15
DJ (disc jockey) ˌdiː'dʒeɪ 73
do [study] du: 32
do a bit/lot of (sightseeing/hiking
   etc.) duː ə bɪt/lɒt ɒv 41, 50
do a course duː ə kɔːs 81
do an Internet search duː æn
   'ɪntənet sɜːtʃ 55
doesn't bother 'dʌzənt 'bɒðə 16
do exercise duː 'eksəsaɪz 41, 81
do homework duː 'həʊmwɜːk
   81
do housework duː
   'haʊswɜːk 16, 81
do not leave bags unattended duː
   nɒt liːv bægz ˌʌnə'tendɪd 30
do research duː rɪ'sɜːtʃ 34
do something/nothing duː
   'sʌmθɪŋ 'nʌθɪŋ 81
do sth up duː 'sʌmθɪŋ ʌp 21
do the shopping duː ðə
   'ʃɒpɪŋ 16
do the washing/ironing (etc.) duː
   ðə 'wɒʃɪŋ/'aɪənɪŋ 16
do well duː wel 33

do your best duː jɔː best 33, 81

do your hair/make-up duː jɔː heə/ meɪk ʌp 81

do/work overtime duː/wɜːk 'əʊvətaɪm 36

do/write an essay duː/raɪt æn 'eseɪ 33

document 'dɒkjəmənt 54

documentary ˌdɒkjə'mentəri 52

dollar 'dɒlə 19

dolphin 'dɒlfɪn 8

don't worry dəʊnt 'wʌri 65

donkey 'dɒŋki 8

dot (in an email address) dɒt 55

double (double four nine) 'dʌbəl 61

double room 'dʌbəl ruːm 48

double-click ˌdʌbəl'klɪk 55

down [further along] daʊn 62

down [to a lower place] daʊn 90

download ˌdaʊn'ləʊd 44, 55

downstairs ˌdaʊn'steəz 17

dozen 'dʌzən 64

Dr 'dɒktə 100

draw (a game) n, v drɔː 42

draw (pictures) drɔː 2

dreadful 'dredfəl 2, 89

dream n, v driːm 72

dress v dres 10, 22, 32

dresses (well) 10

dress in dres ɪn 22

dress up dres ʌp 45

drop (of milk) drɒp 64

drought draʊt 58

drummer 'drʌmə 44

drums drʌmz 44

due to djuː tuː 94

dull dʌl 26

during 'djʊərɪŋ 60

duty free 'djuːti friː 47

duvet 'duːveɪ 18

e.g. iː'dʒiː 100

early (20s/30s, etc.) 'ɜːli 14

earn ɜːn 19, 36

earrings 'ɪərɪŋz 21, 73

east iːst 6

Earth [planet] ɜːθ 6

eat in/out iːt ɪn aʊt 16

economics ˌiːkə'nɒmɪks 34

economist ɪ'kɒnəmɪst 34, 71

economy ɪ'kɒnəmi 40

effect ɪ'fekt 12, 58, 97

efficient ɪ'fɪʃənt 58

Egypt 'iːdʒɪpt 5

Egyptian ɪ'dʒɪpʃən 5

elbow 'elbəʊ 9

elder 'eldə 13

elderly 'eldəli 14, 57

elect ɪ'lekt 57

election ɪ'lekʃən 57

electrical ɪ'lektrɪkəl 72

electrician ˌɪlek'trɪʃən 35

elephant 'elɪfənt 8

embarrassed ɪm'bærəst 89

embarrassing ɪm'bærəsɪŋ 89

emergency ɪ'mɜːdʒənsi 53

emergency services ɪ'mɜːdʒənsi 'sɜːvɪsɪz 35

emotion ɪ'məʊʃən 12

emotional ɪ'məʊʃənəl 12

emphasise 'emfəsaɪz 3

employ sb ɪm'plɔɪ 'sʌmbɒdi 37

employee ɪm'plɔiː 39

en suite ˌɒn'swiːt 18

enclose ɪn'kləʊz 98

encourage ɪn'kʌrɪdʒ 88

endangered animals ɪn'deɪndʒəd 'ænɪməlz 8

end up end ʌp 29

enemy 'enəmi 59

energetic ˌenə'dʒetɪk 12

energy 'enədʒi 58

engaged [busy] ɪn'geɪdʒd 53

engagement ɪn'geɪdʒmənt 15

engineer ˌendʒɪ'nɪə 35

engineering ˌendʒɪ'nɪərɪŋ 34

English 'ɪŋglɪʃ 5

enjoy (+ -ing) ɪn'dʒɔɪ 2, 87

enjoyable ɪn'dʒɔɪəbəl 72

enormous ɪ'nɔːməs 62, 89

enquire about sth ɪn'kwaɪə ə'baʊt 'sʌmθɪŋ 98

enrolment form ɪn'rəʊlmənt fɔːm 96

enter (a password) 'entə 54

entertain ˌentə'teɪn 43

entertainer ˌentə'teɪnə 43

entertainment ˌentə'teɪnmənt 43

entrance 'entrəns 1, 23

entry form 'entri fɔːm 96

environment ɪn'vaɪrənmənt 58

e-paper iː 'peɪpə 52

equal adj 'iːkwəl 57

equals v 'iːkwəlz 61

equipment ɪ'kwɪpmənt 86

escape ɪ'skeɪp 56

essay 'eseɪ 34

essential ɪ'senʃəl 55, 89

etc. et 'setərə 100

EU ˌiː'juː 100

euro 'jʊərəʊ 19

Europe 'jʊərəp 5

even though 'iːvən ðəʊ 93

eventually ɪ'ventʃuəli 92

ever since 'evə sɪns 13

exam ɪg'zæm 100

except for ɪk'sept fɔː 75

excess baggage ɪk'ses 'bægɪdʒ 47

excessive ɪk'sesɪv 58

excuse n ɪk'skjuːs 65

excuse me [attract attention] ɪk'skjuːz miː 69

excuse me [say sorry] ɪk'skjuːz miː 65

ex-girlfriend/wife (etc.) eks 'gɜːlfrend/waɪf 13

exhausted ɪg'zɔːstɪd 26, 89

exist ɪg'zɪst 58

existence ɪg'zɪstəns 58

existing ɪg'zɪstɪŋ 54

exit (stop using an application)

v 'eksɪt 54

expand ɪk'spænd 1, 39

expect ɪk'spekt 88

expecting a baby ɪk'spektɪŋ ə 'beɪbi 74

experience [knowledge] ɪk'spɪəriəns 37, 86

experience [sth that happens to you] ɪk'spɪəriəns 86

experiment v ɪk'sperɪmənt 34

expert 'ekspɜːt 41

explain ɪk'spleɪn 31

explain the difference between X and Y ɪk'spleɪn ðə 'dɪfərəns bɪ'twiːn eks ænd waɪ 31

explanation ˌeksplə'neɪʃən 2, 31

explode ɪk'spləʊd 59

explore ɪk'splɔː 50

extremely ɪk'striːmli 7, 91

facilities fə'sɪlətiz 48

fail (an exam) v feɪl 33

fair [equal] feə 57

fair [hair] feə 10

fairly 'feəli 91

fall n, v fɔːl 40

fall asleep fɔːl ə'sliːp 16

fall in love fɔːl ɪn lʌv 74

fall over fɔːl 'əʊvə 19, 79

family holiday 'fæmli 'hɒlədeɪ 46

famous feɪməs 72

fancy (doing) sth 'fænsi 'sʌmθɪŋ 43, 66, 99

FAQs ˌefeɪ'kjuːz 54

Far East ˌfɑːr 'iːst 5

fare feə 28

farewell ˌfeə'wel 69

farmhouse 'fɑːmhaʊs 27

farming 'fɑːmɪŋ 27

fascinating 'fæsɪneɪtɪŋ 89

fashionable 'fæʃənəbəl 72

fast asleep fɑːst ə'sliːp 74

fasten 'fɑːsən 47

fear n fɪə 40

fee(s) iː 19

feed fiːd 16, 30

feel [believe] fiːl 67

feel [experience] n, v fiːl 85

feel bad about sth fiːl bæd ə'baʊt 'sʌmθɪŋ 76

feel sick fiːl sɪk 20

feelings 'fiːlɪŋz 12

feet [measurement] fiːt 62

female 'fiːmeɪl 32, 69

fence fens 27

festival 'festɪvəl 45

fiction 'fɪkʃən 43

field fiːld 27

fifty-pence piece 'fɪfti pens piːs 19

fight faɪt 59

figures (number) 'fɪgəz 40

file (computer) faɪl 54

file menu faɪl 'menjuː 54
files faɪlz 38
filing cabinet 'faɪlɪŋ 'kæbɪnət 38
fill sth in fɪl 'sʌmθɪŋ ɪn 96
film director fɪlm dɪ'rektə 43
film-maker fɪlm 'meɪkə 73
filthy 'fɪlθi 1
final n 'faɪnəl 42
finally 'faɪnəli 92
find out faɪnd aʊt 79
fine n faɪn 56
fire brigade faɪə brɪ'ɡeɪd 35
fireman/firefighter 'faɪəmən
  'faɪəfaɪtə 35
fireworks 'faɪəwɜːks 45
firm adj fɜːm 18
firm n fɜːm 39
first language fɜːst 'læŋɡwɪdʒ 5
first of all fɜːst ɒv ɔːl 92
first(ly) fɜːst 92
fit adj fɪt 71
fit v fɪt 22
fitness 'fɪtnəs 71
fix fɪks 35
fixed (hours) fɪkst 36
flag flæɡ 63
flat n flæt 17
flautist 'flɔːtɪst 44
flavour 'fleɪvə 24
flight flaɪt 28
flight number flaɪt 'nʌmbə 47
flood flʌd 58
floor flɔː 18
flu fluː 20, 100
fluent 'fluːənt 33
flute fluːt 44
fly n flaɪ 8
fly v flaɪ 28
fog fɒɡ 7
foggy 'fɒɡi 7
fold your arms fəʊld jɔːr ɑːmz 9
folk music fəʊk 'mjuːzɪk 44
footballer 'fʊtbɔːlə 71
footpath 'fʊtpɑːθ 27
for fɔː 60
for a start fɔːr ə stɑːt 92
for ages fɔːr 'eɪdʒɪz 60
for example fɔːr ɪɡ'zɑːmpəl 100
for fun fɔː fʌn 42
for instance fɔːr 'ɪnstəns 75
for one thing fɔː wʌn θɪŋ 92
for pleasure fɔː 'pleʒə 41
for the time being fɔː ðə taɪm
  'biːɪŋ 60
forehead 'fɔːhed 9
forget fə'ɡet 2
former 'fɔːmə 39
fortnight 'fɔːtnaɪt 60
fortunately 'fɔːtʃənətli 16
forum 'fɔːrəm 52
fossil fuel 'fɒsəl 'fjuːəl 58
fountain 'faʊntɪn 50
fraction 'frækʃən 61
fragile 'frædʒaɪl 30
France frɑːns 5
freezing 'friːzɪŋ 7
French frentʃ 5

frequency 'friːkwəntsi 91
frequently 'friːkwəntli 91
fresh freʃ 23
fresh air freʃ eə 27
fridge frɪdʒ 100
fridge/freezer frɪdʒ 'friːzə 18
friendly 'frendli 11
friendship 'frendʃɪp 13
frightened 'fraɪtənd 12
frog frɒɡ 8
front door frʌnt dɔː 17
fry fraɪ 25
frying pan 'fraɪɪŋ pæn 25
full stop fʊl stɒp 4, 73
full-time ˌfʊl'taɪm 37
fully-booked 'fʊli bʊkt 48
fur fɜː 63
furniture 'fɜːnɪtʃə 86
garlic 'ɡɑːlɪk 24
gate ɡeɪt 27
gate (3/5/10, etc.)
  (airport) ɡeɪt 47
gather 'ɡæðə 45
general election 'dʒenərəl
  ɪ'lekʃən 57
generalisation
  ˌdʒenərəlaɪ'zeɪʃən 97
generation ˌdʒenəreɪʃən 39
generous 'dʒenərəs 11
German 'dʒɜːmən 5
Germany 'dʒɜːməni 5
get [answer] ɡet 83
get [arrive] ɡet 83
get [become] ɡet 83
get [do a task] ɡet 83
get [fetch] ɡet 83
get a job ɡet ə dʒɒb 32
get away [escape] ɡet ə'weɪ 56,
  59
get better ɡet 'betə 83
get divorced ɡet dɪ'vɔːst 15
get dressed ɡet drest 21, 70
get engaged ɡet ɪn'ɡeɪdʒd 15
get in [arrive] ɡet ɪn 80, 83
get in [enter] ɡet ɪn 28, 83
get in touch ɡet ɪn tʌtʃ 83
get into trouble ɡet 'ɪntə 'trʌbəl
  32
get lost ɡet lɒst 29, 50
get married to sb ɡet 'mærid tuː
  'sʌmbɒdi 13, 15
get off (a bus) ɡet ɒf 28
get on (a bus) ɡet ɒn 28
get on (with sb) ɡet ɒn 13, 79
get out [leave] ɡet aʊt 28, 83
get over sth ɡet 'əʊvə 'sʌmθɪŋ
  80
get rid of sth ɡet rɪd ɒv 'sʌmθɪŋ
  75, 83
get sth back ɡet 'sʌmθɪŋ bæk 83
get sth done ɡet 'sʌmθɪŋ dʌn 83
get sth wrong ɡet 'sʌmθɪŋ rɒŋ
  33, 83
get stuck ɡet stʌk 26, 61
get through [make contact]
  ɡet θruː 53

get through sth [finish]
  ɡet θruː 'sʌmθɪŋ 33
get to know sb ɡet tuː nəʊ
  'sʌmbɒdi 13, 15, 83
get to sleep ɡet tuː sliːp 83
get together ɡet tə'ɡeðə 83, 99
get undressed ɡet ʌn'drest 70
get up ɡet ʌp 16
get used to sth ɡet juːst tuː
  'sʌmθɪŋ 68
get worse ɡet wɜːs 83
giant 'dʒaɪənt 62
giraffe dʒɪ'rɑːf 8
give [cause an effect] ɡɪv 82
give a speech/lecture (etc.) ɡɪv ə
  spiːtʃ/'lektʃə 82
give my regards/love to … ɡɪv maɪ
  rɪ'ɡɑːdz/lʌv tuː 99
give sb advice ɡɪv 'sʌmbɒdi
  əd'vaɪs 36
give sb a hand ɡɪv 'sʌmbɒdi ə
  hænd 82
give sb a hug ɡɪv 'sʌmbɒdi ə hʌɡ
  72
give sb a ring ɡɪv 'sʌmbɒdi ə rɪŋ
  53, 82
give sb a shock ɡɪv 'sʌmbɒdi ə
  ʃɒk 82
give sb the sack ɡɪv 'sʌmbɒdi ðə
  sæk 37
give sth away ɡɪv 'sʌmθɪŋ ə'weɪ
  79
give sth a push ɡɪv 'sʌmθɪŋ ə pʊʃ
  82
give up (sth) [stop doing an
  activity] ɡɪv ʌp 42, 79
give up sth [leave a job]
  ɡɪv ʌp 'sʌmθɪŋ 15
global warming
  'ɡləʊbəl 'wɔːmɪŋ 58
go [disappear] ɡəʊ 84
go [lead somewhere] ɡəʊ 84
go (out) for a walk/drive (etc.)
  ɡəʊ fɔːr ə wɔːk/draɪv 84
go (swimming/shopping, etc.)
  ɡəʊ 16, 41, 84
go and get [fetch] ɡəʊ ænd ɡet
  83, 84
go away [go on holiday]
  ɡəʊ ə'weɪ 79, 84
go away [leave] ɡəʊ ə'weɪ 79
go back ɡəʊ bæk 79, 84
go by bike/car (etc.) ɡəʊ baɪ/baɪk
  kɑː 28
go down ɡəʊ daʊn 40
go for [choose] ɡəʊ fɔː 84
go for (a swim/drive, etc.)
  ɡəʊ fɔː 51, 84
go grey/bald/deaf (etc.) ɡəʊ ɡreɪ/
  bɔːld/def 84
go into business ɡəʊ 'ɪntə 'bɪznɪs
  34
go mad [become angry]
  ɡəʊ mæd 84
go off [electricity] ɡəʊ ɒf 79
go off [explode] ɡəʊ ɒf 79
go off [go bad] ɡəʊ ɒf 79

go off [ring]   gəʊ ɒf   79
go on [happen]   gəʊ ɒn   26, 84
go on (to do sth)   gəʊ ɒn   32, 34
go on a cruise   gəʊ ɒn ə kruːz   46
go on a diet   gəʊ ɒn ə 'daɪət   74
go online   gəʊ ˌɒn'laɪn   55
go out [social activity]   gəʊ aʊt   16, 50
go out [stop working]   gəʊ aʊt   84
go out with sb   gəʊ aʊt wɪð 'sʌmbɒdi   15
go sightseeing   gəʊ 'saɪtsiːɪŋ   50
go through   gəʊ θruː   47
go to bed   gəʊ tuː bed   16
go to sleep   gəʊ tuː sliːp   16
go up   gəʊ ʌp   40
go well/badly   gəʊ wel/'bædli   84
go with sth   gəʊ wɪð 'sʌmθɪŋ   22
go wrong   gəʊ rɒŋ   15, 84
goalkeeper   'gəʊl,kiːpə   41
goat   gəʊt   8
golf course   gɒlf kɔːs   41
good luck   gʊd lʌk   69
good/bad at sth   gʊd/bæd æt 'sʌmθɪŋ   25, 77
good-looking   ˌgʊd'lʊkɪŋ   10
gorgeous   'gɔːdʒəs   10
govern   'gʌvən   71
government   'gʌvənmənt   57, 71
GP   ˌdʒiː'piː   35
grade   greɪd   33, 34
gradual(ly)   'grædʒuəl   40
graduate   n   'grædʒuət   34, 98
grant [allow]   grɑːnt   95
grapes   greɪps   24
grass   grɑːs   27
great   greɪt   95
great fun   greɪt fʌn   74
great importance   greɪt ɪm'pɔːtəns   74
Greece   griːs   5
Greek   griːk   5
greenhouse effect   'griːnhaʊs ɪ'fekt   58
greenhouse gases   'griːnhaʊs 'gæsɪz   58
greet   griːt   69
greeting   'griːtɪŋ   69
grey   greɪ   63
grill   n, v   grɪl   25
ground   graʊnd   27
growing   'grəʊɪŋ   39, 40
guess   n, v   ges   3, 72
guidebook   'gaɪdbʊk   50
guilty   'gɪlti   56
guitar   gɪ'tɑː   44
guitarist   gɪ'tɑːrɪst   44
gun   gʌn   37, 59
gym   dʒɪm   41, 100
haggle   'hægəl   23
hair   heə   10
haircut   'heəkʌt   73
hairdresser   'heə,dresə   73
hairdryer   'heə,draɪə   73
half   hɑːf   61
half a dozen   hɑːf ə 'dʌzən   64

hand luggage   hænd 'lʌgɪdʒ   47
hand sth out   hænd 'sʌmθɪŋ aʊt   80
handle   v   'hændəl   36
handsome   'hænsəm   10
handwriting   'hænd,raɪtɪŋ   96
hang around   hæŋ ə'raʊnd   80
happiness   'hæpɪnəs   71
harbour   'hɑːbə   45
hard drive/disk   hɑːd draɪv/dɪsk   54
hard work   hɑːd wɜːk   33
hardly ever   'hɑːdli 'evə   91
hard-working   ˌhɑːd'wɜːkɪŋ   11
hate   heɪt   68, 87
have a (swim/drink, etc.)   hæv ə   51
have a bath   hæv ə bɑːθ   16
have a good ear for language   hæv ə gʊd ɪə fɔː 'læŋgwɪdʒ   33
have a great/nice/terrible time   hæv ə greɪt/naɪs/'terəbəl taɪm   50
have a late night   hæv ə leɪt naɪt   16
have a look   hæv ə lʊk   81
have a look round   hæv ə lʊk raʊnd   50
have a sleep   hæv ə sliːp   16
have a wash/shower etc.   hæv ə wɒʃ/ʃaʊə   16, 81
have a word with sb   hæv ə wɜːd wɪð 'sʌmbɒdi   76
have an early night   hæv æn 'ɜːli naɪt   16
have children   hæv 'tʃɪldrən   74
have got sth on   hæv gɒt 'sʌmθɪŋ ɒn   22
have no idea   hæv nəʊ aɪ'dɪə   76
have something/nothing in common   hæv 'sʌmθɪŋ/'nʌθɪŋ ɪn 'kɒmən   68
have time for sth   hæv taɪm fɔː 'sʌmθɪŋ   60
headache   'hedeɪk   20
headline   'hedlaɪn   52
headquarters   ˌhed'kwɔːtəz   39
hear   hɪə   85
heart [in the body]   hɑːt   20
heart of somewhere   hɑːt ɒv 'sʌmweə   48, 59
heart attack   hɑːt ə'tæk   20
heat   v   hiːt   17
heat up   hiːt ʌp   49
heavy (rain)   'hevi   7
heavy (traffic)   'hevi   74
Hebrew   'hiːbruː   5
heel   hiːl   9
height   haɪt   10, 62
held [organised]   held   45
help   help   88
helpful   'helpfəl   71
hen   hen   24
herbal tea   'hɜːbl tiː   49
hi   haɪ   99

hide   haɪd   59
high (mountain)   haɪ   62
highlight   'haɪlaɪt   31
highlighter pen   'haɪˌlaɪtə pen   1, 31
hill   hɪl   27
hip   hɪp   9
hire   'haɪə   19
historic monument   hɪ'stɒrɪk 'mɒnjəmənt   50
hit   hɪt   56
hold an election   həʊld æn ɪ'lekʃən   57
hold on [wait]   həʊld ɒn   80
hold-up   həʊld ʌp   65
honest   'ɒnɪst   11, 70
honeymoon   'hʌnimuːn   15
hope that …   həʊp ðæt   88
hope to do sth   həʊp tuː duː 'sʌmθɪŋ   87, 99
hopeful   'həʊpfəl   12
hopeless   'həʊpləs   27
horrible   'hɒrəbəl   25
horror film   'hɒrə fɪlm   43
hot chocolate   hɒt 'tʃɒklət   49
housework   'haʊswɜːk   16
How about …? [making a suggestion]   haʊ ə'baʊt   66, 69
How about you? [asking sb sth]   haʊ ə'baʊt juː   69
How are things?   haʊ ɑː θɪŋz   69
How do you feel about …?   haʊ duː juː fiːl ə'baʊt   67
How long/wide (etc.) is …?   haʊ lɒŋ/waɪd x ɪz   62
How's it going?   haʊz ɪt 'gəʊɪŋ   69
however   haʊ'evə   93, 97
hug   hʌg   82
huge   hjuːdʒ   62, 89
humid   'hjuːmɪd   7
hundred   'hʌndrəd   61
hurry (up)   'hʌri   79
hurt   v   hɜːt   20
I am pleased to inform you …   aɪ æm pliːzd tuː ɪn'fɔːm juː   98
I am writing in response to …   aɪ ˌæm 'raɪtɪŋ ɪn rɪ'spɒns tuː   98
I am writing to …   aɪ æm 'raɪtɪŋ tuː   98
I beg your pardon   aɪ beg jɔː 'pɑːdən   65
I bet   aɪ bet   95
I don't believe it   aɪ dəʊnt bɪ'liːv ɪt   76
I don't fancy that   aɪ dəʊnt 'fænsi ðæt   66
I don't mind   aɪ dəʊnt maɪnd   66
I look forward to hearing from you   aɪ lʊk 'fɔːwəd tuː 'hɪərɪŋ frɒm juː   98
I must apologise for …   aɪ mʌst ə'pɒlədʒaɪz fɔː   65
I regret to inform you …   aɪ rɪ'gret tuː ɪn'fɔːm juː   98

I see what you mean   aɪ siː wɒt juː miːn   67

I suppose so   aɪ sə'pəʊz səʊ   76

I was wondering if you could …   aɪ wɒz 'wʌndərɪŋ ɪf juː kʊd   66

I wonder if you could …   aɪ 'wʌndər ɪf juː kʊd   66

I would be grateful if you could …   aɪ wʊd biː 'greɪtfəl ɪf juː kʊd   98

i.e.   aɪ'iː   100

I'd rather …   aɪd 'rɑːðə   66

I'll have (chicken/fish, etc.)   aɪl hæv   48

I'll leave it   aɪl liːv ɪt   22

I'll take it   aɪl teɪk ɪt   22

I'm afraid I can't   aɪm ə'freɪd aɪ kɑːnt   66

I'm being served   aɪm 'biːɪŋ sɜːvd   22

I'm looking for …   aɪm 'lʊkɪŋ fɔː   22

I'm sorry   aɪm 'sɒri   65

I'm sorry I'm late   aɪm 'sɒri aɪm leɪt   65

ice   aɪs   7

ice hockey   aɪs 'hɒki   41, 73

icon   'aɪkɒn   54

icy   'aɪsi   7

ID   aɪ'diː   100

ID card   aɪ'diː kɑːd   73

if I were you   ɪf aɪ wɜː juː   75

if you like   ɪf juː laɪk   66

ill   ɪl   70

illegal   ɪ'liːgəl   70

illness   'ɪlnəs   20, 71

image   'ɪmɪdʒ   39

imagine   ɪ'mædʒɪn   87

immediately   ɪ'miːdiətli   55

impatient   ɪm'peɪʃənt   11

improve   ɪm'pruːv   71

improvement   ɪm'pruːvmənt   71

in [place]   ɪn   90

in a hurry   ɪn ə 'hʌri   26, 78

in a moment   ɪn ə 'məʊmənt   78

in a row   ɪn ə rəʊ   40

in a week's/month's (etc.) time   ɪn ə wiːks/mʌnθs taɪm   60, 75, 99

in addition (to)   ɪn ə'dɪʃən   93

in advance   ɪn əd'vɑːns   48

in black/blue/brown (etc.)   ɪn blæk/bluː/braʊn   21

in business   ɪn 'bɪznɪs   78

in case   ɪn keɪs   94

in charge of   ɪn tʃɑːdʒ ɒv   36

in contrast   ɪn 'kɒntrɑːst   97

in credit   ɪn 'kredɪt   19

in detail   ɪn 'diːteɪl   78

in fact   ɪn fækt   99

in fashion   ɪn 'fæʃən   22

in future   ɪn 'fjuːtʃə   78

in general   ɪn 'dʒenərəl   75, 97

in large quantities   ɪn lɑːdʒ 'kwɒntətiz   64

in love   ɪn lʌv   15

in my opinion   ɪn maɪ ə'pɪnjən   67

in order to   ɪn 'ɔːdə tuː   94

in other words   ɪn 'ʌðə wɜːdz   100

in progress   ɪn 'prəʊgres   30

in response to   ɪn rɪ'spɒns tuː   98

in spite of   ɪn spaɪt ɒv   93

in tears   ɪn tɪəz   78

in that case   ɪn ðæt keɪs   76

in the end   ɪn ði end   14, 78, 92

in the past   ɪn ðə pɑːst   32, 97

in the south   ɪn ðə saʊθ   6

in the wild   ɪn ðə waɪld   8

in the world   ɪn ðə wɜːld   6

in time   ɪn taɪm   60, 78

in writing   ɪn 'raɪtɪŋ   98

in your teens   ɪn jɔː tiːnz   14

inability   ˌɪnə'bɪləti   71

inch   ɪntʃ   62

include   ɪn'kluːd   48

income   'ɪŋkʌm   36

income tax   'ɪŋkʌm tæks   36, 73

incorrect   ˌɪnkər'ekt   70

increase   n   'ɪnkriːs   33, 40

increase   v   ɪn'kriːs   40

incredible   ɪn'kredɪbəl   42

incredibly   ɪn'kredɪbli   91

indefinite article   ɪn'defɪnət 'ɑːtɪkəl   4

individual   ˌɪndɪ'vɪdʒuəl   42

inflation   ɪn'fleɪʃən   40

ingredients   ɪn'griːdiənts   25

injure   'ɪndʒə   30

injury   'ɪndʒəri   29

innocent   'ɪnəsənt   56

insect   'ɪnsekt   8

inside lane   'ɪnsaɪd leɪn   29

insist on doing sth   ɪn'sɪst ɒn 'duːɪŋ 'sʌmθɪŋ   87

install   ɪn'stɔːl   35, 54

instant messaging   'ɪnstənt 'mesɪdʒɪŋ   55

instead   ɪn'sted   16

intelligent   ɪn'telɪdʒənt   11

intend   ɪn'tend   87

interest   n   'ɪntrəst   40

interest   v   'ɪntrəst   68

interest rate   'ɪntrəst reɪt   40

interested in   'ɪntrəstɪd ɪn   68, 77

interests   'ɪntrəsts   68, 96

Internet access   'ɪntənet 'ækses   48

interrupt   ˌɪntə'rʌpt   65

interview   'ɪntəvjuː   37

into   'ɪntə   90

introduce sb   ˌɪntrə'djuːs 'sʌmbɒdi   69

invent   ɪn'vent   71, 80

invention   ɪn'venʃən   71

invoice   'ɪnvɔɪs   38

involve   ɪn'vɒlv   38, 45

iron   aɪən   46

ironing   'aɪənɪŋ   16

irregular   ɪ'regjələ   70

irregular (verb)   ɪ'regjələ   4

Is that (Joe, Emma, etc …?)   ɪz ðæt   53

-ish   ɪʃ   10

ISP   ˌaɪes'piː   55, 100

Israel   'ɪzreɪl   5

Israeli   ɪz'reɪli   5

it/that depends   ɪt/ðæt dɪ'pendz   76

it said in   ɪt sed ɪn   52

it seems to me   ɪt siːmz tuː miː   97

Italian   ɪ'tæliən   5

Italy   'ɪtəli   5

item   'aɪtəm   23, 55

jail   dʒeɪl   56

jacket   'dʒækɪt   21

Japan   dʒə'pæn   5

Japanese   ˌdʒæpə'niːz   5

jar   dʒɑ   64

jeans   dʒiːnz   21

jealous   'dʒeləs   12

jealousy   'dʒeləsi   12

jogging   'dʒɒgɪŋ   41

join [become a member]   dʒɔɪn   35

join [do sth with others]   dʒɔɪn   99

journalist   'dʒɜːnəlɪst   52

journey   'dʒɜːni   28

judge   dʒʌdʒ   56

jug   dʒʌg   64

jumper   'dʒʌmpə   21

junction   'dʒʌŋkʃən   31

junk mail   dʒʌŋk meɪl   55

jury   'dʒʊəri   56

just as   dʒʌst æz   92

keen on   kiːn ɒn   68

keep [look after]   kiːp   27

keep [stay in a place/condition]   kiːp   82

keep (on) doing sth   kiːp 'duːɪŋ 'sʌmθɪŋ   82

keep a secret   kiːp ə 'siːkrət   82

keep in touch   kiːp ɪn tʌtʃ   82

keep off sth   kiːp ɒf 'sʌmθɪŋ   30

keep right/left   kiːp raɪt/left   30

keep sb fit   kiːp 'sʌmbɒdi fɪt   41

keep (pets)   kiːp   8

keep sth up   kiːp 'sʌmθɪŋ ʌp   82

kettle   'ketəl   18

keyboard   'kiːbɔːd   38, 44, 54

keyboard player   'kiːbɔːd 'pleɪə   44

(I'm/you're, etc.) kidding   'kɪdɪŋ   76

kids   kɪdz   95

kill   kɪl   59

kind   kaɪnd   1, 11

kind of   kaɪnd ɒv   76

Kind regards   kaɪnd rɪ'gɑːdz   98

kitten   'kɪtən   2

knee   niː   9

knowledge (of sth)   'nɒlɪdʒ   86

Korean   kə'riːən   5

lab   læb   34, 100

laboratory   lə'bɒrətəri   34

ladder 'lædə 63
lamb læm 24
land v lænd 47
landing 'lændɪŋ 47
landing card 'lændɪŋ kɑːd 96
landline 'lændlaɪn 53
landscape 'lændskeɪp 6
lane (on a road) leɪn 29
laptop 'læptɒp 54
large lɑːdʒ 49
large number/amount
   lɑːdʒ 'nʌmbə/ə'maʊnt 19, 74
last v lɑːst 34, 45, 60
last long lɑːst lɒŋ 60
late (50s/60s, etc.) leɪt 14
lately 'leɪtli 60
latest 'leɪtɪst 43
latte 'læteɪ 49
laugh v lɑːf 9
law lɔː 34
lawyer 'lɔɪə 35
lazy 'leɪzi 11
lead [be in front] liːd 42
leader 'liːdə 57
league liːg 42
lean liːn 30
leather 'leðə 63
leave [end a relationship] liːv 15
leave (a place) liːv 32
leave a message liːv ə
   'mesɪdʒ 53
leave sb/sth out liːv
   'sʌmbɒdi/'sʌmθɪŋ aʊt 80
leaves (on a tree) liːvz 27
lecturer 'lektʃərə 34, 35
legal 'liːgəl 70
lemon 'lemən 24
lend lend 31
length leŋθ 62
leopard 'lepəd 8
let [allow] let 14
let you know let juː nəʊ 99
lettuce 'letɪs 24
library 'laɪbrəri 34
lie down laɪ daʊn 79
lift n lɪft 17
light [not dark] laɪt 17
light [not much] laɪt 7, 74
light lunch laɪt lʌntʃ 16
light (rain/shower) laɪt 7
lightning 'laɪtnɪŋ 7
like [similar to] laɪk 85
likely 'laɪkli 23
limited number/amount/choice
   'lɪmɪtɪd 'nʌmbə/ə'maʊnt/tʃɔɪs
   74
limited vocabulary
   'lɪmɪtɪd və'kæbjələri 74
link (computer) lɪŋk 55
link word lɪŋk wɜːd 4
lion 'laɪən 8
lips lɪps 9
listen [pay attention] 'lɪsən 85
literature 'lɪtrətʃə 43
live adj laɪv 44
lively 'laɪvli 26, 50

liver 'lɪvə 20
loads of sth ləʊdz ɒv 'sʌmθɪŋ 38
loan ləʊn 40
location ləʊ'keɪʃən 17
lock v lɒk 70
log in/on lɒg ɪn/ɒn 54
log off/out lɒg ɒf/aʊt 54
longish 'lɒŋɪʃ 10
look n, v lʊk 85
look after sb lʊk 'ɑːftə
   'sʌmbɒdi 80
look sth up lʊk 'sʌmθɪŋ ʌp 3,
   31, 79
loose luːs 22
lorry 'lɒri 28
lose (a game) luːz 42
lose weight luːz weɪt 74
loser 'luːzə 42
loss lɒs 40
lots of character lɒts əv
   'kæræktə 17
loud noise laʊd nɔɪz 74
love v lʌv 68
Love (greeting) lʌv 99
luckily 'lʌkəli 16
luggage 'lʌgɪdʒ 47
lung cancer lʌŋ 'kænsə 20
lungs lʌŋz 20
lyrics 'lɪrɪks 44
mad about sb mæd ə'baʊt
   'sʌmbɒdi 77
magnificent mæg'nɪfɪsənt 50
main course meɪn kɔːs 48
main meal meɪn miːl 16
main road meɪn rəʊd 29
mainly 'meɪnli 53
majority mə'dʒɒrəti 61
make [cause sb to do sth] meɪk
   23, 81
make [force sb to do
   sth] meɪk 81
make a comparison meɪk ə
   kəm'pærɪsən 97
make a decision meɪk ə
   dɪ'sɪʒən 81
make a mistake meɪk ə mɪ'steɪk
   81
make a noise meɪk ə nɔɪz 81
make a profit/loss
   meɪk ə 'prɒfɪt/lɒs 40
make an effort meɪk æn 'efət 81
make friends meɪk frendz 81
make generalisations
   meɪk ˌdʒenərəlaɪ'zeɪʃənz 97
make it meɪk ɪt 95
make (money) meɪk 36
make sth up meɪk 'sʌmθɪŋ
   ʌp 80
make the bed meɪk ðə bed 16
make up your mind
   meɪk ʌp jɔː maɪnd 75, 81
make yourself understood
   meɪk jɔː'self ˌʌndə'stʊd 33
make-up 'meɪkʌp 16
male meɪl 32, 69
manage [run a business]
   'mænɪdʒ 71

manage [succeed in doing sth]
   'mænɪdʒ 14
management 'mænɪdʒmənt 71
Mandarin 'mændərɪn 5
marital status 'mærɪtəl
   'steɪtəs 96
mark [grade] mɑːk 33
market 'mɑːkɪt 50
marry 'mæri 15
marvellous 'mɑːvələs 89
match v mætʃ 22
mate meɪt 13, 95
material mə'tɪəriəl 63
maths mæθs 100
me neither miː 'naɪðə 68
me too miː tuː 68
meal miːl 16
mean adj miːn 11
mean v miːn 31
meaning 'miːnɪŋ 31
measure 'meʒə 31
mechanic mɪ'kænɪk 37
media reporting
   'miːdiə rɪ'pɔːtɪŋ 52
medicine [the
   subject] 'medsən 34
medicine [to treat an illness]
   'medsən 20
medium [meat] 'miːdiəm 48
medium height 'miːdiəm haɪt 10
melon 'melən 24
mend mend 35
mention 'menʃən 88
mess mes 2
metal 'metəl 62
mice maɪs 8
microwave 'maɪkrəweɪv 18
mid (30s/40s, etc.) mɪd 14
Middle East ˌmɪdəl 'iːst 5
middle-aged ˌmɪdəl'eɪdʒd 14
mild maɪld 7
mile maɪl 62
milkshake 'mɪlkʃeɪk 49
million 'mɪljən 61
mind v maɪnd 68
mind (+ -ing) maɪnd 87
mind the step maɪnd ðə step 30
mind your head maɪnd jɔː
   hed 30
minimum wage
   'mɪnɪməm weɪdʒ 36
minor (offence) 'maɪnə 56
minority maɪ'nɒrəti 61
minus 'maɪnəs 6
minus adj 'maɪnəs 61
miserable 'mɪzərəbəl 12
mishear mɪs'hɪə 70
miss [avoid] mɪs 82
miss [not hear] mɪs 82
miss sb mɪs 'sʌmbɒdi 82
miss a chance/opportunity
   mɪs ə tʃɑːns/ˌɒpə'tjuːnəti 82
miss the bus/train (etc.)
   mɪs ðə bʌs/treɪn 28, 74
missing 'mɪsɪŋ 59
misunderstand ˌmɪsʌndə'stænd
   70

mix n mɪks 26
mix sth up mɪks 'sʌmθɪŋ ʌp 2
mobile edition 'məʊbaɪl ɪ'dɪʃən 52
mobile number 'məʊbaɪl 'nʌmbə 53
monkey 'mʌŋki 8
monthly 'mʌntθli 52
mood muːd 12
mosque mɒsk 50
mosquito mə'skiːtəʊ 8
mostly 'məʊstli 53
mother tongue 'mʌðə tʌŋ 73
mother/brother/son-in-law 'mʌðə/'brʌðə/sʌn ɪn lɔː 13
motorbike 'məʊtəbaɪk 30
mouse (animal) maʊs 8
mouse (computer) maʊs 54
mouse mat maʊs mæt 54
move muːv 17
MP ˌem'piː 57, 100
Mr 'mɪstə 100
Mrs 'mɪsɪz 100
muffin 'mʌfɪn 49
multiplication ˌmʌltɪplɪ'keɪʃən 61
multiplied by 'mʌltɪplaɪd baɪ 61
murder n, v 'mɜːdə 56
murderer 'mɜːdərə 56
mushroom 'mʌʃruːm 24
musical 'mjuːzɪkəl 72
mussels 'mʌsəlz 24
my view/feeling is maɪ vjuː/'fiːlɪŋ ɪz 67
napkins 'næpkɪns 49
narrow 'nærəʊ 10, 62
national 'næʃənəl 52, 63, 72
navy [army] 'neɪvi 35
navy blue 'neɪvi bluː 63
nearby nɪə'baɪ 46
nearest 'nɪərɪst 46, 62
nearly 'nɪəli 14
necessary 'nesəsəri 2
neck nek 9
necklace 'nekləs 21
negative 'negətɪv 11
neither do/am/can I 'naɪðə duː/æm/kæn aɪ 68
nephew 'nefjuː 13
nervous 'nɜːvəs 11
net net 41
never mind 'nevə maɪnd 65
news njuːz 52, 86
next time nekst taɪm 60
nice naɪs 11
nice to meet you naɪs tuː miːt juː 69
niece niːs 13
night after night naɪt 'ɑːftə naɪt 75
nightlife 'naɪtlaɪf 26
nil nɪl 42
nine-to-five adj naɪn tuː faɪv 36
no entry nəʊ 'entri 30
no exit nəʊ 'eksɪt 30
no parking nəʊ 'pɑːkɪŋ 30

no problem nəʊ 'prɒbləm 66, 65
no vacancies nəʊ 'veɪkənsiz 30
no way/chance nəʊ weɪ/tʃɑːns 76
nod your head nɒd jɔː hed 9
normal 'nɔːməl 72
north nɔːθ 6
north-east nɔːθ 'iːst 6
north-west nɔːθ 'west 6
not at all nɒt æt ɔːl 65
not (so) bad nɒt bæd 69
not really nɒt 'rɪəli 76
note [money] nəʊt 19
note down nəʊt daʊn 2
nothing to declare 'nʌθɪŋ tuː dɪ'kleə 47
notice n 'nəʊtɪs 30
notice v 'nəʊtɪs 88
noticeboard 'nəʊtɪsbɔːd 38
nought nɔːt 61
noun naʊn 4
novel 'nɒvəl 43
now and again naʊ ænd ə'gen 69
now and then naʊ ænd ðen 75
nowadays 'naʊədeɪz 60, 97
nowhere to park 'nəʊweə tuː pɑːk 26
nurse nɜːs 35
nursery school 'nɜːsəri skuːl 32
obesity ə'biːsəti 97
object n 'ɒbdʒɪkt 63
occasionally ə'keɪʒənəli 91
ocean 'əʊʃən 6
octopus 'ɒktəpəs 8
of course ɒv kɔːs 66
off [absent] ɒf 36, 38
offence ə'fens 56
offer 'ɒfə 87
official ə'fɪʃəl 3
oh [0] əʊ 61
oil [fuel] ɔɪl 58
oil [on food] ɔɪl 24
old friend əʊld frend 13
olives 'ɒlɪvz 24
omit ə'mɪt 80
on [place] ɒn 90
on and off ɒn ænd ɒf 75
on board ɒn bɔːd 78
on business ɒn 'bɪznɪs 78
on display ɒn dɪ'spleɪ 78
on earth ɒn ɜːθ 6
on fire ɒn 'faɪə 78
on my/your own ɒn maɪ/jɔːr əʊn 15, 96
on purpose ɒn 'pɜːpəs 78
on record ɒn 'rekɔːd 58
on strike ɒn straɪk 78
on the first/second (etc.) floor ɒn ðə fɜːst/'sekənd flɔː 17
on the Internet ɒn ði 'ɪntənet 55
on the one hand ɒn ðə wʌn hænd 97
on the other hand ɒn ði 'ʌðə hænd 97
on the outskirts ɒn ði 'aʊtskɜːts 17

on the phone ɒn ðə fəʊn 53, 78
on the way ɒn ðə weɪ 31
on the whole ɒn ðə həʊl 75, 97
on time ɒn taɪm 60, 78
once wʌns 69
once a week/month (etc.) wʌns ə wiːk/mʌnθ 16
once again wʌns ə'gen 99
once or twice wʌns ɔː twaɪs 75
one day wʌn deɪ 60
one pound coin wʌn paʊnd kɔɪn 19
one of the advantages of … wʌn ɒv ði əd'vɑːntɪdʒɪz ɒv 97
onion 'ʌnjən 24
only child 'əʊnli tʃaɪld 13
open space 'əʊpən speɪs 27
opera (singer) 'ɒpərə 44
operate on sb 'ɒpəreɪt ɒn 'sʌmbɒdi 35
operating system 'ɒpəreɪtɪŋ 'sɪstəm 54
operation ˌɒpər'eɪʃən 20
opposite 'ɒpəzɪt 1
or so ɔː səʊ 95
orchestra 'ɔːkɪstrə 44
ordinary 'ɔːdɪnəri 10
organisation ˌɔːgənaɪ'zeɪʃən 38
organise 'ɔːgənaɪz 38
otherwise 'ʌðəwaɪz 94
out [not there] aʊt 53
out of aʊt ɒv 90
out of order aʊt ɒv 'ɔːdə 19, 30
out of the blue aʊt ɒv ðə bluː 75
out of work aʊt ɒv wɜːk 39
out-of-date ˌaʊtəv'deɪt 78
outside lane 'aʊtsaɪd leɪn 29
outstanding ˌaʊt'stændɪŋ 42
oven 'ʌvən 18, 25
over [more than] 'əʊvə 6
over [movement] 'əʊvə 90
overcharge ˌəʊvə'tʃɑːdʒ 70
overhead locker ˌəʊvəhed 'lɒkə 47
oversleep ˌəʊvə'sliːp 65
overtake ˌəʊvə'teɪk 29
overtime 'əʊvətaɪm 36
overweight ˌəʊvə'weɪt 10
owe əʊ 19
own adj əʊn 18, 37
own v əʊn 17, 26, 37
owner 'əʊnə 37
pack pæk 70
package holiday 'pækɪdʒ 'hɒlədeɪ 46
packed 'pækt 50
packet 'pækɪt 64
pain peɪn 20
painful 'peɪnfəl 20, 72
painless 'peɪnləs 72
pair peə 64
palace 'pælɪs 50
panini pə'niːni 49
paper [newspaper] 'peɪpə 52
paperwork 'peɪpəwɜːk 38
parade pə'reɪd 45
parcel 'pɑːsəl 29

parked car pɑːkt kɑː 29
parrot 'pærət 8
part of speech pɑːt ɒv spiːtʃ 3
partly 'pɑːtli 67
partner 'pɑːtnə 31
part-time ˌpɑːt'taɪm 37
pass an exam pɑːs æn ɪg'zæm 33
passenger 'pæsəndʒə 47
password 'pɑːswɜːd 54
paste peɪst 54
patient adj 'peɪʃənt 11
patient n 'peɪʃənt 20
pause pɔːz 4
pavement 'peɪvmənt 29
pay n, v peɪ 36
pay attention peɪ ə'tenʃən 76
pay back peɪ bæk 19, 40
pay rise peɪ raɪz 37
PC ˌpiː'siː 54, 100
peace and quiet piːs ænd 'kwaɪət 75
peaceful 'piːsfəl 72
peach piːtʃ 24
pear peə 24
peas piːz 24
pedestrian pə'destriən 29
pedestrian crossing pə'destriən 'krɒsɪŋ 29
peel piːl 25
pencil sharpener 'pensəl 'ʃɑːpənə 31
per cent pə sent 40, 61
percentage pə'sentɪdʒ 40
perform pə'fɔːm 44
performance pə'fɔːməns 44
permanent 'pɜːmənənt 1
permission pə'mɪʃən 66
personal (opinion) 'pɜːsənəl 72
personal details 'pɜːsənəl 'diːteɪlz 96
personal statement 'pɜːsənəl 'steɪtmənt 96
personally 'pɜːsənəli 67
persuade pə'sweɪd 88
pet pet 8
phone fəʊn 100
phone sb back fəʊn 'sʌmbɒdi bæk 53
phonemic symbol fə'niːmɪk 'sɪmbəl 3, 4
photo 'fəʊtəʊ 100
photocopier 'fəʊtəʊˌkɒpiə 38
phrasal verb 'freɪzəl vɜːb 4
phrase freɪz 3, 4
pianist 'piːənɪst 44
piano pi'ænəʊ 44
pick pɪk 27
pick sb up [collect sb] pɪk 'sʌmbɒdi ʌp 79
pick sth up [learn] pɪk 'sʌmθɪŋ ʌp 33
pick sth up [collect sth] pɪk 'sʌmθɪŋ ʌp 46
pick sth up [lift sth from the floor] pɪk 'sʌmθɪŋ ʌp 79
pie paɪ 25
piece piːs 64, 86

pill pɪl 20
pillow 'pɪləʊ 18
pilot 'paɪlət 35
pineapple 'paɪnæpəl 24
pink pɪŋk 63
pipe paɪp 35
pitch pɪtʃ 41
place [town/building] pleɪs 50
plan plæn 35
plane pleɪn 100
planet 'plænɪt 6
plant n plɑːnt 27
plant v plɑːnt 58
plastic 'plæstɪk 63
platform 'plætfɔːm 28
play (a game) pleɪ 41
play against sb pleɪ ə'genst 'sʌmbɒdi 42
pleasant 'plezənt 11
Please accept our apologies for … pliːz ək'sept 'aʊər ə'pɒlədʒiz fɔː 98
Please could you …? pliːz kʊd juː 98
plenty 'plenti 51, 64
plug plʌg 31
plug sth in plʌg 'sʌmθɪŋ ɪn 31
plumber 'plʌmə 35
plus plʌs 61
PM ˌpiː'em 100
pocket 'pɒkɪt 21
pocket money 'pɒkɪt 'mʌni 86
podcast 'pɒdkɑːst 52
poet 'pəʊɪt 43
poetry 'pəʊɪtri 43
point [decimal point] pɔɪnt 61
point [idea] pɔɪnt 67
point of view pɔɪnt ɒv vjuː 97
pointed 'pɔɪntɪd 63
Poland 'pəʊlənd 5
police force pə'liːs fɔːs 35
police officer pə'liːs 'ɒfɪsə 35
policy 'pɒləsi 57
Polish 'pəʊlɪʃ 5
polite pə'laɪt 66
politely pə'laɪtli 91
political pə'lɪtɪkəl 57
political party pə'lɪtɪkəl 'pɑːti 57
pollution pə'luːʃən 26
pop music pɒp 'mjuːzɪk 44
popular 'pɒpjələ 44, 71
popularity ˌpɒpjə'lærəti 71
population ˌpɒpjə'leɪʃən 5
pork pɔːk 24
Portuguese ˌpɔːtʃə'giːz 5
positive 'pɒzətɪv 11
post n [different meanings] pəʊst 3
post [message] pəʊst 55
postgraduate ˌpəʊst'grædʒuət 34
postpone pəʊst'pəʊn 80
pour (with rain) pɔː 7
powerful 'paʊəfəl 57
prawns prɔːnz 24
predict (the future) prɪ'dɪkt 74
prefer prɪ'fɜː 68
prefix 'priːfɪks 4

pregnancy 'pregnənsi 15
pregnant 'pregnənt 15
preparation ˌprepər'eɪʃən 33
preposition ˌprepə'zɪʃən 4
pretty [attractive] 'prɪti 10
pretty [rather] 'prɪti 91
pride praɪd 12
primary school 'praɪməri skuːl 32
Prime Minister praɪm 'mɪnɪstə 57
print prɪnt 54
print sth out prɪnt 'sʌmθɪŋ aʊt 54
printer 'prɪntə 54
prison 'prɪzən 56
private 'praɪvət 32
proceed prə'siːd 95
produce v prə'djuːs 36, 38
product 'prɒdʌkt 36
production prə'dʌkʃən 38
profession prə'feʃən 35
profit 'prɒfɪt 40
progress n 'prəʊgres 86
promise (+ obj) that 'prɒmɪs ðæt 88
promise to do sth 'prɒmɪs tuː duː 'sʌmθɪŋ 88
promote prə'məʊt 37
promotion prə'məʊʃən 37
pronoun 'prəʊnaʊn 4
pronounce prə'naʊns 31
pronunciation prəˌnʌnsi'eɪʃən 31
properly 'prɒpəli 19
protect prə'tekt 8, 59
protection prə'tekʃən 51
proud praʊd 12
proud (of) 12
provide prə'vaɪd 57
psychologist saɪ'kɒlədʒɪst 36
psychology saɪ'kɒlədʒi 36
public transport 'pʌblɪk 'trænspɔːt 27, 28, 73
publish 'pʌblɪʃ 52
punctuation ˌpʌŋktʃu'eɪʃən 4
punish 'pʌnɪʃ 32, 56
punishment 'pʌnɪʃmənt 56
pupil 'pjuːpəl 32
purchase 'pɜːtʃəs 95
purple 'pɜːpəl 63
purpose 'pɜːpəs 94
push pʊʃ 82
put on make-up pʊt ɒn 'meɪkʌp 16
put on weight pʊt ɒn weɪt 74
put sb through pʊt 'sʌmbɒdi θruː 53
put sth back pʊt 'sʌmθɪŋ bæk 79
put sth off pʊt 'sʌmθɪŋ ɒf 80
put sth on [make equipment work] pʊt 'sʌmθɪŋ ɒn 79
put sth up [raise] pʊt 'sʌmθɪŋ ʌp 79
put sth on [put clothes on your body] pʊt 'sʌmθɪŋ ɒn 21, 79, 80

qualification ˌkwɒlɪfɪˈkeɪʃən 34, 96
qualified ˈkwɒlɪfaɪd 34
qualify ˈkwɒlɪfaɪ 34
quality ˈkwɒləti 39
quantity ˈkwɒntəti 64
quarter [one quarter] ˈkwɔːtə 61
quarter [three months] ˈkwɔːtə 40
question mark ˈkwestʃən mɑːk 4
queue n kjuː 23, 28
queue v kjuː 30
quiet ˈkwaɪət 26
quietly ˈkwaɪətli 91
quit kwɪt 37
quite kwaɪt 91
quite a bit kwaɪt ə bɪt 95
quite a long way kwaɪt ə lɒŋ weɪ 62
quite likely kwaɪt ˈlaɪkli 74
quite often kwaɪt ˈɒfən 91
rabbit ˈræbɪt 8
race n reɪs 42
race v reɪs 41
racing driver ˈreɪsɪŋ ˈdraɪvə 41
rain n, v reɪn 7
rainforest ˈreɪnˌfɒrɪst 6
raise reɪz 40
range reɪndʒ 23
rare [meat] reə 47
rare [unusual] reə 8
rarely ˈreəli 91
rather ˈrɑːðə 91
raw rɔː 2, 25
real rɪəl 63
realise ˈrɪəlaɪz 88
reality TV show ri'ælətɪ ˌtiːˈviː ʃəʊ 52
really [very] ˈrɪəli 89
really? [to express surprise] ˈrɪəli 68
reason ˈriːzən 94
reasonable ˈriːzənəbəl 19, 22,
reasonable (amount) 19
recently ˈriːsəntli 60
reception [in a hotel] rɪˈsepʃən 48
reception [wedding party] rɪˈsepʃən 15
recession rɪˈseʃən 40
recipe ˈresɪpi 25
recommend rekəˈmend 46, 51
recommend (+ -ing) ˌrekəˈmend 87
recommend + that ˌrekəˈmend ðæt 51, 88
record n ˈrekɔːd 42
record v rɪˈkɔːd 44
recording studio rɪˈkɔːdɪŋ ˈstjuːdiəʊ 44
red pepper red ˈpepə 24
reduce rɪˈdjuːs 57, 58
reduction rɪˈdʌkʃən 57
reference ˈrefərəns 96
refund n ˈriːfʌnd 23
regarding rɪˈgɑːdɪŋ 95, 98

region ˈriːdʒən 6
regional ˈriːdʒənəl 52
registration form ˌredʒɪˈstreɪʃən fɔːm 96
regret n, v rɪˈgret 98
regular ˈregjələ 49
regular (verb) ˈregjələ 4
regularly ˈregjələli 55
reject v rɪˈdʒekt 80
relating to rɪˈleɪtɪŋ tuː 3
relations rɪˈleɪʃənz 13
relationship rɪˈleɪʃənʃɪp 15
relatives ˈrelətɪvz 13
relax rɪˈlæks 71
relaxation ˌriːlækˈseɪʃən 71
relaxed rɪˈlækst 32
relevant ˈreləvənt 96
reliable rɪˈlaɪəbəl 11, 28, 72
rely on rɪˈlaɪ ɒn 77
remarry ˌriːˈmæri 13
remind rɪˈmaɪnd 88
rent n, v rent 17, 19
repair rɪˈpeə 35
repeat rɪˈpiːt 31
repetition ˌrepɪˈtɪʃən 31
replace rɪˈpleɪs 23
reply n, v rɪˈplaɪ 55, 66
report rɪˈpɔːt 52
reporter rɪˈpɔːtə 52
represent ˌreprɪˈzent 35
request n rɪˈkwest 66
require rɪˈkwaɪə 95, 96
research n rɪˈsɜːtʃ 34
reserve rɪˈzɜːv 48
resign rɪˈzaɪn 37
resignation ˌrezɪgˈneɪʃən 37
responsible for rɪˈspɒnsəbəl fɔː 36
result [consequence] rɪˈzʌlt 58, 97
result [in a competition] rɪˈzʌlt 42
retake sth ˌriːˈteɪk ˈsʌmθɪŋ 33
retire rɪˈtaɪə 37
retired rɪˈtaɪəd 14
retirement rɪˈtaɪəmənt 14, 37
review rɪˈvjuː 46, 52
reviewer rɪˈvjuːə 43
revise rɪˈvaɪz 1, 33
revision rɪˈvɪʒən 33
rewrite ˈriːraɪt 70
ride [a bike] raɪd 28
right [exactly] raɪt 90
right away raɪt əˈweɪ 75
ring v rɪŋ 53
ring [jewellery] n rɪŋ 21
ring a bell rɪŋ ə bel 75
rink rɪŋk 41
rise n, v raɪz 40
road sign rəʊd saɪn 29
roast rəʊst 25
rob rɒb 56
robber ˈrɒbə 56
robbery ˈrɒbəri 56
rock rɒk 51
rock climbing rɒk ˈklaɪmɪŋ 41
romantic comedy rəʊˈmæntɪk ˈkɒmədi 43

room [space] ruːm 86
room service ruːm ˈsɜːvɪs 48
roots ruːts 27
rough (sea) rʌf 51
roughly ˈrʌfli 10, 14
round [movement] raʊnd 90
round [shape] raʊnd 63
round the corner raʊnd ðə ˈkɔːnə 28, 62
routine ruːˈtiːn 1
rub sth out rʌb ˈsʌmθɪŋ aʊt 1, 31
rubber ˈrʌbə 1, 31, 63
rubbish ˈrʌbɪʃ 86
rucksack ˈrʌksæk 21
rug rʌg 18
ruler ˈruːlə 31
run [manage] rʌn 36, 39
run [use applications] rʌn 54
run out of sth rʌn aʊt ɒv ˈsʌmθɪŋ 38
runway ˈrʌnweɪ 47
rush hour rʌʃ ˈaʊə 26
Russia ˈrʌʃə 5
Russian ˈrʌʃən 5
sack n, v sæk 37
safe seɪf 26
sail seɪl 41
sailing ˈseɪlɪŋ 41
sailor ˈseɪlə 35, 41
salad ˈsæləd 24
salad dressing ˈsæləd ˈdresɪŋ 24
salary ˈsæləri 36
sales rep seɪlz rep 100
salmon ˈsæmən 24
same to you seɪm tuː juː 69
sand sænd 51
sandy ˈsændi 51
satisfied with ˈsætɪsfaɪd wɪð 77
saucepan ˈsɔːspən 25
Saudi Arabia ˈsaʊdi əˈreɪbiə 5
Saudi Arabian ˈsaʊdi əˈreɪbiən 5
save [keep] seɪv 54, 58
save (up) seɪv 19, 79
saxophone ˈsæksəfəʊn 44
saxophonist sækˈsɒfənɪst 44
say [give information in writing] seɪ 52, 67
say + that seɪ ðæt 88
Scandinavia ˌskændɪˈneɪviə 5
scared skeəd 12
scarf skɑːf 21
scenery ˈsiːnəri 27, 86
science ˈsaɪəns 34
science fiction ˈsaɪəns ˈfɪkʃən 43
scientist ˈsaɪəntɪst 71
score a goal skɔːr ə gəʊl 74
search n, v sɜːtʃ 55, 59
seaside resort ˈsiːsaɪd rɪˈzɔːt 51
season (in the year) ˈsiːzən 27
season ticket ˈsiːzən ˈtɪkɪt 28
seat belt siːt belt 47
second (time) ˈsekənd 60
secondary school ˈsekəndəri skuːl 32
secondly ˈsekəndli 92
secret ˈsiːkrət 57
see [find out] siː 3

see [use your eyes]   si: 85
see the sights   si: ðə saɪts   50
seem   si:m   85
seldom   'seldəm   91
semi-circle   'semi 'sɜ:kəl   63
send my regards/love to
    send maɪ rɪ'gɑ:dz/lʌv tu: 99
sense of humour
    sens ɒv 'hju:mə   11
sensible   'sentsɪbəl   11
series   'sɪəri:z   52
serious [bad]   'sɪəriəs   20, 74
serious [important]   'sɪəriəs   15
serious [quiet]   'sɪəriəs   11
serve   v   sɜ:v   22
service   'sɜ:vɪs   48
set off   set ɒf   80
set sth up   set 'sʌmθɪŋ ʌp   36, 39
several   'sevərəl   64
shade   ʃeɪd   51
shake hands   ʃeɪk hændz   9, 69
shake your head   ʃeɪk jɔ: hed   9
shall we …?   ʃæl wi: 66
share   ʃeə   18, 31
shark   ʃɑ:k   8
sharp(ly)   ʃɑ:p   40
sharpen   'ʃɑ:pən   31
shave   ʃeɪv   16
sheet [of a bed]   ʃi:t   18
sheet [of paper]   ʃi:t   64
shelf   ʃelf   23
shine   ʃaɪn   7
shining   7
shocked   ʃɒkt   89
shocking   'ʃɒkɪŋ   89
shoot   ʃu:t   59
shop   v   ʃɒp   22
shop assistant   ʃɒp ə'sɪstənt   22
shopping centre   'ʃɒpɪŋ
    'sentə   23
shore   ʃɔ: 51
short of sth   ʃɔ:t ɒv 'sʌmθɪŋ   77
shoulder   'ʃəʊldə   9
shout at/to sb   ʃaʊt æt/tu:
    'sʌmbɒdi   77
show sb around   ʃəʊ 'sʌmbɒdi
    ə'raʊnd   38
shower [bath]   'ʃaʊə   16
shower [of rain]   'ʃaʊə   7
shy   ʃaɪ   11
sight   saɪt   85
sights   saɪts   50
sightseeing   'saɪtsi:ɪŋ   50
sign   n   saɪn   29
sign   v   saɪn   98
sign (of sth happening)   saɪn   40
signature   'sɪgnətʃə   96, 98
signed   saɪnd   96
significance   sɪg'nɪfɪkəns   72
silence   'saɪləns   30
silently   'saɪləntli   1
silk   sɪlk   63
silly   'sɪli   11
similar   'sɪmɪlə   71, 77
similarity   ˌsɪmɪ'lærɪti   71
simple   'sɪmpəl   33
since [conjunction]   sɪns   94, 99

since [preposition]   sɪns   60
singer   'sɪŋə   71
single [record]   'sɪŋgəl   43
single room   'sɪŋgəl ru:m   48
sink   sɪŋk   18
sister-in-law   'sɪstərɪnlɔ: 13
situation   ˌsɪtju'eɪʃən   69
size   saɪz   22, 62
ski   v   ski: 41
skiing holiday   'ski:ɪŋ 'hɒlədeɪ   46
skills   skɪlz   96
skin   skɪn   9
skirt   skɜ:t   21
skis   ski:z   41
sky   skaɪ   7
sleep   n   sli:p   16
sleeping bag   'sli:pɪŋ bæg   86
sleeve   sli:v   21
slice   slaɪs   64
slight   slaɪt   40
slightly   'slaɪtli   40, 91
smart [well-dressed]   smɑ:t
    10, 21, 32
smell   n, v   smel   85
smile   v   smaɪl   9
smooth   smu:ð   1
smoothie   'smu:ði   49
snack   snæk   16
snake   sneɪk   8
snow   v   snəʊ   7
snowing   'snəʊɪŋ   7
snowy   'snəʊi   7
so   səʊ   94
so do/am I   səʊ du:/æm aɪ   68
so that   səʊ ðæt   94
soap opera   səʊp 'ɒpərə   52
sociable   'səʊʃəbəl   72
social networking site
    'səʊʃəl 'netwɜ:kɪŋ saɪt   55
socket   'sɒkɪt   31
sofa   'səʊfə   18
soft   sɒft   18
software   'sɒftweə   54
sold out   səʊld aʊt   30
soldier   'səʊldʒə   35, 59
solo artist   'səʊləʊ 'ɑ:tɪst   44
solution   sə'lu:ʃən   58
some people believe …
    sʌm 'pi:pəl bɪ'li:v   97
something wrong with
    'sʌmθɪŋ rɒŋ wɪð   77
songwriter   'sɒŋˌraɪtə   44
sooner or later   'su:nər ɔ: 'leɪtə
    75
sore throat   sɔ: θrəʊt   20
sorry to disturb you
    'sɒri tu: dɪ'stɜ:b ju: 65
sorry to keep you waiting
    'sɒri tu: ki:p ju: 'weɪtɪŋ   65
sort of   sɔ:t ɒv   76
sort sth out   sɔ:t 'sʌmθɪŋ aʊt   79
sound   saʊnd   85
sour   'saʊə   25
south   saʊθ   6
South America   saʊθ ə'merɪkə   5
South Korea   saʊθ kə'ri:ə   5
south-east   saʊθ 'i:st   6

south-west   saʊθ 'west   6
souvenir   ˌsu:vən'ɪə   51
space   speɪs   17
spacebar   'speɪsbɑ: 54
Spain   speɪn   5
spam   spæm   55
Spanish   'spænɪʃ   5
spare room   speə ru:m   18
spare time   speə taɪm   16
sparkling   'spɑ:kəlɪŋ   48
speaking [on the
    phone]   'spi:kɪŋ   53
special offer   'speʃəl 'ɒfə   23
spectacular   spek'tækjələ   45
speech   spi:tʃ   82
speed limit   spi:d 'lɪmɪt   29
spell   spel   31
spelling   'spelɪŋ   31
spend (money) on   spend ɒn   77
spend time   spend taɪm   51, 74
spicy   'spaɪsi   25
spider   'spaɪdə   8
spill   spɪl   19
spinach   'spɪnɪtʃ   24
spoonful   'spu:nfʊl   64
square   adj, n   skweə   63
St   seɪnt/stri:t   100
stadium   'steɪdiəm   41
stall   stɔ:l   23
star [famous actor]   stɑ: 43
starter   'stɑ:tə   48
state education
    steɪt ˌedʒʊ'keɪʃən   32
station
    [broadcasting]   'steɪʃən   52
statue   'stætʃu: 50
stay   n   steɪ   48
stay at school   steɪ æt sku:l   32
stay behind   steɪ bɪ'haɪnd   32
stay in   steɪ ɪn   16
stay out late   steɪ aʊt leɪt   14
stay the same   steɪ ðə seɪm   40
steal   sti:l   56
stepfather   'step,fɑ:ðə   13
steps   steps   17
sterling   'stɜ:lɪŋ   19
stick   stɪk   41
still [continuing]   stɪl   93
still [of water]   stɪl   48
stir   stɜ: 25
stomach ache   'stʌmək eɪk   20
store   stɔ: 54
storm   stɔ:m   7
straight   streɪt   10
straight away   streɪt ə'weɪ   75
stranger   'streɪndʒə   69
strawberry   'strɔ:bəri   24
street market   stri:t 'mɑ:kɪt   23
stress [emphasis]   stres   4
stress [worry]   stres   12
stressed   strest   26
stressful   'stresfʊl   26
strict   strɪkt   14, 32
stripe   straɪp   63
stroll   strəʊl   51
strong (wind)   strɒŋ   7
study   n   'stʌdi   18

stuff stʌf 95
student loan 'stjuːdənt ləʊn 19
stupid 'stjuːpɪd 11, 71
stupidity stjuː'pɪdəti 71
student loan 19
stylish 'staɪlɪʃ 21, 63
subject 'sʌbdʒɪkt 32
subtraction səb'trækʃən 61
succeed (in doing sth) sək'siːd 34, 37
success sək'ses 37
successful sək'sesfəl 34, 37
suddenly 'sʌdənli 91
suffer 'sʌfə 58
suffer from sth 'sʌfə frɒm 'sʌmθɪŋ 20
suffix 'sʌfɪks 4
suggest (+ -ing) sə'dʒest x 87
suggest + that sə'dʒest ðæt 88
suggestion sə'dʒestʃən 66
suit n suːt 21
suit v suːt 21, 22
suitable 'suːtəbəl 72
suitcase 'suːtkeɪs 47
sun sʌn 7
sunbathe 'sʌnbeɪð 51
sunbathing 'sʌnbeɪðɪŋ 51
sunburn 'sʌnbɜːn 51
sun cream sʌn kriːm 51
sunglasses 'sʌnˌglɑːsɪz 73
sunny 'sʌni 7
sunscreen/sunblock 'sʌnskriːn/'sʌnblɒk 51
sunset 'sʌnset 27
sunshine 'sʌnʃaɪn 51
suntan 'sʌntæn 51
superb suː'pɜːb 42
support [help] sə'pɔːt 57, 98
sure ʃɔː 66
surf the web sɜːf ðə web 55
surface 'sɜːfɪs 6
surfing 'sɜːfɪŋ 51
surgeon 'sɜːdʒən 20, 35
surgery [an operation] 'sɜːdʒəri 20
surgery [a place] 'sɜːdʒəri 35
surrounded by sə'raʊndɪd baɪ 27
swap (places) swɒp 31
sweater 'swetə 21
sweets swiːts 23
swerve swɜːv 29
swimmer 'swɪmə 41
swimming costume 'swɪmɪŋ 'kɒstjuːm 41
Swiss swɪs 5
switch sth off swɪtʃ 'sʌmθɪŋ ɒf 58
switch sth on swɪtʃ 'sʌmθɪŋ ɒn 46, 79
Switzerland 'swɪtsələnd 5
syllable 'sɪləbəl 4
synonym 'sɪnənɪm 1
system 'sɪstəm 32
tablet 'tæblət 20
take [accept sth] teɪk 81
take [remove sth] teɪk 81
take [steal] teɪk 56, 81

take [write down] teɪk 81
take (size 12) teɪk 81
take (time) teɪk 60
take a break teɪk ə breɪk 81
take a course teɪk ə kɔːs 81
take/make a decision teɪk/meɪk ə dɪ'sɪʒən 81
take a look teɪk ə lʊk 81
take a photo teɪk ə 'fəʊtəʊ 81
take/have a shower teɪk/hæv ə 'ʃaʊə 16, 81
take action teɪk 'ækʃən 58
take away teɪk ə'weɪ 49
take/do an exam teɪk/duː æn ɪg'zæm 33
take care teɪk keə 69
take/do exercise teɪk/duː 'eksəsaɪz 16, 81
take over sth teɪk 'əʊvə 'sʌmθɪŋ 39
take part teɪk pɑːt 42
take sb on teɪk 'sʌmbɒdi ɒn 79
take sth back teɪk 'sʌmθɪŋ bæk 79
take sth off teɪk 'sʌmθɪŋ ɒf 21, 80
take sth up teɪk 'sʌmθɪŋ ʌp 39
take things/it easy teɪk θɪŋz ɪt 'iːzi 81
takeaway 'teɪkəweɪ 16
take-off 'teɪkɒf 47
talent 'tælənt 11
talented 'tæləntɪd 11
tallish (person) 'tɔː.lɪʃ 10
tall person/tree/building tɔːl 'pɜːsən/triː/'bɪldɪŋ 62
tap tæp 18, 58
taste [flavour] n, v teɪst 25, 85
taste [what you like] teɪst 44
tasty 'teɪsti 25
tax tæks 57
taxi rank 'tæksi ræŋk 28
teaching 'tiːtʃɪŋ 34
team tiːm 42, 96
tear v teə 19
teenager 'tiːnˌeɪdʒə 14
teens tiːnz 14
tell + obj + that tel ðæt 88
tell sb a joke tel 'sʌmbɒdi ə dʒəʊk 74
telly 'teli 100
temperature 'temprətʃə 6, 20
temple 'tempəl 50
ten pound note ten paʊnd nəʊt 19
tent tent 41, 86
term tɜːm 32
terminal (building) 'tɜːmɪnəl 47
terribly sorry 'terəbli 'sɒri 65, 74
terrific tə'rɪfɪk 89, 95
terrifying 'terəfaɪɪŋ 89
text v tekst 53
texting 'tekstɪŋ 53
Thai taɪ 5
Thailand 'taɪlænd 5
thank goodness/God θæŋk 'gʊdnəs/gɒd 69
thank sb (for sth) θæŋk 'sʌmbɒdi

98
thanks (very much) θæŋks 65
that/it depends ðæt/ɪt dɪ'pendz 76
that sort/kind of thing ðæt sɔːt/kaɪnd ɒv θɪŋ 76
that's a great idea ðæts ə greɪt aɪ'dɪə 66
that's a pity ðæts ə 'pɪti 22
that's a shame ðæts ə ʃeɪm 22
that's all right/okay ðæts ɔːl raɪt ə'keɪ 65
that's to say ðæts tuː seɪ 100
that's very kind of you ðæts 'veri kaɪnd ɒv juː 65
the best/worst thing about … ðə best/wɜːst θɪŋ ə'baʊt 27
the cold ðə kəʊld 7
the last time ðə lɑːst taɪm 60
the news ðə njuːz 52
the other day ðɪ 'ʌðə deɪ 60
the thing is … ðə θɪŋ ɪz 95
theft θeft 56
there's something wrong with … ðeəz 'sʌmθɪŋ rɒŋ wɪð 19
therefore 'ðeəfɔː 94
these days ðiːz deɪz 60
thick [not thin] θɪk 62
thick fog θɪk fɒg 7
thief θiːf 56
thin θɪn 62
think of (+ -ing) θɪŋk ɒv 77, 87
though ðəʊ 93
thousand 'θaʊzənd 61
three quarters θriː 'kwɔːtəz 61
thriller 'θrɪlə 43
through θruː 90
throw sth away θrəʊ 'sʌmθɪŋ ə'weɪ 23, 58
throw sth to/at sb θrəʊ 'sʌmθɪŋ tuː/æt 'sʌmbɒdi 77
thumb θʌm 9
thunder 'θʌndə 7
thunderstorm 'θʌndəstɔːm 7
tick tɪk 3
tie taɪ 21
tiger 'taɪgə 8
tight taɪt 22
tights taɪts 21
tiles taɪlz 18
time (for us) to go/leave (etc.) taɪm tuː gəʊ/liːv 60
times taɪmz 61
timetable 'taɪmˌteɪbəl 32
tin (of fruit, etc.) tɪn 64
tiny 'taɪni 62, 89
tip [advice] tɪp 2, 96
tip [money] tɪp 2
tired 'taɪəd 89
tired of sth taɪəd ɒv 'sʌmθɪŋ 77
tiring 'taɪərɪŋ 89
tissue 'tɪʃuː 63
to be honest tuː biː 'ɒnɪst 75
to begin with tuː bɪ'gɪn wɪð 92
to some extent tuː sʌm ɪk'stent 67
toast təʊst 86
toastie 'təʊsti 49

toddler ˈtɒdlə 14
toe təʊ 9
tomato təˈmɑːtəʊ 24
too tuː 93
toothbrush ˈtuːθbrʌʃ 73
toothpaste ˈtuːθpeɪst 73
top tɒp 21
top floor tɒp flɔː 17
topic ˈtɒpɪk 2
totally ˈtəʊtəli 67, 91
touch n, v tʌtʃ 85
tournament ˈtʊənəmənt 42
towards təˈwɔːdz 90
town centre taʊn ˈsentə 26
toy tɔɪ 63
track [music] træk 43
track [sport] træk 41
tractor ˈtræktə 27
trade treɪd 40
tradition trəˈdɪʃən 44
traditional trəˈdɪʃənəl 45, 72
traffic jam ˈtræfɪk dʒæm 26
traffic light(s) ˈtræfɪk laɪt 29, 73
trainers ˈtreɪnəz 21
training ˈtreɪnɪŋ 37
translate (sth into
    sth) trænzˈleɪt 2, 71, 77
translation trænzˈleɪʃən 2, 71
translator trænzˈleɪtə 71
travel agent ˈtrævəl ˈeɪdʒənt 73
tray treɪ 49
treat triːt 35
tree triː 27
trend trend 40
trolley ˈtrɒli 23, 47
trousers ˈtraʊzəz 21
truck trʌk 28
trumpet ˈtrʌmpɪt 44
trumpeter ˈtrʌmpɪtə 44
trunk trʌŋk 8
trust trʌst 11
try sth on traɪ ˈsʌmθɪŋ ɒn 22
try/do your best traɪ/duː jɔː
    best 33
T-shirt ˈtiːʃɜːt 21, 73
tube tjuːb 64
tune tjuːn 44
Turkey ˈtɜːki 5
Turkish ˈtɜːkɪʃ 5
turn sth down [reduce volume]
    tɜːn ˈsʌmθɪŋ daʊn 31
turn sth/sb down [reject] tɜːn
    ˈsʌmθɪŋ ˈsʌmbɒdi daʊn 80
turn sth off tɜːn ˈsʌmθɪŋ ɒf 80
turn sth on tɜːn ˈsʌmθɪŋ ɒn 80
turn sth up tɜːn ˈsʌmθɪŋ ʌp 31
turning ˈtɜːnɪŋ 29
twenty-euro note 19
twentyish 10
twice twaɪs 69
twin(s) twɪn 13
twin room twɪn ruːm 48
type v taɪp 38, 96
ugly ˈʌgli 10
UK ˌjuːˈkeɪ 5
UN ˌjuːˈen 100
unable ʌnˈeɪbəl 70

unbelievable ˌʌnbɪˈliːvəbəl 72
uncle ˈʌŋkəl 13
uncomfortable ʌnˈkʌmftəbəl
    70, 72
uncountable
    (noun) ʌnˈkaʊntəbəl 4
under [movement] ˈʌndə 90
under arrest ˈʌndər əˈrest 56
under one roof ˈʌndə wʌn
    ruːf 23
undergraduate ˌʌndəˈgrædʒuət
    34
underneath ˌʌndəˈniːθ 90
undo ʌnˈduː 21
unemployed ˌʌnɪmˈplɔɪd 37
unemployment ˌʌnɪmˈplɔɪmənt
    37
unfair ʌnˈfeə 70
unfashionable ʌnˈfæʃənəbəl 72
unforgettable ˌʌnfəˈgetəbəl 72
unfriendly ʌnˈfrendli 11
uniform ˈjuːnɪfɔːm 32
United States of America
    juːˈnaɪtɪd steɪts ɒv əˈmerɪkə 5
unkind ʌnˈkaɪnd 11
unless ənˈles 94
unlikely ʌnˈlaɪkli 70
unlock ʌnˈlɒk 70
unlucky ʌnˈlʌki 70
unnecessary ʌnˈnesəsəri 2
unpack ʌnˈpæk 70
unpleasant ʌnˈplezənt 11
unreasonable ʌnˈriːzənəbəl 72
unreliable ˌʌnrɪˈlaɪəbəl 11, 72
unsociable ʌnˈsəʊʃəbəl 72
unsuccessful ˌʌnsəkˈsesfəl 34
unsuitable ʌnˈsuːtəbəl 72
untidy ʌnˈtaɪdi 2
until ənˈtɪl 60
up [further along] ʌp 62
up [not in bed] ʌp 27
up and down ʌp ænd daʊn 76
up to ʌp tuː 45
upload ʌpˈləʊd 55
upset adj ʌpˈset 12
upstairs ʌpˈsteəz 17
up-to-date ˌʌptəˈdeɪt 78
urgently ˈɜːdʒəntli 91
USA juːˌesˈeɪ 5
use n juːs 31
use v juːz 31
used to ˈjuːst tuː 68
useful ˈjuːsfəl 72
useless ˈjuːsləs 72
username ˈjuːzəneɪm 54
utility room juːˈtɪləti ruːm 18
valley ˈvæli 27
value ˈvælju 40
value for money
    ˈvælju fɔː ˈmʌni 19, 26
van væn 28
variety vəˈraɪəti 26, 39
vase vɑːz 64
vast majority vɑːst
    məˈdʒɒrəti 61
veal viːl 24
vegetarian ˌvedʒɪˈteəriən 24, 49

vehicle ˈvɪəkəl 28
verb vɜːb 4
vet vet 36, 100
via ˈvaɪə 29
victory ˈvɪktəri 42
video clip ˈvɪdiəʊ klɪp 55
view vjuː 17
village ˈvɪlɪdʒ 27
vinegar ˈvɪnɪgə 24
violence ˈvaɪələns 59
violent ˈvaɪələnt 59
violin ˌvaɪəˈlɪn 44
violinist ˌvaɪəˈlɪnɪst 44
virus [computer] ˈvaɪrəs 54
visa application form
    ˈviːzə ˌæplɪˈkeɪʃən fɔːm 96
vitally important ˈvaɪtəli
    ɪmˈpɔːtənt 74
vocational training vəʊˈkeɪʃənəl
    ˈtreɪnɪŋ 32
volleyball ˈvɒlibɔːl 51
vote vəʊt 57
vowel ˈvaʊəl 33
wage weɪdʒ 36
waffle ˈwɒfl 49
waist weɪst 9
wait and see weɪt ænd siː 76
wake (up) weɪk 79
wake (sb) up weɪk ʌp 16
war wɔː 59
wardrobe ˈwɔːdrəʊb 22
warn (+ obj + inf) wɔːn 88
warning ˈwɔːnɪŋ 30
wash n, v wɒʃ 16
washbasin ˈwɒʃˌbeɪsən 18
washing [dirty
    clothes] ˈwɒʃɪŋ 16
washing machine ˈwɒʃɪŋ
    məˈʃiːn 18
waste weɪst 19, 58
waste of money weɪst əv
    ˈmʌni 19
watch wɒtʃ 85
waterfall ˈwɔːtəfɔːl 6
wave to somebody
    weɪv tuː ˈsʌmbədi 9
waves (in the sea) weɪvz 51
wavy ˈweɪvi 10
way [route] weɪ 29
we could … wiː kʊd 66
weak wiːk 71
weakness ˈwiːknəs 71
wear weə 32
weather forecast
    ˈweðə ˈfɔːkɑːst 52
webcam ˈwebkæm 55
website ˈwebsaɪt 55
wedding ˈwedɪŋ 15
weekend break ˈwiːkend
    breɪk 46
weekly ˈwiːkli 1, 52
weigh weɪ 10, 47
weight weɪt 10
well wel 10
well aware wel əˈweə 74
well done [meat] wel dʌn 48
well known wel nəʊn 52

west   west   6
wet   wet   7
whale   weɪl   8
What are you up to?   wɒt ɑː juː ʌp
   tuː   95
What do you do?
   wɒt duː juː duː   36
What do you do for a living?
   wɒt duː juː duː fɔːr ə ˈlɪvɪŋ   36
What do you think of/about …?
   wɒt duː juː θɪŋk ɒv/əˈbaʊt   67
What does he/she look like?
   wɒt dʌz hiː/ʃiː lʊk laɪk   10
What does that involve?   wɒt dʌz
   ðæt ɪnˈvɒlv   36
What does X mean?
   wɒt dʌz eks miːn   31
What does X stand for?   wɒt dʌz
   eks stænd fɔː   100
What for?   wɒt fɔː   76
what if   wɒt ɪf   76
What's he/she/it like?   wɒts hiː/
   ʃiː/ɪt laɪk   11
what's more   wɒts mɔː   93
What's on?   wɒts ɒn   43
What's your job?   wɒts jɔː
   dʒɒb   36
wheelchair   ˈwiːltʃeə   73
whereas   weəˈræz   93
whether   ˈweðə   94

while [comparing]   ˈwaɪl   93
while [during]   ˈwaɪl   92
Who's calling?   huːz ˈkɔːlɪŋ   53
Why don't we …?   waɪ dəʊnt wiː
   66
Why not?   waɪ nɒt   76
wide [not narrow]   waɪd   62
wide awake   waɪd əˈweɪk   74
wide choice   waɪd tʃɔɪs   74
wide range   waɪd reɪndʒ   23
wide vocabulary
   waɪd vəˈkæbjələri   33, 74
widow   ˈwɪdəʊ   13
width   wɪtθ   62
wi-fi password   waɪ.faɪ
   ˈpɑːswɜːd   46
wild (animals)   waɪld   8
willing   ˈwɪlɪŋ   33
win   wɪn   42
wind   n   wɪnd   7
windsurfing   ˈwɪndsɜːfɪŋ   51
windy   ˈwɪndi   7
wing   wɪŋ   8
winner   ˈwɪnə   42
wish   wɪʃ   11
won't be long   wəʊnt biː lɒŋ   65
wonderful   ˈwʌndəfəl   89
wood   wʊd   35
wooden   ˈwʊdən   18, 63
woods   wʊdz   27

work [function]   wɜːk   19, 38
work experience
   wɜːk ɪkˈspɪəriəns   96
work on sth   wɜːk ɒn ˈsʌmθɪŋ   33
work out   wɜːk aʊt   41
work sth out   wɜːk ˈsʌmθɪŋ aʊt
   61
worry about sth   ˈwʌri əˈbaʊt
   ˈsʌmθɪŋ   77
worth [value]   wɜːθ   56
worth (+ noun/-ing)   wɜːθ   50
would rather   wʊd ˈrɑːðə   68
wow   waʊ   31
wrap   ræp   49
wrist   rɪst   9
write down   raɪt daʊn   2
wrong number   rɒŋ ˈnʌmbə   53
yard   jɑːd   62
yawn   jɔːn   9
yet   jet   93
yoga   ˈjəʊɡə   41
you (don't) get …   juː get   26, 27
you know   juː nəʊ   76
you must be joking   juː mʌst biː
   ˈdʒəʊkɪŋ   76
Yours faithfully/sincerely
   jɔːz ˈfeɪθfəli/sɪnˈsɪəli   98
zero   ˈzɪərəʊ   61
zip   zɪp   21
zoo   zuː   8

Acknowledgements

The authors and publishers acknowledge the following sources of copyright material and are grateful for the permissions granted. While every effort has been made, it has not always been possible to identify the sources of all the material used, or to trace all copyright holders. If any omissions are brought to our notice, we will be happy to include the appropriate acknowledgements on reprinting & in the next update to the digital edition, as applicable.

Key: B = Below, BL = Below Left, BR = Below Right, BC = Below Centre, C = Centre, CL = Centre Left, CR = Centre Right, L = Left, R = Right, T = Top, TR = Top Right, TL = Top Left.

Photographs

All the photographs are sourced from GettyImages.

p. 10 (Kazuo): Siri Stafford/DigitalVision; p. 10 (Eun): Layland Masuda/Moment; p. 10 (Andrey): Neustockimages/E+; p. 10 (Donata): Lava; p. 10 (Rafael): Jon Feingersh/Blend Images; p. 14: Bertrand Demee/photographer's Choice RF; p. 18 (TL): Stephen Alvarez/National Geographic; p. 18 (CL): Keren Su/China Span/China Span; p. 18 (BL): Jane Sweeney/The Image Bank; p. 18 (R): Oleksiy Maksymenko; p. 22 (parrot): Zedcor Wholly Owned/photoObjects.net/Getty Images Plus; p. 22 (rabbit): Life On White/photodisc; p. 22 (mouse): Joseph Zellner/iStock/Getty Images Plus; p. 22 (donkey): Ralf Kraft/Hemera/Getty Images Plus; p. 22 (snake): Simon Murrell/Cultura; p. 22 (frog): Miroslaw Kijewski/E+; p. 22 (bull): nicolasprimola/iStock/Getty Images Plus; p. 22 (spider): Thomas Bedenk/iStock/Getty Images Plus; p. 22 (goat): Eric Issele/iStock/Getty Images Plus; p. 22 (monkey): Catherine Ledner/Stone; p. 22 (camel): jamesbenet/E+; p. 22 (giraffe): kotomiti/iStock/Getty Images Plus; p. 22 (tiger): luamduan/iStock/Getty Images Plus; p. 22 (lion) & p. 22 (bee): GlobalP/iStock/Getty Images Plus; p. 22 (leopard): Eric Issele/iStock/Getty Images Plus; p. 22 (bear): JackF/iStock/Getty Images Plus; p. 22 (elephant): DaddyBit/iStock/Getty Images Plus; p. 22 (ant): Henrik_L/iStock/Getty Images Plus; p. 22 (mosquito): Anest/iStock/Getty Images Plus; p. 22 (fly): Antagain/iStock/Getty Images Plus; p. 22 (butterfly): AmbientIdeas/iStock/Getty Images Plus; p. 22 (whale): freestylephoto/iStock/Getty Images Plus; p. 22 (dolphin): DrPAS/iStock/Getty Images Plus; p. 22 (shark), p. 134 (paper), p. 135 (Ex 64.2.3) & p. 135 (Ex 64.2.9): Dorling Kindersley; p. 22 (octopus): Mike Hargreaves/photolibrary; p. 26 (straight): Mike Harrington/Stone; p. 26 (wavy): Nick Dolding/Stone; p. 26 (curly), p. 138 (photo 6) & p. 138 (photo 12): Plume Creative/DigitalVision; p. 26 (hair): VladTeodor/iStock/Getty Images Plus; p. 28: Tempura/E+; p. 30: Patrick Foto/Moment; p. 32 (T), p. 92 (comedies), p. 92 (complicated), p. 112 (BL), p. 116 (B), p. 140 (CL), p. 136 (photo 3) & p. 138 (photo 7): Hero Images; p. 32 (B): Dave Nagel/The Image Bank; p. 34: H. Armstrong Roberts/ClassicStock/Archive photos; p. 37: Jupiterimages/Stockbyte; p. 39: Erik Isakson; p. 40: David Clapp/Oxford Scientific; p. 44 (10 pound): Bank of England; p. 44 (20 euro): The European Central bank; p. 44 (50 dollar): malerapaso/Getty Images Plus; p. 44 (one pound): claudiodivizia/iStock/Getty Images Plus; p. 44 (one euro), p. 89 (skiing) & p. 89 (swimming): Westend61/iStock/Getty Images Plus; p. 44 (one dollar): Usmint.gov; p. 44 (woman): ariwasabi/iStock/Getty Images Plus; p. 44 (cashpoint): Ken Welsh/Design Pics; p. 48 (TL): Vincent Besnault/DigitalVision; p. 48 (TR): David Lees/DigitalVision; p. 48 (CL): Thomas Barwick/DigitalVision; p. 48 (BL): vgajic/E+; p. 48 (CR): Klaus Vedfelt/DigitalVision; p. 50 (B): Monkey Business Images/Stockbroker/Monkey Business/Getty Images Plus; p. 50 (T): Nurphoto; p. 50 (customer 1): 4x6; p. 50 (customer 3): Ivanko_Brnjakovic; p. 51: Thomas Barwick/Iconica; p. 52 (T): Cultura RM Exclusive/Line Klein/Cultura Exclusive; p. 52 (B): Apeloga AB/Cultura; p. 53: Ken Welsh/Design Pics/Perspectives; p. 54 (peach): yvdavyd/iStock/Getty Images Plus; p. 54 (pear) & (garlic): RedHelga/E+; p. 54 (pineapple): Tim Hawley/photolibrary; p. 54 (strawberry): Rosemary Calvert/photographer's Choice; p. 54 (melon): Smneedham/photolibrary; p. 54 (grapes): JazzIRT/E+; p. 54 (lemon): Davies and Starr/The Image Bank; p. 54 (olives): Laszlo Selly/photolibrary; p. 54 (coconut): Viktar Malyshchyts/iStock/Getty Images Plus; p. 54 (beans): fotogal/iStock/Getty Images Plus; p. 54 (aubergine): mr_Prof/iStock/Getty Images Plus; p. 54 (peas): li jingwang/E+; p. 54 (courgette): Daniel Loiselle/E+; p. 54 (onion): Natikka/iStock/Getty Images Plus; p. 54 (bell pepper): Lew Robertson/StockFood Creative; p. 54 (cabbage): chengyu zheng/iStock/Getty Images Plus; p. 54 (carrot): rimglow/iStock/Getty Images Plus; p. 54 (broccoli): loops7/E+; p. 54 (mushrooms): MaxRiesgo/iStock/Getty Images Plus; p. 54 (spinach): Florea Marius Catalin/E+; p. 54 (lettuce): Craig Allsop/iStock/Getty Images Plus; p. 54 (tomato): Stuart Minzey/photographer's Choice RF; p. 54 (cucumber): JohnGollop/iStock/Getty Images Plus; p. 54 (olive oil): hilmi_m/E+; p. 54 (vinegar): Blaz Kure/Hemera/Getty Images Plus; p. 54 (prawns): Ermin Gutenberger/E+; p. 54 (mussels): Floortje/E+; p. 54 (crab): malerapaso/E+; p. 54 (fish): italiaStock/artzooks; p. 56 (barbecue): Steve Wisbauer/photolibrary; p. 56 (grill): monkeybusinessimages/iStock/Getty Images Plus; p. 56 (saucepan): schulzie/iStock/Getty Images Plus; p. 56 (pan): Paul Poplis/photolibrary; p. 56 (oven): gerenme/iStock/Getty Images Plus; p. 56 (apple pie): Zoonar/S.Heap/Zoonar/Getty Images Plus; p. 58: Danita Delimont/Gallo Images; p. 59: Tim Graham/Getty Images News; p. 62 (bus): sound35/iStock/Getty Images Plus; p. 62 (coach), p. 63 (Ex 28.2.1) & p. 63 (Ex 28.2.5): mladn61/E+; p. 62 (lorry): deepblue4you/iStock/Getty Images Plus; p. 62 (van): Dmitry Vereshchagin/Hemera/Getty Images Plus; p. 62 (bicycle): Nikada/iStock/Getty Images Plus; p. 62 (motorbike) & p. 63 (Ex 28.2.3): Rawpixel Ltd/iStock/Getty Images Plus; p. 62 (T): Frank P wartenberg/Picture Press; p. 62 (C): William King/Taxi; p. 62 (B): Rubberball/Mike Kemp; p. 63 (Ex 28.2.2): DarthArt/iStock/Getty Images Plus; p. 63 (Ex 28.2.4): RistoArnaudov/iStock/Getty Images Plus; p. 63 (Ex 28.2.6): VladislavStarozhilov/iStock/Getty Images Plus; p. 66 (museum): Grzegorz Wozniak/EyeEm; p. 66 (out of order): Sharon Pruitt/EyeEm; p. 66 (sold out): Marcus Brodt/EyeEm; p. 66 (no vacancies): Richard Coombs/EyeEm; p. 66 (goat): Karl Schatz/Aurora; p. 70 (lipstick): bravo1954/E+; p. 72: Andersen Ross/photodisc; p. 73: BrianAJackson/iStock/Getty Images Plus; p. 75: Peopleimages/E+; p. 76 (soldier): JOHN GOMEZ/iStock/Getty Images Plus; p. 76 (sailor): Michael Peuckert/imageBROKER; p. 76 (pilot): Stocktrek Images/Stocktrek Images; p. 76 (police): Peter Dazeley/photographer's Choice RF; p. 76 (firefighter): Elliot Elliot/Johner Images; p. 78 (TL), p. 92 (film director) & p. 136 (photo 10): Richard Drury/Stone; p. 78 (CR): Neustockimages/iStock/Getty Images Plus; p. 78 (BL) & p. 136 (photo 14): Tim Robberts/The Image Bank; p. 78 (TR): Rick Gomez/Blend Images; p. 78 (CL) & p. 78 (BR): drbimages/iStock/Getty Images Plus; p. 80: Jose Luis Pelaez/Iconica; p. 84: Oleksiy Maksymenko/All Canada photos; p. 89 (boxer): Hill Street Studios; p. 89 (sailor): Glow Images, Inc/Glow; p. 89 (runner): Pete Saloutos/Blend Images; p. 90: ADRIAN DENNIS/AFP; p. 92 (horror film): Colin Hawkins/Stone; p. 92 (good review): David Schaffer/Caiaimage; p. 92 (big star): Owen Richards/Stone; p. 92 (fancy): Caiaimage/Sam Edwards/OJO+; p. 94 (piano): filo/iStock/Getty Images Plus; p. 94 (violin): C Squared Studios/photodisc; p. 94 (cello): futureimage/iStock/Getty Images Plus; p. 94 (trumpet): Tetra Images; p. 94 (guitar): Dorling Kindersley/Dorling Kindersley; p. 94 (drums): Nerthuz/iStock/Getty Images Plus; p. 94 (saxophone): Andreas Herpens/E+; p. 94 (keyboard): tiler84/iStock/Getty Images Plus; p. 94 (bass guitar): Cenker Atila/iStock/Getty Images Plus; p. 94 (flute), p. 132